Honorifics Explained

Throughout the Del Rey Manga books, you will find Japanese honorifics left intact in the translations. For those not familiar with how the Japanese use honorifics and, more important, how they differ from American honorifics, we present this brief overview.

Politeness has always been a critical facet of Japanese culture. Ever since the feudal era, when Japan was a highly stratified society, use of honorifics—which can be defined as polite speech that indicates relationship or status—has played an essential role in the Japanese language. When addressing someone in Japanese, an honorific usually takes the form of a suffix attached to one's name (example: "Asuna-san"), is used as a title at the end of one's name, or appears in place of the name itself (example: "Negi-sensei," or simply "Sensei!").

Honorifics can be expressions of respect or endearment. In the context of manga and anime, honorifics give insight into the nature of the relationship between characters. Many English translations leave out these important honorifics and therefore distort the feel of the original Japanese. Because Japanese honorifics contain nuances that English honorifics lack, it is our policy at Del Rey not to translate them. Here, instead, is a guide to some of the honorifics you may encounter in Del Rey Manga.

-*san*: This is the most common honorific and is equivalent to Mr., Miss, Ms., or Mrs. It is the all-purpose honorific and can be used in any situation where politeness is required.

-*sama*: This is one level higher than "-san" and is used to confer great respect.

-*dono*: This comes from the word "tono," which means "lord." It is an even higher level than "-sama" and confers utmost respect.

-*kun*: This suffix is used at the end of boys' names to express familiarity or endearment. It is also sometimes used by men

among friends, or when addressing someone younger or of a lower station.

-chan: This is used to express endearment, mostly toward girls. It is also used for little boys, pets, and even among lovers. It gives a sense of childish cuteness.

Bōzu: This is an informal way to refer to a boy, similar to the English terms "kid" and "squirt."

Sempai/Senpai: This title suggests that the addressee is one's senior in a group or organization. It is most often used in a school setting, where underclassmen refer to their upperclassmen as "sempai." It can also be used in the workplace, such as when a newer employee addresses an employee who has seniority in the company.

Kohai: This is the opposite of "sempai" and is used toward underclassmen in school or newcomers in the workplace. It connotes that the addressee is of a lower station.

Sensei: Literally meaning "one who has come before," this title is used for teachers, doctors, or masters of any profession or art.

Anesan (or *nesan*): A generic term for a girl, usually older, that means "sister."

Ojōsama: A way of referring to the daughter or sister of someone with high political or social status.

-[blank]: This is usually forgotten in these lists, but it is perhaps the most significant difference between Japanese and English. The lack of honorific means that the speaker has permission to address the person in a very intimate way. Usually, only family, spouses, or very close friends have this kind of permission. Known as *yobisute*, it can be gratifying when someone who has earned the intimacy starts to call one by one's name without an honorific. But when that intimacy hasn't been earned, it can be very insulting.

A Word from the Author

I bring you *Negima!* volume 22. There was kind of a lot of eros in the last volume (^^;). But I've repented of that, so this time we're focusing on *battles*!

In order to defeat his arch-nemesis, Fate, Negi decides to train under a new master. Will he really be able to master such a powerful finishing move!?

And what is dark magic, really!?

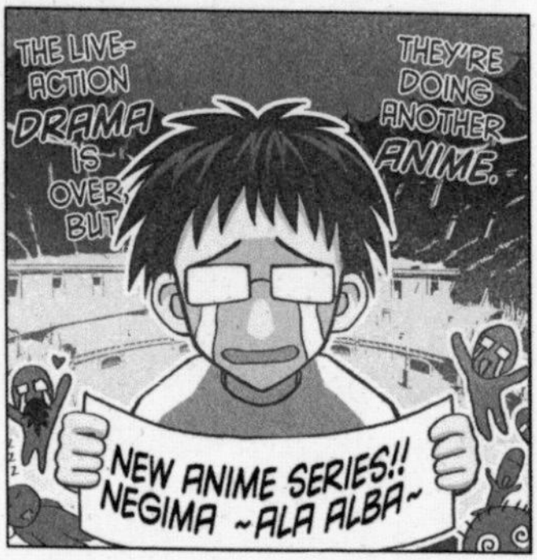
THE LIVE-ACTION DRAMA IS OVER, BUT
THEY'RE DOING ANOTHER ANIME.
NEW ANIME SERIES!! NEGIMA ~ALA ALBA~

Now, another new anime is about to begin!

First, the next three volumes, starting with volume 23, will have limited editions that come with DVDs! (*For preorder only)

This time, they're staying true to the original and animating the manga's summer vacation arc. The theme song will be *that* song. Please look forward to it!

Ken Akamatsu
www.ailove.net

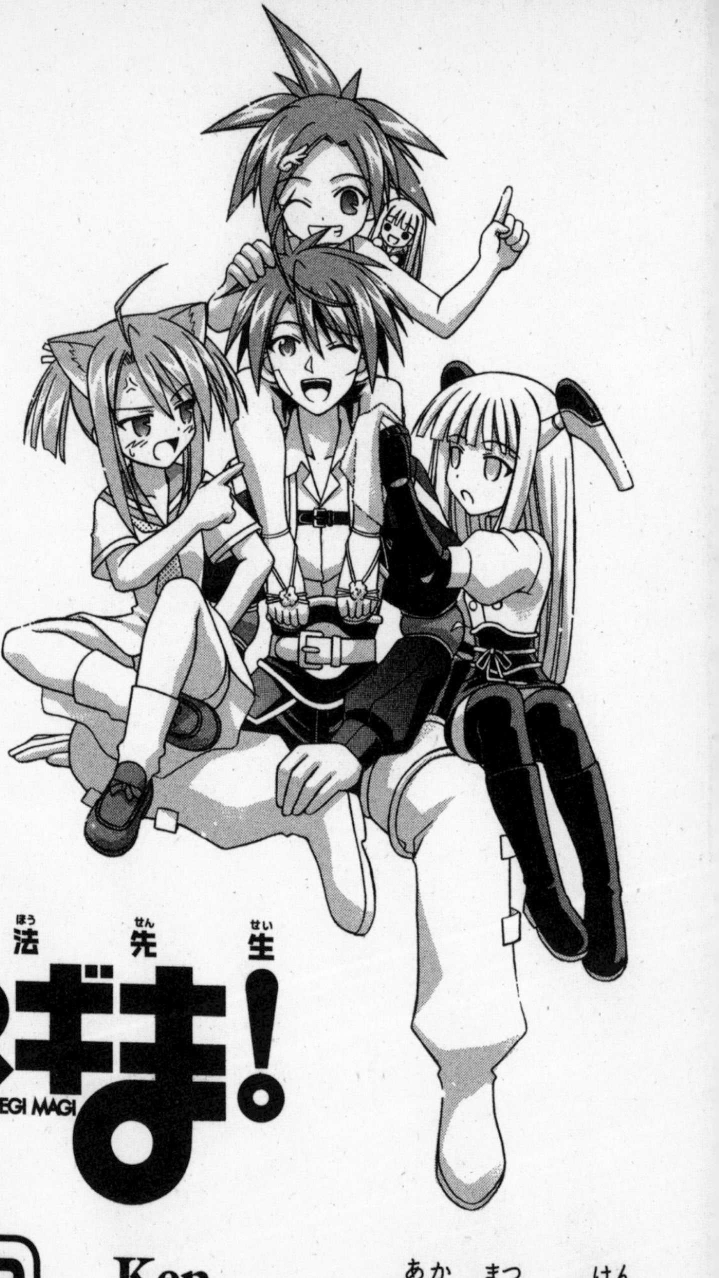

魔法先生ネギま!

MAGISTER NEGI MAGI

22

Ken Akamatsu

赤松健

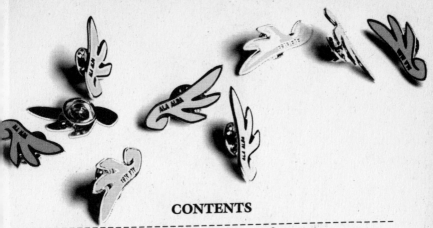

CONTENTS

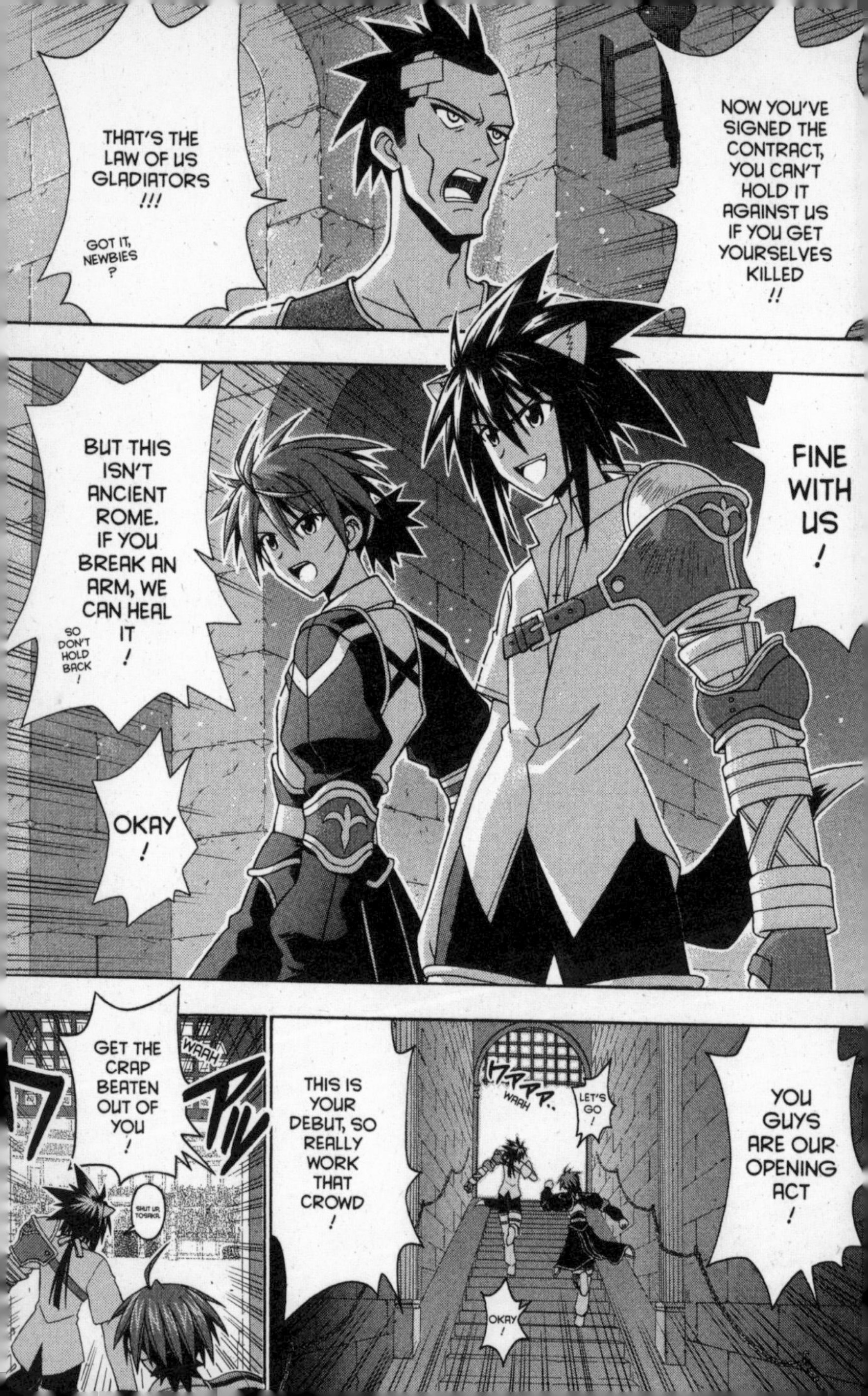
NOW YOU'VE SIGNED THE CONTRACT, YOU CAN'T HOLD IT AGAINST US IF YOU GET YOURSELVES KILLED!!
THAT'S THE LAW OF US GLADIATORS!!!
GOT IT, NEWBIES?
FINE WITH US!
BUT THIS ISN'T ANCIENT ROME. IF YOU BREAK AN ARM, WE CAN HEAL IT!
SO DON'T HOLD BACK!
OKAY!!
YOU GUYS ARE OUR OPENING ACT!
WAAH
LET'S GO!
THIS IS YOUR DEBUT, SO REALLY WORK THAT CROWD!
OKAY!
GET THE CRAP BEATEN OUT OF YOU!
WAAH
SHUT UP, TOSAKA.

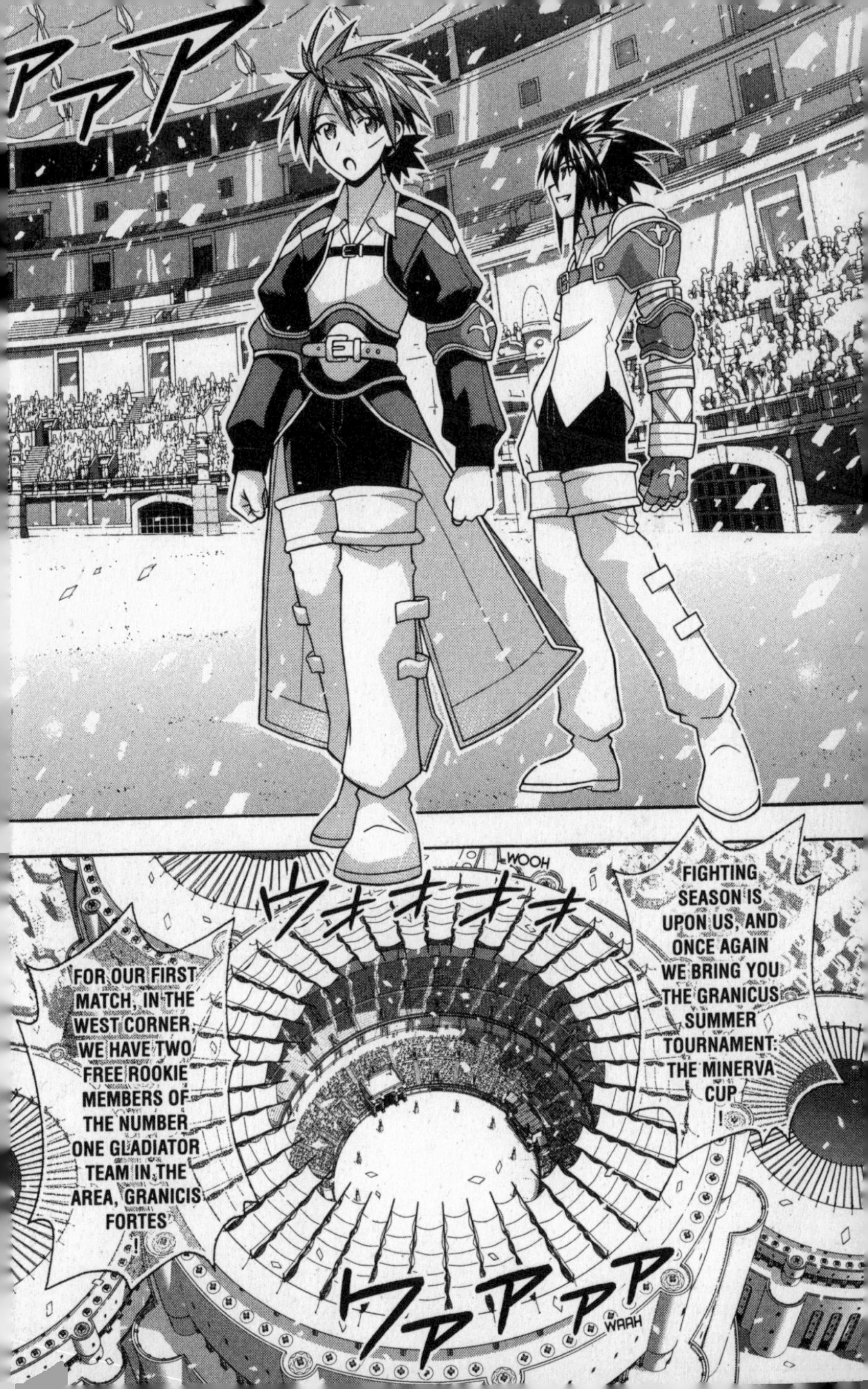

アァア
FIGHTING SEASON IS UPON US, AND ONCE AGAIN WE BRING YOU THE GRANICUS SUMMER TOURNAMENT: THE MINERVA CUP!
ウォォォォ
WOOH
FOR OUR FIRST MATCH, IN THE WEST CORNER, WE HAVE TWO FREE ROOKIE MEMBERS OF THE NUMBER ONE GLADIATOR TEAM IN THE AREA, GRANICIS FORTES!
ワァァァ
WAAH

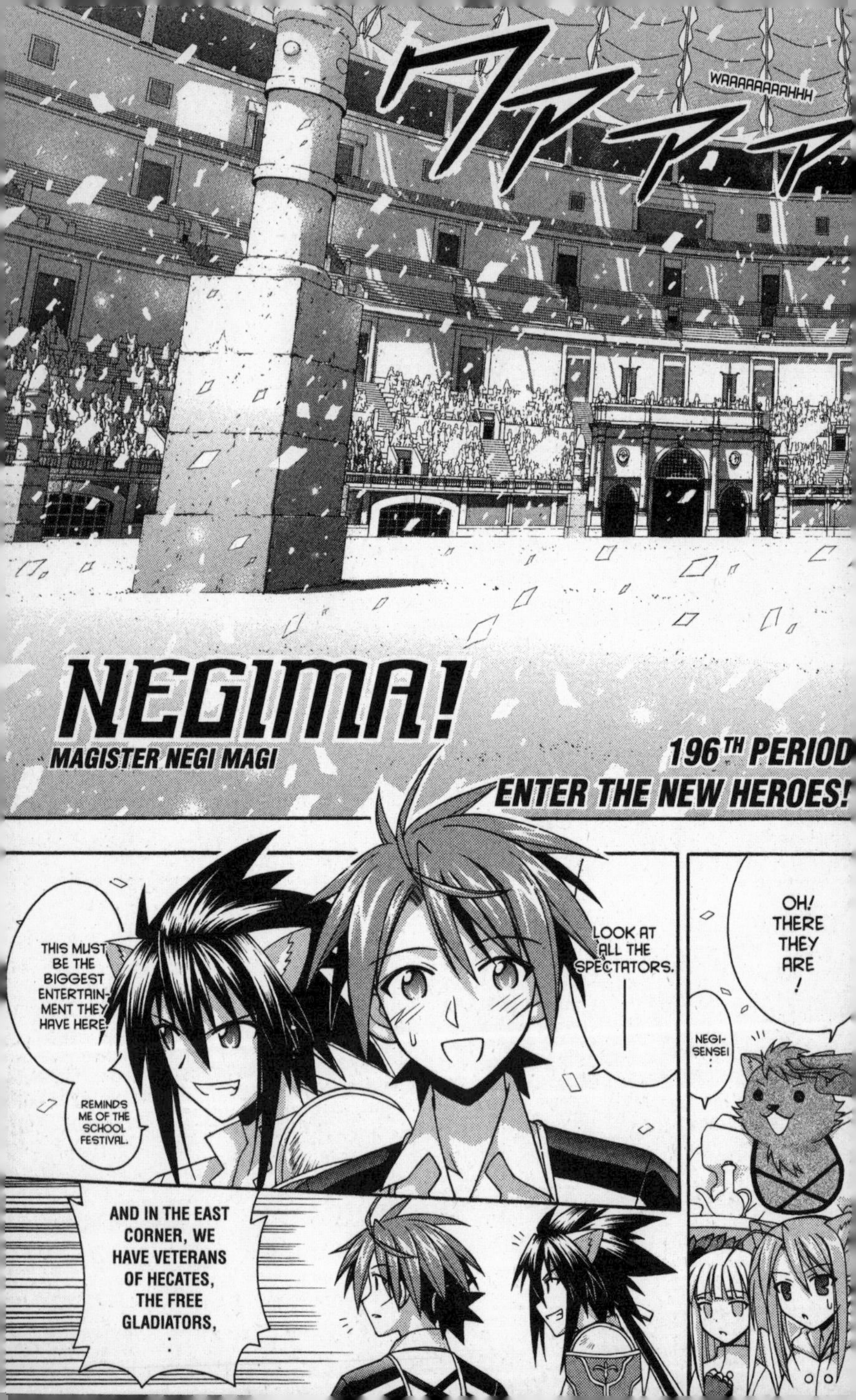
WAAAAAAAAAHHH
NEGIMA!
MAGISTER NEGI MAGI
196TH PERIOD
ENTER THE NEW HEROES!
OH! THERE THEY ARE!
NEGI-SENSEI :
LOOK AT ALL THE SPECTATORS.
THIS MUST BE THE BIGGEST ENTERTAINMENT THEY HAVE HERE.
REMINDS ME OF THE SCHOOL FESTIVAL.
AND IN THE EAST CORNER, WE HAVE VETERANS OF HECATES, THE FREE GLADIATORS, :

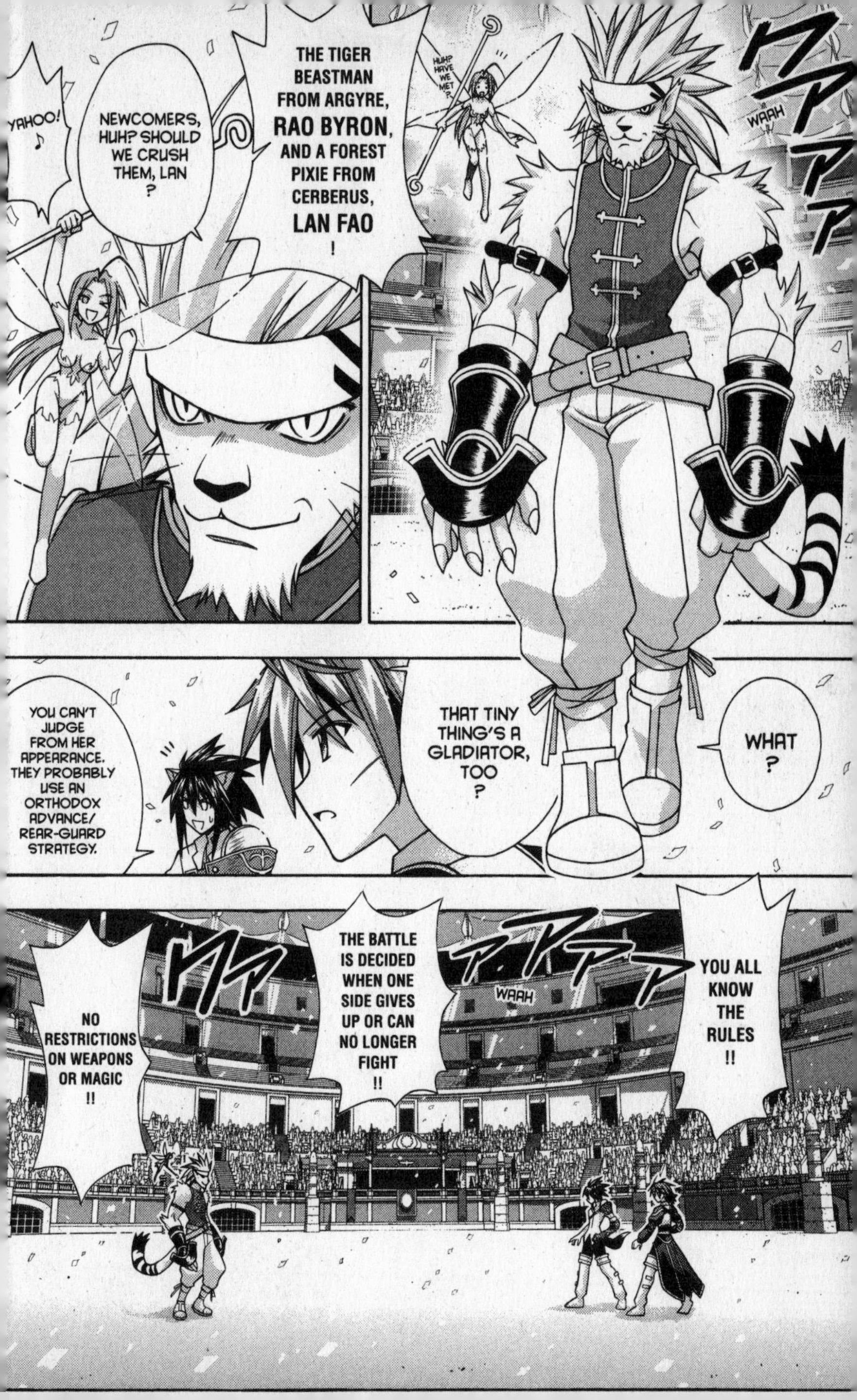
WAAH
HUH? HAVE WE MET?
THE TIGER BEASTMAN FROM ARGYRE, RAO BYRON, AND A FOREST PIXIE FROM CERBERUS, LAN FAO!
NEWCOMERS, HUH? SHOULD WE CRUSH THEM, LAN?
YAHOO! ♪
WHAT?
THAT TINY THING'S A GLADIATOR, TOO?
YOU CAN'T JUDGE FROM HER APPEARANCE. THEY PROBABLY USE AN ORTHODOX ADVANCE/ REAR-GUARD STRATEGY.
YOU ALL KNOW THE RULES!!
WAAH
THE BATTLE IS DECIDED WHEN ONE SIDE GIVES UP OR CAN NO LONGER FIGHT!!
NO RESTRICTIONS ON WEAPONS OR MAGIC!!

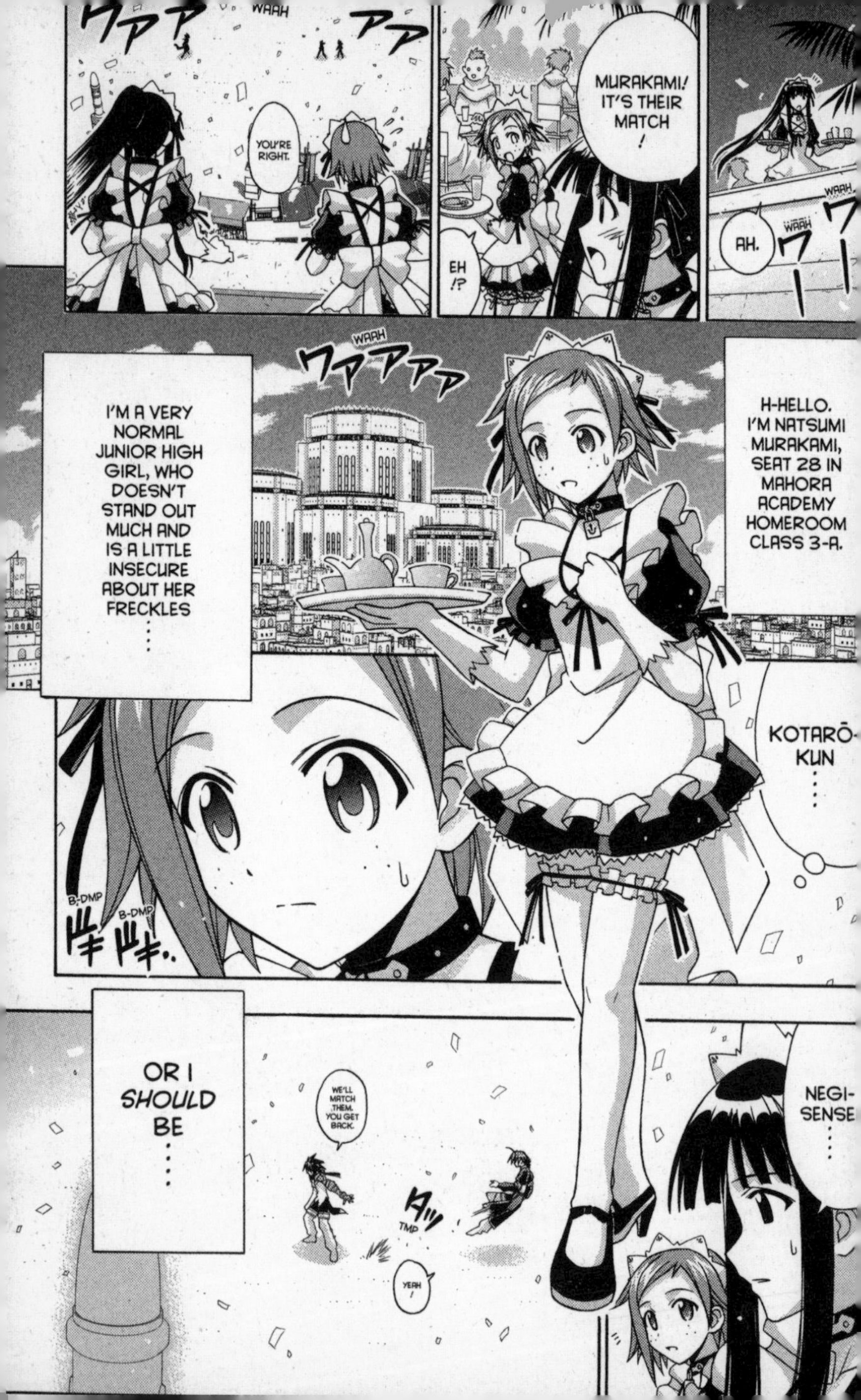
WAAH
WAAH
AH.
MURAKAMI! IT'S THEIR MATCH!
EH!?
WAAH
YOU'RE RIGHT.
H-HELLO. I'M NATSUMI MURAKAMI, SEAT 28 IN MAHORA ACADEMY HOMEROOM CLASS 3-A.
WAAH
I'M A VERY NORMAL JUNIOR HIGH GIRL, WHO DOESN'T STAND OUT MUCH AND IS A LITTLE INSECURE ABOUT HER FRECKLES...
KOTARŌ-KUN...
B-DMP B-DMP
NEGI-SENSE...
YEAH!
TMP
WE'LL MATCH THEM. YOU GET BACK.
OR I SHOULD BE...

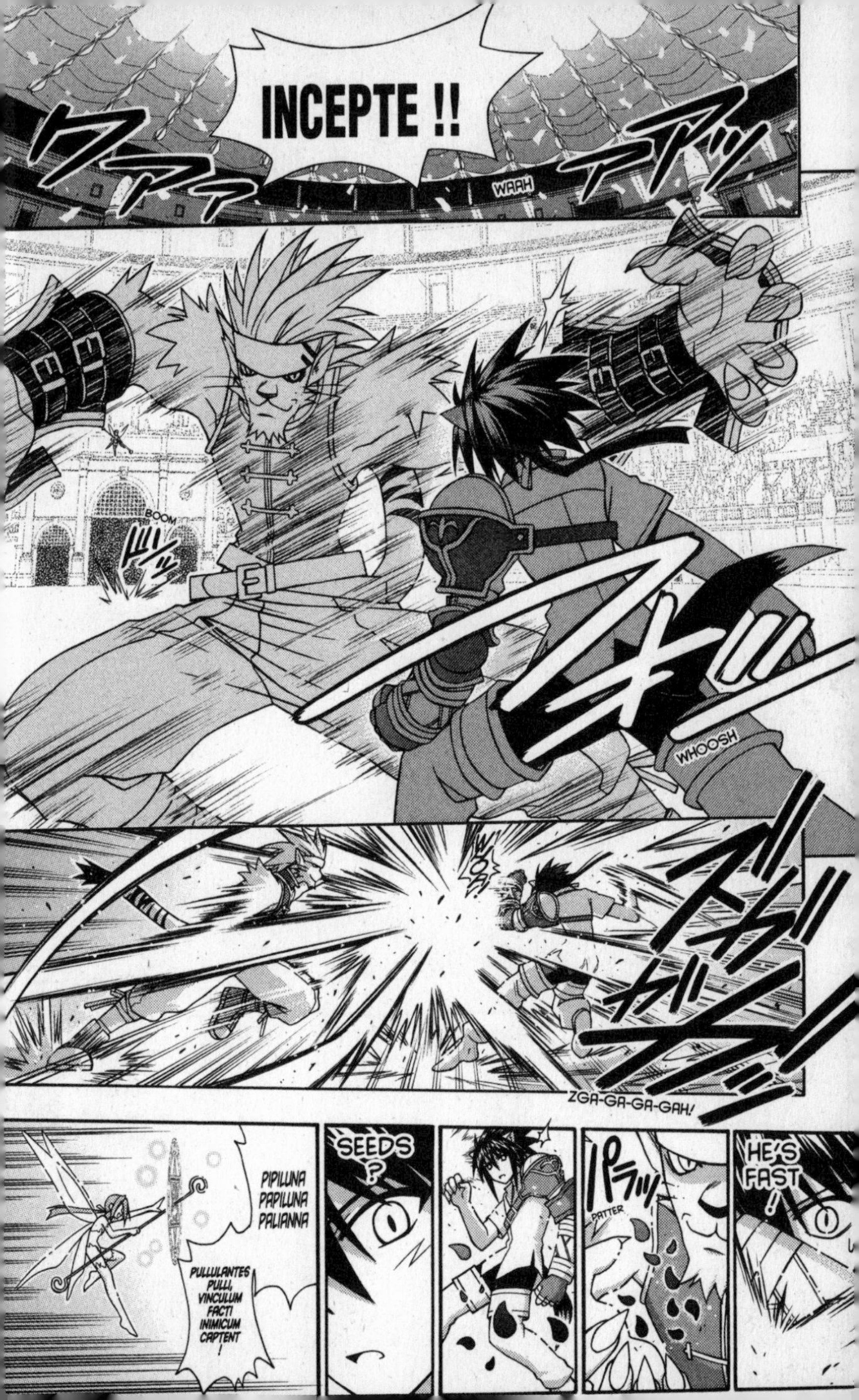
INCEPTE !!
WAAH
WHOOSH
BOOM
ZGA-GA-GA-GAH!
HE'S FAST !
PATTER
SEEDS ?
PIPILUNA PAPILUNA PALIANNA
PULLULANTES PULLI, VINCULUM FACTI INIMICUM CAPTENT !

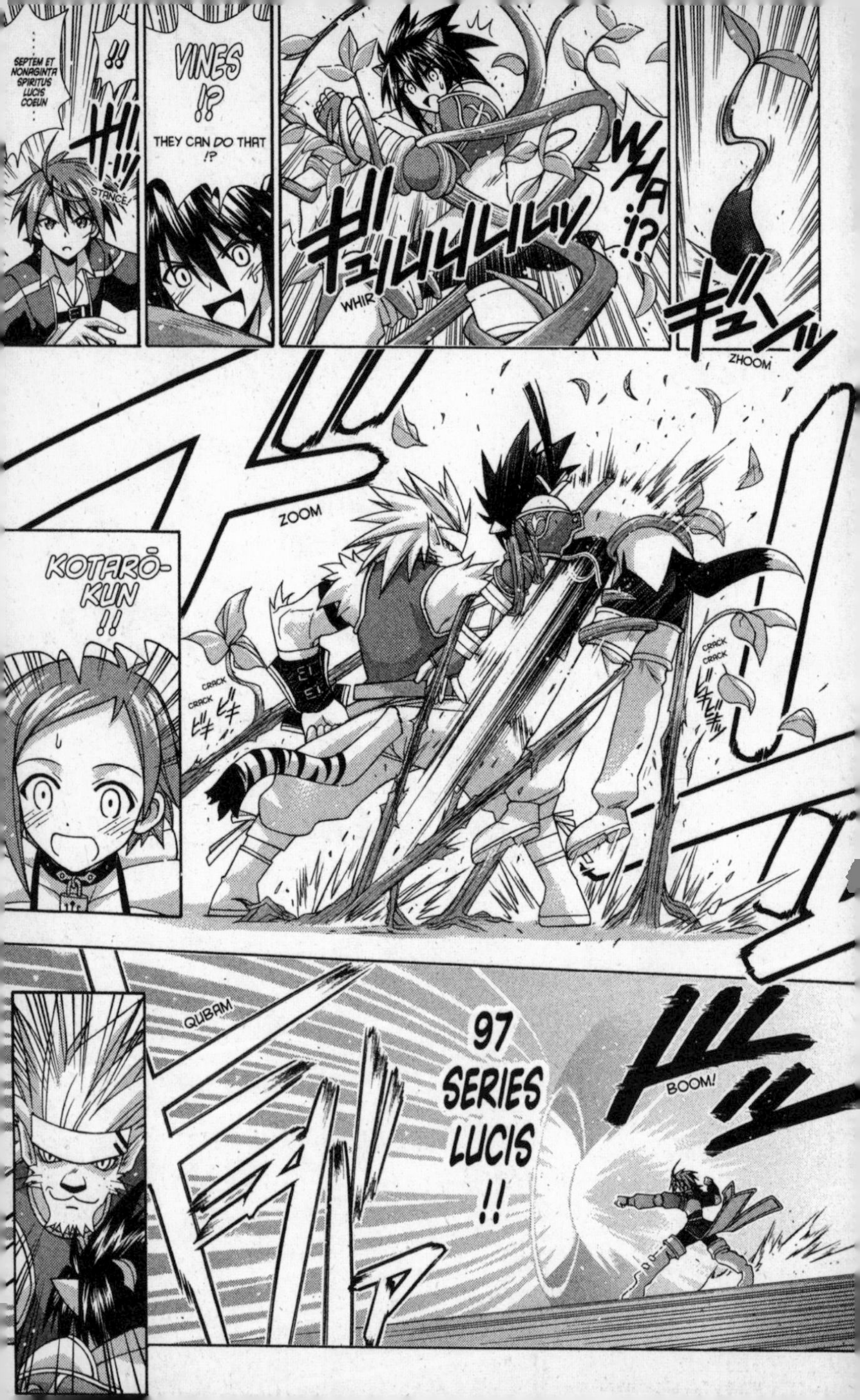
ZHOOM
WHA!?
WHIR
VINES!?
THEY CAN DO THAT!?
...SEPTEM ET NONAGINTA SPIRITUS LUCIS COEUN...
!!
STANCE!
ZOOM
CRACK CRACK
CRACK CRACK
KOTARŌ-KUN!!
BOOM!
97 SERIES LUCIS!!
QUBAM

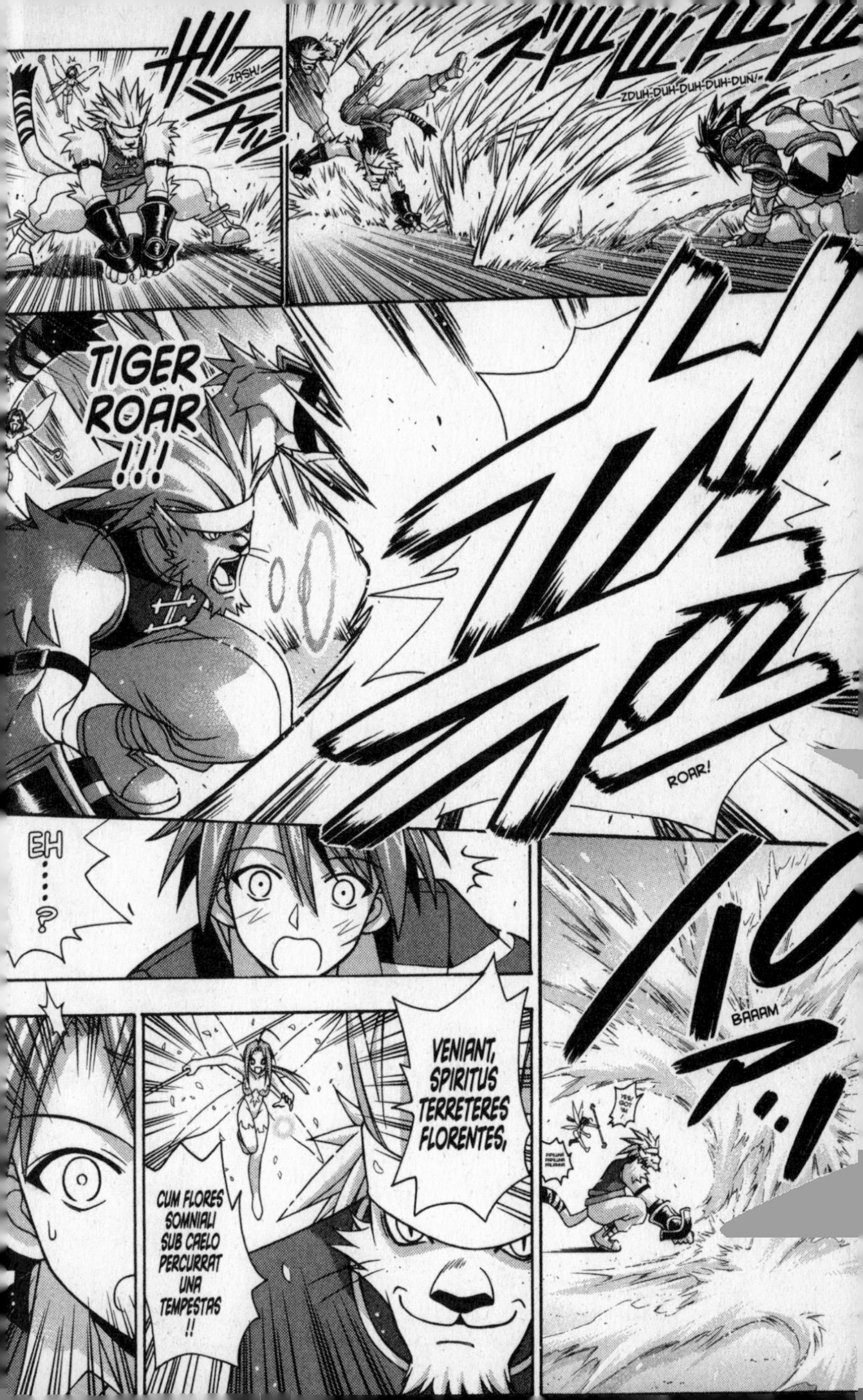
ZDUH-DUH-DUH-DUH-DUN!
ZASH!
TIGER ROAR!!!
ROAR!
BAAAM
YES! GOT 'IM!
EH....?
VENIANT, SPIRITUS TERRETERES FLORENTES,
CUM FLORES SOMNIALI SUB CAELO PERCURRAT UNA TEMPESTAS!!

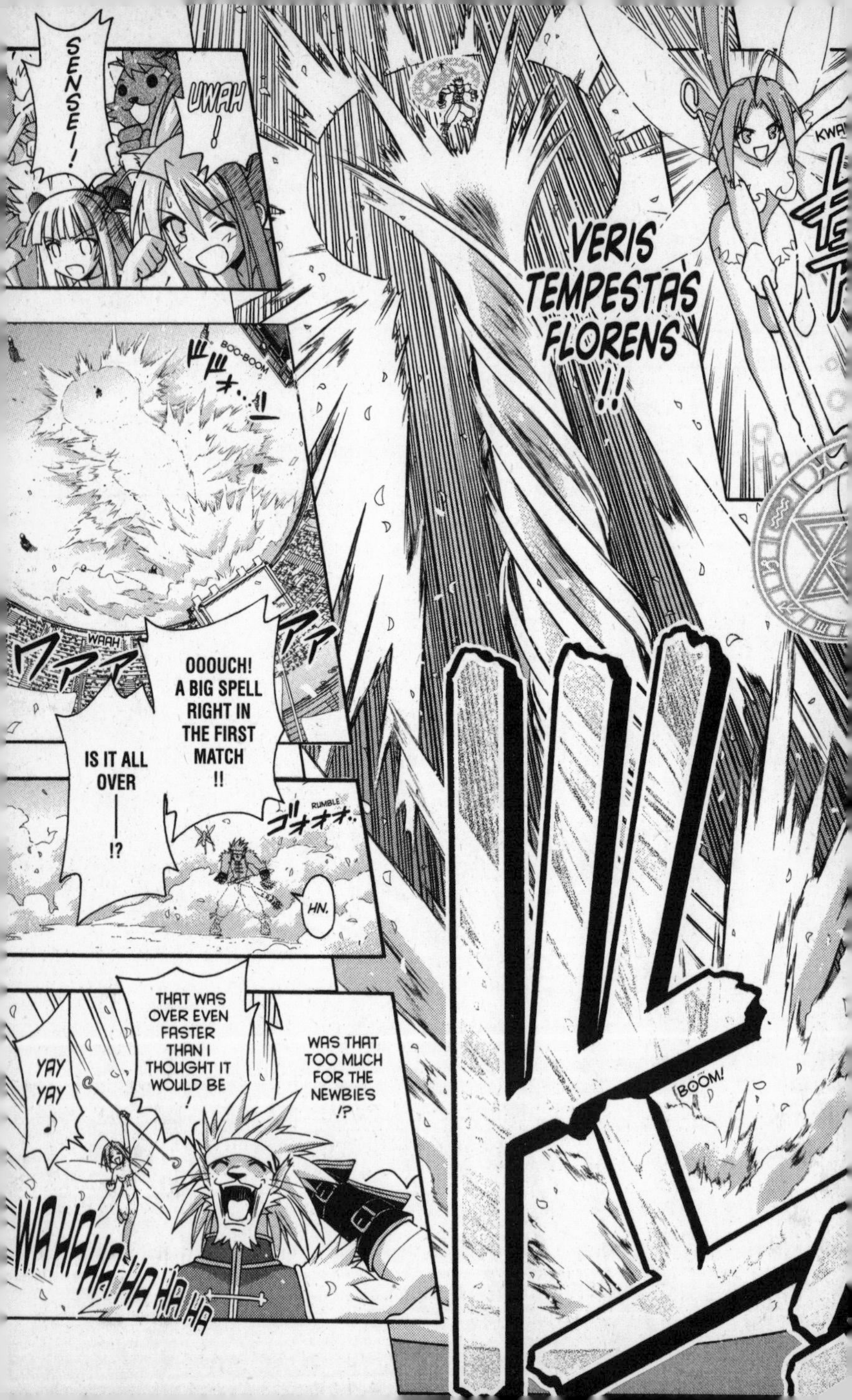
KWA
VERIS TEMPESTAS FLORENS !!
BOOM!
SENSEI!!
UWAH !
BOO-BOOM
WAAH
OOOUCH! A BIG SPELL RIGHT IN THE FIRST MATCH !!
IS IT ALL OVER —— !?
RUMBLE
HN.
WAS THAT TOO MUCH FOR THE NEWBIES !?
THAT WAS OVER EVEN FASTER THAN I THOUGHT IT WOULD BE !
YAY YAY ♪
WA HA HA HA HA HA HA HA HA

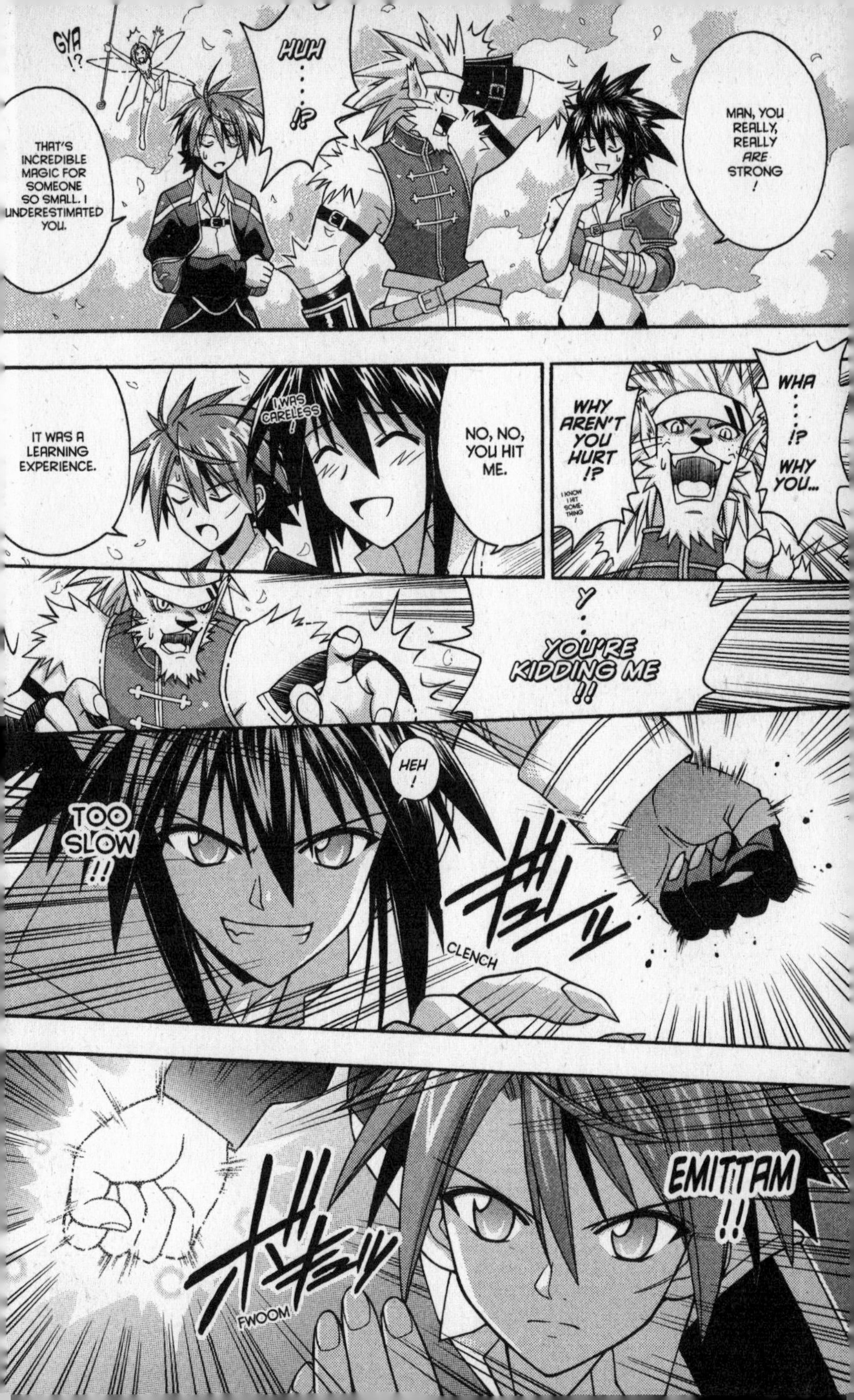
MAN, YOU REALLY, REALLY ARE STRONG!
HUH...!?
GYA!?
THAT'S INCREDIBLE MAGIC FOR SOMEONE SO SMALL. I UNDERESTIMATED YOU.
WHA...!? WHY YOU...
WHY AREN'T YOU HURT!?
I KNOW I HIT SOMETHING!
NO, NO, YOU HIT ME.
I WAS CARELESS!
IT WAS A LEARNING EXPERIENCE.
Y... YOU'RE KIDDING ME!!
HEH!
TOO SLOW!!
CLENCH
EMITTAM!!
FWOOM

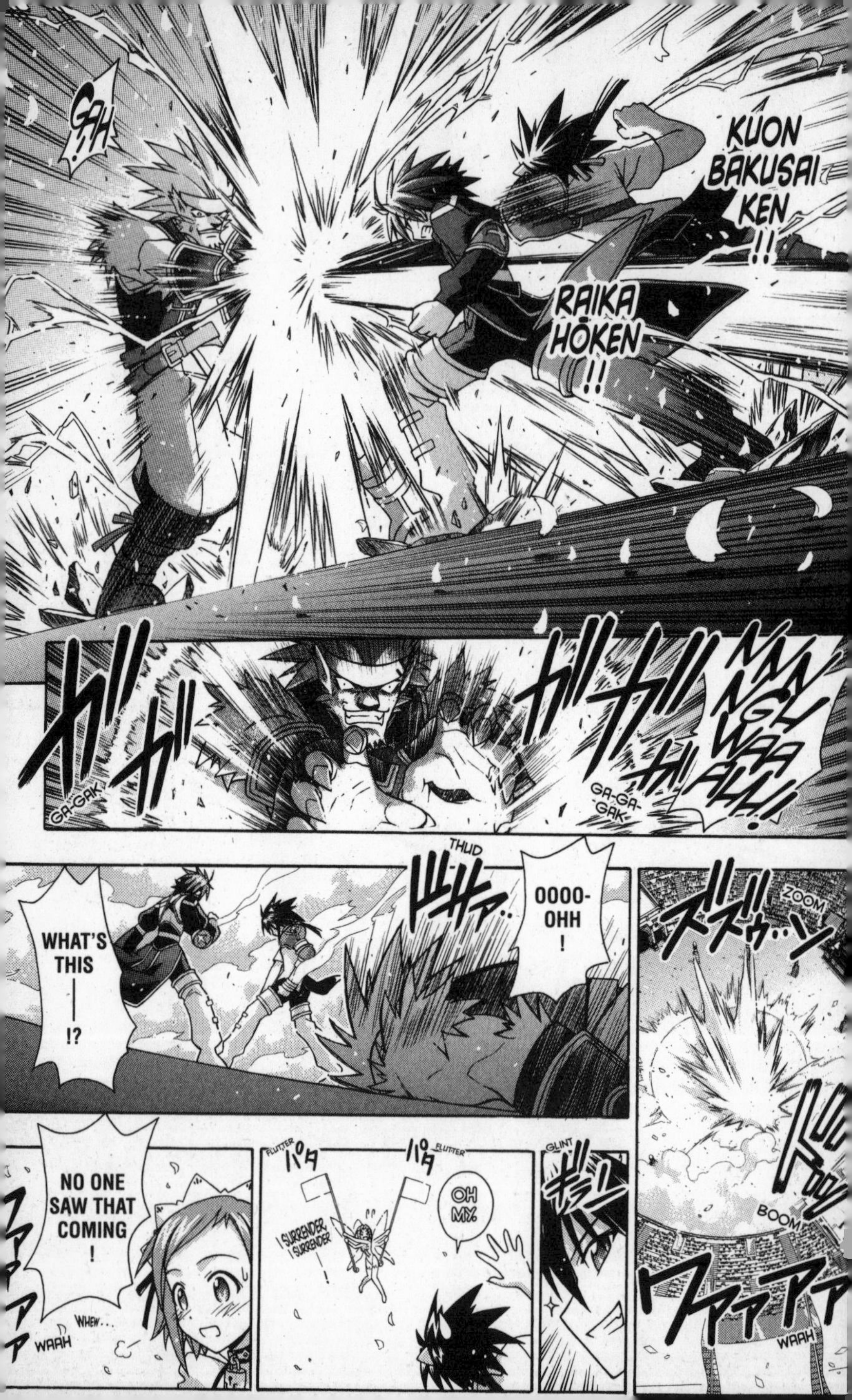
KUON BAKUSAI KEN!!
RAIKA HŌKEN!!
GAH!
MNNNGH WAAAHHH!!
GA-GA-GAK
GA-GAK
ZOOM
BOOM
WAAH
THUD
OOOO-OHH!
WHAT'S THIS—!?
GLINT
FLUTTER
FLUTTER
OH MY.
I SURRENDER I SURRENDER!
NO ONE SAW THAT COMING!
WHEW...
WAAH

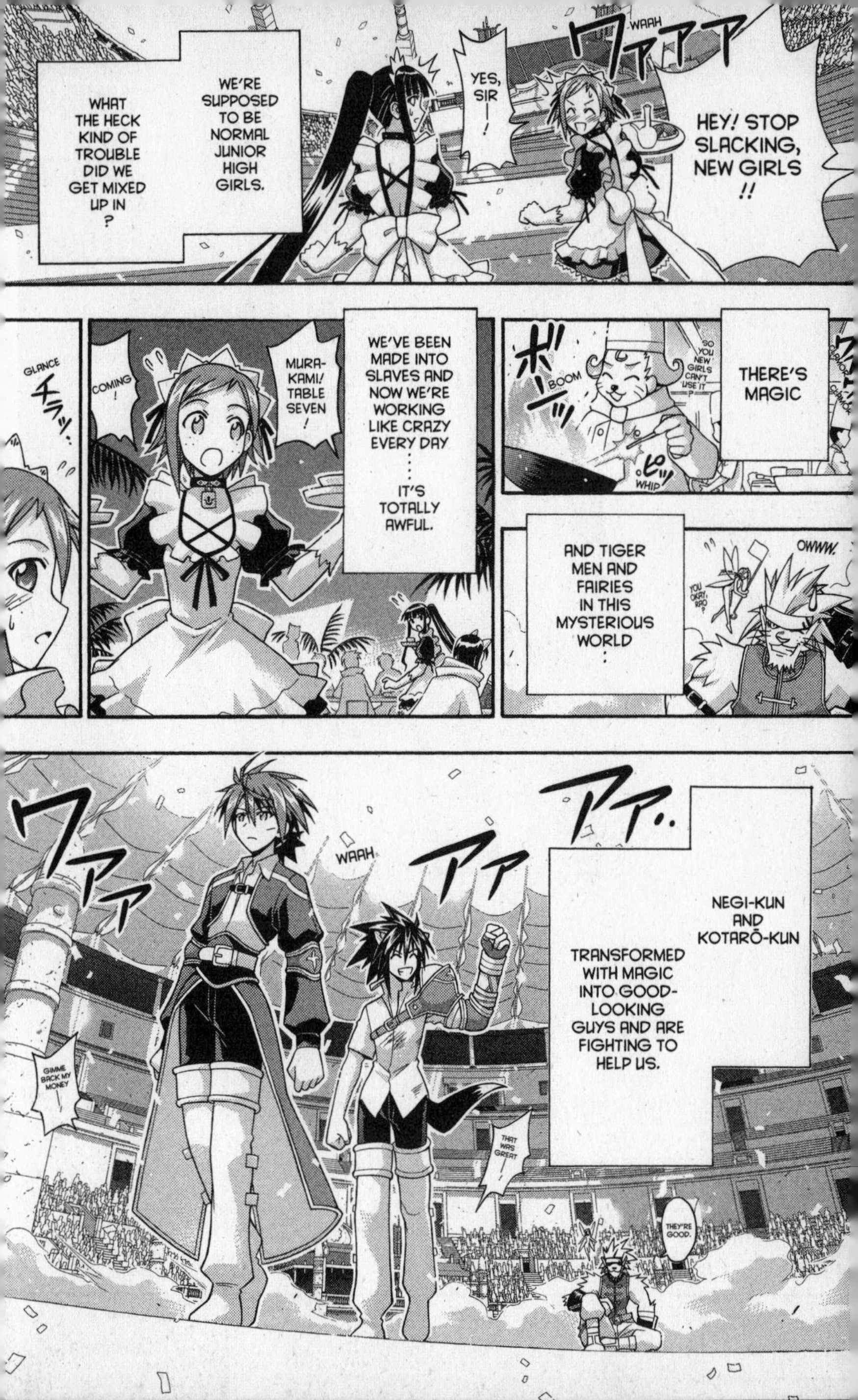
WAAH
HEY! STOP SLACKING, NEW GIRLS!!
YES, SIR!
WE'RE SUPPOSED TO BE NORMAL JUNIOR HIGH GIRLS.
WHAT THE HECK KIND OF TROUBLE DID WE GET MIXED UP IN?
THERE'S MAGIC
CLAMOR CLAMOR
SO YOU NEW GIRLS CAN'T USE IT?
BOOM
WHIP
AND TIGER MEN AND FAIRIES IN THIS MYSTERIOUS WORLD...
OWWW.
YOU OKAY, RAO?
WE'VE BEEN MADE INTO SLAVES AND NOW WE'RE WORKING LIKE CRAZY EVERY DAY... IT'S TOTALLY AWFUL.
MURA-KAMI! TABLE SEVEN!
COMING!
GLANCE
NEGI-KUN AND KOTARŌ-KUN
TRANSFORMED WITH MAGIC INTO GOOD-LOOKING GUYS AND ARE FIGHTING TO HELP US.
WAAH
THEY'RE GOOD.
THAT WAS GREAT!
GIMME BACK MY MONEY!

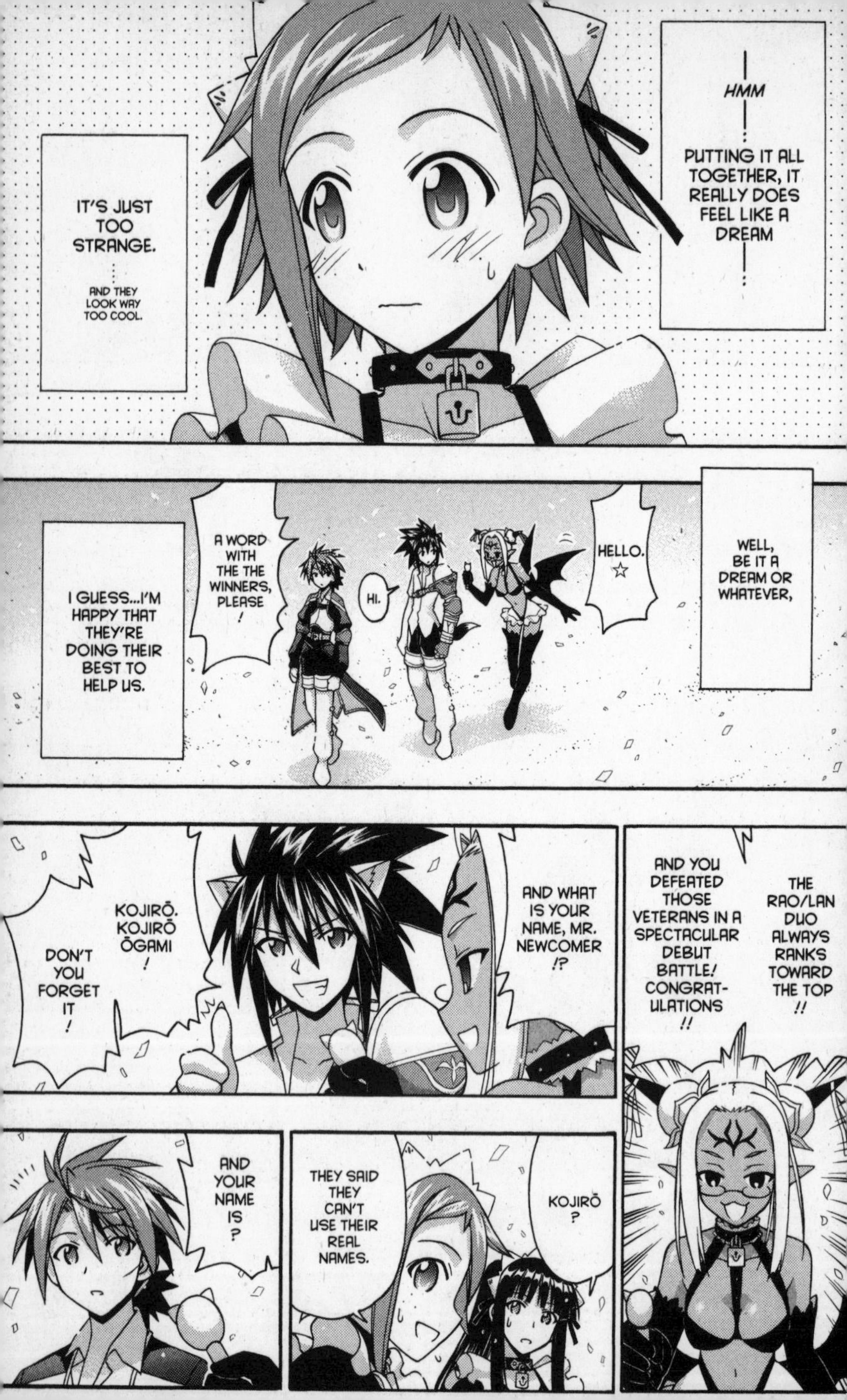
HMM
PUTTING IT ALL TOGETHER, IT REALLY DOES FEEL LIKE A DREAM
IT'S JUST TOO STRANGE.
AND THEY LOOK WAY TOO COOL.
WELL, BE IT A DREAM OR WHATEVER,
HELLO. ☆
HI.
A WORD WITH THE THE WINNERS, PLEASE!
I GUESS...I'M HAPPY THAT THEY'RE DOING THEIR BEST TO HELP US.
THE RAO/LAN DUO ALWAYS RANKS TOWARD THE TOP!!
AND YOU DEFEATED THOSE VETERANS IN A SPECTACULAR DEBUT BATTLE! CONGRAT-ULATIONS!!
AND WHAT IS YOUR NAME, MR. NEWCOMER!?
KOJIRŌ. KOJIRŌ ŌGAMI!
DON'T YOU FORGET IT!
KOJIRŌ?
THEY SAID THEY CAN'T USE THEIR REAL NAMES.
AND YOUR NAME IS?

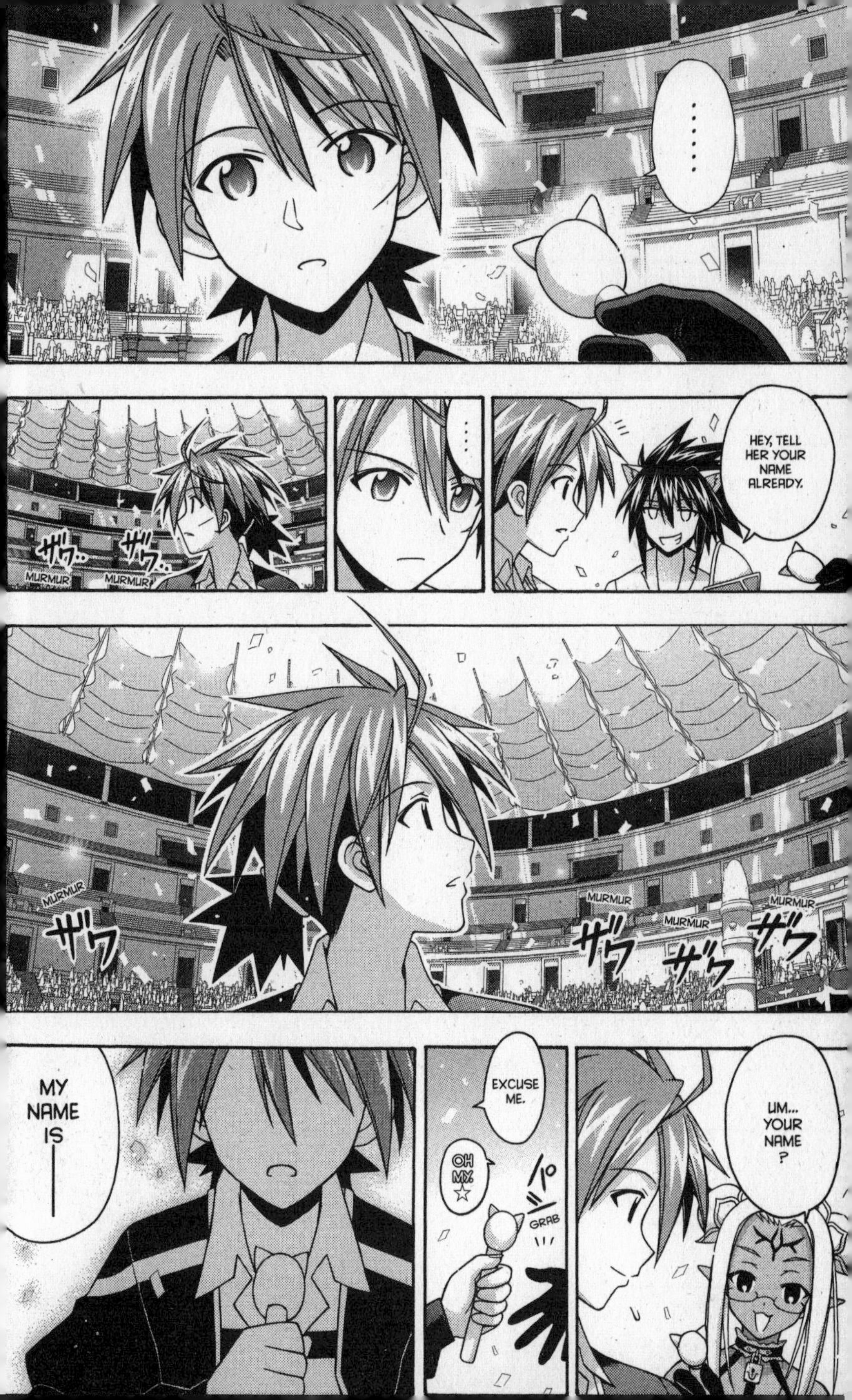
......
HEY, TELL HER YOUR NAME ALREADY.
....
ザワ.. ザワ..
MURMUR MURMUR
MURMUR ザワ ザワ ザワ
MURMUR MURMUR MURMUR
ザワ
UM... YOUR NAME?
EXCUSE ME.
OH MY.☆
GRAB
MY NAME IS—

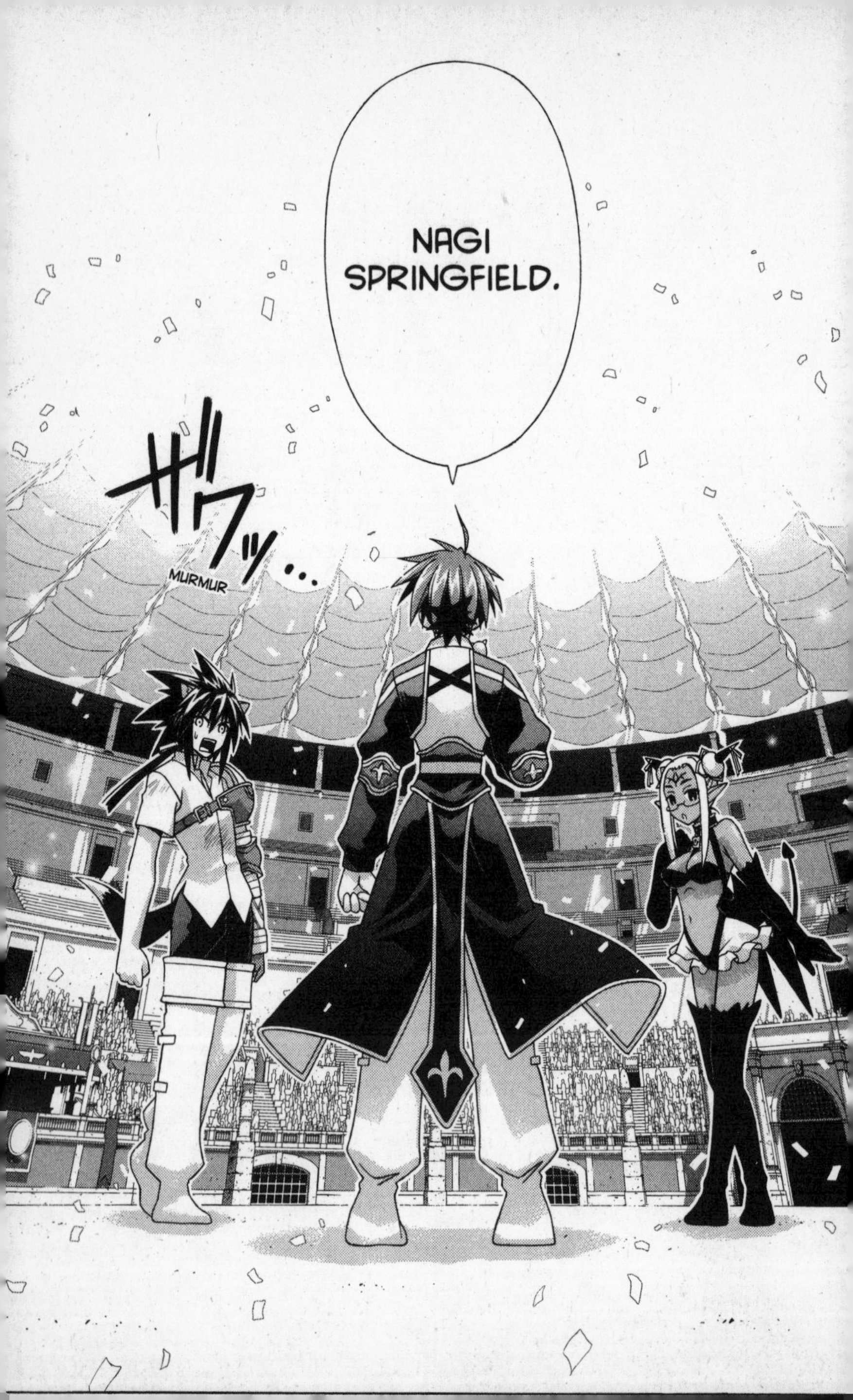
NAGI SPRINGFIELD.
ザワッ…
MURMUR

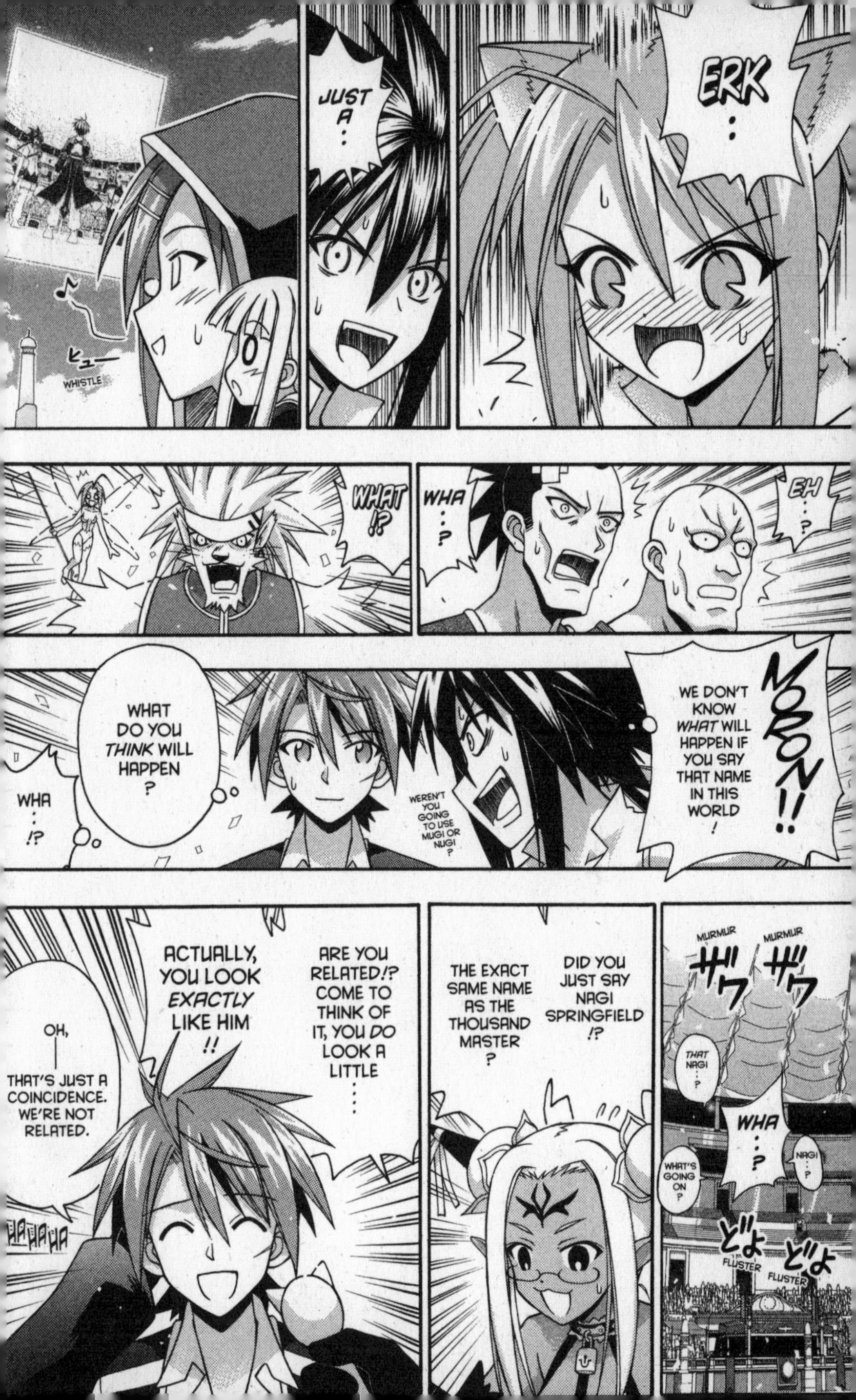
ERK...
JUST A...
ヒュー
WHISTLE
EH...?
WHA...?
WHAT!?
MORON!!
WE DON'T KNOW *WHAT* WILL HAPPEN IF YOU SAY THAT NAME IN THIS WORLD!
WEREN'T YOU GOING TO USE MUGI OR NUGI?
WHAT DO YOU *THINK* WILL HAPPEN?
WHA...!?
ザワ ザワ
MURMUR MURMUR
THAT NAGI...?
NAGI...?
WHA...?
WHAT'S GOING ON?
どよ どよ
FLUSTER FLUSTER
DID YOU JUST SAY NAGI SPRINGFIELD!?
THE EXACT SAME NAME AS THE THOUSAND MASTER?
ARE YOU RELATED!? COME TO THINK OF IT, YOU *DO* LOOK A LITTLE...
ACTUALLY, YOU LOOK *EXACTLY* LIKE HIM!!
OH, — THAT'S JUST A COINCIDENCE. WE'RE NOT RELATED.
HAHAHA

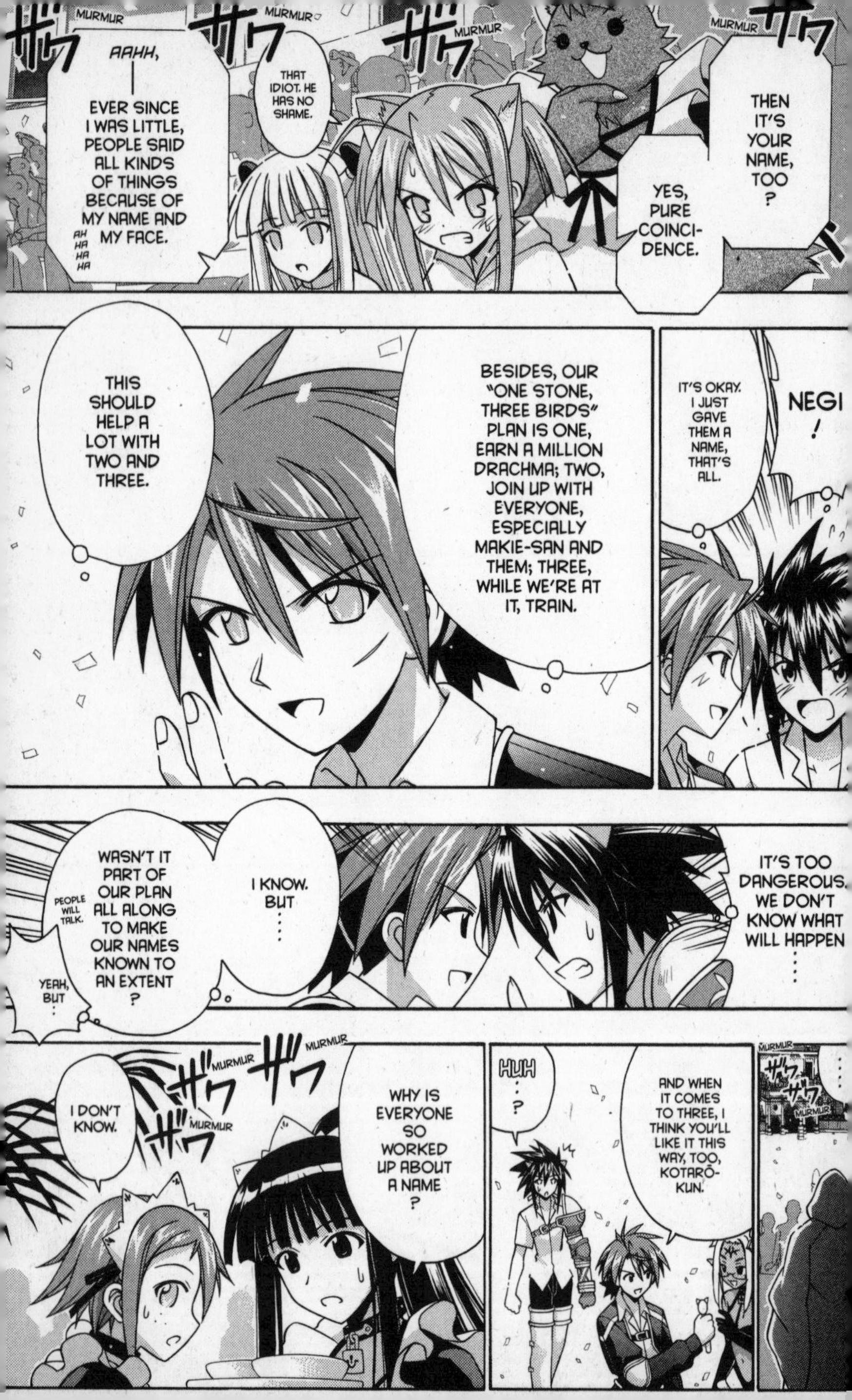

ザワ ザワ ザワ ザワ
MURMUR
MURMUR
MURMUR
MURMUR
THEN IT'S YOUR NAME, TOO?
YES, PURE COINCIDENCE.
THAT IDIOT. HE HAS NO SHAME.
AAHH, EVER SINCE I WAS LITTLE, PEOPLE SAID ALL KINDS OF THINGS BECAUSE OF MY NAME AND MY FACE.
AH HA HA HA
NEGI!
IT'S OKAY. I JUST GAVE THEM A NAME, THAT'S ALL.
BESIDES, OUR "ONE STONE, THREE BIRDS" PLAN IS ONE, EARN A MILLION DRACHMA; TWO, JOIN UP WITH EVERYONE, ESPECIALLY MAKIE-SAN AND THEM; THREE, WHILE WE'RE AT IT, TRAIN.
THIS SHOULD HELP A LOT WITH TWO AND THREE.
IT'S TOO DANGEROUS. WE DON'T KNOW WHAT WILL HAPPEN....
I KNOW. BUT....
WASN'T IT PART OF OUR PLAN ALL ALONG TO MAKE OUR NAMES KNOWN TO AN EXTENT?
PEOPLE WILL TALK.
YEAH, BUT...
MURMUR
ザワ ザワ
MURMUR
...
AND WHEN IT COMES TO THREE, I THINK YOU'LL LIKE IT THIS WAY, TOO, KOTARŌ-KUN.
HUH...?
MURMUR
ザワ ザワ
MURMUR
MURMUR
WHY IS EVERYONE SO WORKED UP ABOUT A NAME?
I DON'T KNOW.

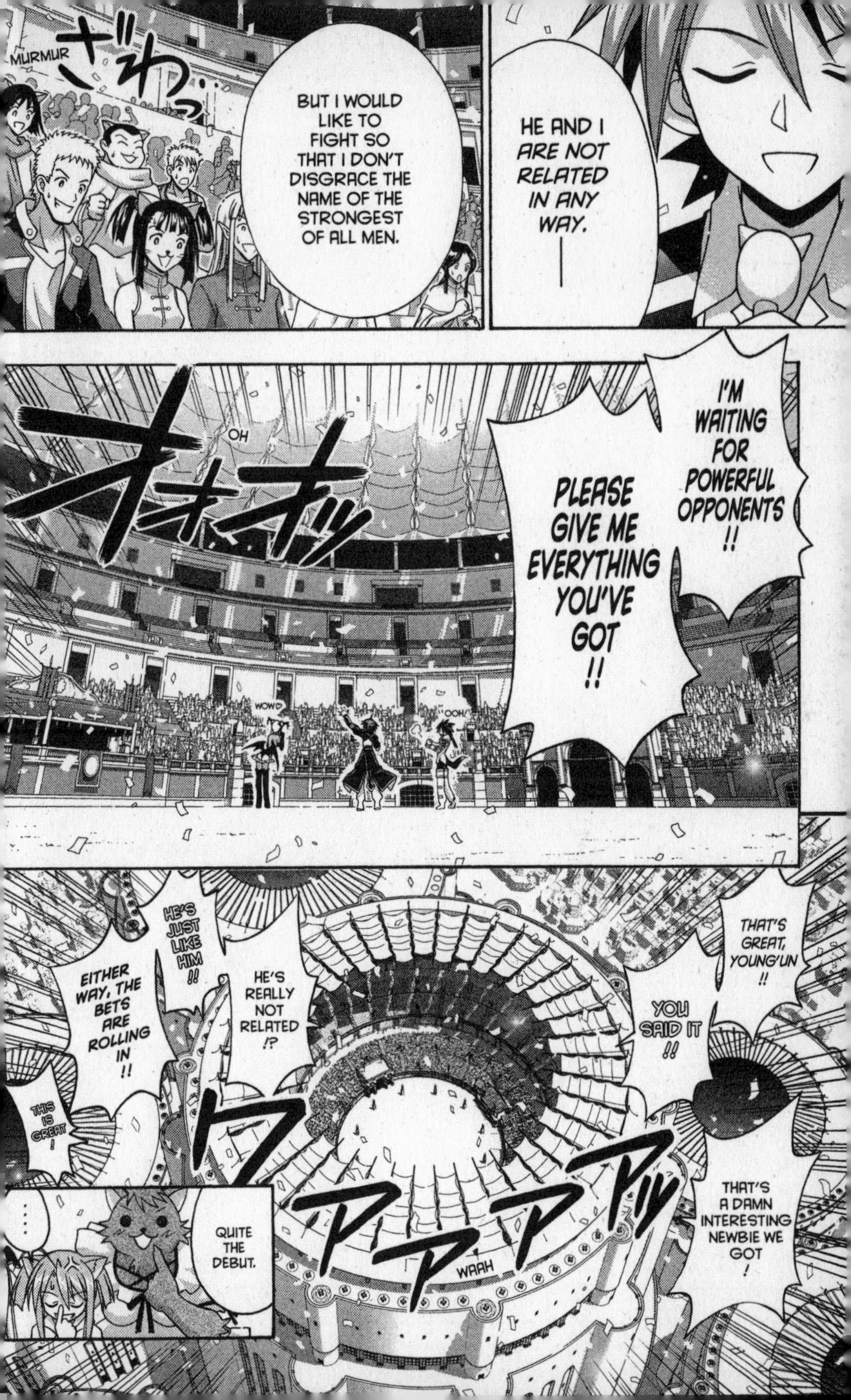
HE AND I ARE NOT RELATED IN ANY WAY.
MURMUR
BUT I WOULD LIKE TO FIGHT SO THAT I DON'T DISGRACE THE NAME OF THE STRONGEST OF ALL MEN.
I'M WAITING FOR POWERFUL OPPONENTS!!
PLEASE GIVE ME EVERYTHING YOU'VE GOT!!
OH
OOH
WOW
THAT'S GREAT, YOUNG'UN!!
YOU SAID IT!!
HE'S REALLY NOT RELATED!?
HE'S JUST LIKE HIM!!
EITHER WAY, THE BETS ARE ROLLING IN!!
THIS IS GREAT!
THAT'S A DAMN INTERESTING NEWBIE WE GOT!
WAAH
QUITE THE DEBUT.
.....

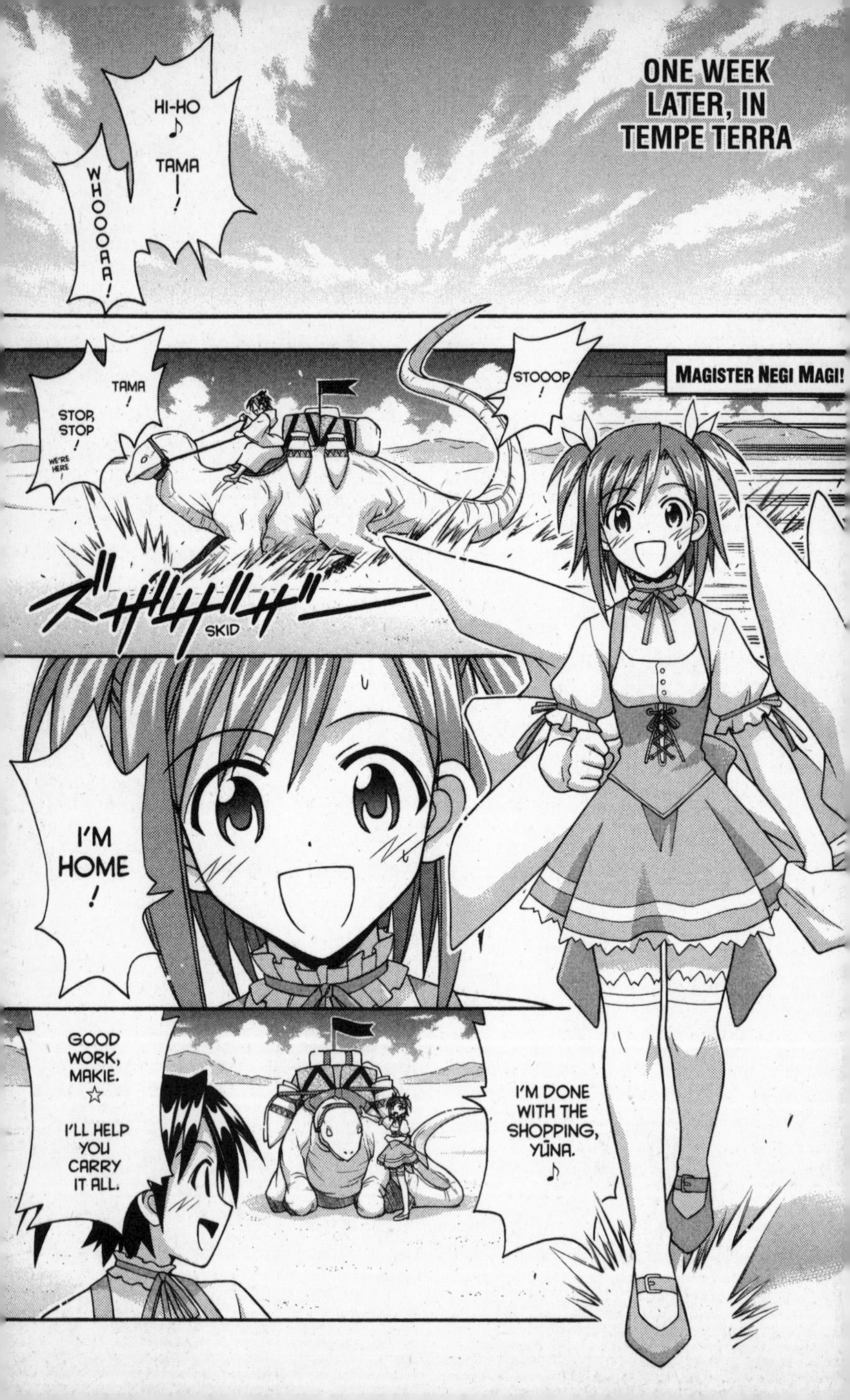
ONE WEEK LATER, IN TEMPE TERRA
HI-HO ♪ TAMA-!
WHOOOOAA!
MAGISTER NEGI MAGI!
STOOOP!
TAMA! STOP, STOP! WE'RE HERE!
SKID
I'M HOME!
I'M DONE WITH THE SHOPPING, YŪNA. ♪
GOOD WORK, MAKIE. ☆ I'LL HELP YOU CARRY IT ALL.

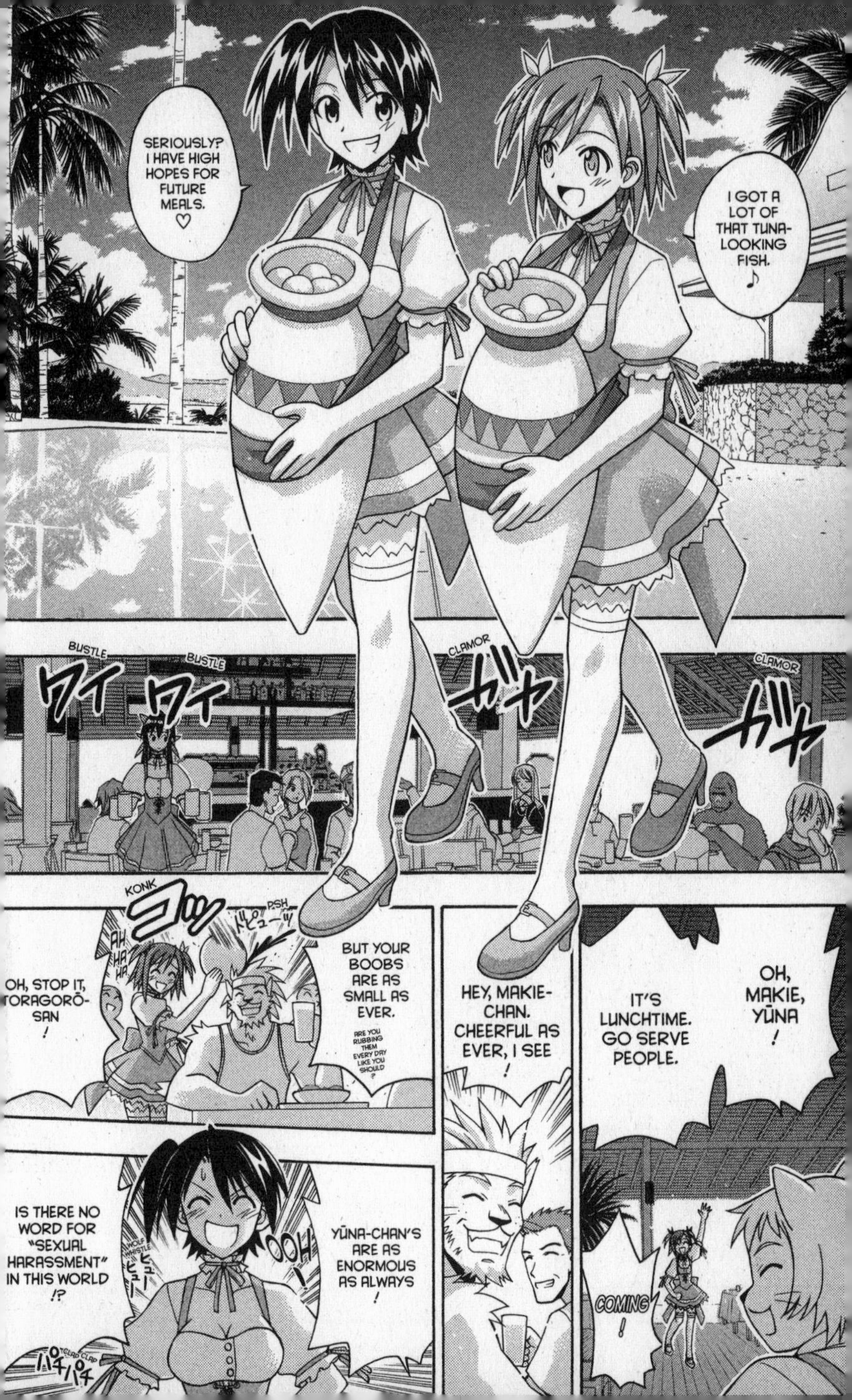
I GOT A LOT OF THAT TUNA-LOOKING FISH. ♪
SERIOUSLY? I HAVE HIGH HOPES FOR FUTURE MEALS. ♡
CLAMOR
ガヤ
CLAMOR
ガヤ
BUSTLE
ワイ
BUSTLE
ワイ
OH, MAKIE, YŪNA!
IT'S LUNCHTIME. GO SERVE PEOPLE.
COMING!
HEY, MAKIE-CHAN. CHEERFUL AS EVER, I SEE!
BUT YOUR BOOBS ARE AS SMALL AS EVER.
ARE YOU RUBBING THEM EVERY DAY LIKE YOU SHOULD!?
PSH
KONK
AH HA HA HA
OH, STOP IT, TORAGORŌ-SAN!
YŪNA-CHAN'S ARE AS ENORMOUS AS ALWAYS!
OOH!
WOLF WHISTLE
IS THERE NO WORD FOR "SEXUAL HARASSMENT" IN THIS WORLD!?
CLAP CLAP

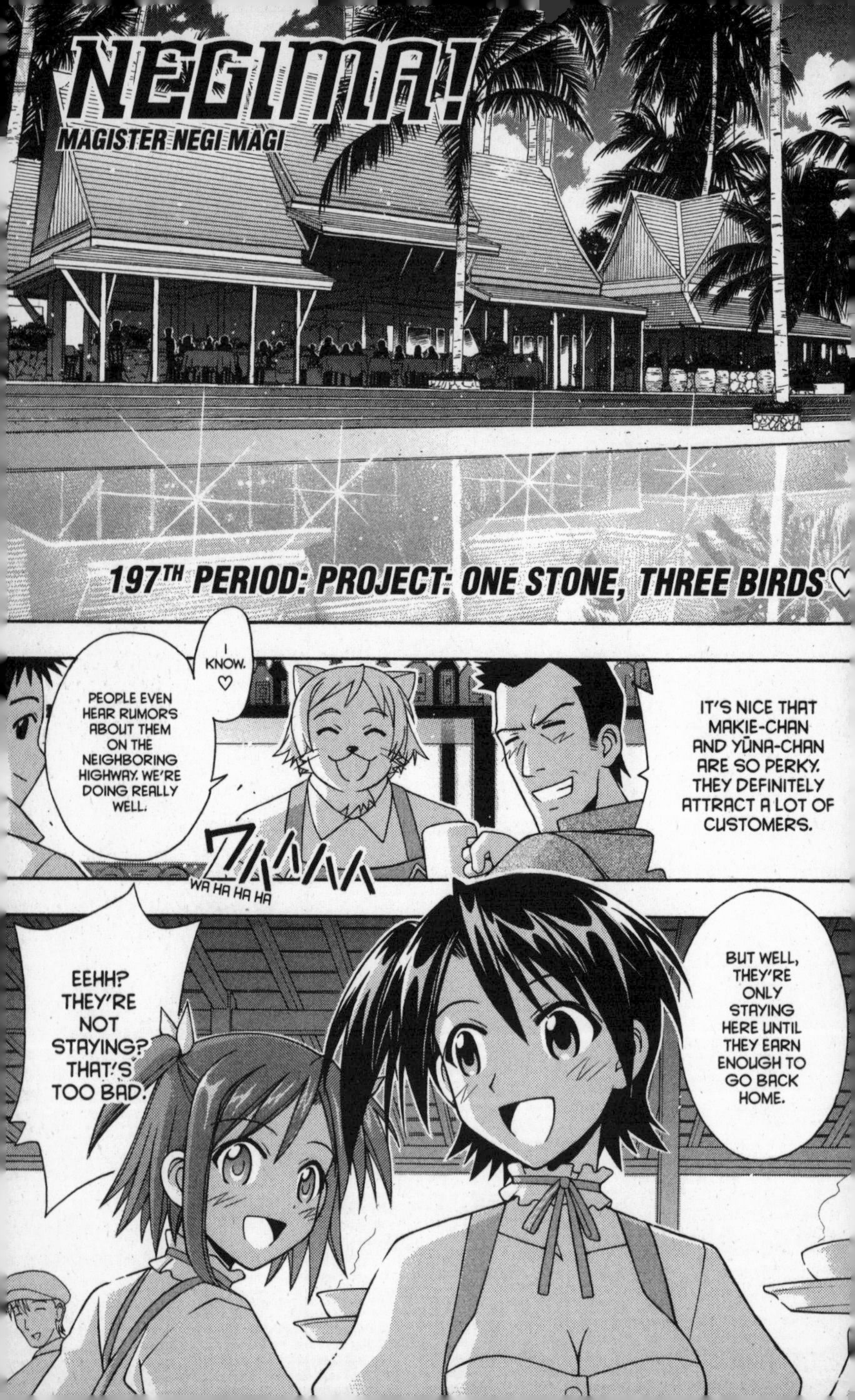
NEGIMA!
MAGISTER NEGI MAGI
197TH PERIOD: PROJECT: ONE STONE, THREE BIRDS ♡
IT'S NICE THAT MAKIE-CHAN AND YŪNA-CHAN ARE SO PERKY. THEY DEFINITELY ATTRACT A LOT OF CUSTOMERS.
I KNOW. ♡
PEOPLE EVEN HEAR RUMORS ABOUT THEM ON THE NEIGHBORING HIGHWAY. WE'RE DOING REALLY WELL.
WA HA HA HA
BUT WELL, THEY'RE ONLY STAYING HERE UNTIL THEY EARN ENOUGH TO GO BACK HOME.
EEHH? THEY'RE NOT STAYING? THAT'S TOO BAD.

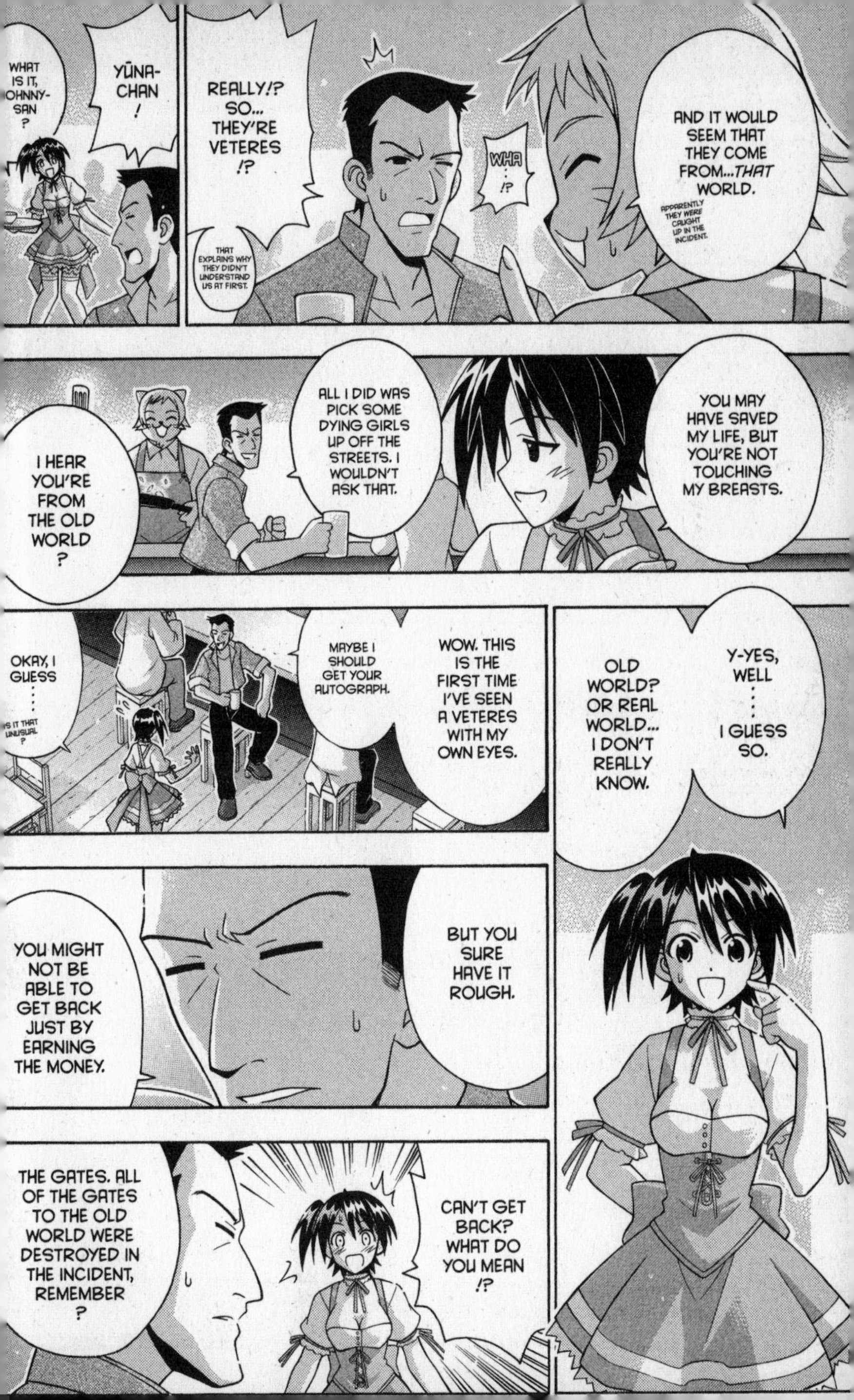
AND IT WOULD SEEM THAT THEY COME FROM...*THAT* WORLD.
APPARENTLY THEY WERE CAUGHT UP IN THE INCIDENT.
WHA...!?
REALLY!? SO... THEY'RE VETERES!?
THAT EXPLAINS WHY THEY DIDN'T UNDERSTAND US AT FIRST.
YŪNA-CHAN!
WHAT IS IT, OHNNY-SAN?
YOU MAY HAVE SAVED MY LIFE, BUT YOU'RE NOT TOUCHING MY BREASTS.
ALL I DID WAS PICK SOME DYING GIRLS UP OFF THE STREETS. I WOULDN'T ASK THAT.
I HEAR YOU'RE FROM THE OLD WORLD?
Y-YES, WELL... I GUESS SO.
OLD WORLD? OR REAL WORLD... I DON'T REALLY KNOW.
WOW. THIS IS THE FIRST TIME I'VE SEEN A VETERES WITH MY OWN EYES.
MAYBE I SHOULD GET YOUR AUTOGRAPH.
OKAY, I GUESS...
S IT THAT UNUSUAL?
BUT YOU SURE HAVE IT ROUGH.
YOU MIGHT NOT BE ABLE TO GET BACK JUST BY EARNING THE MONEY.
CAN'T GET BACK? WHAT DO YOU MEAN!?
THE GATES. ALL OF THE GATES TO THE OLD WORLD WERE DESTROYED IN THE INCIDENT, REMEMBER?

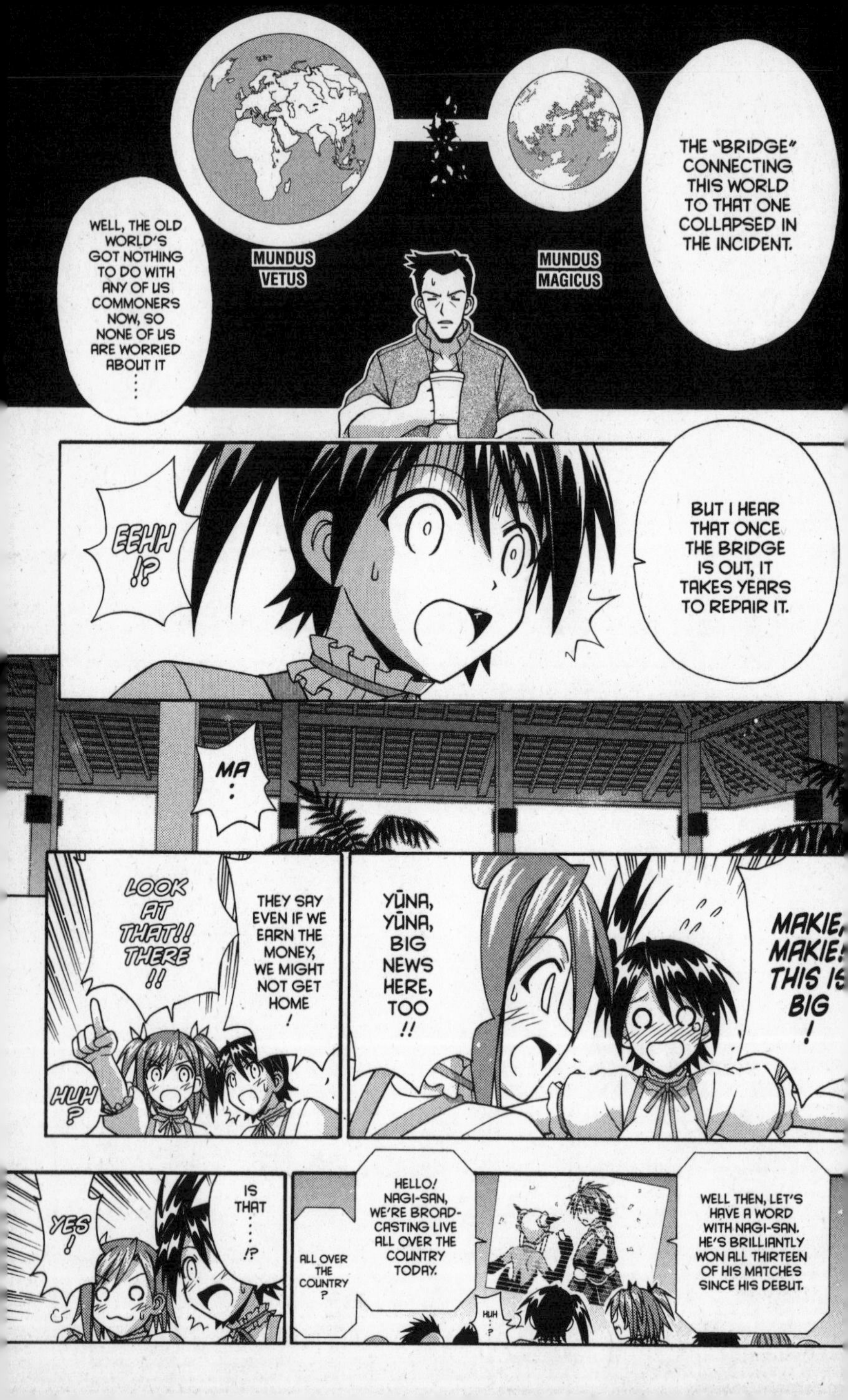
THE "BRIDGE" CONNECTING THIS WORLD TO THAT ONE COLLAPSED IN THE INCIDENT.
MUNDUS MAGICUS
MUNDUS VETUS
WELL, THE OLD WORLD'S GOT NOTHING TO DO WITH ANY OF US COMMONERS NOW, SO NONE OF US ARE WORRIED ABOUT IT....
BUT I HEAR THAT ONCE THE BRIDGE IS OUT, IT TAKES YEARS TO REPAIR IT.
EEHH!?
MA..
MAKIE, MAKIE! THIS IS BIG!
YŪNA, YŪNA, BIG NEWS HERE, TOO!!
THEY SAY EVEN IF WE EARN THE MONEY, WE MIGHT NOT GET HOME!
LOOK AT THAT!! THERE!!
HUH?
WELL THEN, LET'S HAVE A WORD WITH NAGI-SAN. HE'S BRILLIANTLY WON ALL THIRTEEN OF HIS MATCHES SINCE HIS DEBUT.
HELLO! NAGI-SAN, WE'RE BROADCASTING LIVE ALL OVER THE COUNTRY TODAY.
ALL OVER THE COUNTRY?
HUH...?
IS THAT......!?
YES!

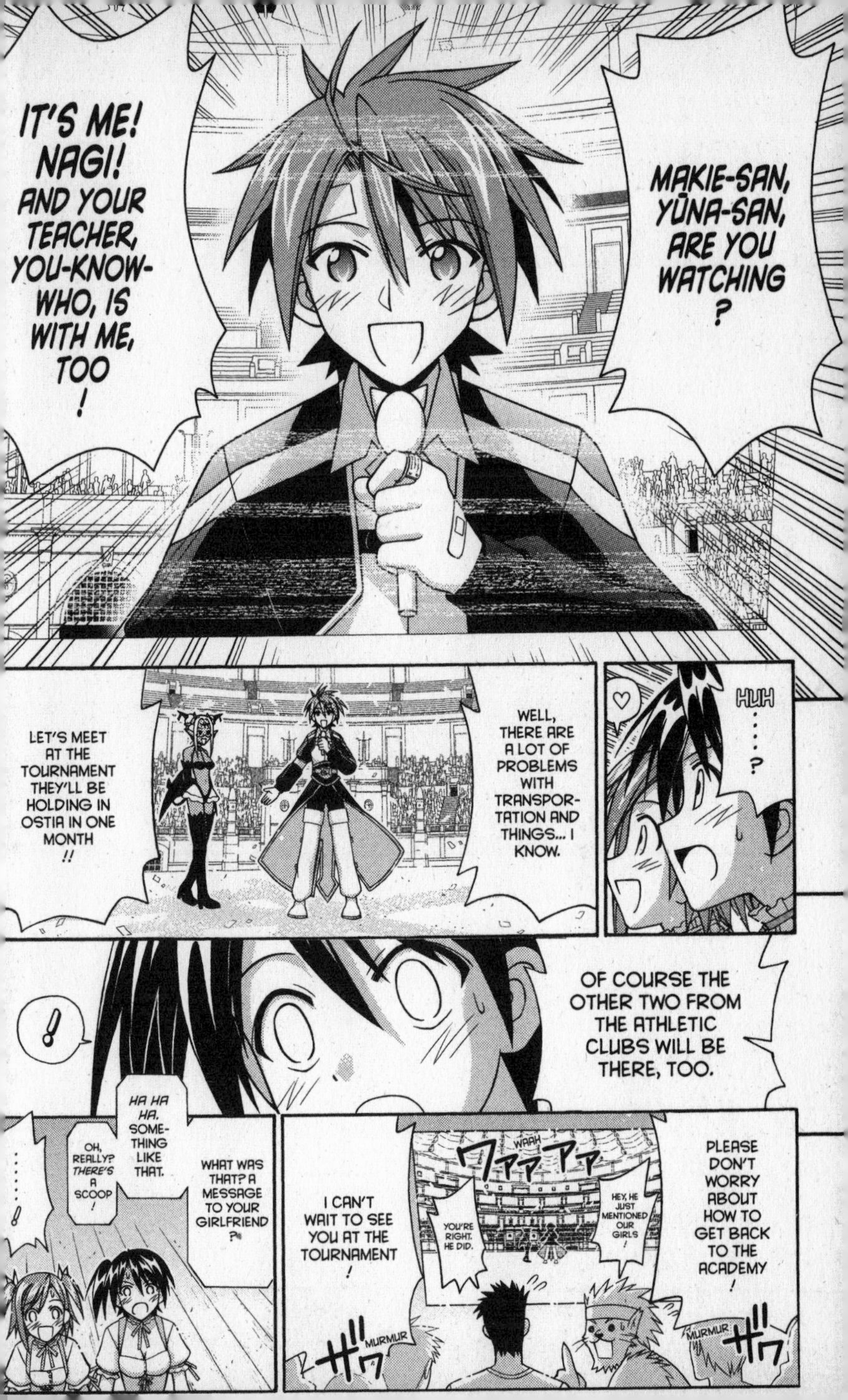
MAKIE-SAN, YŪNA-SAN, ARE YOU WATCHING?
IT'S ME! NAGI! AND YOUR TEACHER, YOU-KNOW-WHO, IS WITH ME, TOO!
HUH....?
WELL, THERE ARE A LOT OF PROBLEMS WITH TRANSPORTATION AND THINGS... I KNOW.
LET'S MEET AT THE TOURNAMENT THEY'LL BE HOLDING IN OSTIA IN ONE MONTH!!
OF COURSE THE OTHER TWO FROM THE ATHLETIC CLUBS WILL BE THERE, TOO.
!
PLEASE DON'T WORRY ABOUT HOW TO GET BACK TO THE ACADEMY!
MURMUR
WAAH
HEY, HE JUST MENTIONED OUR GIRLS!
YOU'RE RIGHT. HE DID.
I CAN'T WAIT TO SEE YOU AT THE TOURNAMENT!
MURMUR
WHAT WAS THAT? A MESSAGE TO YOUR GIRLFRIEND?
HA HA HA. SOMETHING LIKE THAT.
OH, REALLY? THERE'S A SCOOP!
......!

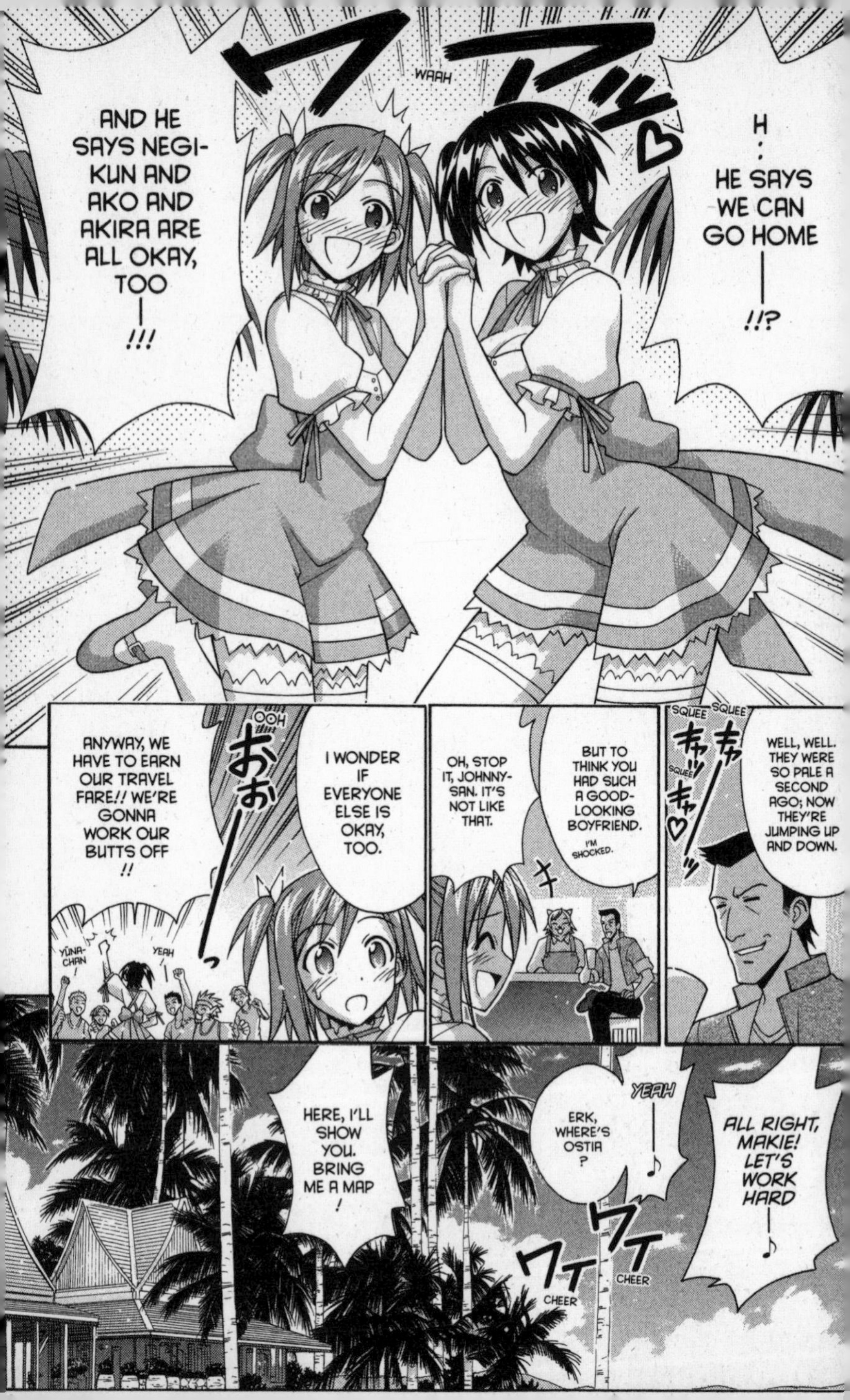
H : HE SAYS WE CAN GO HOME—!!?
WAAH
AND HE SAYS NEGI-KUN AND AKO AND AKIRA ARE ALL OKAY, TOO—!!!
SQUEE SQUEE SQUEE
WELL, WELL. THEY WERE SO PALE A SECOND AGO; NOW THEY'RE JUMPING UP AND DOWN.
BUT TO THINK YOU HAD SUCH A GOOD-LOOKING BOYFRIEND.
I'M SHOCKED.
OH, STOP IT, JOHNNY-SAN. IT'S NOT LIKE THAT.
OOH
I WONDER IF EVERYONE ELSE IS OKAY, TOO.
ANYWAY, WE HAVE TO EARN OUR TRAVEL FARE!! WE'RE GONNA WORK OUR BUTTS OFF!!
YEAH!
YŪNA-CHAN!
ALL RIGHT, MAKIE! LET'S WORK HARD—♪
YEAH—♪
ERK, WHERE'S OSTIA?
CHEER
CHEER
HERE, I'LL SHOW YOU. BRING ME A MAP!

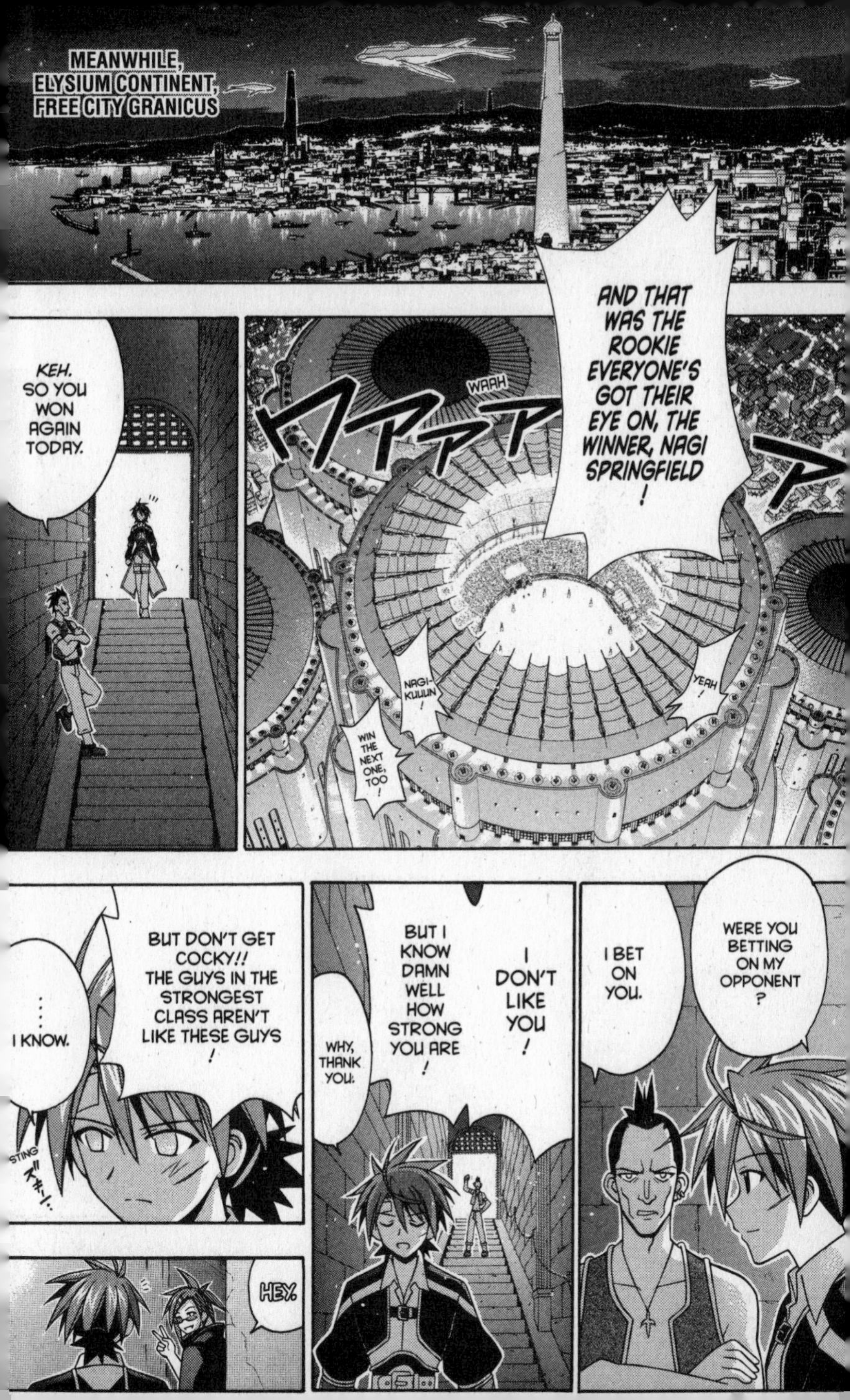
MEANWHILE, ELYSIUM CONTINENT, FREE CITY GRANICUS
AND THAT WAS THE ROOKIE EVERYONE'S GOT THEIR EYE ON, THE WINNER, NAGI SPRINGFIELD!
WAAH
NAGI-KUUUN!
YEAH!
WIN THE NEXT ONE, TOO!
KEH. SO YOU WON AGAIN TODAY.
WERE YOU BETTING ON MY OPPONENT?
I BET ON YOU.
I DON'T LIKE YOU!
BUT I KNOW DAMN WELL HOW STRONG YOU ARE!
WHY, THANK YOU.
BUT DON'T GET COCKY!! THE GUYS IN THE STRONGEST CLASS AREN'T LIKE THESE GUYS!
...I KNOW.
STING
HEY.

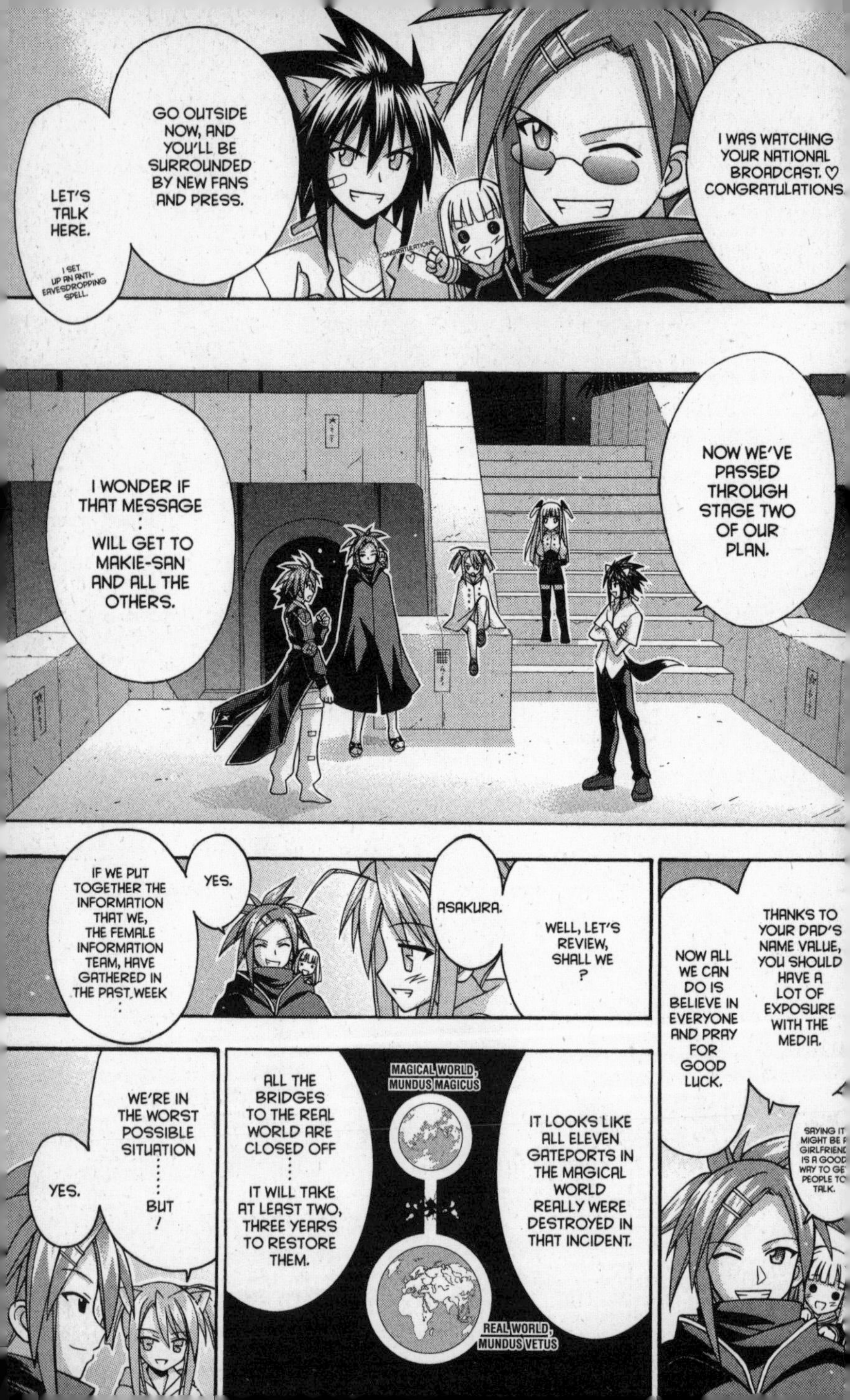
I WAS WATCHING YOUR NATIONAL BROADCAST. ♡ CONGRATULATIONS.
CONGRATULATIONS ♡
GO OUTSIDE NOW, AND YOU'LL BE SURROUNDED BY NEW FANS AND PRESS.
LET'S TALK HERE.
I SET UP AN ANTI-EAVESDROPPING SPELL.
NOW WE'VE PASSED THROUGH STAGE TWO OF OUR PLAN.
I WONDER IF THAT MESSAGE : WILL GET TO MAKIE-SAN AND ALL THE OTHERS.
THANKS TO YOUR DAD'S NAME VALUE, YOU SHOULD HAVE A LOT OF EXPOSURE WITH THE MEDIA.
NOW ALL WE CAN DO IS BELIEVE IN EVERYONE AND PRAY FOR GOOD LUCK.
SAYING IT MIGHT BE A GIRLFRIEND IS A GOOD WAY TO GET PEOPLE TO TALK.
WELL, LET'S REVIEW, SHALL WE?
ASAKURA.
YES.
IF WE PUT TOGETHER THE INFORMATION THAT WE, THE FEMALE INFORMATION TEAM, HAVE GATHERED IN THE PAST WEEK :
IT LOOKS LIKE ALL ELEVEN GATEPORTS IN THE MAGICAL WORLD REALLY WERE DESTROYED IN THAT INCIDENT.
MAGICAL WORLD, MUNDUS MAGICUS
REAL WORLD, MUNDUS VETUS
ALL THE BRIDGES TO THE REAL WORLD ARE CLOSED OFF : IT WILL TAKE AT LEAST TWO, THREE YEARS TO RESTORE THEM.
WE'RE IN THE WORST POSSIBLE SITUATION ...... BUT!
YES.

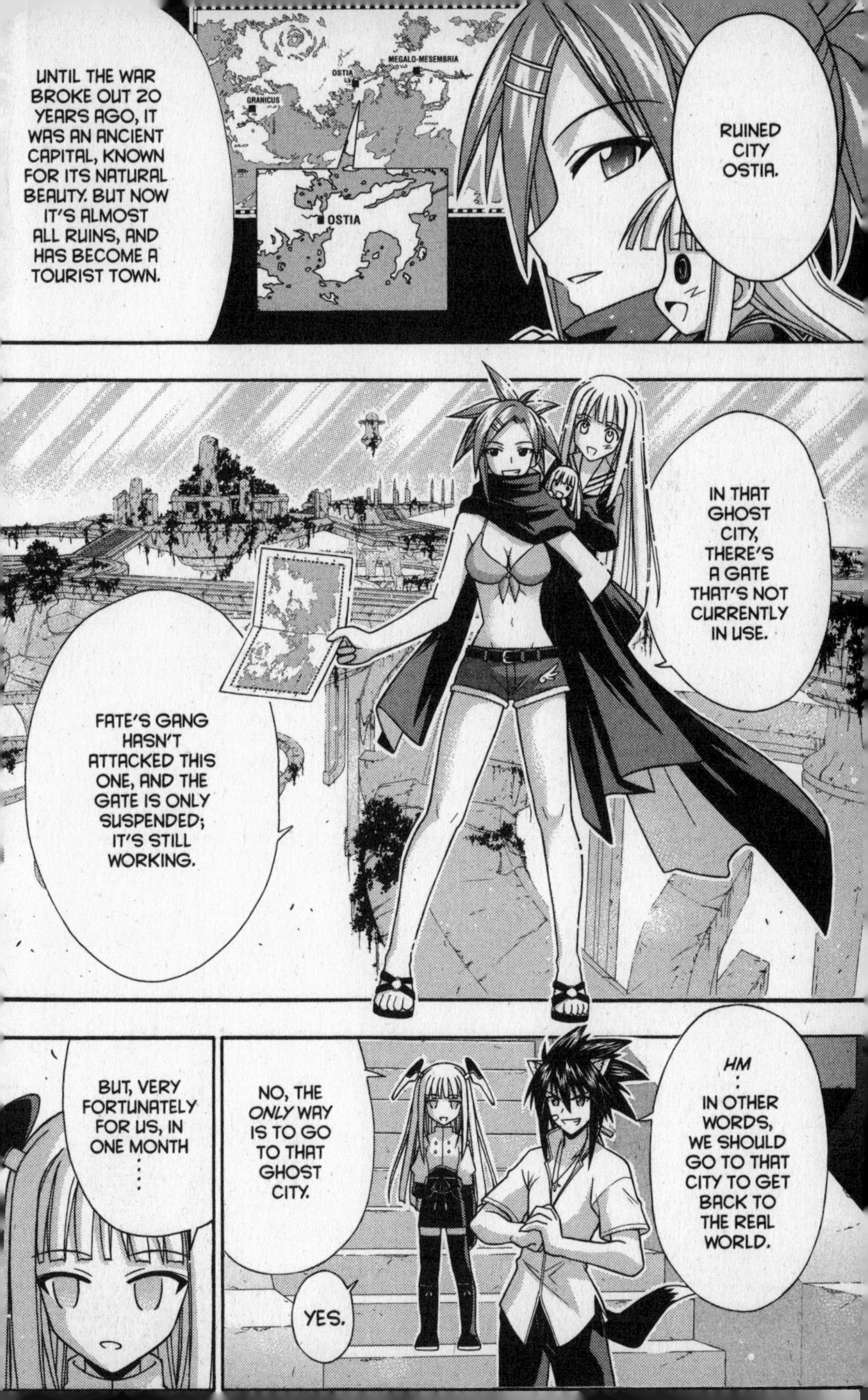
RUINED CITY OSTIA.
MEGALO-MESEMBRIA
OSTIA
GRANICUS
OSTIA
UNTIL THE WAR BROKE OUT 20 YEARS AGO, IT WAS AN ANCIENT CAPITAL, KNOWN FOR ITS NATURAL BEAUTY. BUT NOW IT'S ALMOST ALL RUINS, AND HAS BECOME A TOURIST TOWN.
IN THAT GHOST CITY, THERE'S A GATE THAT'S NOT CURRENTLY IN USE.
FATE'S GANG HASN'T ATTACKED THIS ONE, AND THE GATE IS ONLY SUSPENDED; IT'S STILL WORKING.
HM: IN OTHER WORDS, WE SHOULD GO TO THAT CITY TO GET BACK TO THE REAL WORLD.
NO, THE *ONLY* WAY IS TO GO TO THAT GHOST CITY.
YES.
BUT, VERY FORTUNATELY FOR US, IN ONE MONTH...

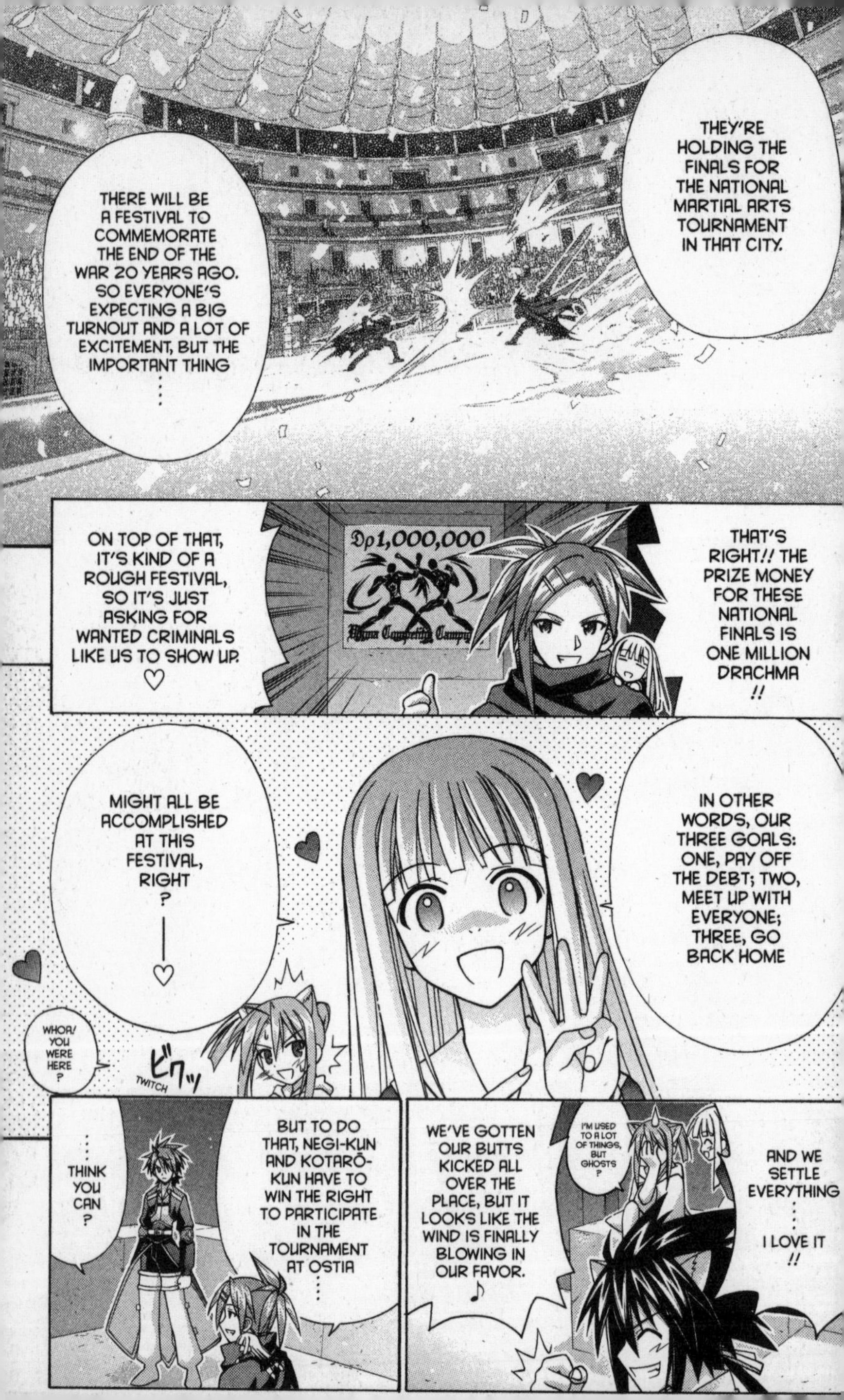
THEY'RE HOLDING THE FINALS FOR THE NATIONAL MARTIAL ARTS TOURNAMENT IN THAT CITY.
THERE WILL BE A FESTIVAL TO COMMEMORATE THE END OF THE WAR 20 YEARS AGO. SO EVERYONE'S EXPECTING A BIG TURNOUT AND A LOT OF EXCITEMENT, BUT THE IMPORTANT THING ...
THAT'S RIGHT!! THE PRIZE MONEY FOR THESE NATIONAL FINALS IS ONE MILLION DRACHMA !!
Dp1,000,000
ON TOP OF THAT, IT'S KIND OF A ROUGH FESTIVAL, SO IT'S JUST ASKING FOR WANTED CRIMINALS LIKE US TO SHOW UP. ♡
IN OTHER WORDS, OUR THREE GOALS: ONE, PAY OFF THE DEBT; TWO, MEET UP WITH EVERYONE; THREE, GO BACK HOME
MIGHT ALL BE ACCOMPLISHED AT THIS FESTIVAL, RIGHT? —♡
WHOA! YOU WERE HERE?
ビクッ
TWITCH
AND WE SETTLE EVERYTHING ... I LOVE IT !!
I'M USED TO A LOT OF THINGS, BUT GHOSTS?
WE'VE GOTTEN OUR BUTTS KICKED ALL OVER THE PLACE, BUT IT LOOKS LIKE THE WIND IS FINALLY BLOWING IN OUR FAVOR. ♪
BUT TO DO THAT, NEGI-KUN AND KOTARŌ-KUN HAVE TO WIN THE RIGHT TO PARTICIPATE IN THE TOURNAMENT AT OSTIA ...
... THINK YOU CAN?

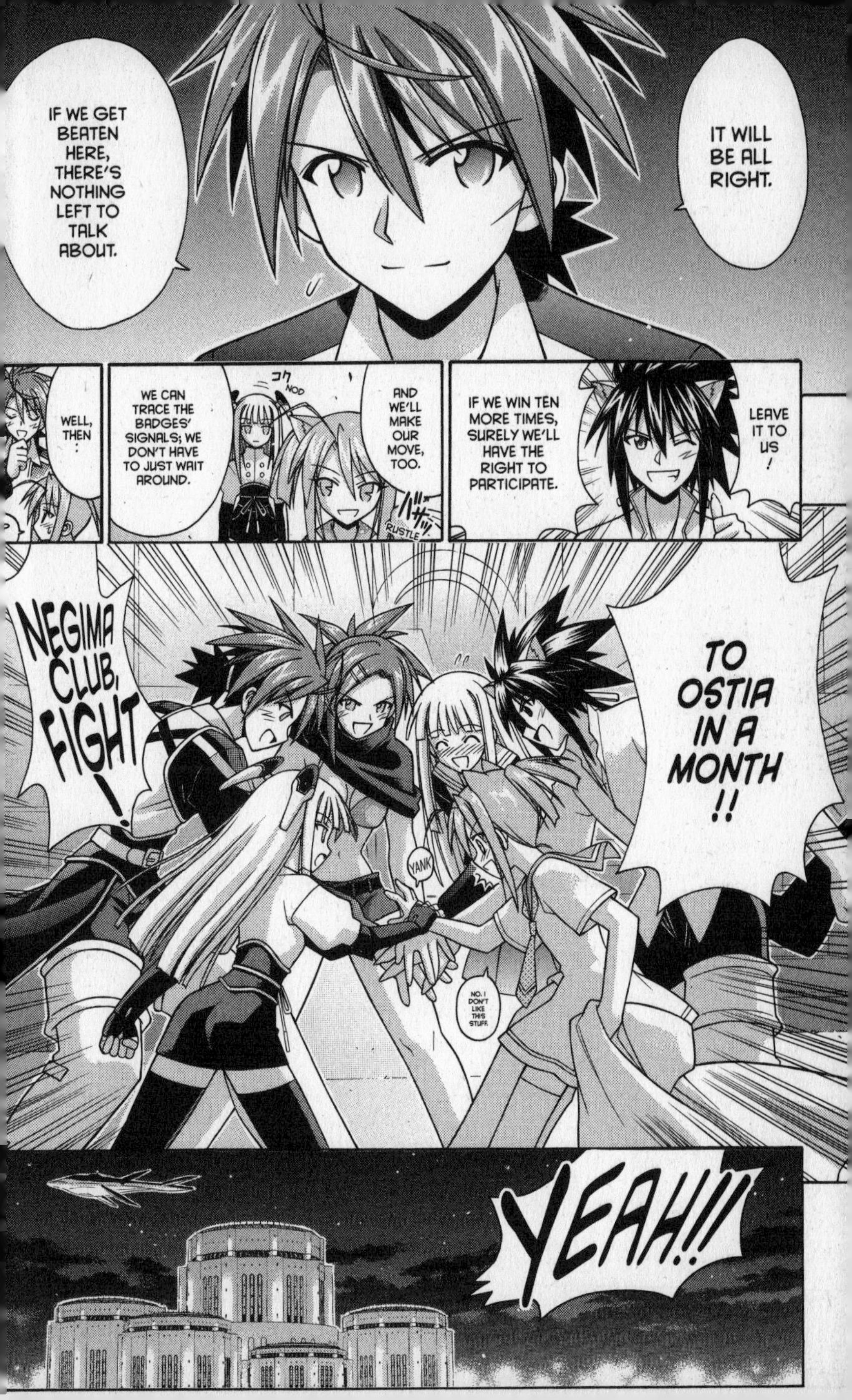
IT WILL BE ALL RIGHT.
IF WE GET BEATEN HERE, THERE'S NOTHING LEFT TO TALK ABOUT.
LEAVE IT TO US!
IF WE WIN TEN MORE TIMES, SURELY WE'LL HAVE THE RIGHT TO PARTICIPATE.
RUSTLE
AND WE'LL MAKE OUR MOVE, TOO.
コク NOD
WE CAN TRACE THE BADGES' SIGNALS; WE DON'T HAVE TO JUST WAIT AROUND.
WELL, THEN :
TO OSTIA IN A MONTH!!
NEGIMA CLUB, FIGHT!
YANK
NO, I DON'T LIKE THIS STUFF.
YEAH!!

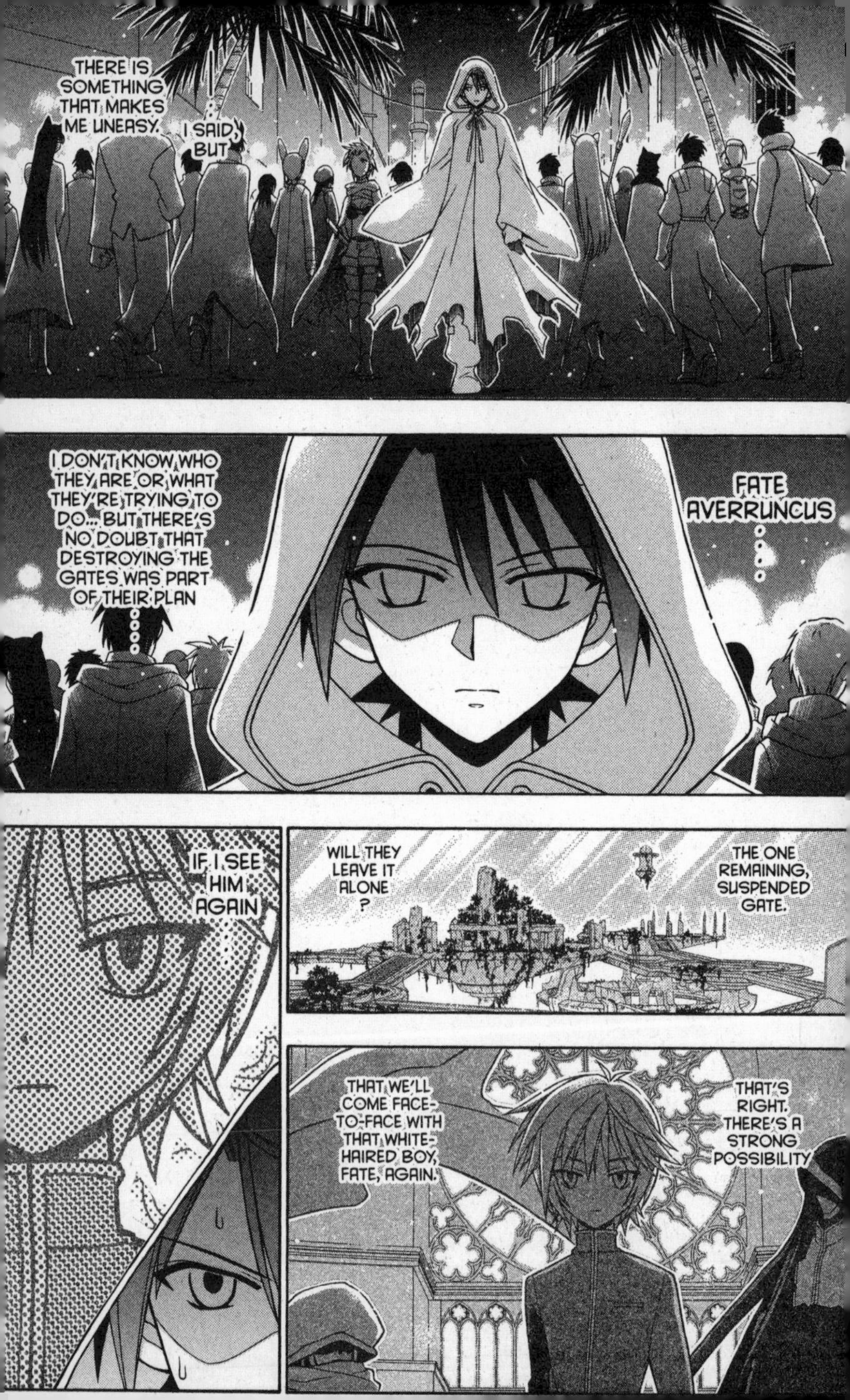
I SAID, BUT
THERE IS SOMETHING THAT MAKES ME UNEASY.
FATE AVERRUNCUS....
I DON'T KNOW WHO THEY ARE OR WHAT THEY'RE TRYING TO DO... BUT THERE'S NO DOUBT THAT DESTROYING THE GATES WAS PART OF THEIR PLAN....
THE ONE REMAINING, SUSPENDED GATE.
WILL THEY LEAVE IT ALONE?
THAT'S RIGHT. THERE'S A STRONG POSSIBILITY
THAT WE'LL COME FACE-TO-FACE WITH THAT WHITE-HAIRED BOY, FATE, AGAIN.
IF I SEE HIM AGAIN

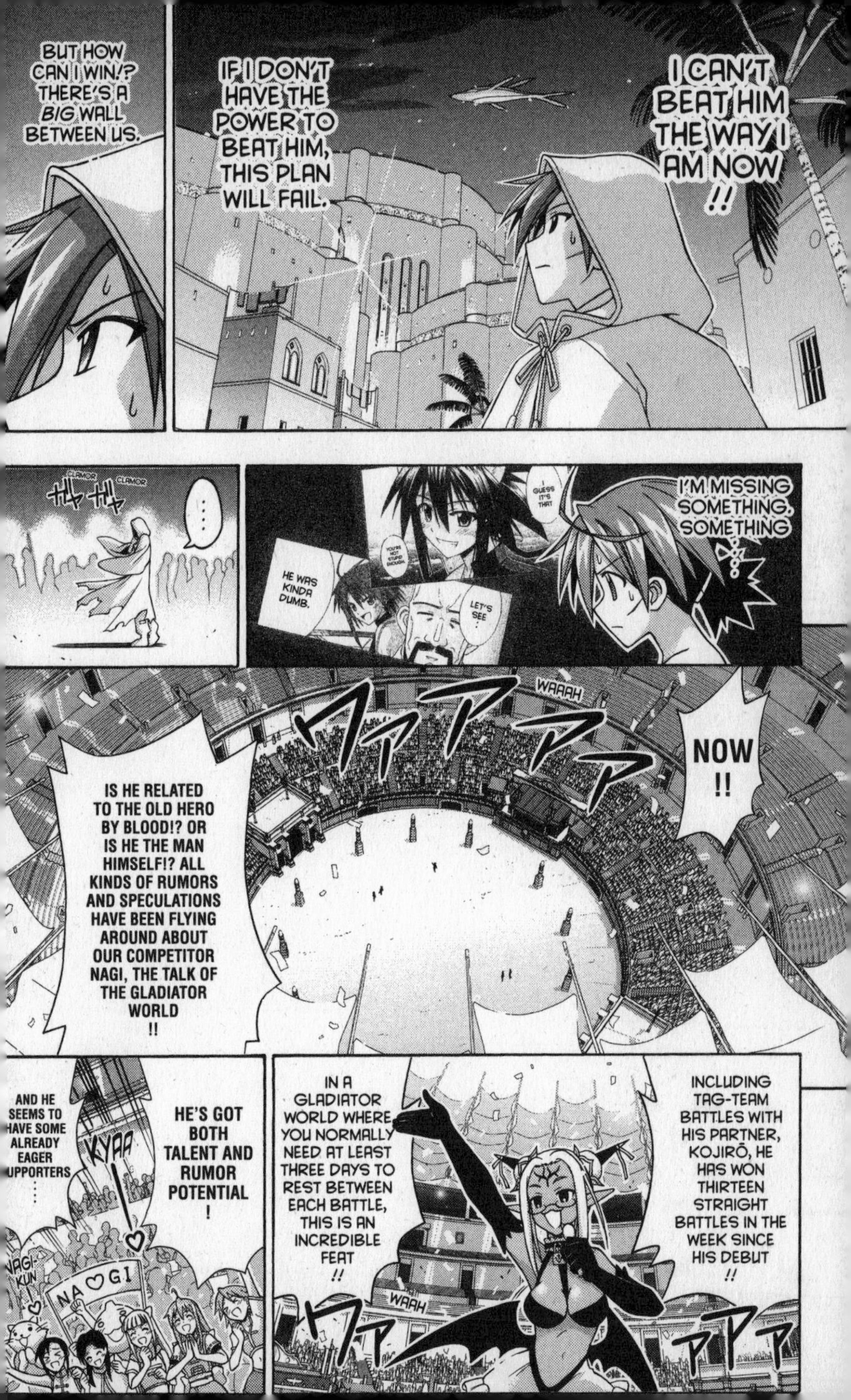
I CAN'T BEAT HIM THE WAY I AM NOW!!
IF I DON'T HAVE THE POWER TO BEAT HIM, THIS PLAN WILL FAIL.
BUT HOW CAN I WIN!? THERE'S A *BIG* WALL BETWEEN US.
I'M MISSING SOMETHING. SOMETHING
I GUESS IT'S THAT
YOU'RE NOT STUPID ENOUGH.
LET'S SEE
HE WAS KINDA DUMB.
CLAMOR
CLAMOR
......
WAAAH
NOW!!
IS HE RELATED TO THE OLD HERO BY BLOOD!? OR IS HE THE MAN HIMSELF!? ALL KINDS OF RUMORS AND SPECULATIONS HAVE BEEN FLYING AROUND ABOUT OUR COMPETITOR NAGI, THE TALK OF THE GLADIATOR WORLD!!
INCLUDING TAG-TEAM BATTLES WITH HIS PARTNER, KOJIRŌ, HE HAS WON THIRTEEN STRAIGHT BATTLES IN THE WEEK SINCE HIS DEBUT!!
IN A GLADIATOR WORLD WHERE YOU NORMALLY NEED AT LEAST THREE DAYS TO REST BETWEEN EACH BATTLE, THIS IS AN INCREDIBLE FEAT!!
WAAH
HE'S GOT BOTH TALENT AND RUMOR POTENTIAL!
AND HE SEEMS TO HAVE SOME ALREADY EAGER UPPORTERS......
KYAA!♡
NAGI-KUN!♡
NA♡GI

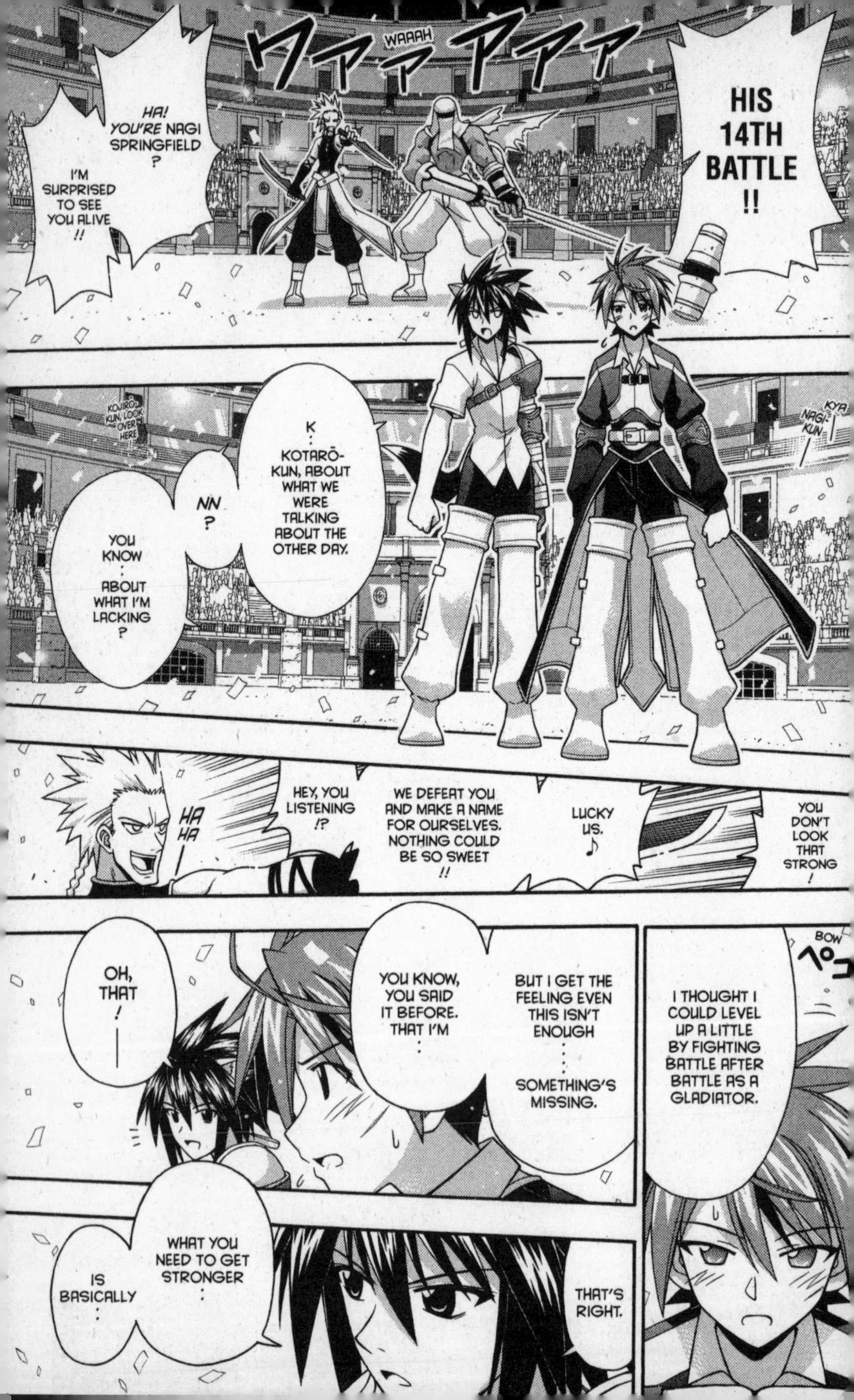
HIS 14TH BATTLE!!
WAAAH
HA! YOU'RE NAGI SPRINGFIELD?
I'M SURPRISED TO SEE YOU ALIVE!!
KYA NAGI-KUN!
KOJIRO-KUN, LOOK OVER HERE!
K... KOTARŌ-KUN, ABOUT WHAT WE WERE TALKING ABOUT THE OTHER DAY.
NN?
YOU KNOW... ABOUT WHAT I'M LACKING?
YOU DON'T LOOK THAT STRONG!
LUCKY US. ♪
WE DEFEAT YOU AND MAKE A NAME FOR OURSELVES. NOTHING COULD BE SO SWEET!!
HEY, YOU LISTENING!?
HA HA!
BOW
I THOUGHT I COULD LEVEL UP A LITTLE BY FIGHTING BATTLE AFTER BATTLE AS A GLADIATOR.
BUT I GET THE FEELING EVEN THIS ISN'T ENOUGH... SOMETHING'S MISSING.
YOU KNOW, YOU SAID IT BEFORE. THAT I'M...
OH, THAT!
THAT'S RIGHT.
WHAT YOU NEED TO GET STRONGER... IS BASICALLY...

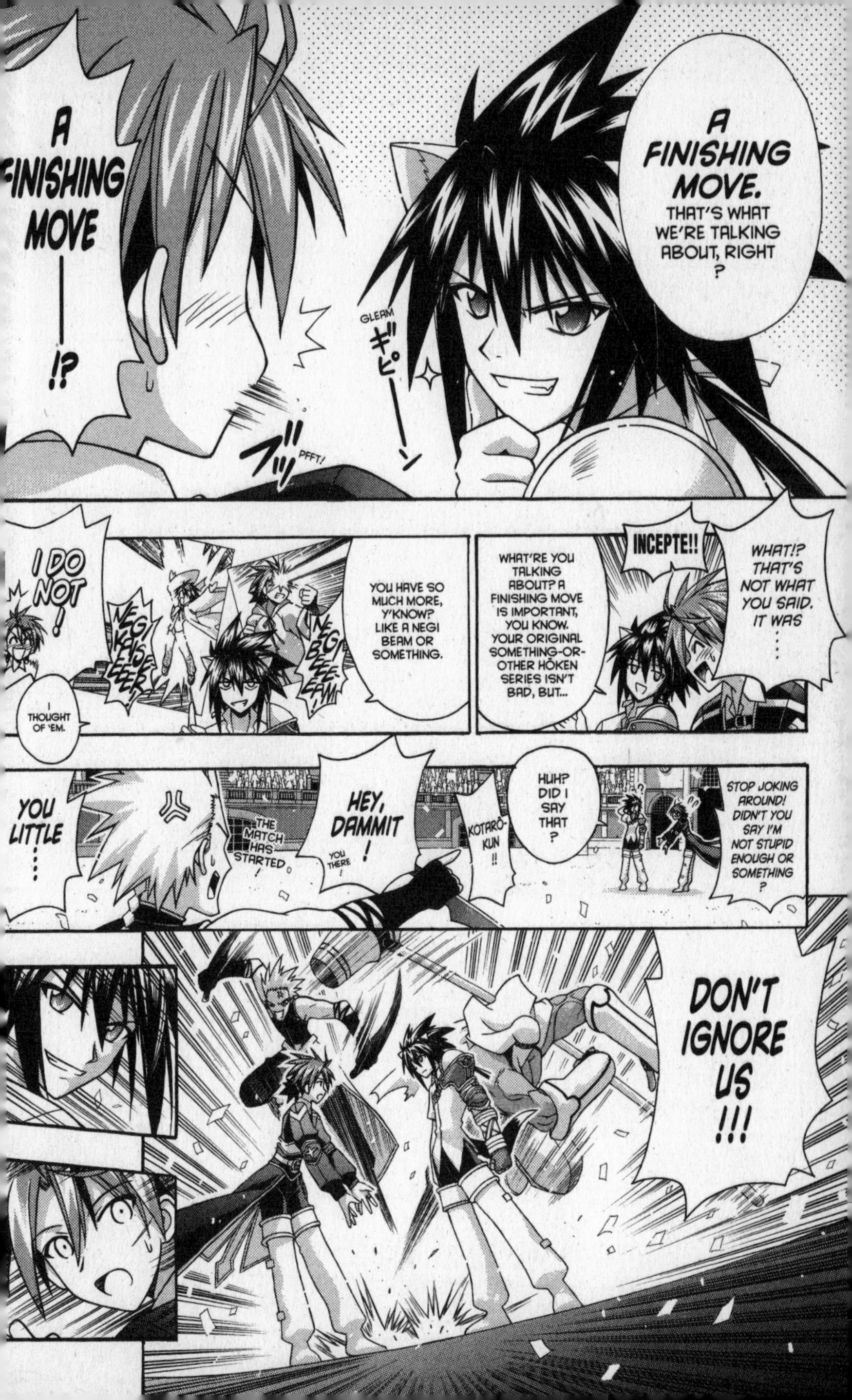
A FINISHING MOVE. THAT'S WHAT WE'RE TALKING ABOUT, RIGHT?
GLEAM
ギピーーン
PFFT!
ブッ
A FINISHING MOVE——!?
INCEPTE!!
WHAT!? THAT'S NOT WHAT YOU SAID. IT WAS...
WHAT'RE YOU TALKING ABOUT? A FINISHING MOVE IS IMPORTANT, YOU KNOW. YOUR ORIGINAL SOMETHING-OR-OTHER HŌKEN SERIES ISN'T BAD, BUT...
YOU HAVE SO MUCH MORE, Y'KNOW? LIKE A NEGI BEAM OR SOMETHING.
NEGI BEEEEEAM!
NEGI KAISEEEER!
I DO NOT!
I THOUGHT OF 'EM.
STOP JOKING AROUND! DIDN'T YOU SAY I'M NOT STUPID ENOUGH OR SOMETHING?
HUH? DID I SAY THAT?
KOTARŌ-KUN!!
HEY, DAMMIT!
YOU THERE!
THE MATCH HAS STARTED!
YOU LITTLE...
DON'T IGNORE US!!!

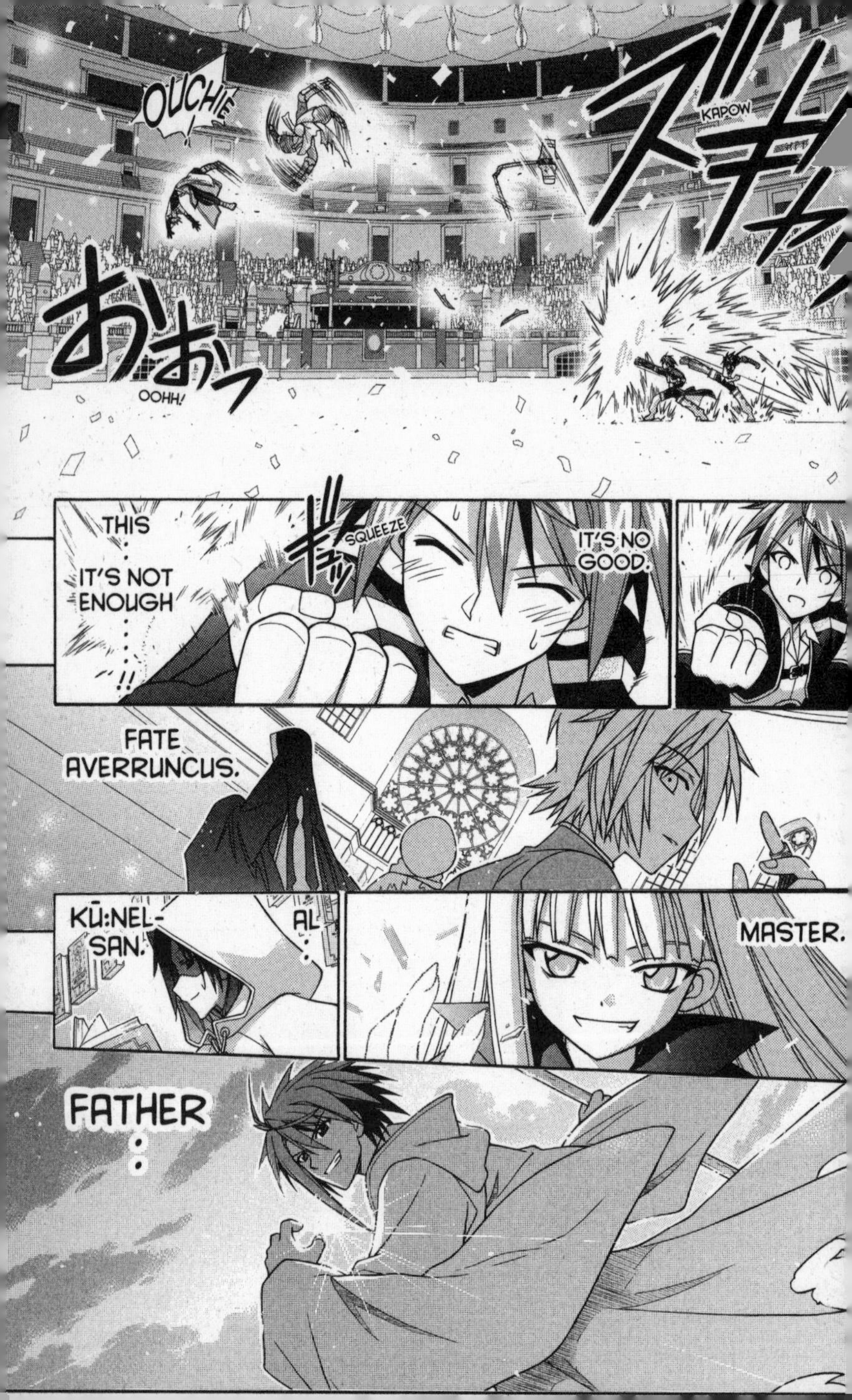

KAPOW
OUCHIE!
おおっ
OOHH!
IT'S NO GOOD.
SQUEEZE
THIS... IT'S NOT ENOUGH......!!
FATE AVERRUNCUS.
MASTER.
AL...
KŪ:NEL-SAN.
FATHER...

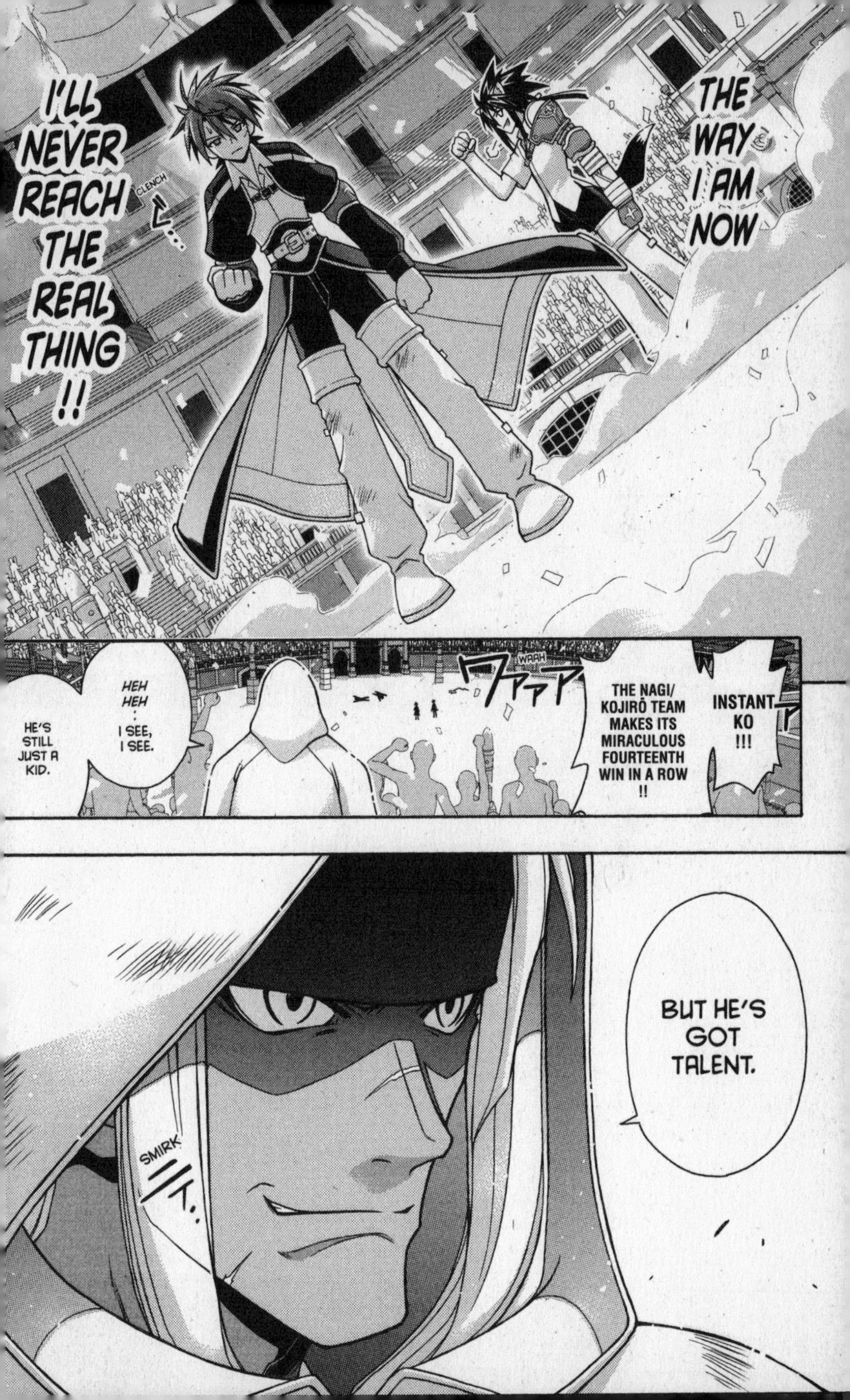
THE WAY I AM NOW
I'LL NEVER REACH THE REAL THING!!
CLENCH
INSTANT KO!!!
THE NAGI/KOJIRŌ TEAM MAKES ITS MIRACULOUS FOURTEENTH WIN IN A ROW!!
ワァァァ
WAAH
HEH HEH... I SEE, I SEE.
HE'S STILL JUST A KID.
BUT HE'S GOT TALENT.
SMIRK

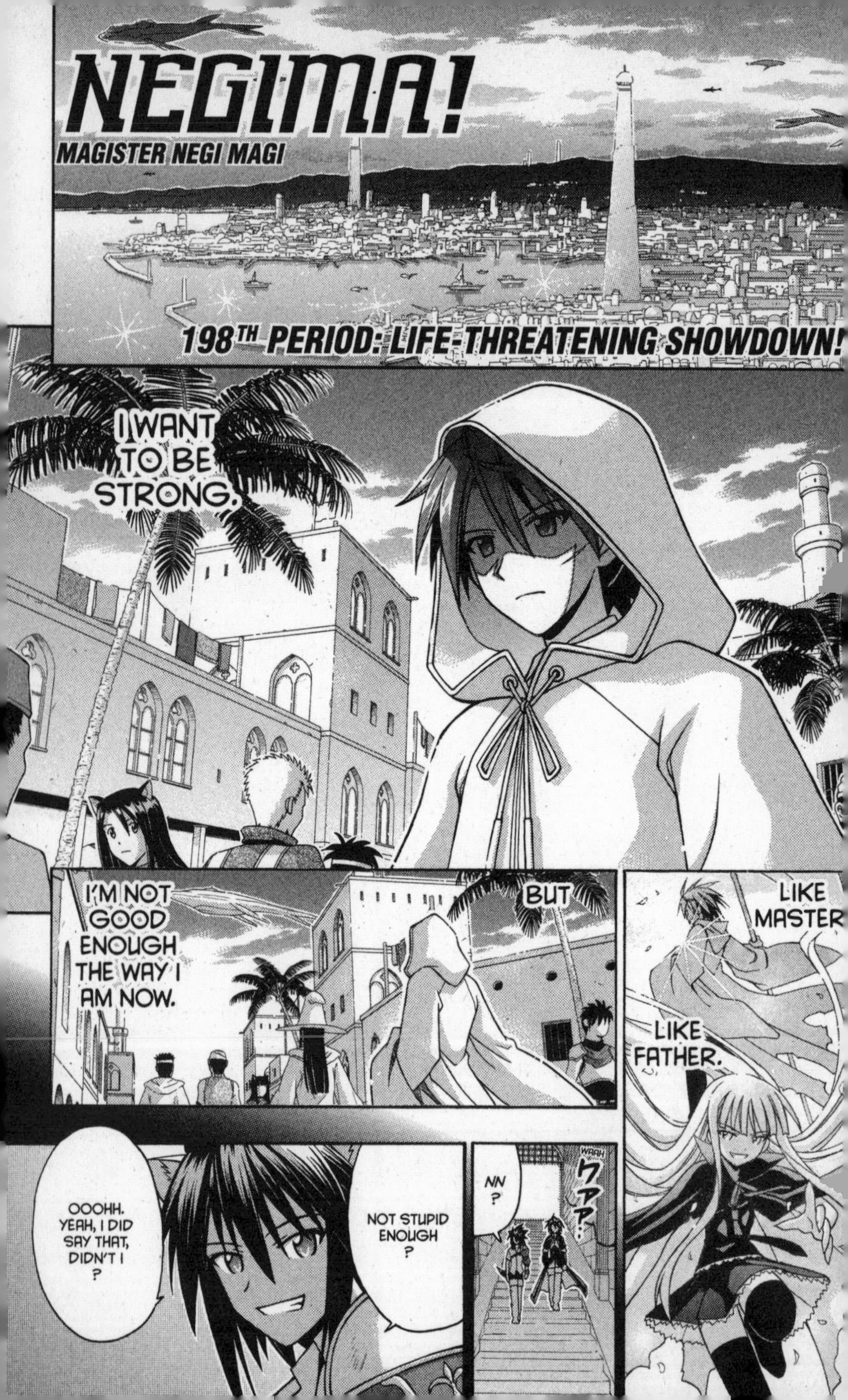
NEGIMA!
MAGISTER NEGI MAGI
198TH PERIOD: LIFE-THREATENING SHOWDOWN!
I WANT TO BE STRONG.
LIKE MASTER
LIKE FATHER.
BUT
I'M NOT GOOD ENOUGH THE WAY I AM NOW.
WAAH
ワァァ…
NN ?
NOT STUPID ENOUGH ?
OOOHH. YEAH, I DID SAY THAT, DIDN'T I ?

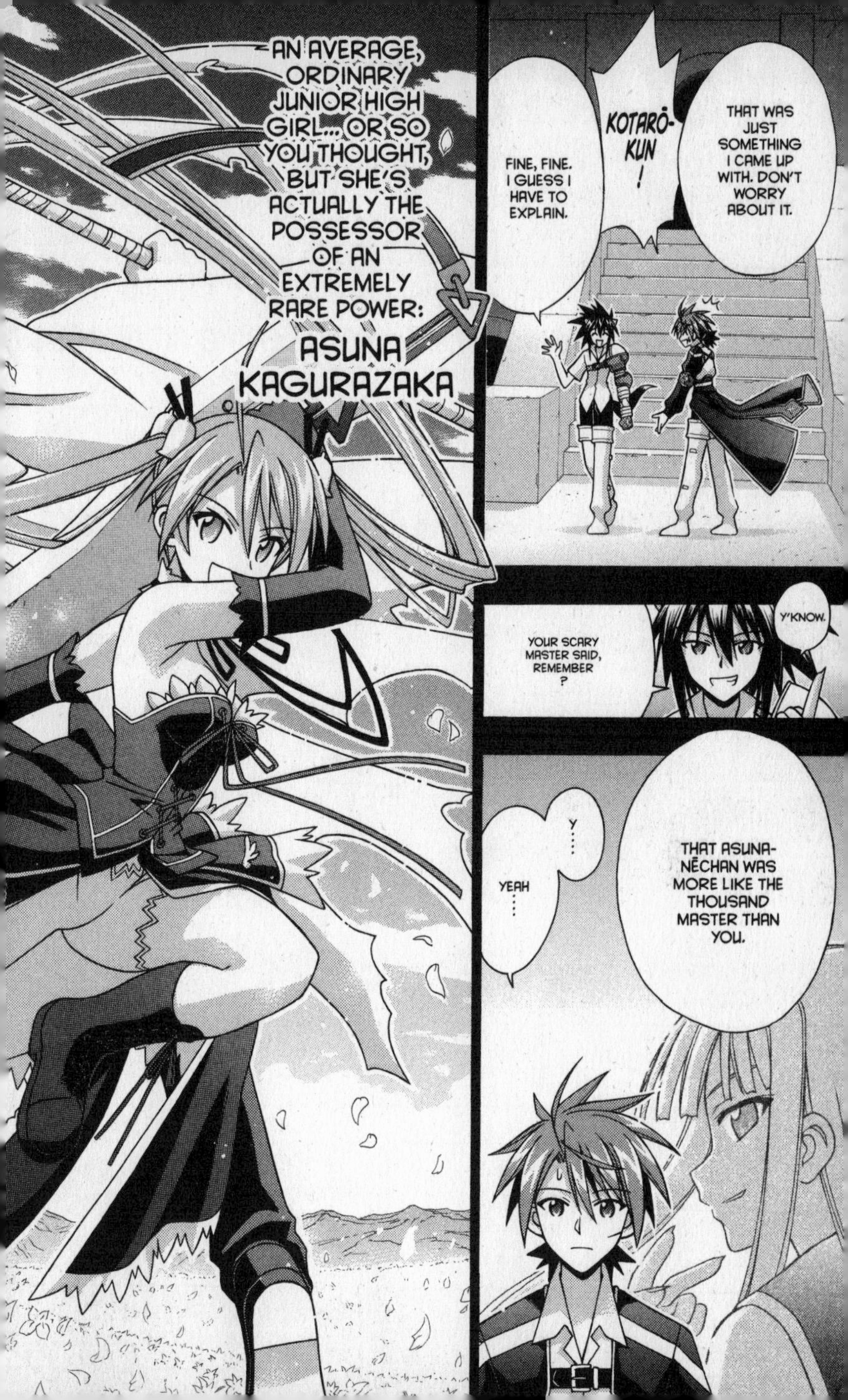
THAT WAS JUST SOMETHING I CAME UP WITH. DON'T WORRY ABOUT IT.
KOTARŌ-KUN!
FINE, FINE. I GUESS I HAVE TO EXPLAIN.
Y'KNOW.
YOUR SCARY MASTER SAID, REMEMBER?
THAT ASUNA-NĒCHAN WAS MORE LIKE THE THOUSAND MASTER THAN YOU.
Y....
YEAH....
AN AVERAGE, ORDINARY JUNIOR HIGH GIRL... OR SO YOU THOUGHT, BUT SHE'S ACTUALLY THE POSSESSOR OF AN EXTREMELY RARE POWER:
ASUNA KAGURAZAKA

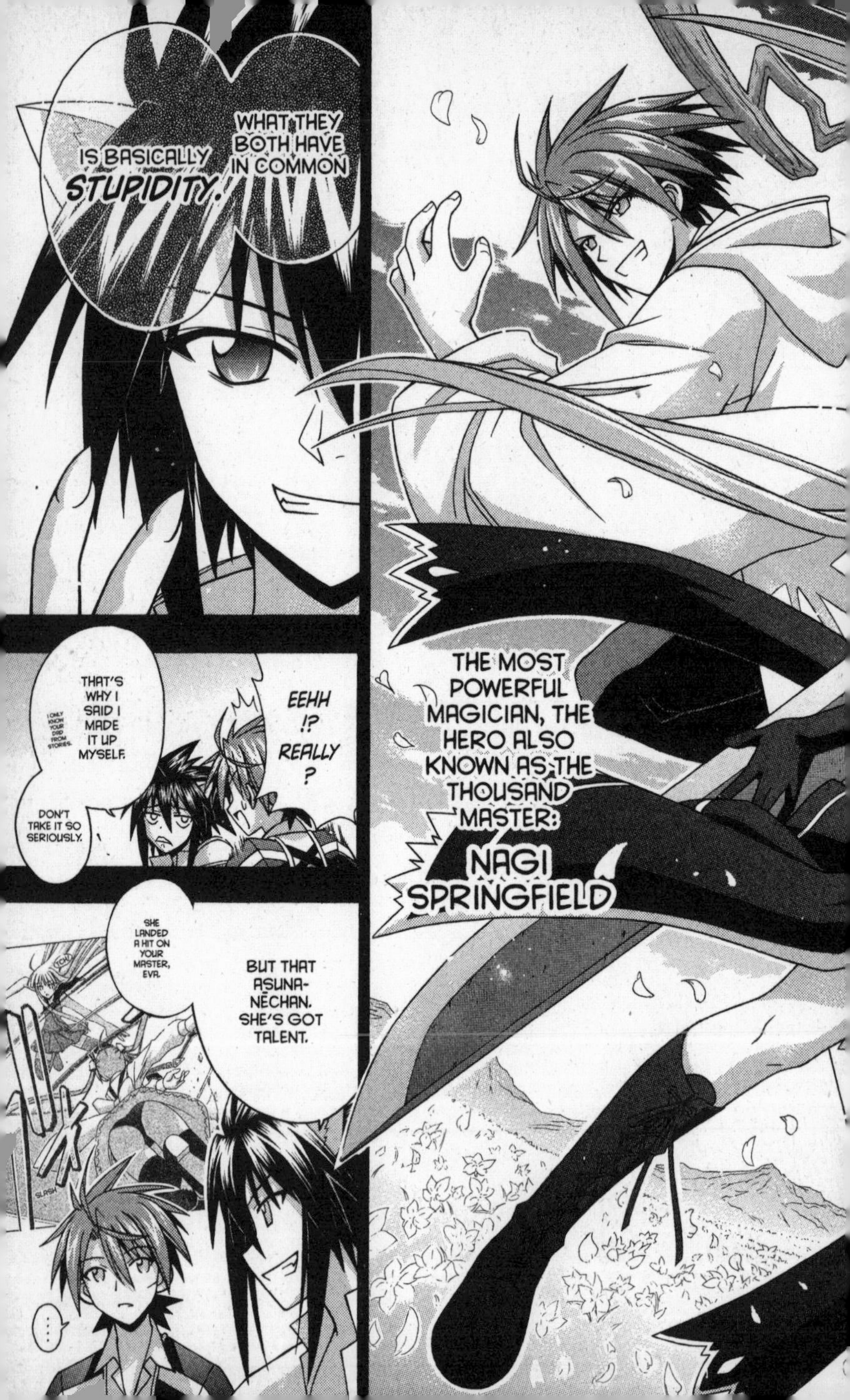
THE MOST POWERFUL MAGICIAN, THE HERO ALSO KNOWN AS THE THOUSAND MASTER:
NAGI SPRINGFIELD
WHAT THEY BOTH HAVE IN COMMON
IS BASICALLY STUPIDITY.
EEHH !? REALLY ?
THAT'S WHY I SAID I MADE IT UP MYSELF.
I ONLY KNOW YOUR DAD FROM STORIES.
DON'T TAKE IT SO SERIOUSLY.
BUT THAT ASUNA-NĒCHAN. SHE'S GOT TALENT.
SHE LANDED A HIT ON YOUR MASTER, EVA.
SLASH
....

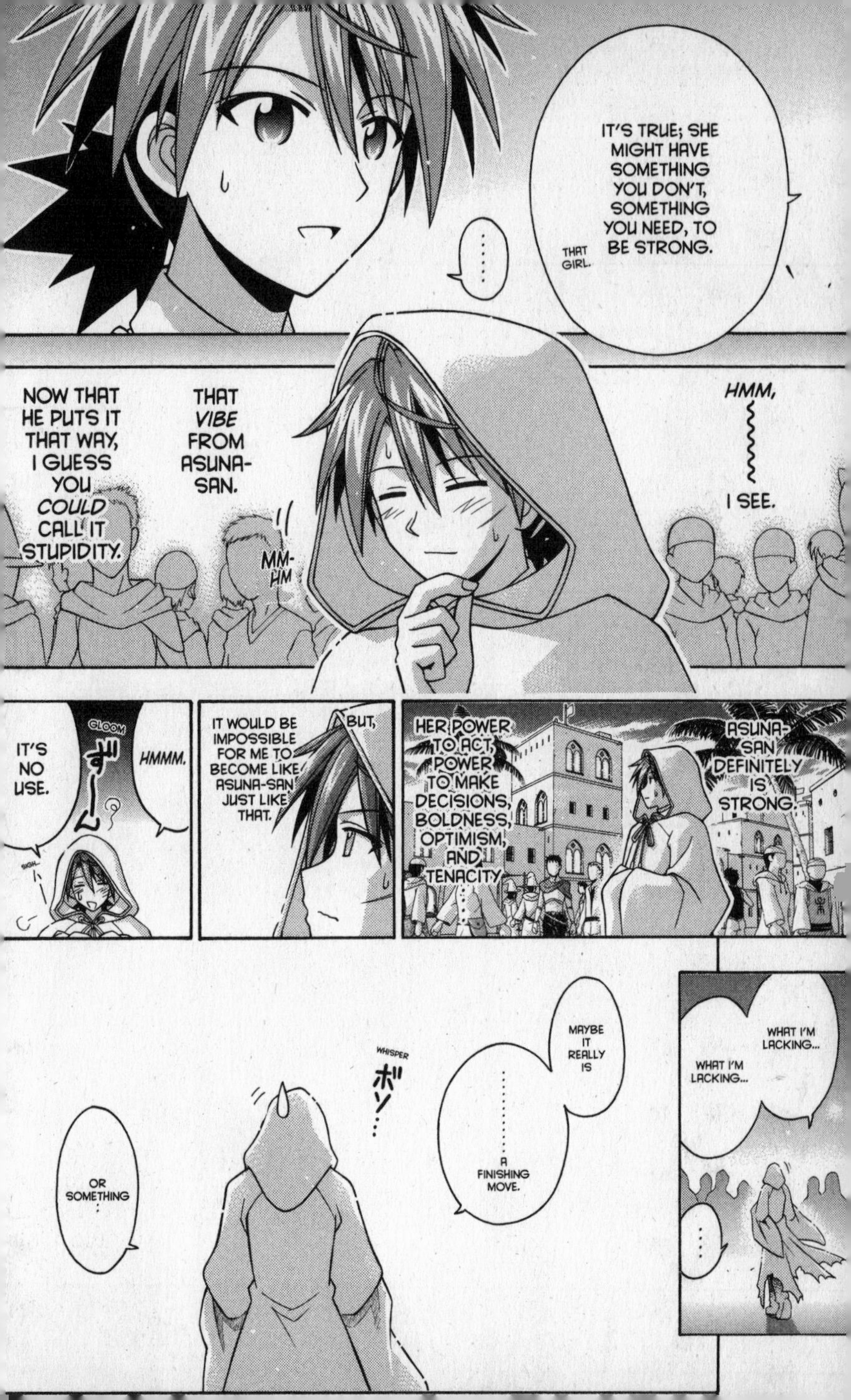
IT'S TRUE; SHE MIGHT HAVE SOMETHING YOU DON'T, SOMETHING YOU NEED, TO BE STRONG.
THAT GIRL.
......
HMM, I SEE.
MM-HM
THAT *VIBE* FROM ASUNA-SAN.
NOW THAT HE PUTS IT THAT WAY, I GUESS YOU *COULD* CALL IT STUPIDITY.
ASUNA-SAN DEFINITELY IS STRONG.
HER POWER TO ACT, POWER TO MAKE DECISIONS, BOLDNESS, OPTIMISM, AND TENACITY
BUT,
IT WOULD BE IMPOSSIBLE FOR ME TO BECOME LIKE ASUNA-SAN JUST LIKE THAT.
HMMM.
GLOOM
ずーん
IT'S NO USE.
SIGH
WHAT I'M LACKING...
WHAT I'M LACKING...
...
MAYBE IT REALLY IS .... A FINISHING MOVE.
WHISPER
ボソ...
OR SOMETHING...

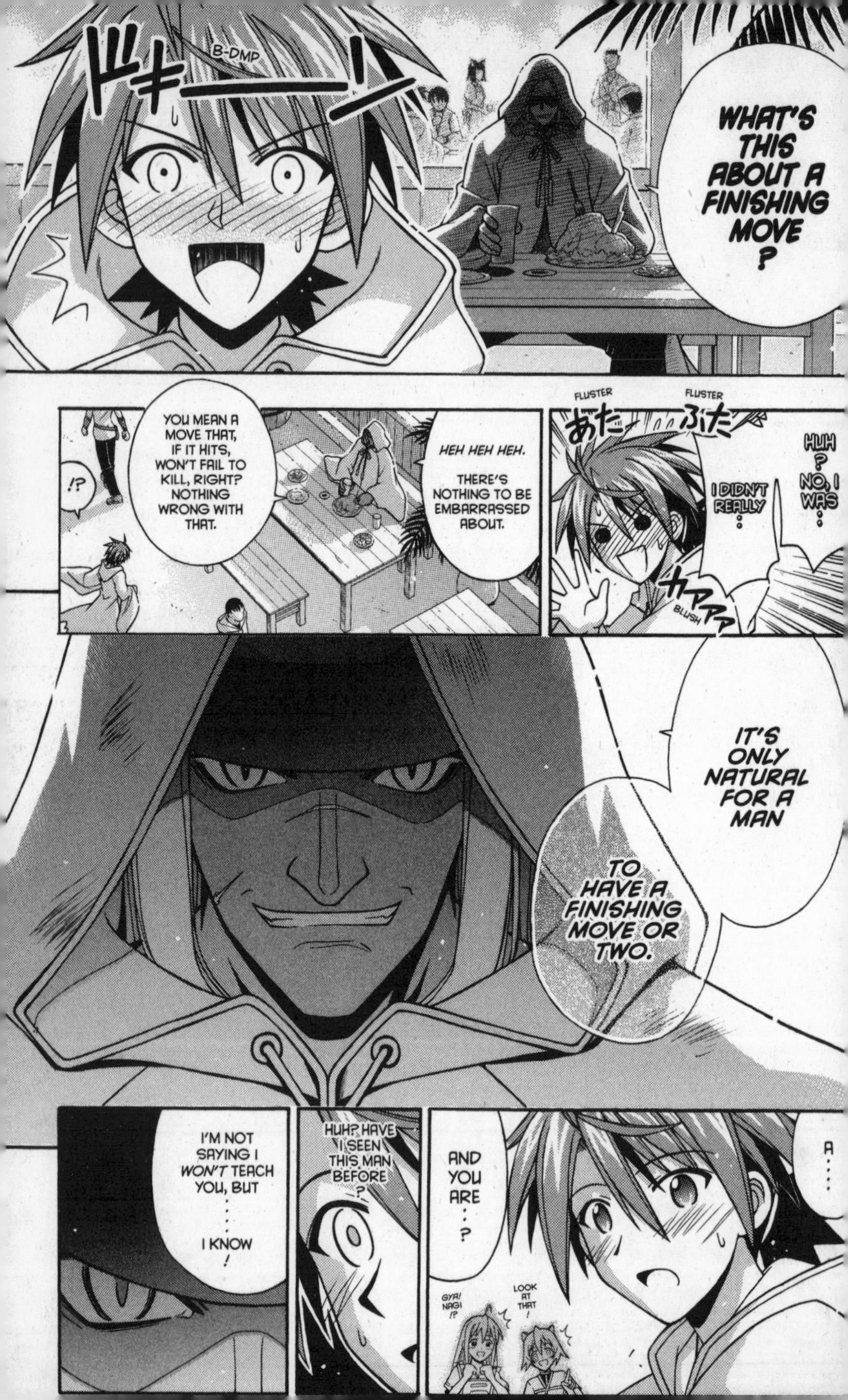
ドキーーーッ
B-DMP
WHAT'S THIS ABOUT A FINISHING MOVE?
FLUSTER あた
FLUSTER ふた
HUH? NO, I WAS...
I DIDN'T REALLY...
カァァァ
BLUSH
HEH HEH HEH.
THERE'S NOTHING TO BE EMBARRASSED ABOUT.
YOU MEAN A MOVE THAT, IF IT HITS, WON'T FAIL TO KILL, RIGHT? NOTHING WRONG WITH THAT.
!?
IT'S ONLY NATURAL FOR A MAN
TO HAVE A FINISHING MOVE OR TWO.
A....
LOOK AT THAT!
GYA! NAGI!?
AND YOU ARE...?
HUH? HAVE I SEEN THIS MAN BEFORE?
I'M NOT SAYING I *WON'T* TEACH YOU, BUT
.....
I KNOW!

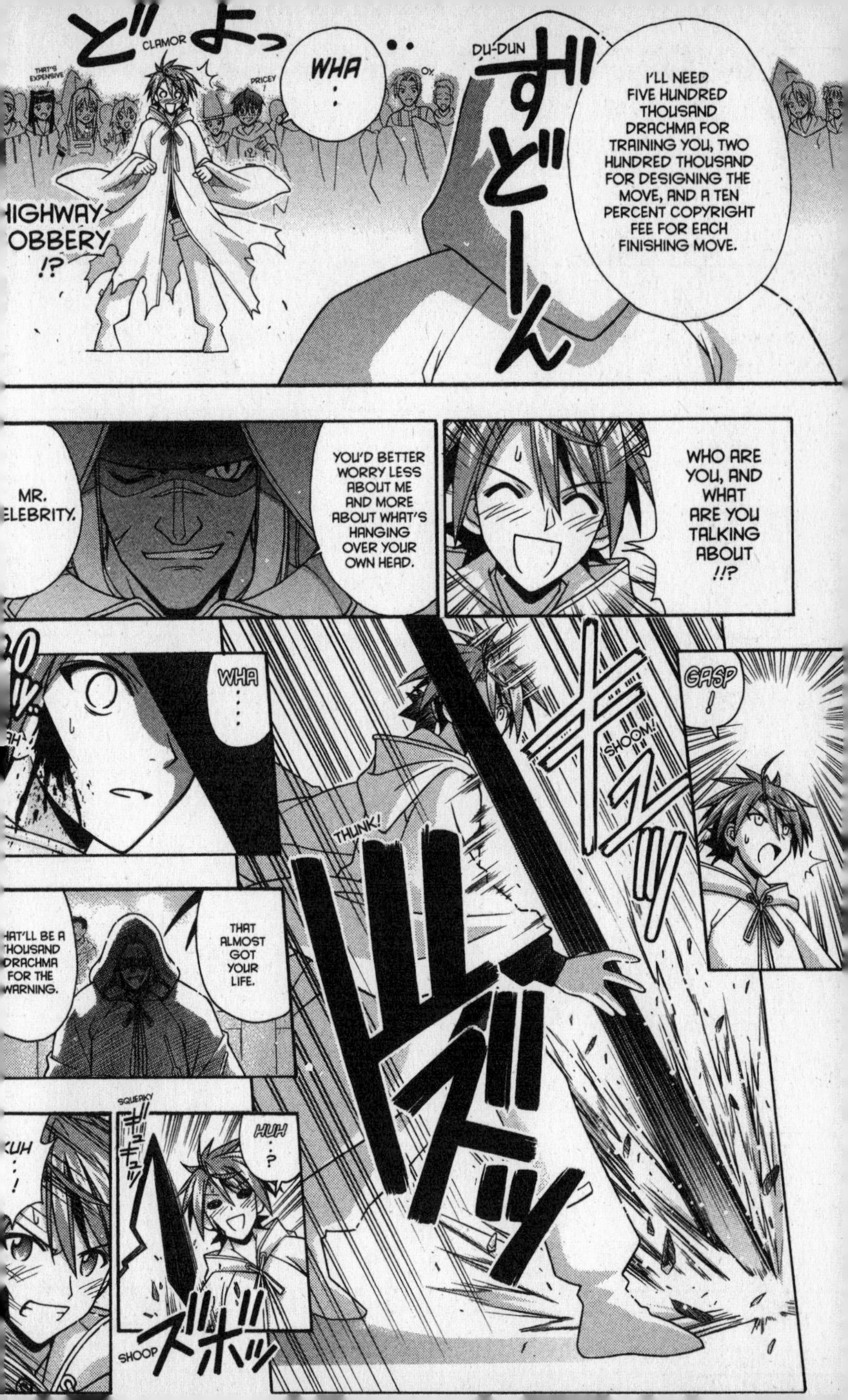
I'LL NEED FIVE HUNDRED THOUSAND DRACHMA FOR TRAINING YOU, TWO HUNDRED THOUSAND FOR DESIGNING THE MOVE, AND A TEN PERCENT COPYRIGHT FEE FOR EACH FINISHING MOVE.
DU-DUN
ずどーん
WHA...
OY.
PRICEY!
CLAMOR
どよっ
THAT'S EXPENSIVE!
HIGHWAY OBBERY!?
WHO ARE YOU, AND WHAT ARE YOU TALKING ABOUT!!?
YOU'D BETTER WORRY LESS ABOUT ME AND MORE ABOUT WHAT'S HANGING OVER YOUR OWN HEAD.
MR. ELEBRITY.
GASP!
SHOOM!
THUNK!
WHA...
THAT ALMOST GOT YOUR LIFE.
HAT'LL BE A THOUSAND DRACHMA FOR THE WARNING.
HUH...?
SQUEAKY
SHOOP
KUH...!

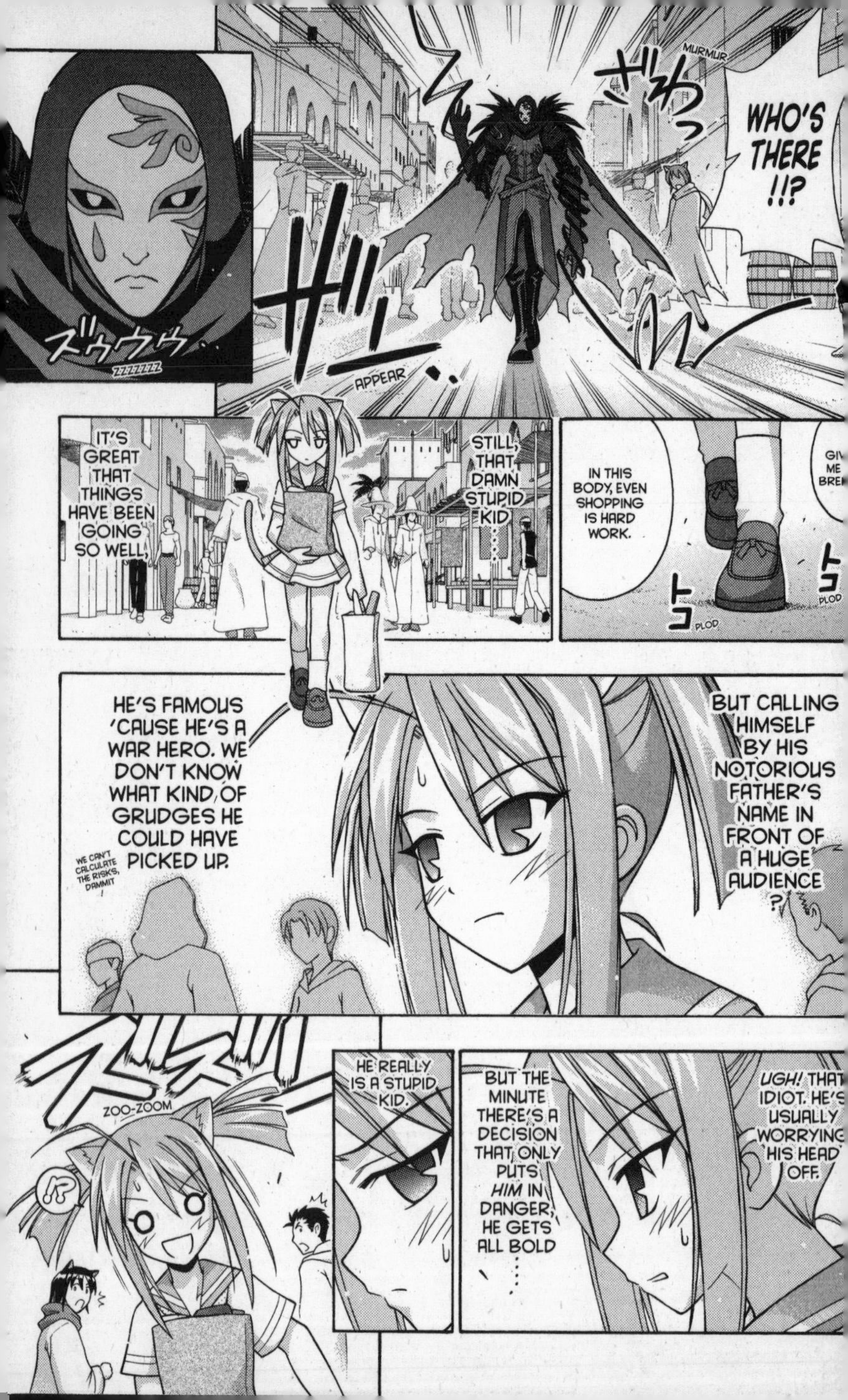

WHO'S THERE!!?
ざわっ
MURMUR
ザッ
APPEAR
ズウウウ
GIV ME BRE
IN THIS BODY, EVEN SHOPPING IS HARD WORK.
トコ
PLOD
トコ
PLOD
STILL, THAT DAMN STUPID KID...
IT'S GREAT THAT THINGS HAVE BEEN GOING SO WELL,
BUT CALLING HIMSELF BY HIS NOTORIOUS FATHER'S NAME IN FRONT OF A HUGE AUDIENCE?
HE'S FAMOUS 'CAUSE HE'S A WAR HERO. WE DON'T KNOW WHAT KIND OF GRUDGES HE COULD HAVE PICKED UP.
WE CAN'T CALCULATE THE RISKS, DAMMIT
UGH! THAT IDIOT. HE'S USUALLY WORRYING HIS HEAD OFF.
BUT THE MINUTE THERE'S A DECISION THAT ONLY PUTS HIM IN DANGER, HE GETS ALL BOLD...
HE REALLY IS A STUPID KID.
ZOO-ZOOM

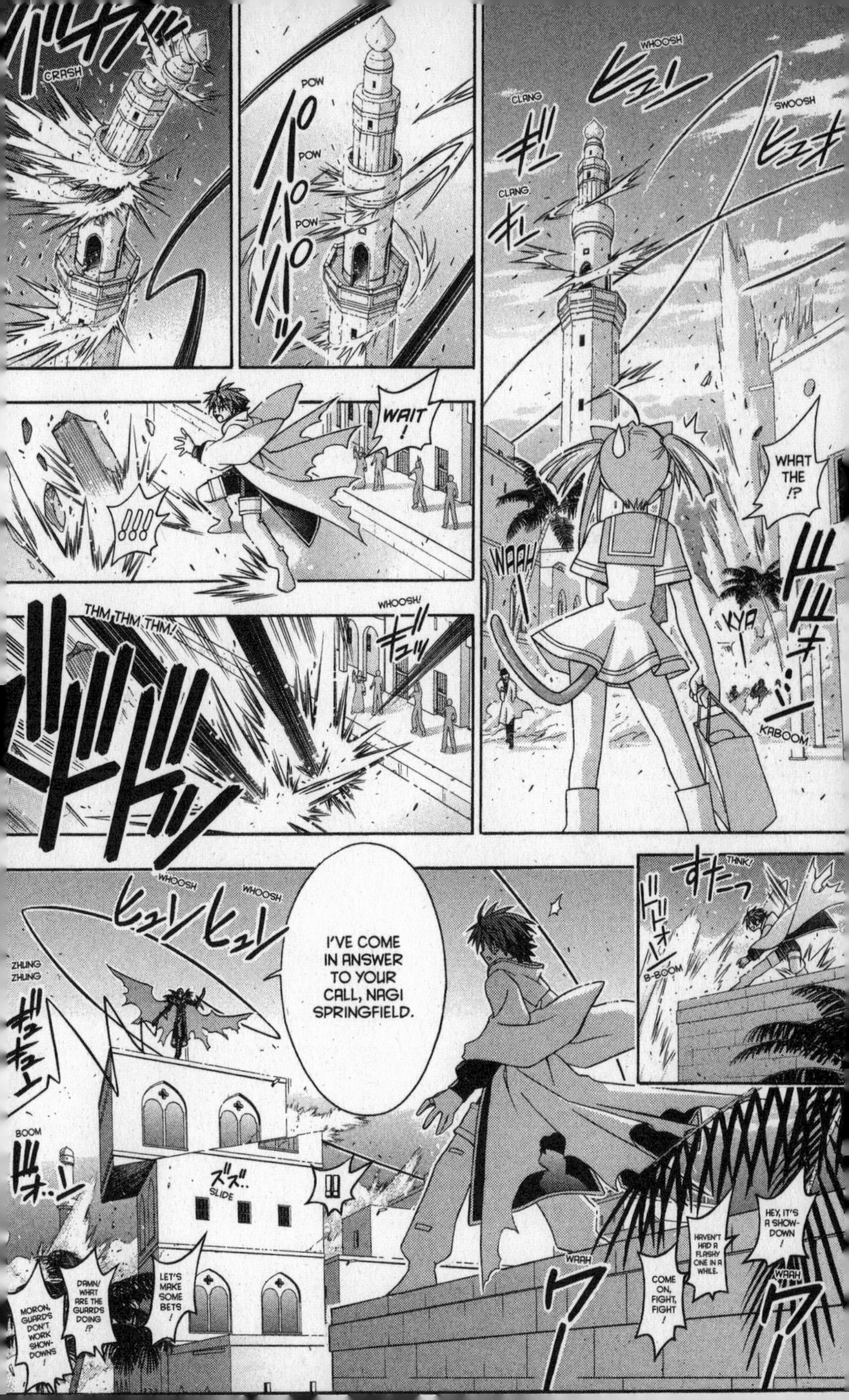
WHOOSH
SWOOSH
CLANG
CLANG
WHAT THE !?
WAAH!
KYA!
KABOOM
POW
POW
POW
CRASH
WAIT!
!!!
WHOOSH!
THM THM THM!
THNK!
B-BOOM
I'VE COME IN ANSWER TO YOUR CALL, NAGI SPRINGFIELD.
WHOOSH
WHOOSH
ZHUNG ZHUNG
BOOM
SLIDE
!!
HEY, IT'S A SHOW-DOWN!
WAAH
HAVEN'T HAD A FLASHY ONE IN A WHILE.
COME ON, FIGHT, FIGHT!
WAAH
LET'S MAKE SOME BETS!
DAMN! WHAT ARE THE GUARDS DOING!?
MORON, GUARDS DON'T WORK SHOW-DOWNS!

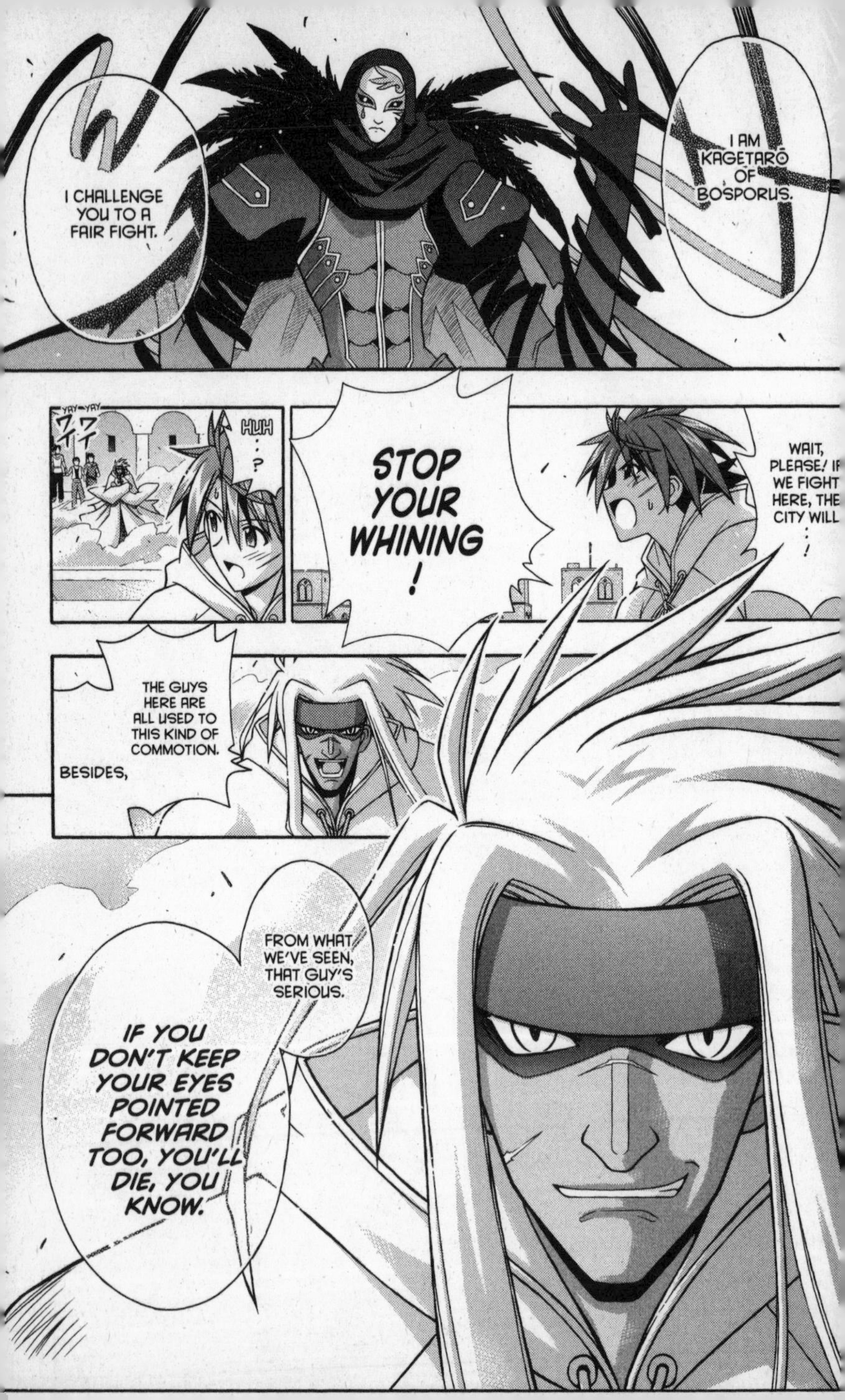
I AM KAGETARŌ OF BOSPORUS.
I CHALLENGE YOU TO A FAIR FIGHT.
WAIT, PLEASE! IF WE FIGHT HERE, THE CITY WILL...!
STOP YOUR WHINING!
YAY YAY
HUH...?
THE GUYS HERE ARE ALL USED TO THIS KIND OF COMMOTION.
BESIDES,
FROM WHAT WE'VE SEEN, THAT GUY'S SERIOUS.
IF YOU DON'T KEEP YOUR EYES POINTED FORWARD TOO, YOU'LL DIE, YOU KNOW.

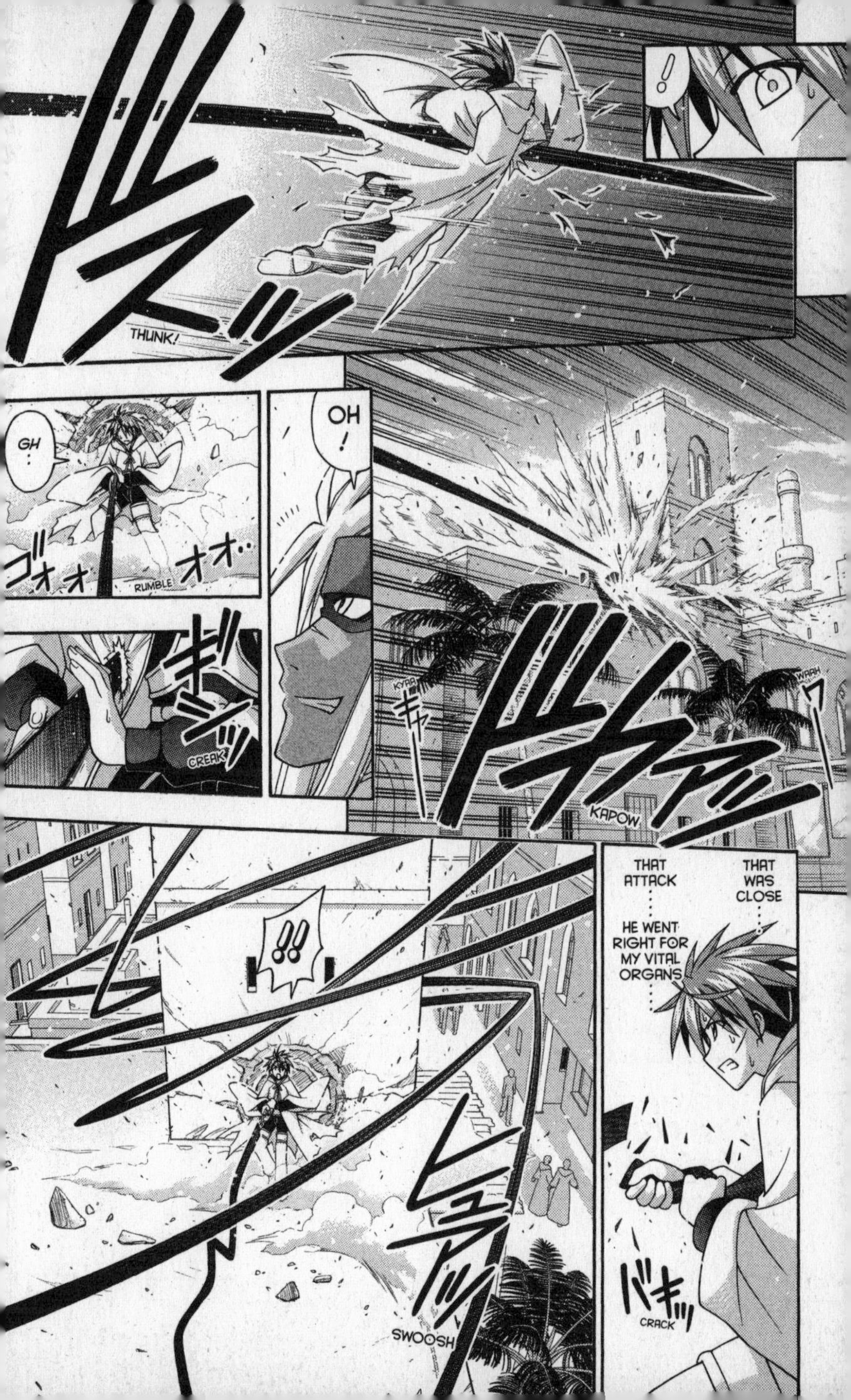
!
THUNK!
KYAA
WAAH
KAPOW
OH!
GH...
RUMBLE
CREAK
THAT WAS CLOSE...
THAT ATTACK...
HE WENT RIGHT FOR MY VITAL ORGANS...
CRACK
!!
SWOOSH

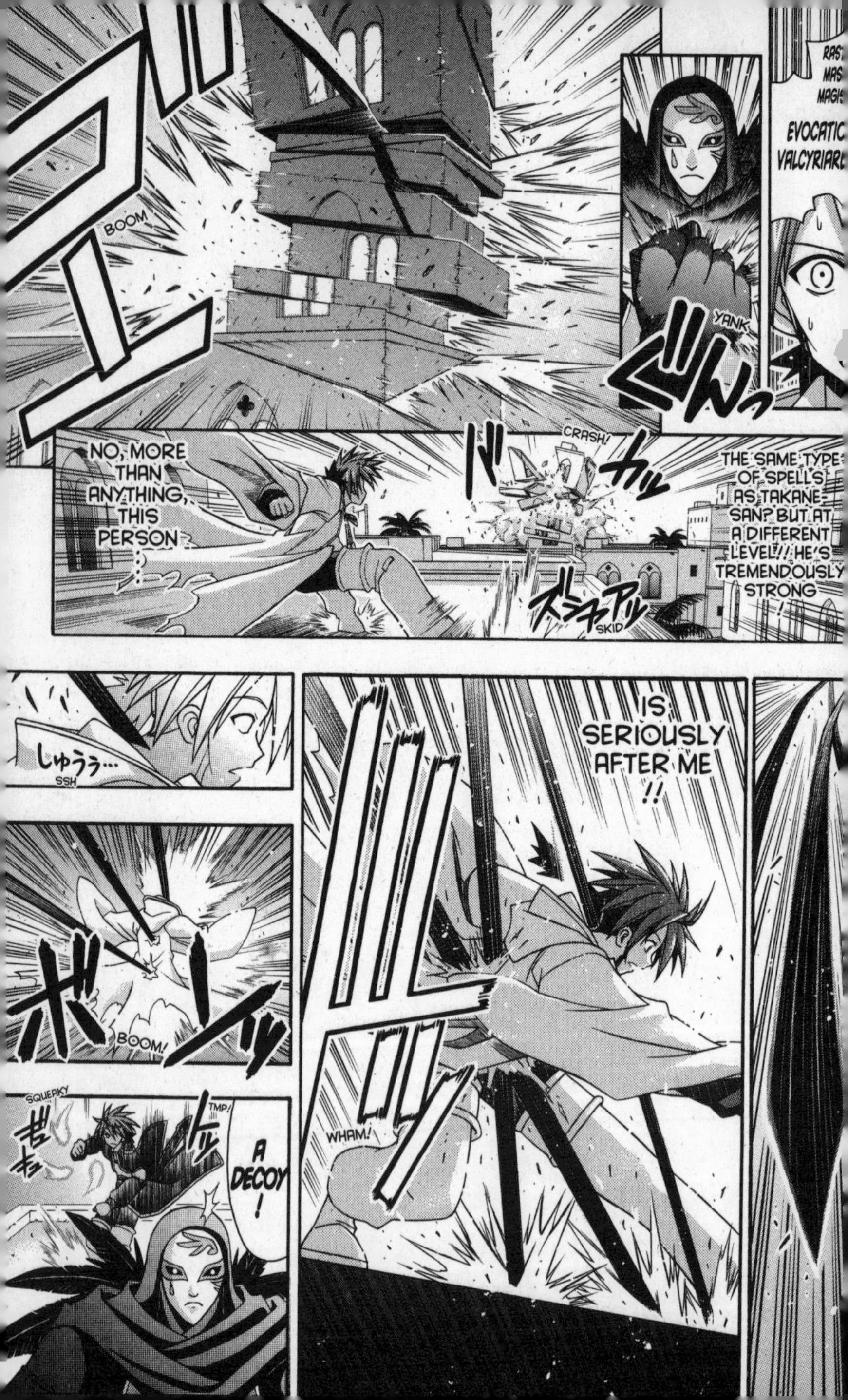
RAST
MAS
MAGIS
EVOCATIO
VALCYRIARE
YANK
BOOM
THE SAME TYPE OF SPELLS AS TAKANE-SAN? BUT AT A DIFFERENT LEVEL!! HE'S TREMENDOUSLY STRONG!
CRASH!
SKID
NO, MORE THAN ANYTHING, THIS PERSON...
IS SERIOUSLY AFTER ME!!
WHAM!
SSH
BOOM!
SQUEAKY
TMP!
A DECOY!

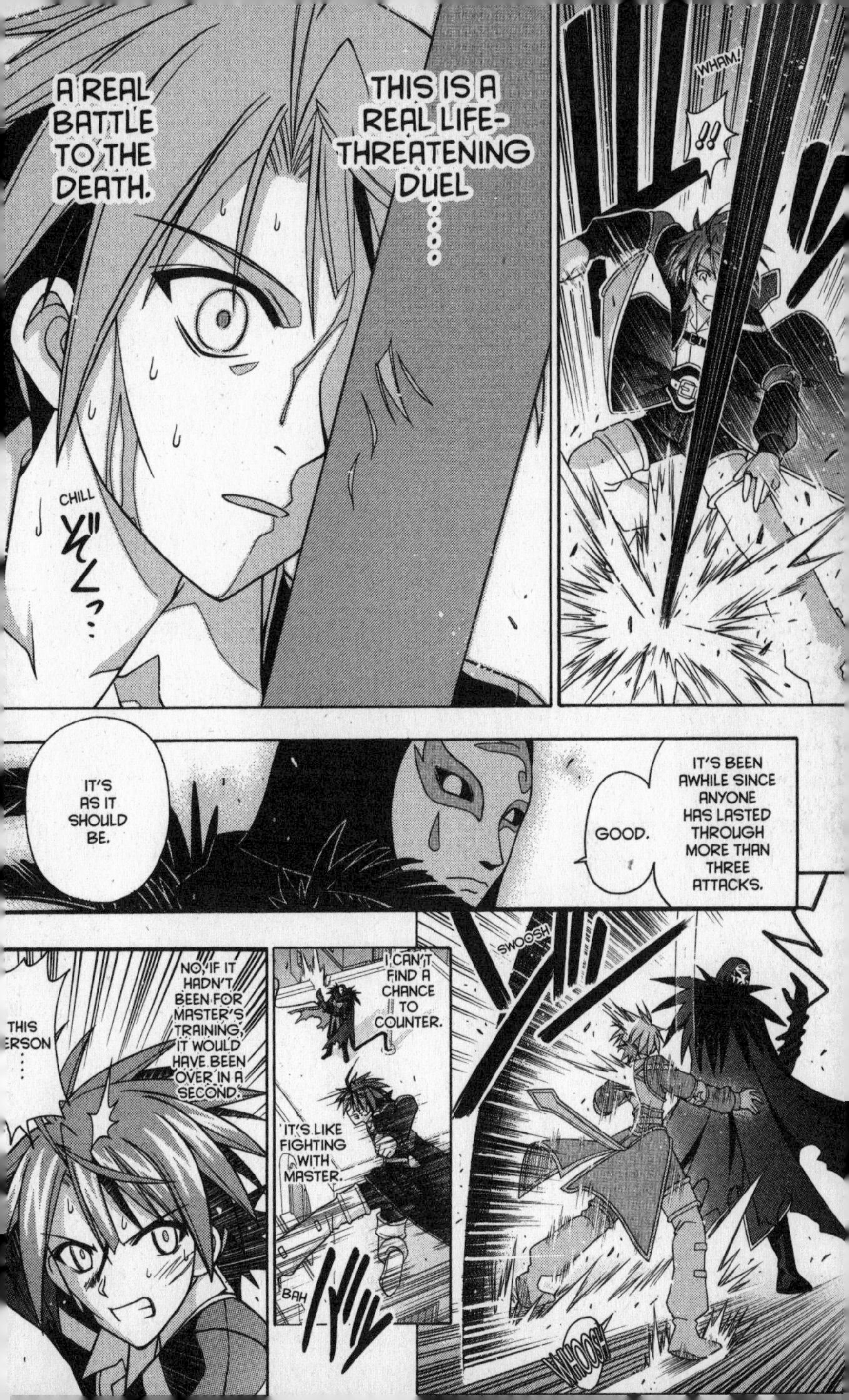
WHAM!
!!
THIS IS A REAL LIFE-THREATENING DUEL....
A REAL BATTLE TO THE DEATH.
CHILL
IT'S BEEN AWHILE SINCE ANYONE HAS LASTED THROUGH MORE THAN THREE ATTACKS.
GOOD.
IT'S AS IT SHOULD BE.
SWOOSH
WHOOSH
I CAN'T FIND A CHANCE TO COUNTER.
IT'S LIKE FIGHTING WITH MASTER.
BAH
NO, IF IT HADN'T BEEN FOR MASTER'S TRAINING, IT WOULD HAVE BEEN OVER IN A SECOND.
THIS ERSON....

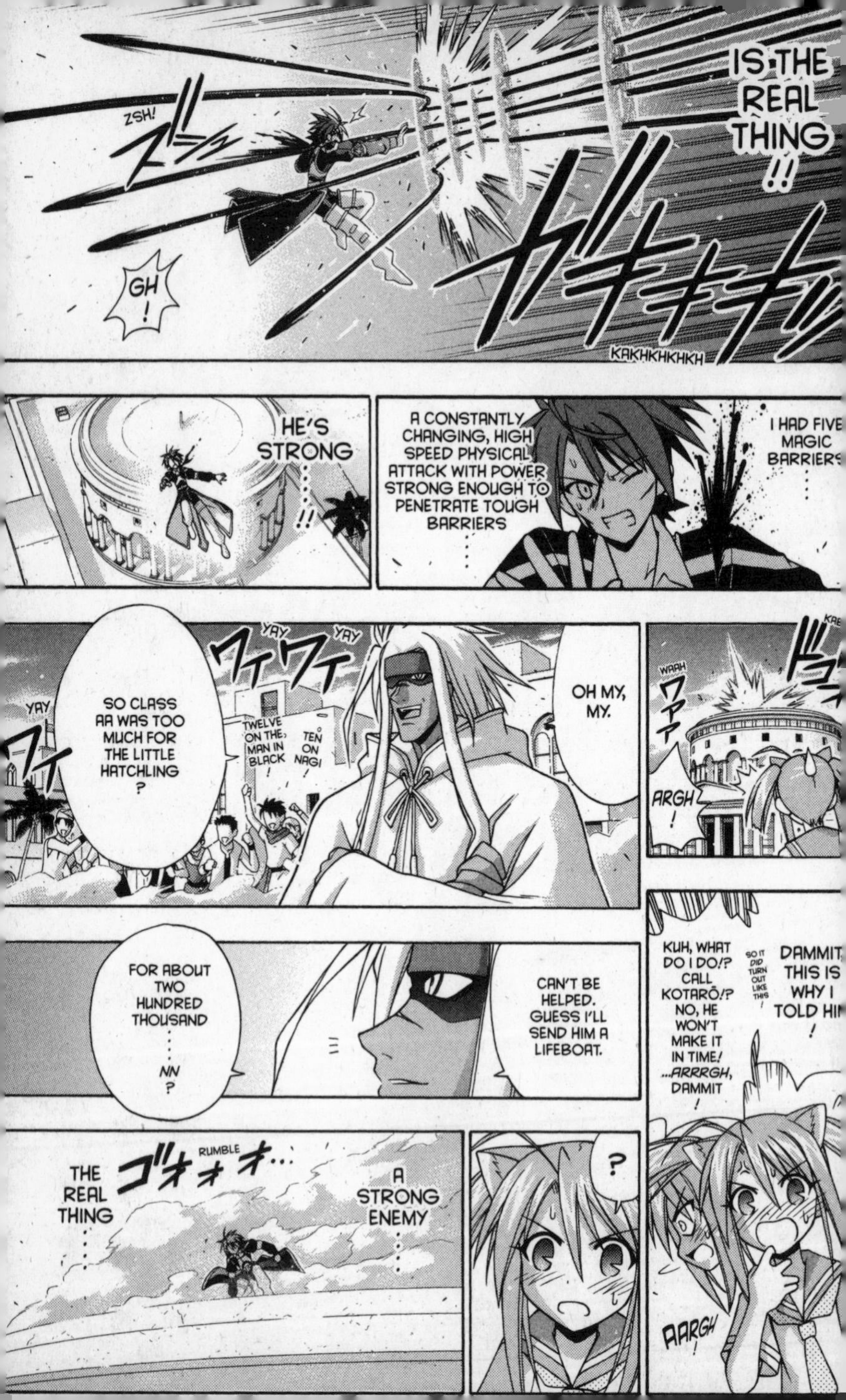
IS THE REAL THING!!
KAKHKHKHKH
ZSH!
GH!
I HAD FIVE MAGIC BARRIERS...
A CONSTANTLY CHANGING, HIGH SPEED PHYSICAL ATTACK WITH POWER STRONG ENOUGH TO PENETRATE TOUGH BARRIERS...
HE'S STRONG...!!
WARH
ARGH!
OH MY, MY.
YAY YAY
TEN ON NAGI!
TWELVE ON THE MAN IN BLACK!
SO CLASS AA WAS TOO MUCH FOR THE LITTLE HATCHLING?
YAY
DAMMIT, THIS IS WHY I TOLD HIM!
SO IT DID TURN OUT LIKE THIS!
KUH, WHAT DO I DO!? CALL KOTARŌ!? NO, HE WON'T MAKE IT IN TIME! ...ARRRGH, DAMMIT!
AARGH!
CAN'T BE HELPED. GUESS I'LL SEND HIM A LIFEBOAT.
FOR ABOUT TWO HUNDRED THOUSAND... NN?
?
A STRONG ENEMY...
RUMBLE
THE REAL THING...

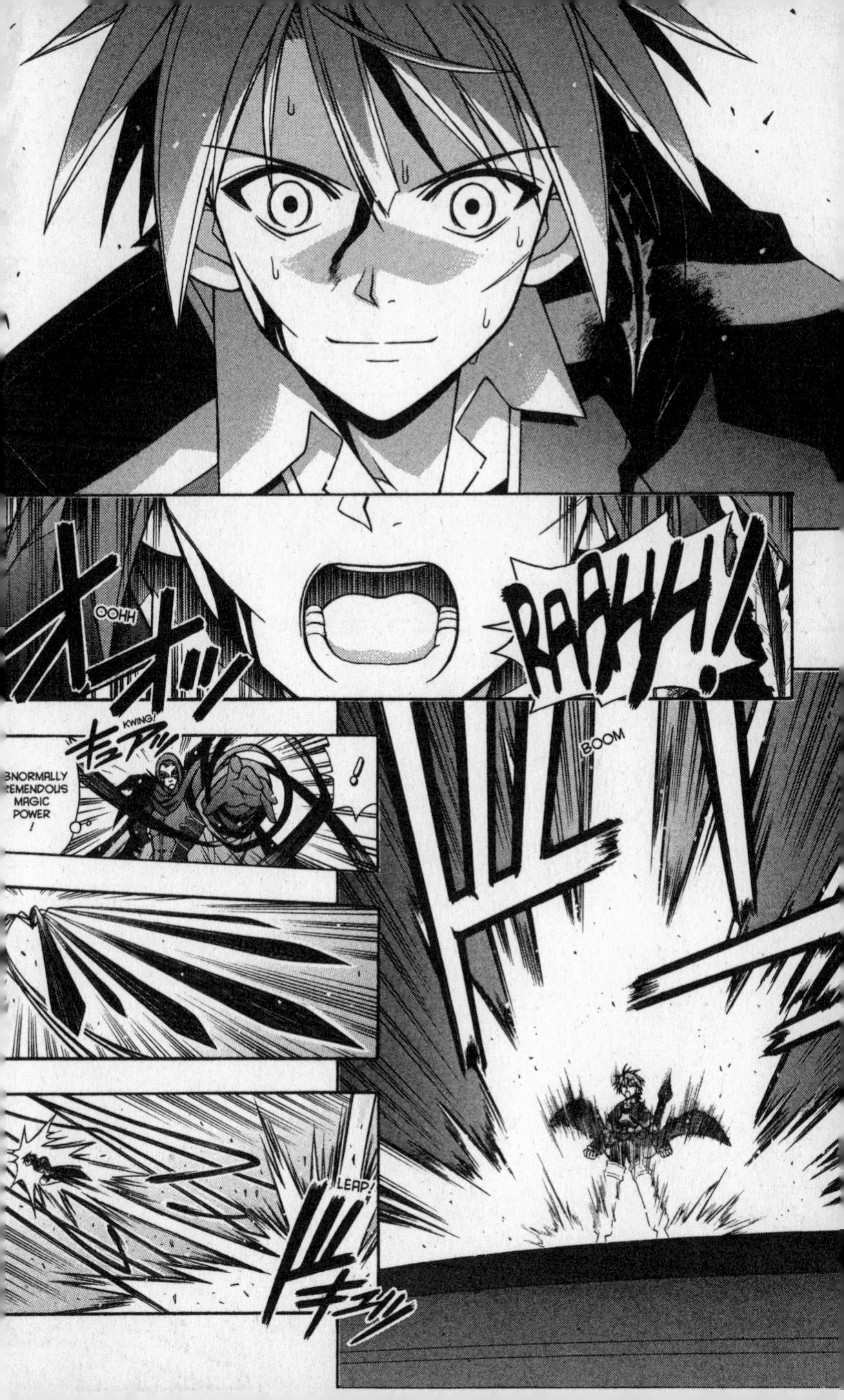
RAAHH!!
OOHH
BOOM
KWING!
!
BNORMALLY REMENDOUS MAGIC POWER !
LEAP!

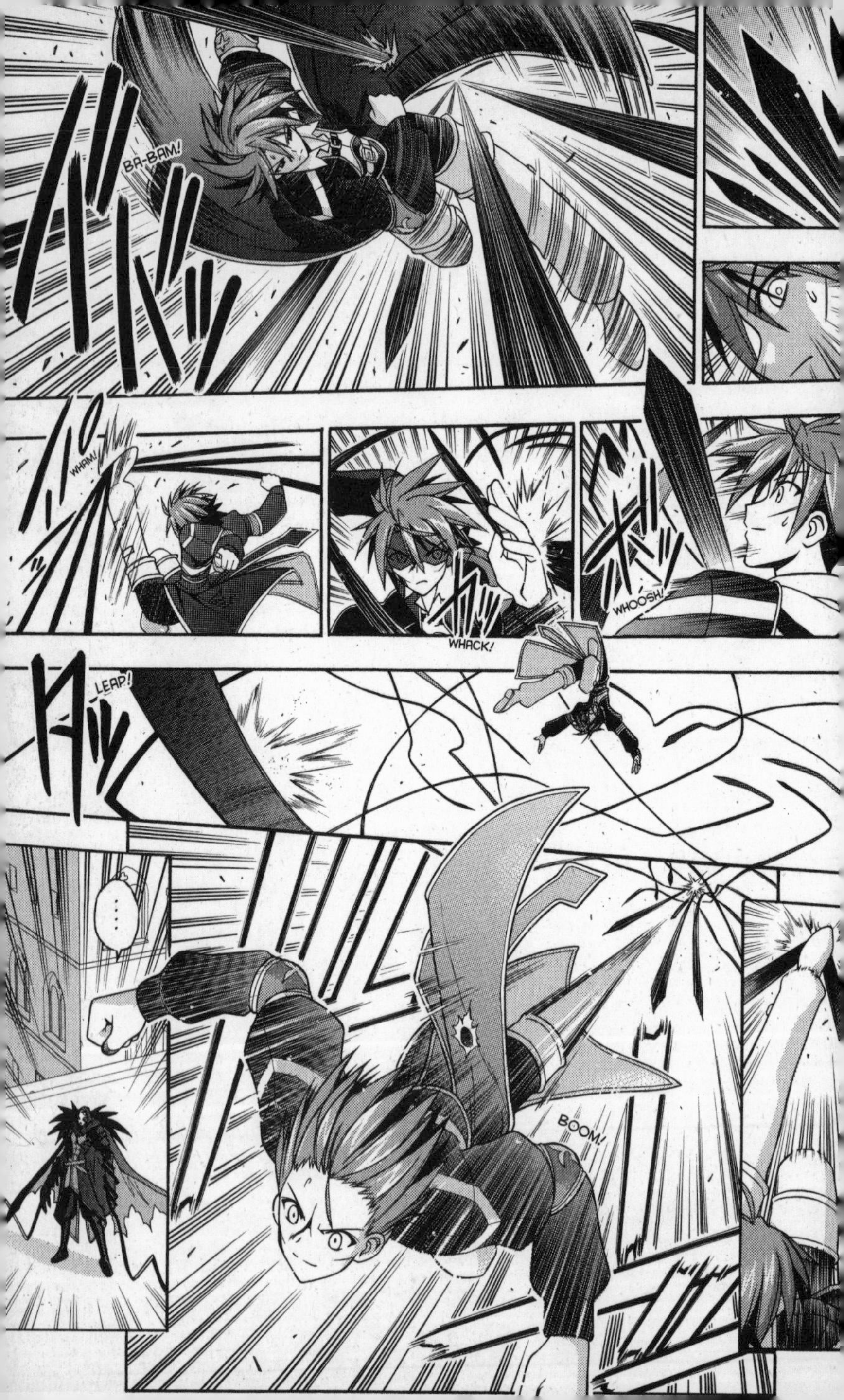
BA-BAM!
WHOOSH!
WHACK!
WHAM!
LEAP!
BOOM!
...

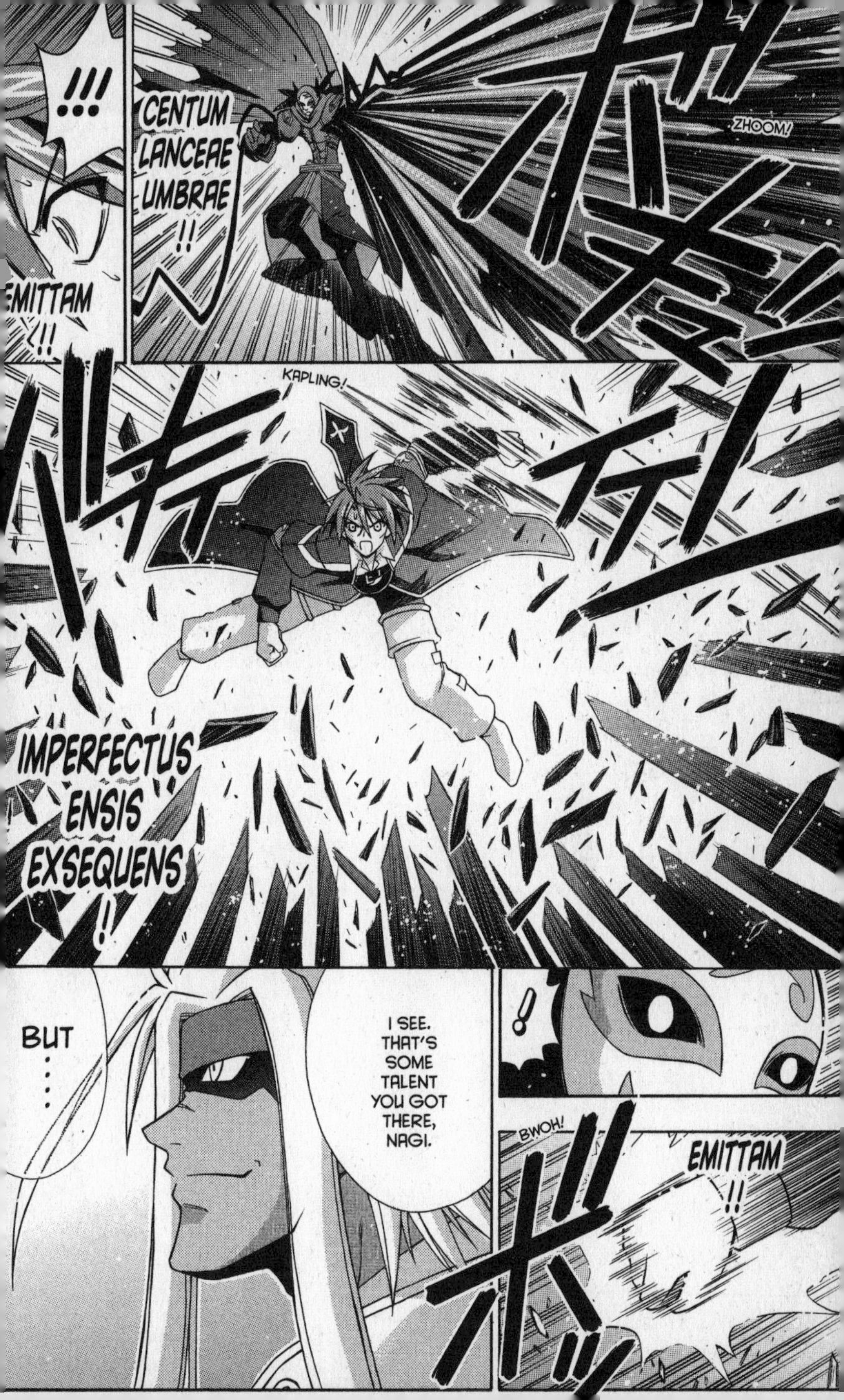
ZHOOM!
CENTUM LANCEAE UMBRAE !!
!!!
EMITTAM !!
KAPLING!
IMPERFECTUS ENSIS EXSEQUENS !!
!
BWOH!
EMITTAM !!
I SEE. THAT'S SOME TALENT YOU GOT THERE, NAGI.
BUT ....

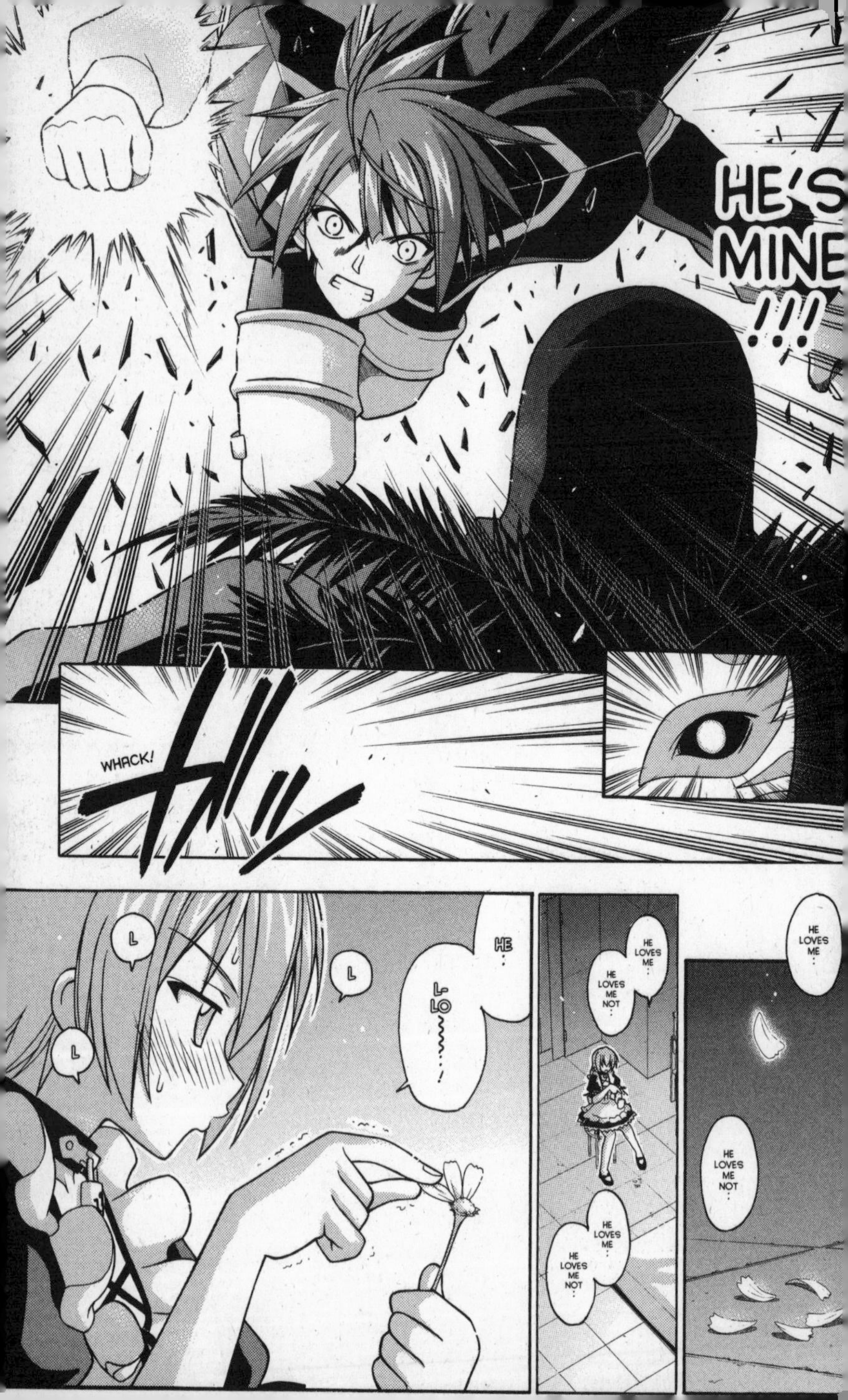
HE'S MINE!!!
WHACK!
HE LOVES ME...
HE LOVES ME NOT...
HE LOVES ME...
HE LOVES ME NOT...
HE LOVES ME...
HE LOVES ME NOT...
HE... L-LO~~...!
L
L
L

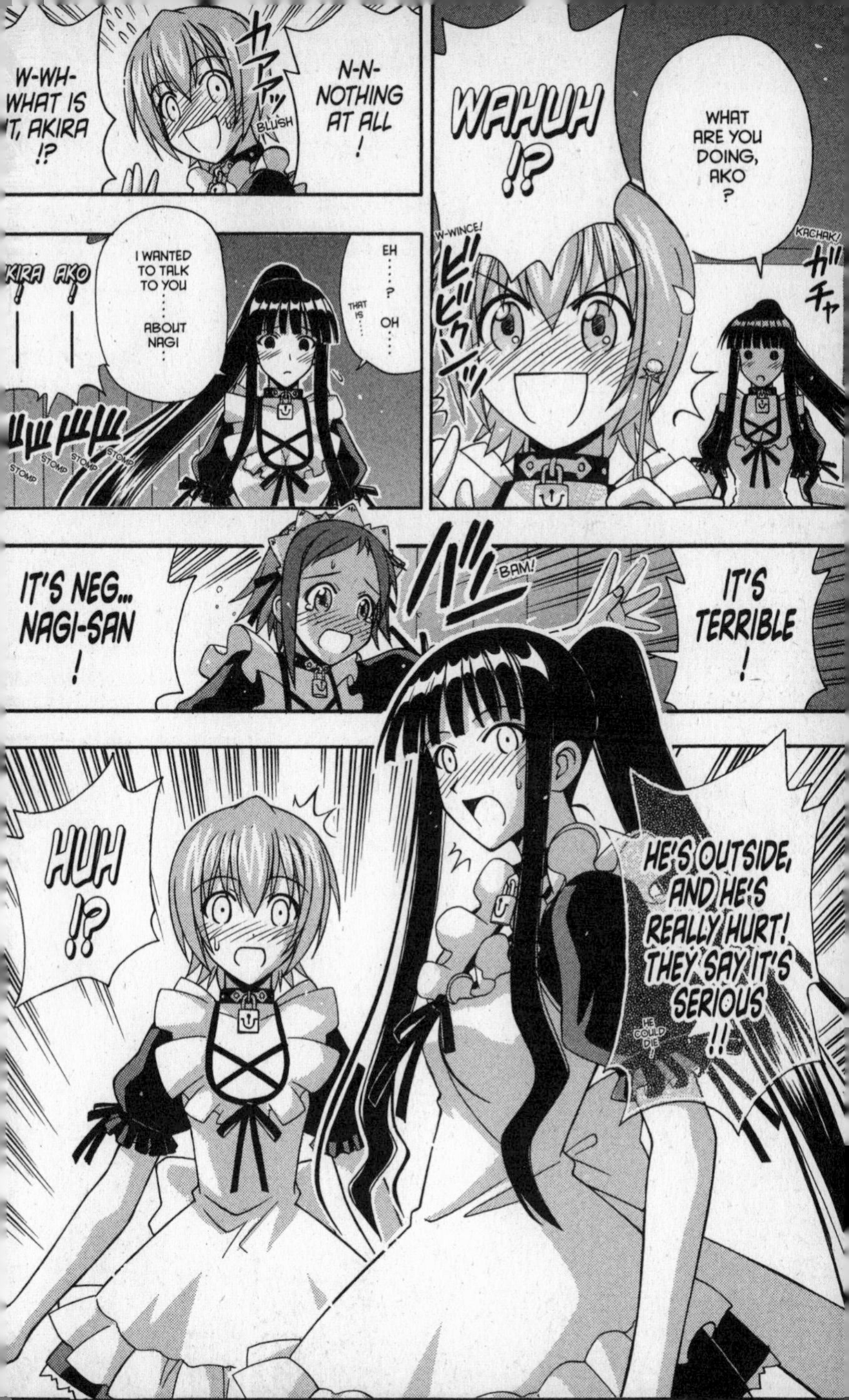
WHAT ARE YOU DOING, AKO?
KACHAK!
WAHUH!?
W-WINCE!
N-N-NOTHING AT ALL!
BLUSH
W-WH-WHAT IS T, AKIRA!?
EH....? OH....
THAT IS....
I WANTED TO TALK TO YOU...... ABOUT NAGI
AKO!
KIRA!
STOMP STOMP STOMP STOMP
IT'S TERRIBLE!
BAM!
IT'S NEG... NAGI-SAN!
HE'S OUTSIDE, AND HE'S REALLY HURT! THEY SAY IT'S SERIOUS!!
HE COULD DIE!
HUH!?

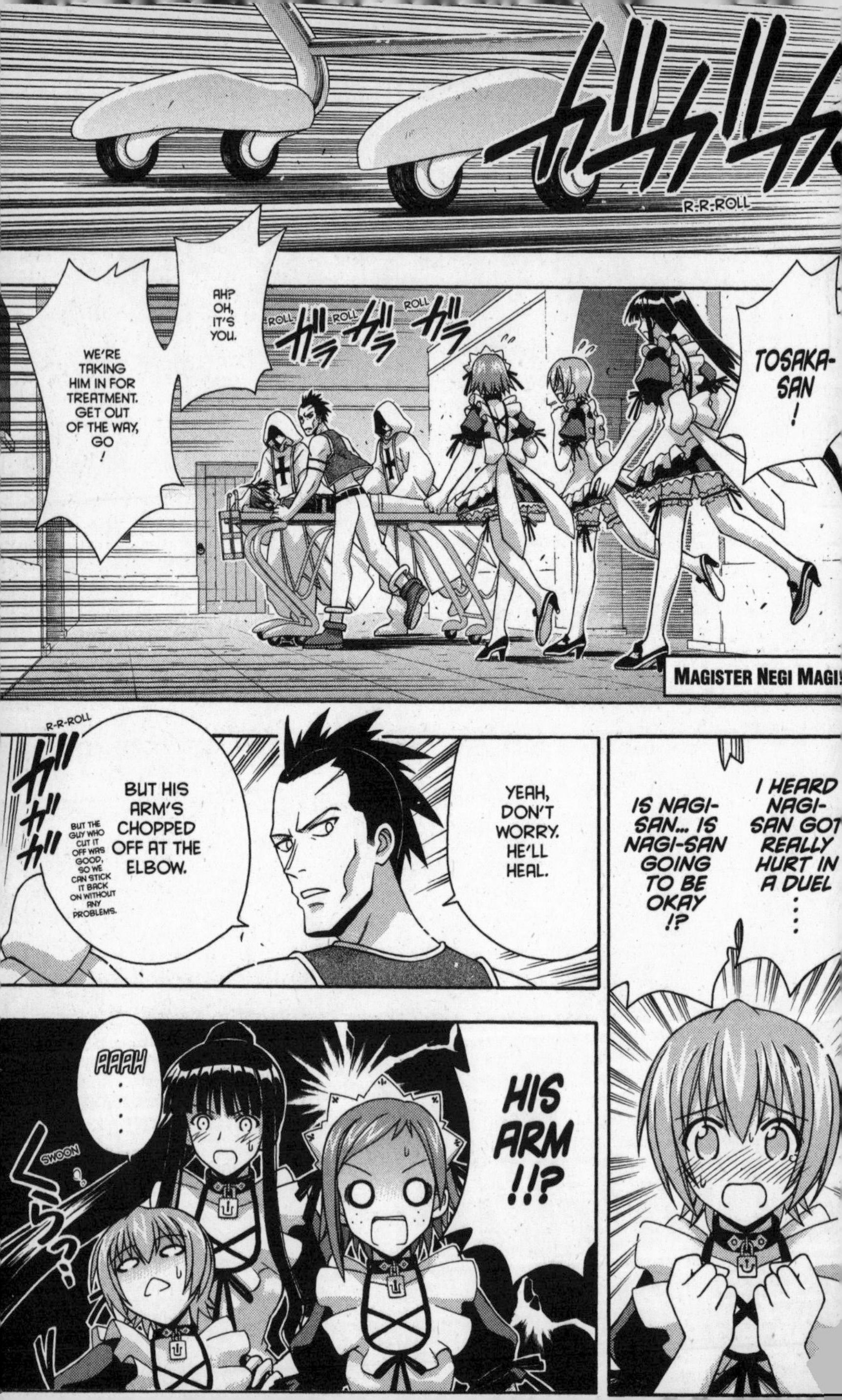

R-R-ROLL
TOSAKA-SAN!
AH? OH, IT'S YOU.
ROLL ROLL ROLL
WE'RE TAKING HIM IN FOR TREATMENT. GET OUT OF THE WAY, GO!
MAGISTER NEGI MAGI!
I HEARD NAGI-SAN GOT REALLY HURT IN A DUEL...
IS NAGI-SAN... IS NAGI-SAN GOING TO BE OKAY!?
YEAH, DON'T WORRY. HE'LL HEAL.
BUT HIS ARM'S CHOPPED OFF AT THE ELBOW.
BUT THE GUY WHO CUT IT OFF WAS GOOD, SO WE CAN STICK IT BACK ON WITHOUT ANY PROBLEMS.
R-R-ROLL
HIS ARM!!?
AAAH...
SWOON

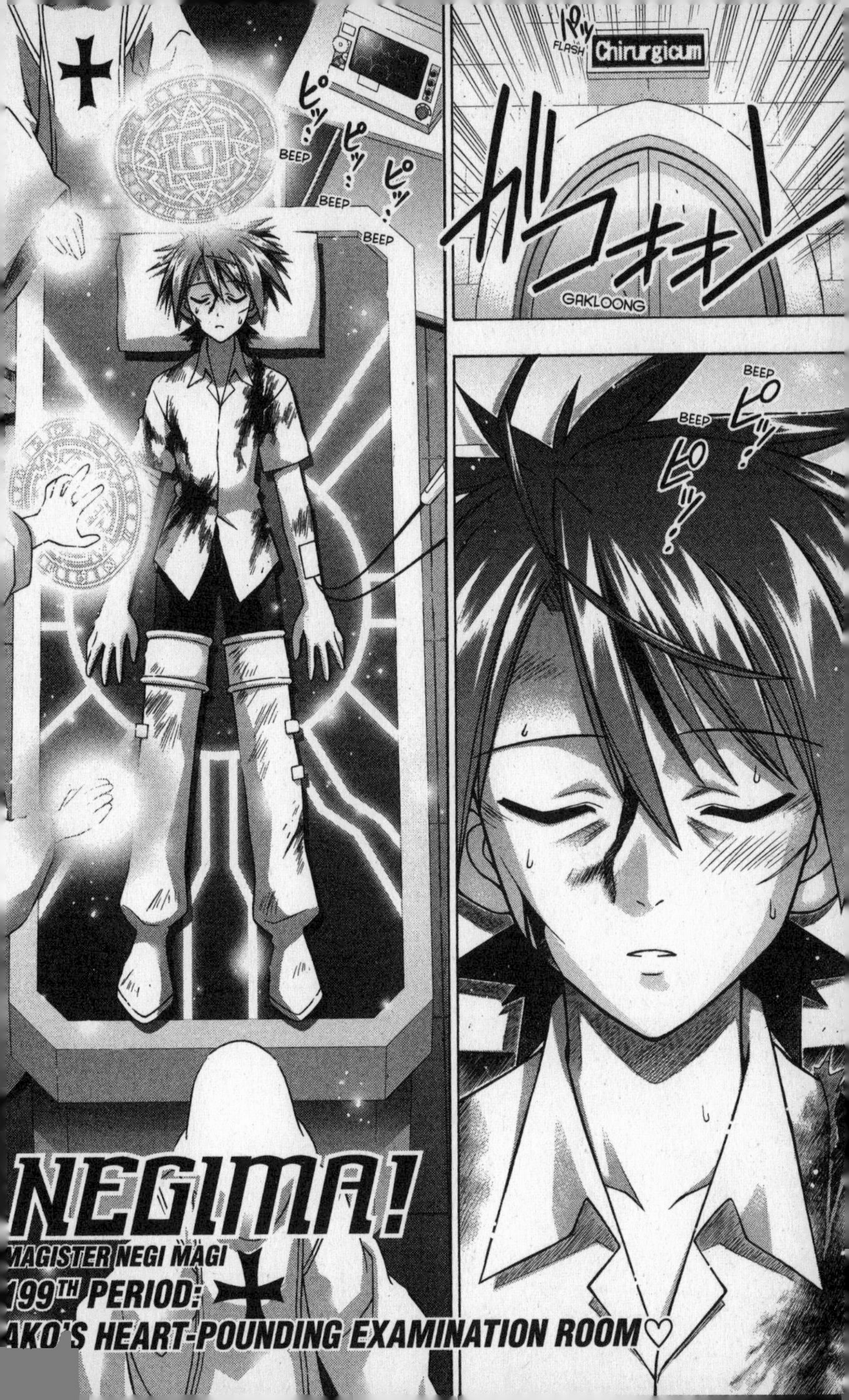
パッ
FLASH
Chirurgicum
がコォン
GAKLOONG
ピッ
BEEP
ピッ
BEEP
ピッ
BEEP
ピッ
BEEP
ピッ
BEEP
NEGIMA!
MAGISTER NEGI MAGI
199TH PERIOD:
AKO'S HEART-POUNDING EXAMINATION ROOM♡

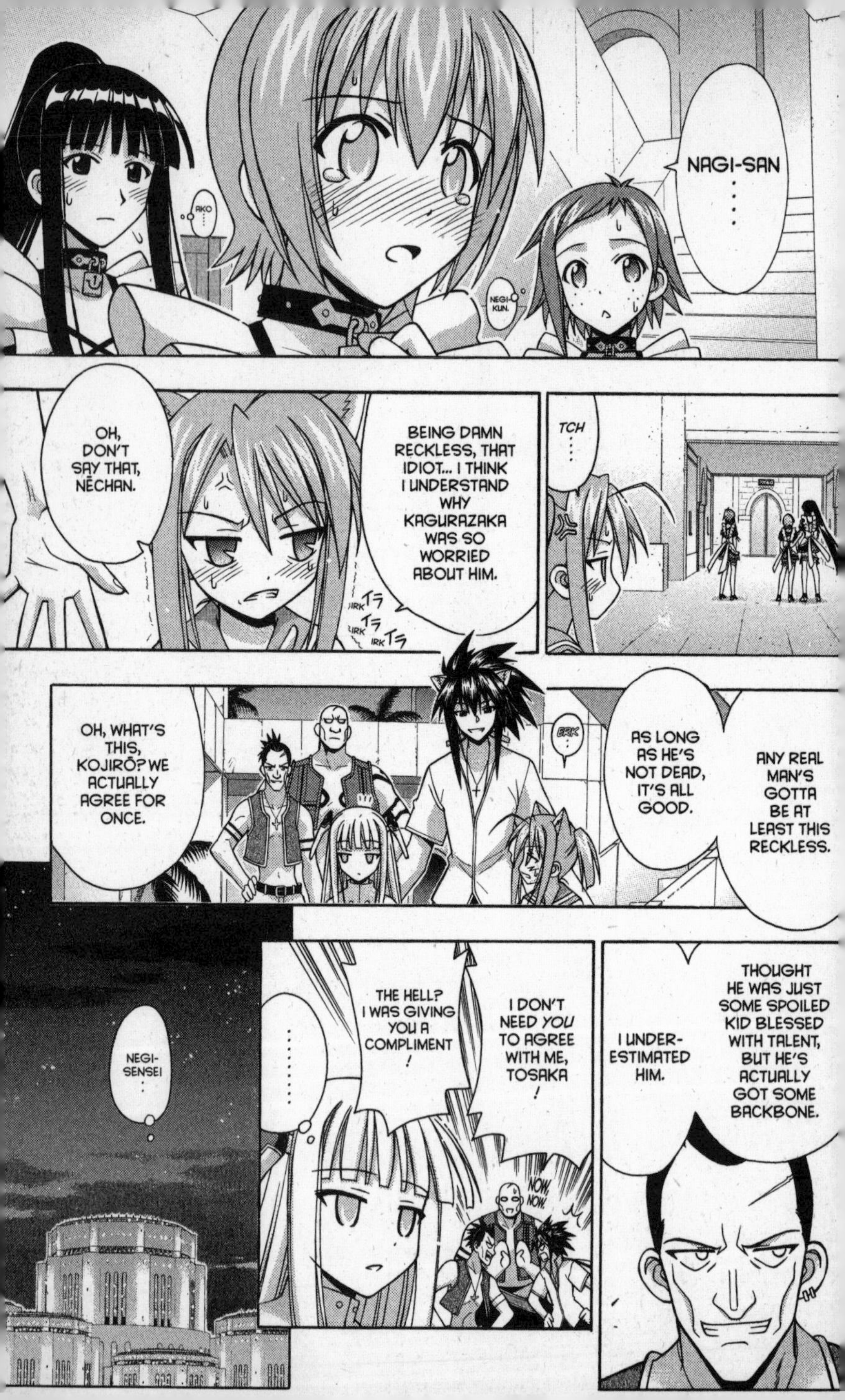
NAGI-SAN ....
NEGI-KUN.
AKO ...
TCH ...
BEING DAMN RECKLESS, THAT IDIOT... I THINK I UNDERSTAND WHY KAGURAZAKA WAS SO WORRIED ABOUT HIM.
IRK イラ IRK イラ IRK イラ
OH, DON'T SAY THAT, NĒCHAN.
ANY REAL MAN'S GOTTA BE AT LEAST THIS RECKLESS.
AS LONG AS HE'S NOT DEAD, IT'S ALL GOOD.
ERK ...
OH, WHAT'S THIS, KOJIRŌ? WE ACTUALLY AGREE FOR ONCE.
THOUGHT HE WAS JUST SOME SPOILED KID BLESSED WITH TALENT, BUT HE'S ACTUALLY GOT SOME BACKBONE.
I UNDER-ESTIMATED HIM.
I DON'T NEED *YOU* TO AGREE WITH ME, TOSAKA!
THE HELL? I WAS GIVING YOU A COMPLIMENT!
NOW, NOW.
......
NEGI-SENSEI ...

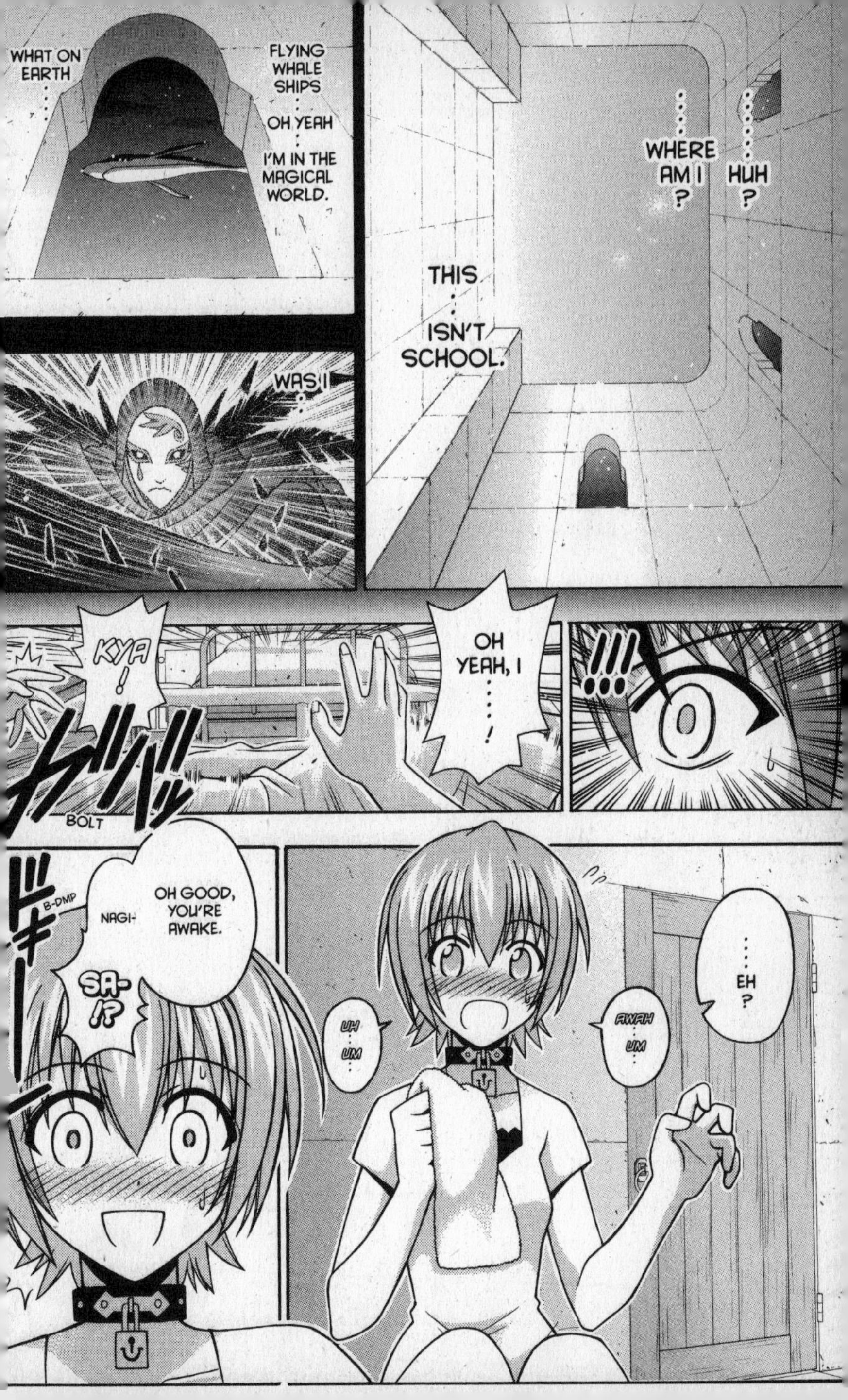
......HUH?
......WHERE AM I?
THIS... ISN'T SCHOOL.
FLYING WHALE SHIPS... OH YEAH... I'M IN THE MAGICAL WORLD.
WHAT ON EARTH...
WAS I...
!!!
OH YEAH, I.....!
KYA!
BOLT
......EH?
AWAH UM
UH... UM...
OH GOOD, YOU'RE AWAKE.
NAGI-
SA-!?
B-DMP

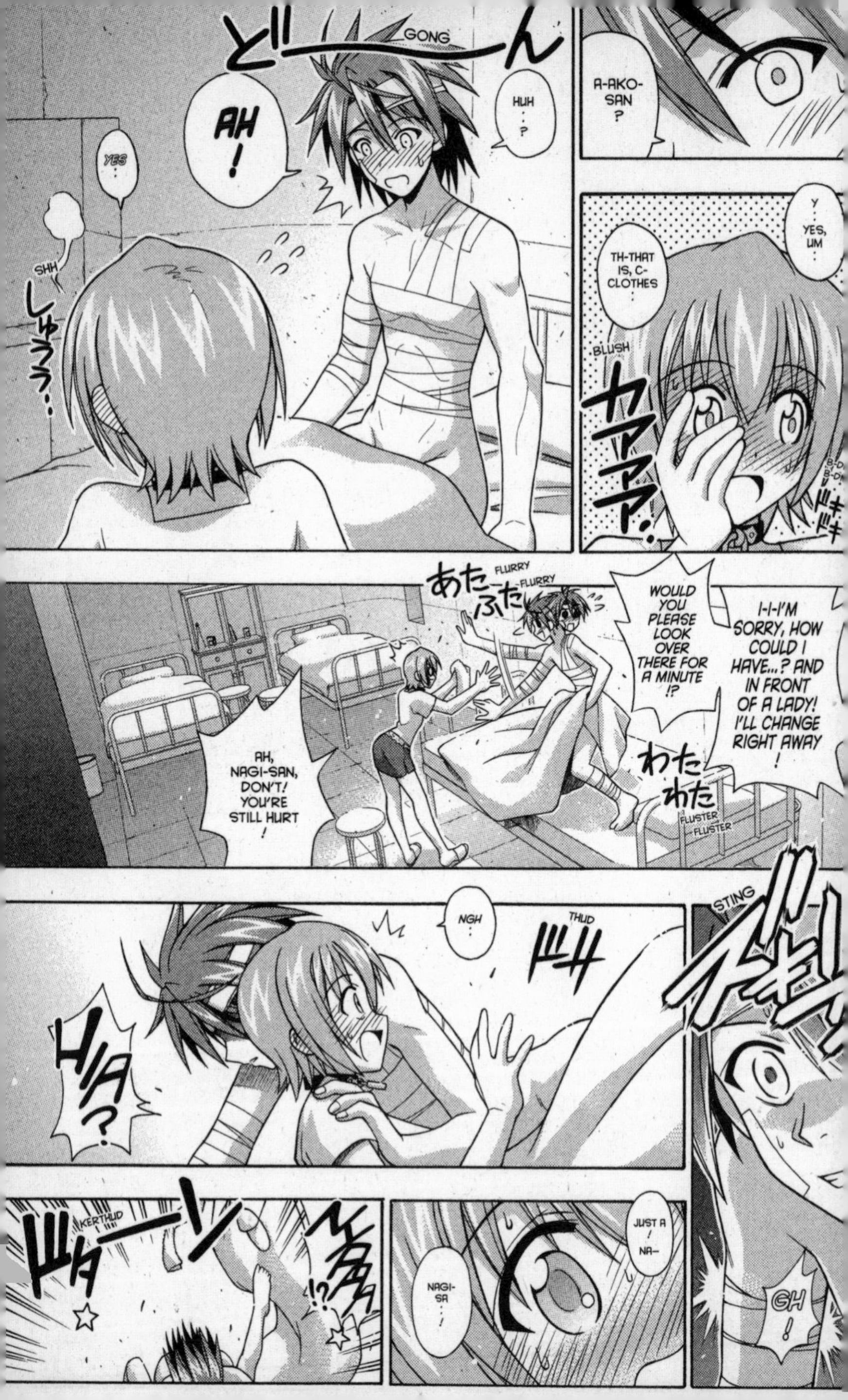
A-AKO-SAN?
Y... YES, UM...
TH-THAT IS, C-CLOTHES...
BLUSH
B-DMP B-DMP
GONG
HUH...?
AH!
YES...
SHH
I-I-I'M SORRY, HOW COULD I HAVE...? AND IN FRONT OF A LADY! I'LL CHANGE RIGHT AWAY!
WOULD YOU PLEASE LOOK OVER THERE FOR A MINUTE!?
あたふた
FLURRY FLURRY
わたわた
FLUSTER FLUSTER
AH, NAGI-SAN, DON'T! YOU'RE STILL HURT!
STING
GH!
NGH...
THUD
HIA?!
JUST A! NA—
NAGI-SA...!
!?
KERTHUD

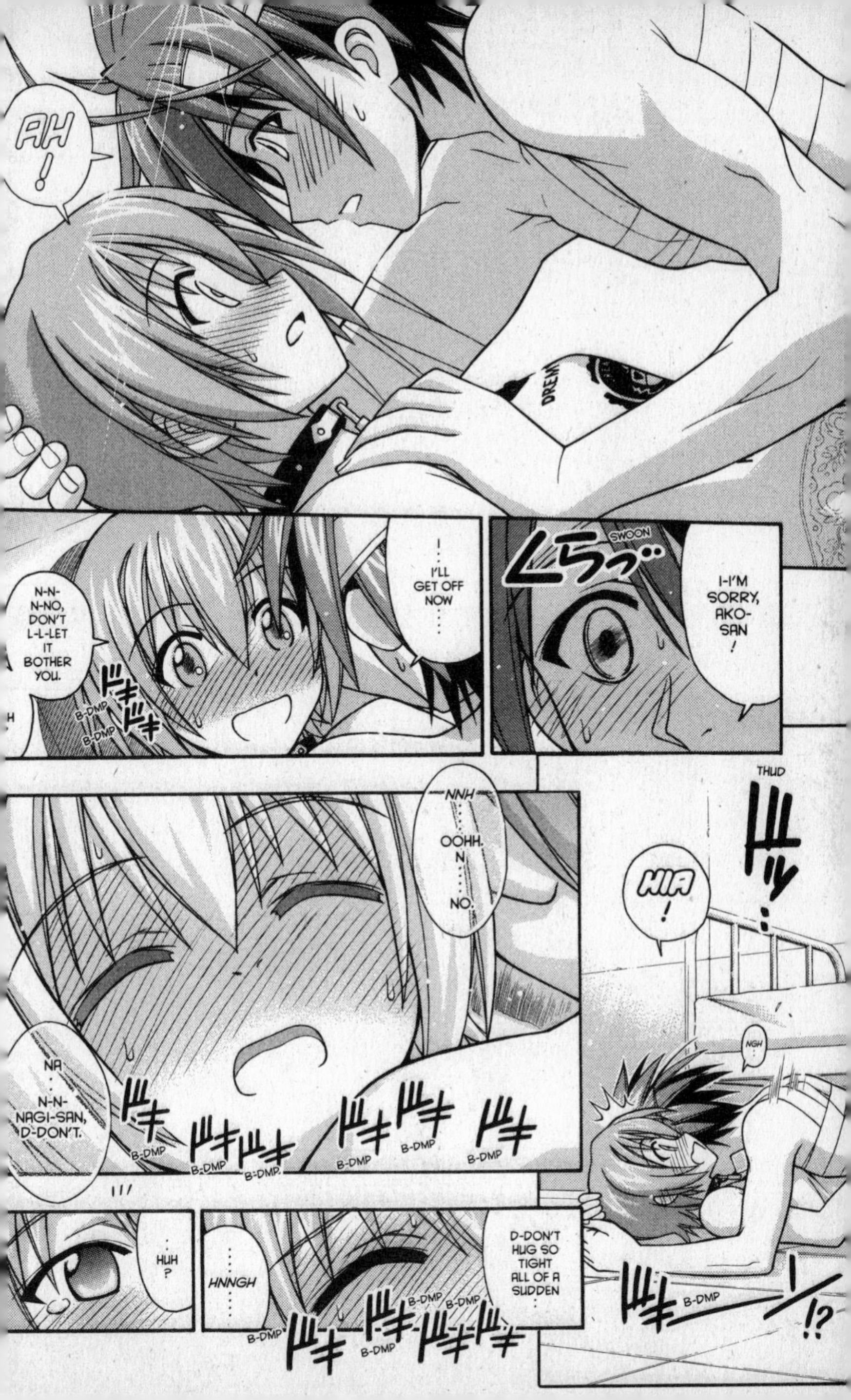
AH!
DREM
SWOON
I-I'M SORRY, AKO-SAN!
...I'LL GET OFF NOW.....
N-N-N-NO, DON'T L-L-LET IT BOTHER YOU.
B-DMP
B-DMP
THUD
HIA!
NGH...
B-DMP
!?
NNH... OOHH. N... NO.
NA... N-N-NAGI-SAN, D-DON'T.
B-DMP
B-DMP
B-DMP
B-DMP
B-DMP
B-DMP
D-DON'T HUG SO TIGHT ALL OF A SUDDEN...
....HNNGH....
...HUH?
B-DMP
B-DMP
B-DMP
B-DMP

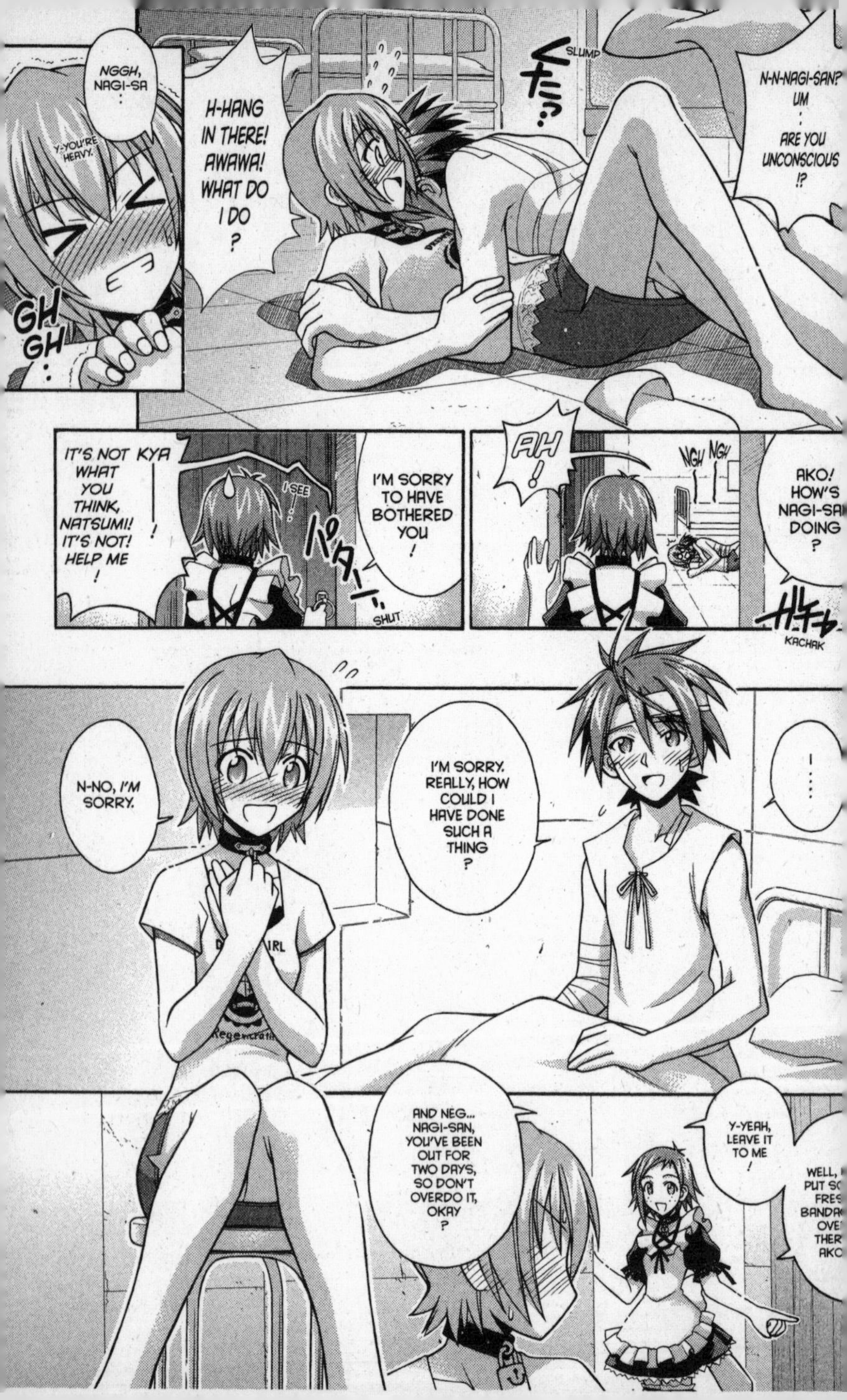
SLUMP
N-N-NAGI-SAN? UM : ARE YOU UNCONSCIOUS !?
H-HANG IN THERE! AWAWA! WHAT DO I DO ?
NGGH, NAGI-SA :
Y-YOU'RE HEAVY.
GH GH :
AKO! HOW'S NAGI-SAN DOING ?
KACHAK
AH !
NGH NGH
I'M SORRY TO HAVE BOTHERED YOU !
SHUT
I SEE
KYA
IT'S NOT WHAT YOU THINK, NATSUMI! IT'S NOT! HELP ME !
I ....
I'M SORRY. REALLY, HOW COULD I HAVE DONE SUCH A THING ?
N-NO, I'M SORRY.
WELL, I PUT SO FRES BANDA OVE THER AKO
Y-YEAH, LEAVE IT TO ME !
AND NEG... NAGI-SAN, YOU'VE BEEN OUT FOR TWO DAYS, SO DON'T OVERDO IT, OKAY ?

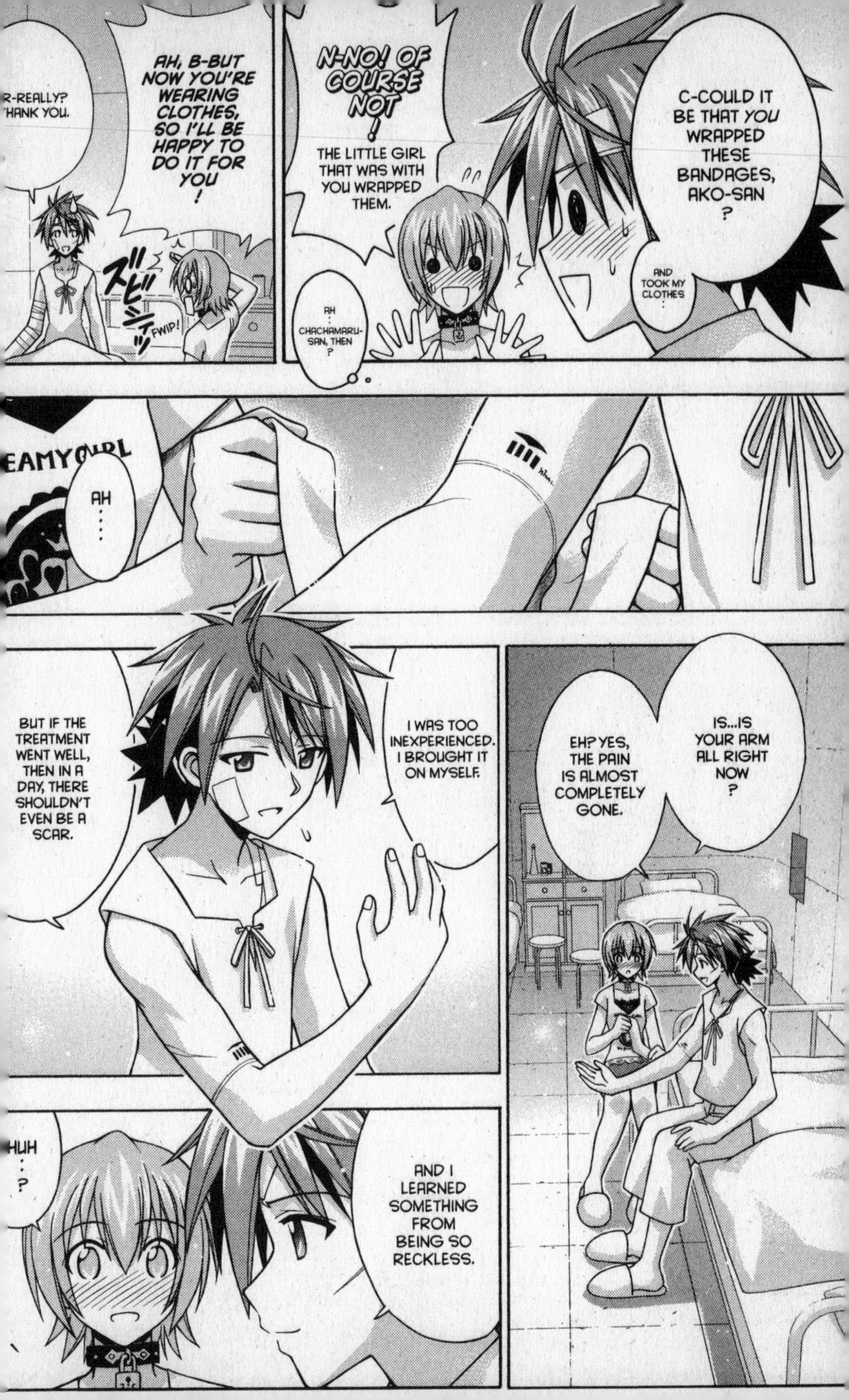
C-COULD IT BE THAT *YOU* WRAPPED THESE BANDAGES, AKO-SAN?
AND TOOK MY CLOTHES...
N-NO! OF COURSE NOT!
THE LITTLE GIRL THAT WAS WITH YOU WRAPPED THEM.
AH... CHACHAMARU-SAN, THEN?
AH, B-BUT NOW YOU'RE WEARING CLOTHES, SO I'LL BE HAPPY TO DO IT FOR YOU!
FWIP!
R-REALLY? THANK YOU.
AH...
IS...IS YOUR ARM ALL RIGHT NOW?
EH? YES, THE PAIN IS ALMOST COMPLETELY GONE.
I WAS TOO INEXPERIENCED. I BROUGHT IT ON MYSELF.
BUT IF THE TREATMENT WENT WELL, THEN IN A DAY, THERE SHOULDN'T EVEN BE A SCAR.
AND I LEARNED SOMETHING FROM BEING SO RECKLESS.
HUH...?

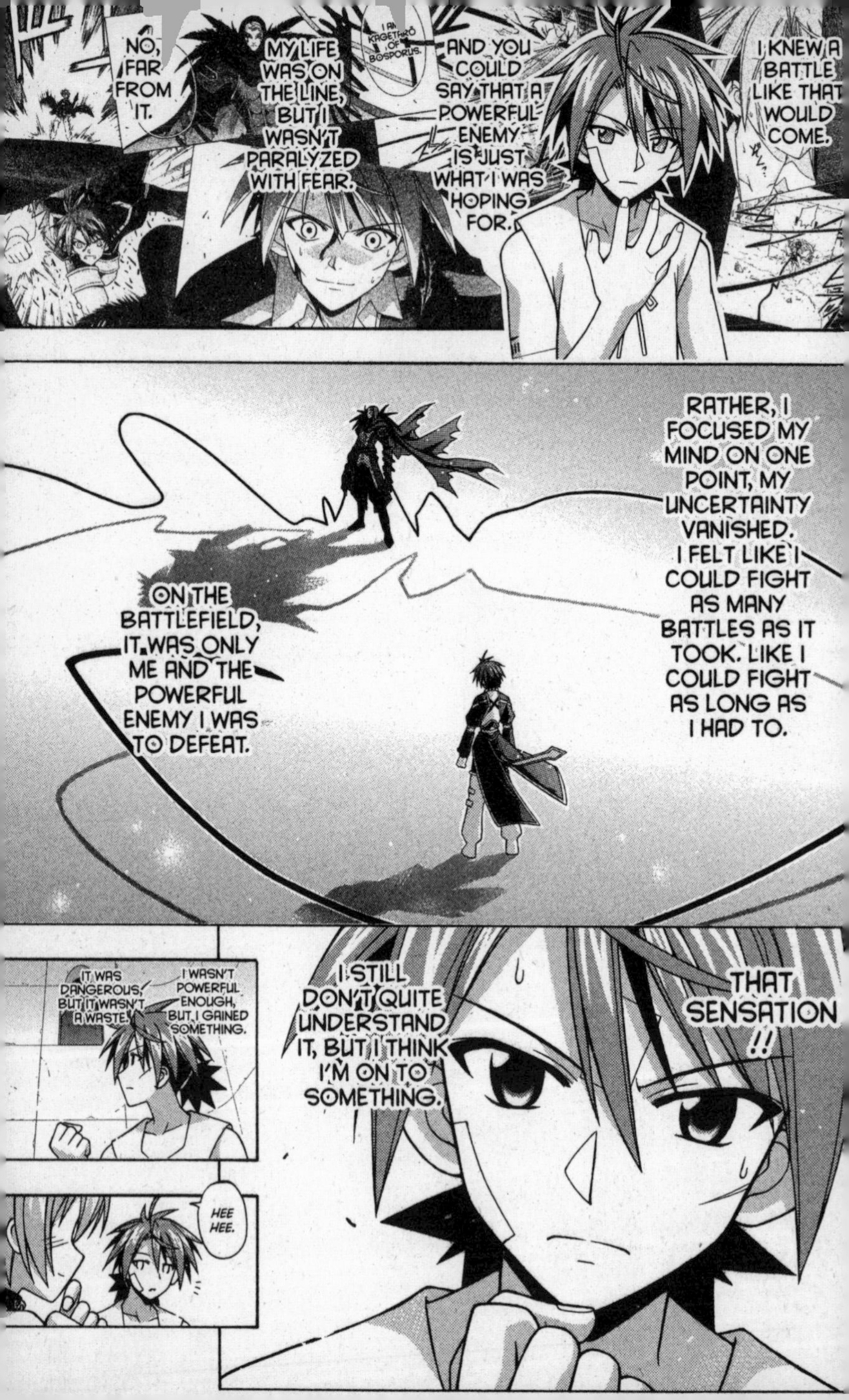

I KNEW A BATTLE LIKE THAT WOULD COME.
AND YOU COULD SAY THAT A POWERFUL ENEMY IS JUST WHAT I WAS HOPING FOR.
I AM KAGETARŌ OF BOSPORUS.
MY LIFE WAS ON THE LINE, BUT I WASN'T PARALYZED WITH FEAR.
NO, FAR FROM IT.
RATHER, I FOCUSED MY MIND ON ONE POINT, MY UNCERTAINTY VANISHED. I FELT LIKE I COULD FIGHT AS MANY BATTLES AS IT TOOK. LIKE I COULD FIGHT AS LONG AS I HAD TO.
ON THE BATTLEFIELD, IT WAS ONLY ME AND THE POWERFUL ENEMY I WAS TO DEFEAT.
THAT SENSATION!!
I STILL DON'T QUITE UNDERSTAND IT, BUT I THINK I'M ON TO SOMETHING.
I WASN'T POWERFUL ENOUGH, BUT I GAINED SOMETHING.
IT WAS DANGEROUS, BUT IT WASN'T A WASTE.
HEE HEE.

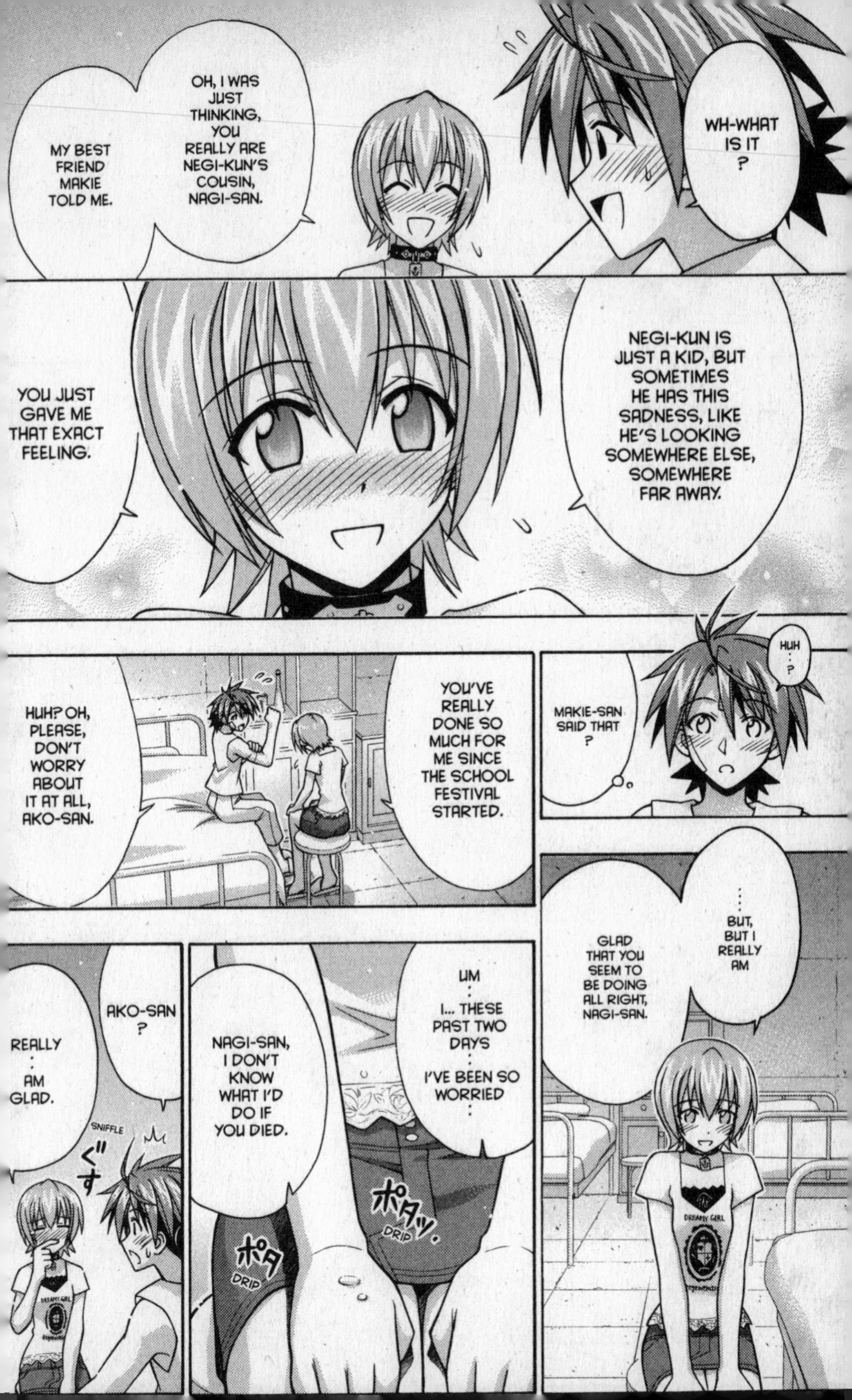
WH-WHAT IS IT ?
OH, I WAS JUST THINKING, YOU REALLY ARE NEGI-KUN'S COUSIN, NAGI-SAN.
MY BEST FRIEND MAKIE TOLD ME.
NEGI-KUN IS JUST A KID, BUT SOMETIMES HE HAS THIS SADNESS, LIKE HE'S LOOKING SOMEWHERE ELSE, SOMEWHERE FAR AWAY.
YOU JUST GAVE ME THAT EXACT FEELING.
HUH : ?
MAKIE-SAN SAID THAT ?
YOU'VE REALLY DONE SO MUCH FOR ME SINCE THE SCHOOL FESTIVAL STARTED.
HUH? OH, PLEASE, DON'T WORRY ABOUT IT AT ALL, AKO-SAN.
: : BUT, BUT I REALLY AM
GLAD THAT YOU SEEM TO BE DOING ALL RIGHT, NAGI-SAN.
UM : I... THESE PAST TWO DAYS : I'VE BEEN SO WORRIED :
NAGI-SAN, I DON'T KNOW WHAT I'D DO IF YOU DIED.
ポタッ
DRIP
ポタ
DRIP
AKO-SAN ?
REALLY : AM GLAD.
SNIFFLE
ぐす

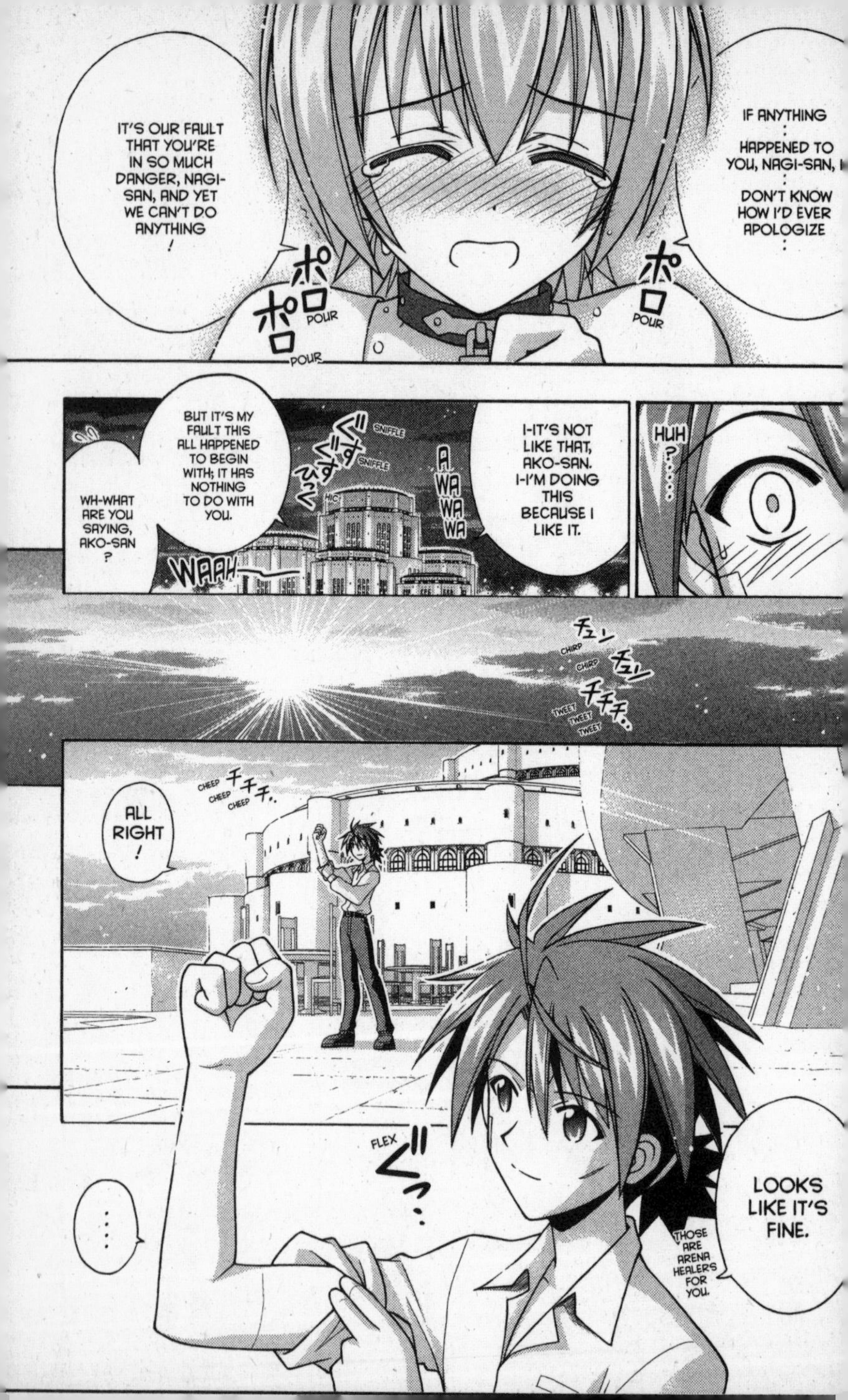
IF ANYTHING : HAPPENED TO YOU, NAGI-SAN, I : DON'T KNOW HOW I'D EVER APOLOGIZE :
ポロ POUR
IT'S OUR FAULT THAT YOU'RE IN SO MUCH DANGER, NAGI-SAN, AND YET WE CAN'T DO ANYTHING !
ポロ POUR
ポロ POUR
HUH ?....
I-IT'S NOT LIKE THAT, AKO-SAN. I-I'M DOING THIS BECAUSE I LIKE IT.
A WA WA WA
ぐすぐす SNIFFLE SNIFFLE
ひっく HIC
BUT IT'S MY FAULT THIS ALL HAPPENED TO BEGIN WITH; IT HAS NOTHING TO DO WITH YOU.
WH-WHAT ARE YOU SAYING, AKO-SAN ?
WAAH
チュンチュン CHIRP CHIRP
チチチ.. TWEET TWEET TWEET
チチチ.. CHEEP CHEEP CHEEP
ALL RIGHT !
LOOKS LIKE IT'S FINE.
THOSE ARE ARENA HEALERS FOR YOU.
ぐっ FLEX
....

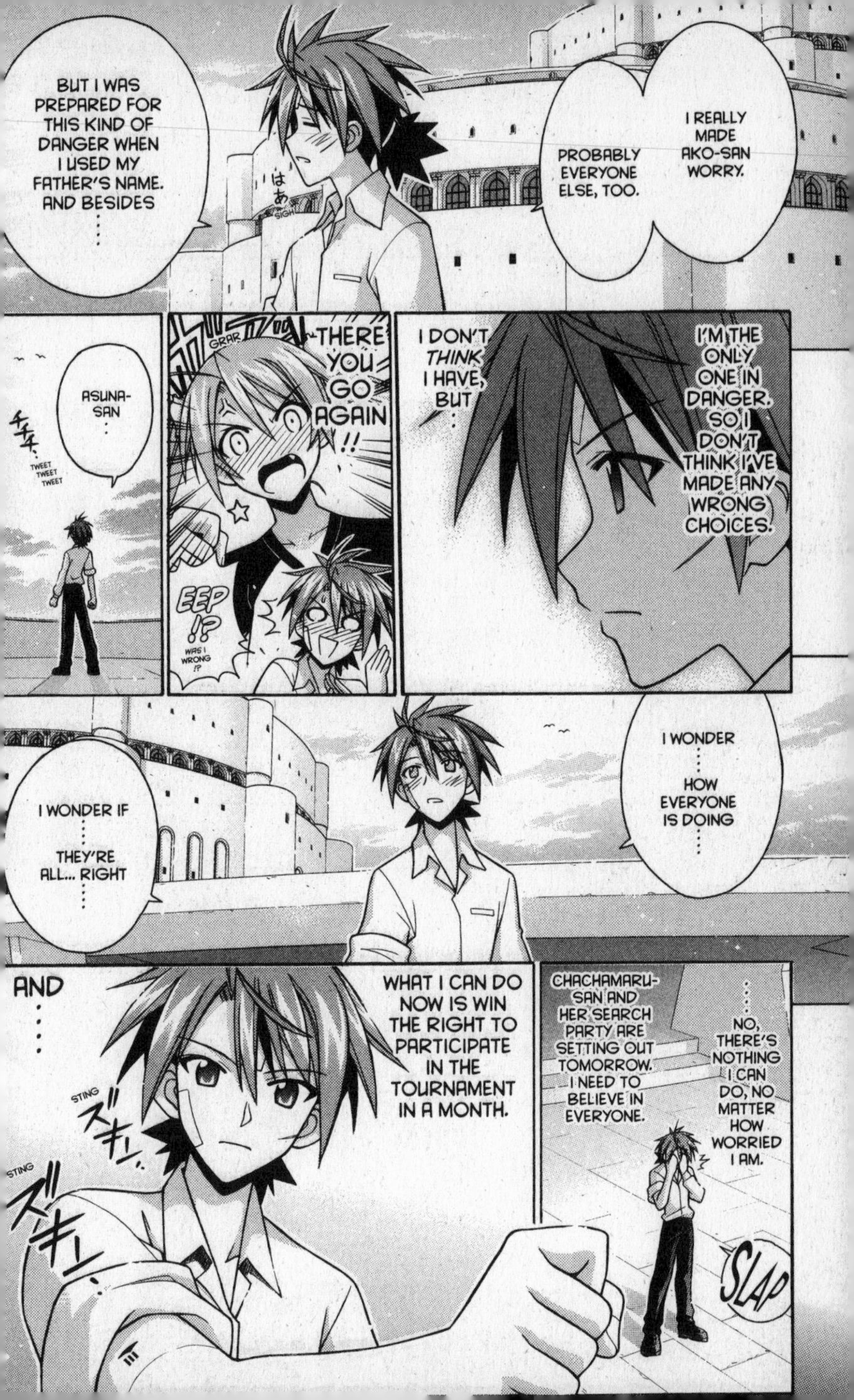
I REALLY MADE AKO-SAN WORRY.
PROBABLY EVERYONE ELSE, TOO.
はあ SIGH
BUT I WAS PREPARED FOR THIS KIND OF DANGER WHEN I USED MY FATHER'S NAME. AND BESIDES ......
I'M THE ONLY ONE IN DANGER. SO I DON'T THINK I'VE MADE ANY WRONG CHOICES.
I DON'T THINK I HAVE, BUT ...
GRAR
THERE YOU GO AGAIN!!
EEP!?
WAS I WRONG!?
ASUNA-SAN ...
チチチ TWEET TWEET TWEET
I WONDER ... HOW EVERYONE IS DOING ...
I WONDER IF ... THEY'RE ALL... RIGHT ...
...... NO, THERE'S NOTHING I CAN DO, NO MATTER HOW WORRIED I AM.
CHACHAMARU-SAN AND HER SEARCH PARTY ARE SETTING OUT TOMORROW. I NEED TO BELIEVE IN EVERYONE.
SLAP
WHAT I CAN DO NOW IS WIN THE RIGHT TO PARTICIPATE IN THE TOURNAMENT IN A MONTH.
AND ....
ズキン STING
ズキン STING

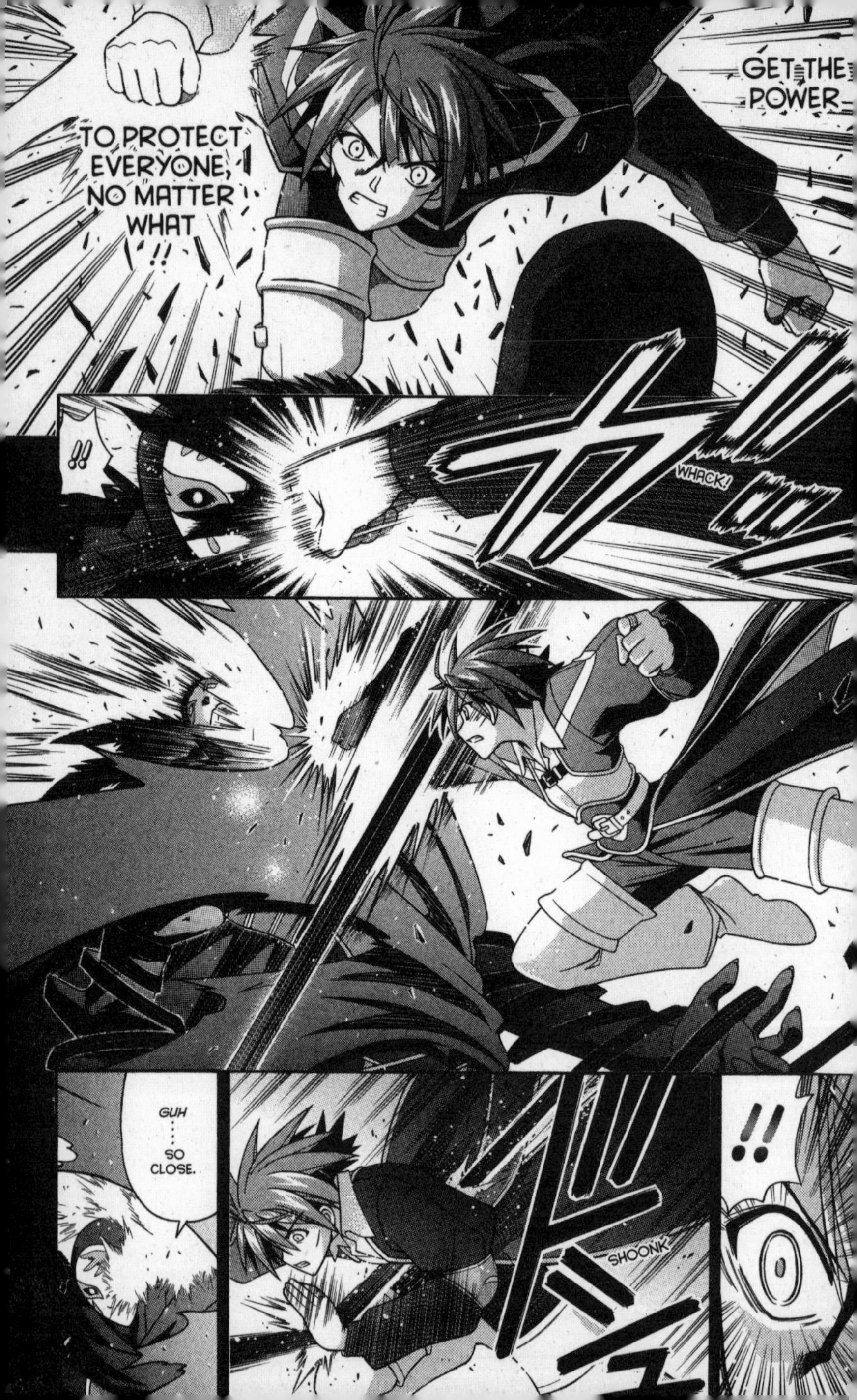
GET THE POWER
TO PROTECT EVERYONE, NO MATTER WHAT !!
!!
WHACK!
!!
SHOONK
GUH ...... SO CLOSE.

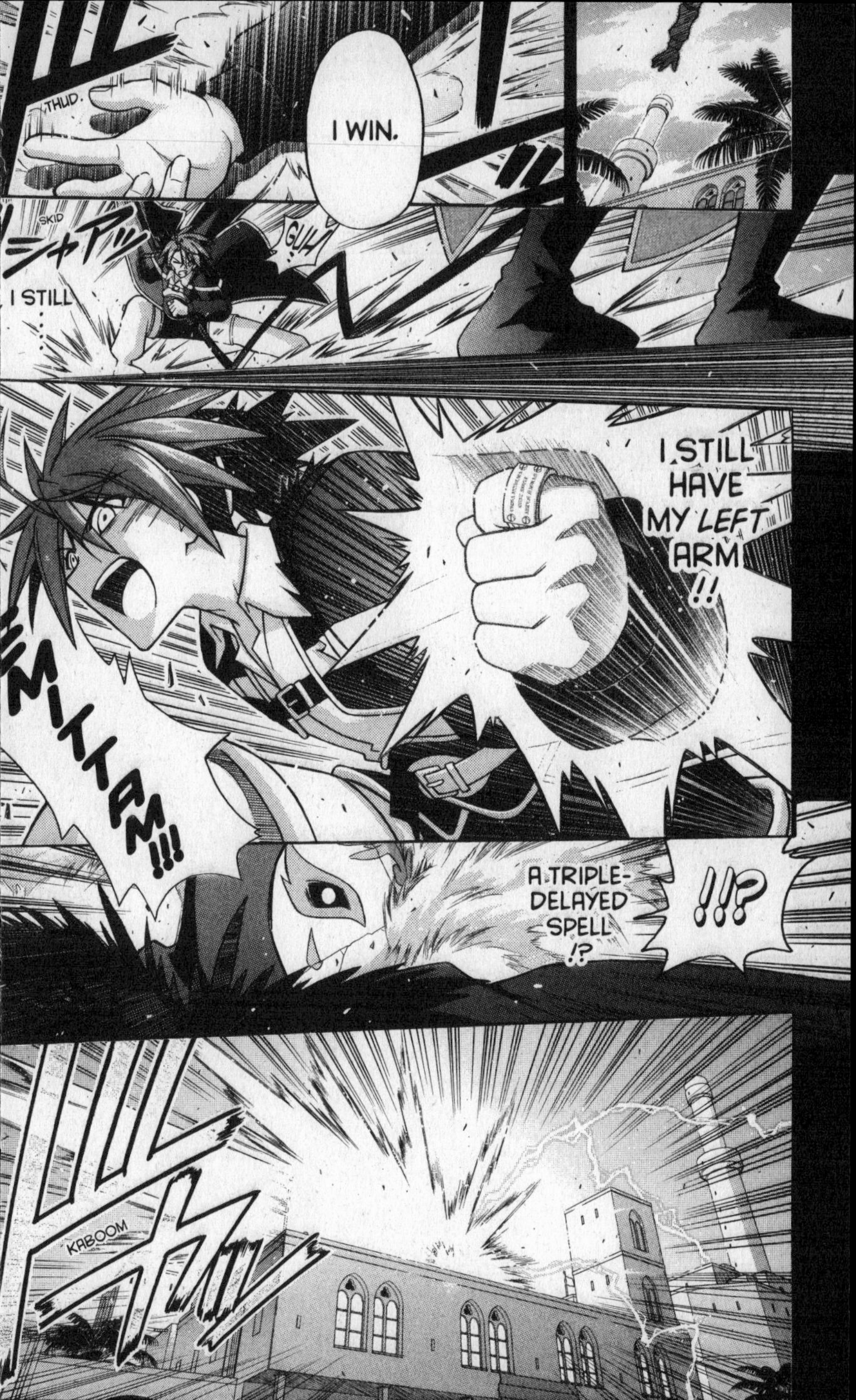

I WIN.
THUD.
GUH!
SKID
I STILL......
I STILL HAVE MY LEFT ARM!!
MIKKAM!!!
!!?
A TRIPLE-DELAYED SPELL!?
KABOOM

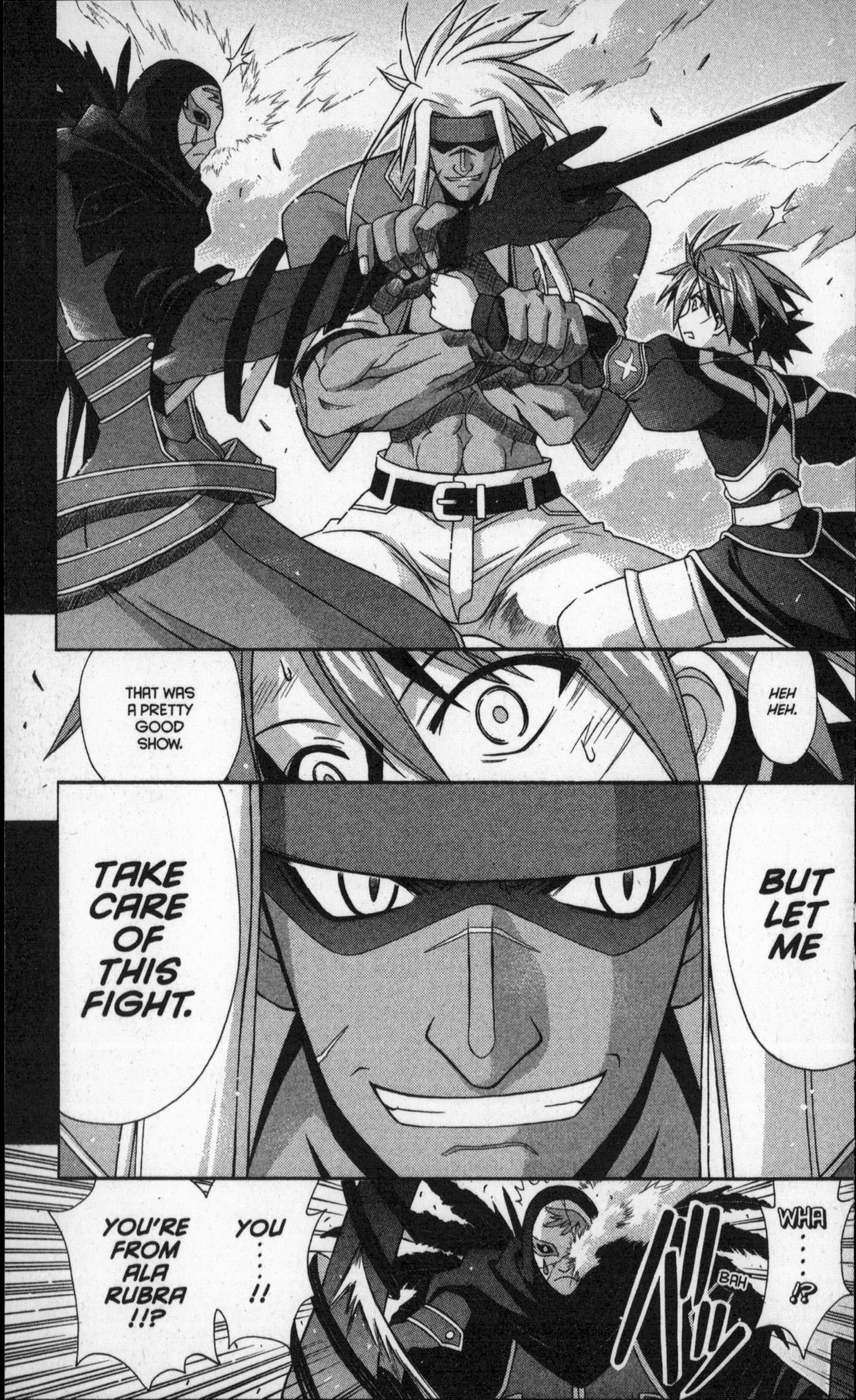
HEH HEH.
THAT WAS A PRETTY GOOD SHOW.
BUT LET ME
TAKE CARE OF THIS FIGHT.
WHA....!?
BAH
YOU....!!
YOU'RE FROM ALA RUBRA!!?

ERMINE MATH

HOW MUCH IS A DRACHMA?

YO! LONG TIME NO SEE, EVERYBODY. THIS IS ALBERT CHAMOMILE, THE ERMINE ELF. YOU ALL KNOW THAT IN THE MAGICAL WORLD, THEY USE A UNIT OF CURRENCY CALLED A DRACHMA (DRACHMA MARK), RIGHT? LET'S THINK ABOUT THIS TODAY. OUR TEACHER WILL BE THE LEADER OF THE BAKA RANGERS, YUECCHI.

 HELLO, I'M SEAT 4, YUE AYASE. NOW, A DRACHMA IS A COIN THAT WAS USED IN ANCIENT GREECE, MADE OF APPROXIMATELY 4.37 GRAMS OF SILVER.

 WOW. AND ABOUT HOW MANY YEN IS THAT?

 PRICES IN GENERAL CHANGED DEPENDING ON TIME AND PLACE, SO I COULDN'T SAY DEFINITIVELY. BUT IN A PLAY BY ARISTOPHANES, THERE'S A TRANSACTION IN WHICH SOMEONE WENT INTO DEBT FOR 1200 DRACHMA TO BUY A FAMOUS RACEHORSE. *1

 WHOA, WHOA!

 ALSO, ACCORDING TO HERODOTUS, DARIUS I, KING OF THE ACHAEMENID PERSIAN EMPIRE, COLLECTED 87,360,000 DRACHMA IN TAXES EVERY YEAR. *2

 THAT AMOUNT IS TOO BIG; THAT DOESN'T TELL ME ANYTHING!

 GOING FORWARD IN TIME TO ROME, IN THE BIBLE'S "PARABLE OF THE WORKERS IN THE VINEYARD," ONE DAY'S WORK WAS WORTH ONE DRACHMA. THE THEORY THAT ONE DRACHMA EQUALS ONE DAY'S WAGES HOLDS UP COMPARATIVELY WELL. *3

 I EARN ABOUT 166 YEN (ABOUT $1.60) A DAY.

 IT IS SAID THAT JESUS WAS SOLD FOR 30 PIECES OF SILVER, BUT IT ONLY SAYS "PIECES OF SILVER," SO WE DON'T KNOW WHICH OF THE FOUR TYPES OF SILVER COINS WERE USED IN THAT ERA—DINARIUS (1 DRACHMA MARK), DRACHMA, DIDRACHMA (2 DRACHMA MARKS), OR STATER (4 DRACHMA MARKS)—THE 30 PIECES WERE. WHICHEVER IT WAS, JESUS WOULD HAVE BEEN SOLD FOR 30 TO 120 DRACHMA. *4

 SO THAT WOULD BE THE AMOUNT OF MONEY YOU WOULD SELL YOUR FRIEND AND TEACHER FOR. OF COURSE JUDAS'S PERSONAL CHARACTER IS ANOTHER PROBLEM. *5

 FURTHERMORE, ACCORDING TO PLUTARCH, IN 75BC, CAESAR, A ROMAN STATESMAN, WAS KIDNAPPED BY PIRATES AND RANSOMED FOR 300,000 DRACHMA.

WHOA. THE REWARD OUT FOR ANIKI WAS 300,000 DRACHMA. BY THE WAY, YUECCHI, THIS IS MORE ABOUT ANCIENT CIVILIZATIONS THAN MATH, DON'T YOU THINK?

....

*1: *THE CLOUDS* 21. *2: *THE HISTORIES* VOLUME 3, CHAPTER 95. *3: "THE GOSPEL ACCORDING TO MATTHEW," 20:1-16. *4: THE SAME, 26:14-16. *5: *PARALLEL LIVES*, CAESAR 2.
* 1 TALENT IS APPROXIMATELY 6,000 DRACHMA. 1 DINARIUS IS EQUAL TO A DRACHMA.

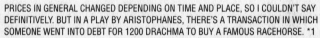

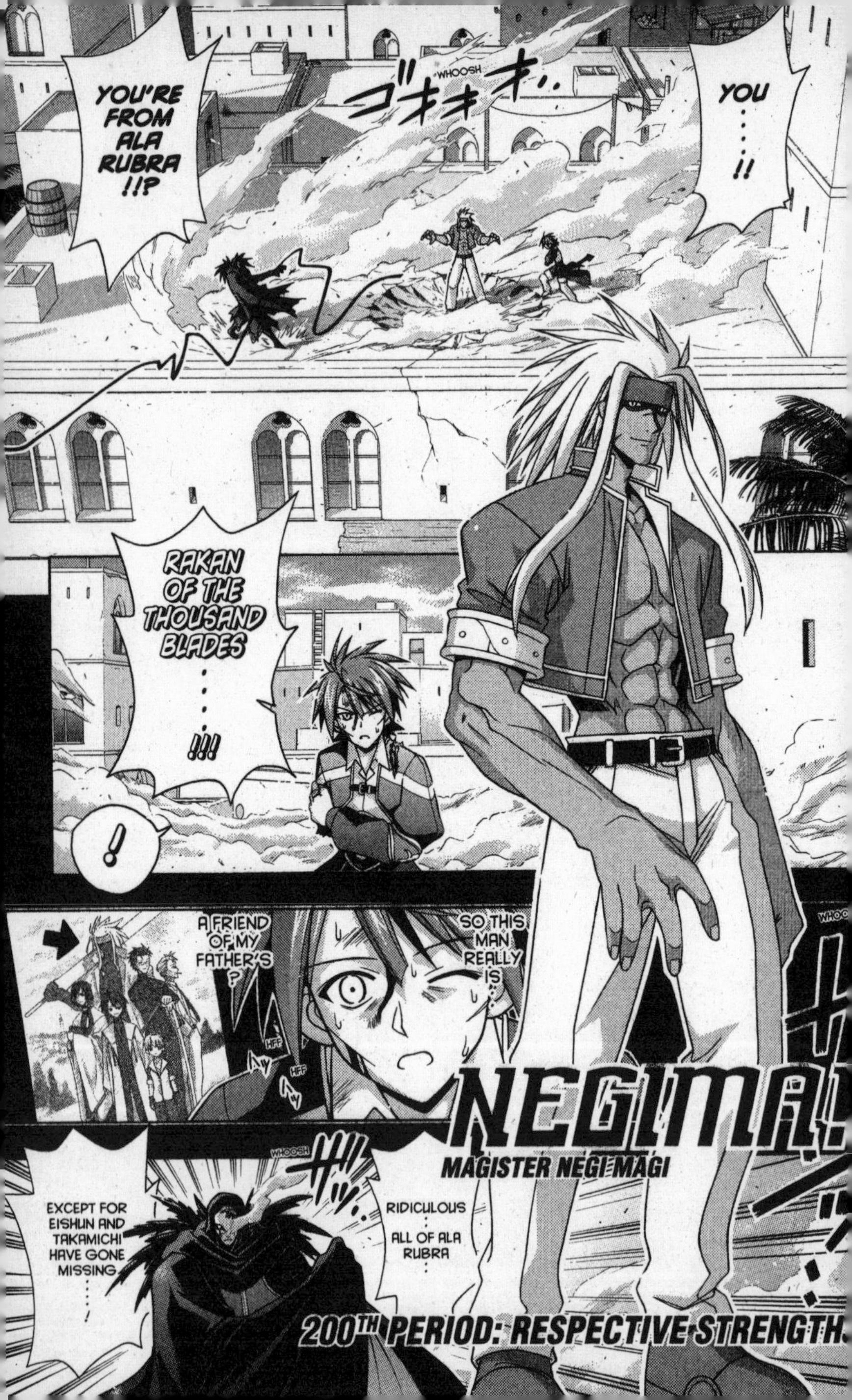
YOU.....!!
WHOOSH
YOU'RE FROM ALA RUBRA!!?
RAKAN OF THE THOUSAND BLADES.....!!!
!
WHOOSH
SO THIS MAN REALLY IS...
A FRIEND OF MY FATHER'S?
HFF
HFF
NEGIMA!
MAGISTER NEGI MAGI
WHOOSH
RIDICULOUS... ALL OF ALA RUBRA
EXCEPT FOR EISHUN AND TAKAMICHI HAVE GONE MISSING.....!
200TH PERIOD: RESPECTIVE STRENGTH

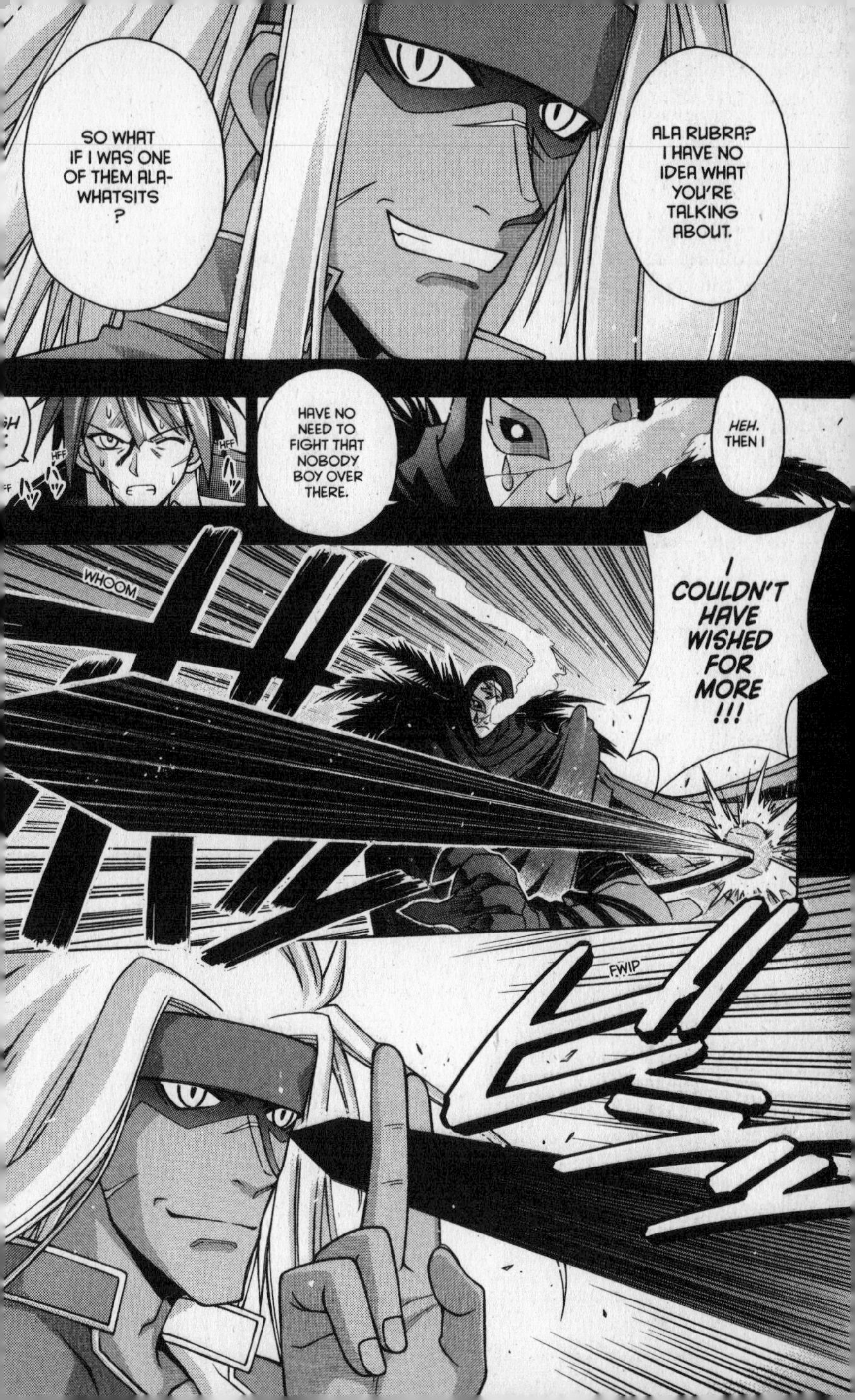
ALA RUBRA? I HAVE NO IDEA WHAT YOU'RE TALKING ABOUT.
SO WHAT IF I WAS ONE OF THEM ALA-WHATSITS?
HEH. THEN I
HAVE NO NEED TO FIGHT THAT NOBODY BOY OVER THERE.
HFF
HFF
I COULDN'T HAVE WISHED FOR MORE!!!
WHOOM
FWIP

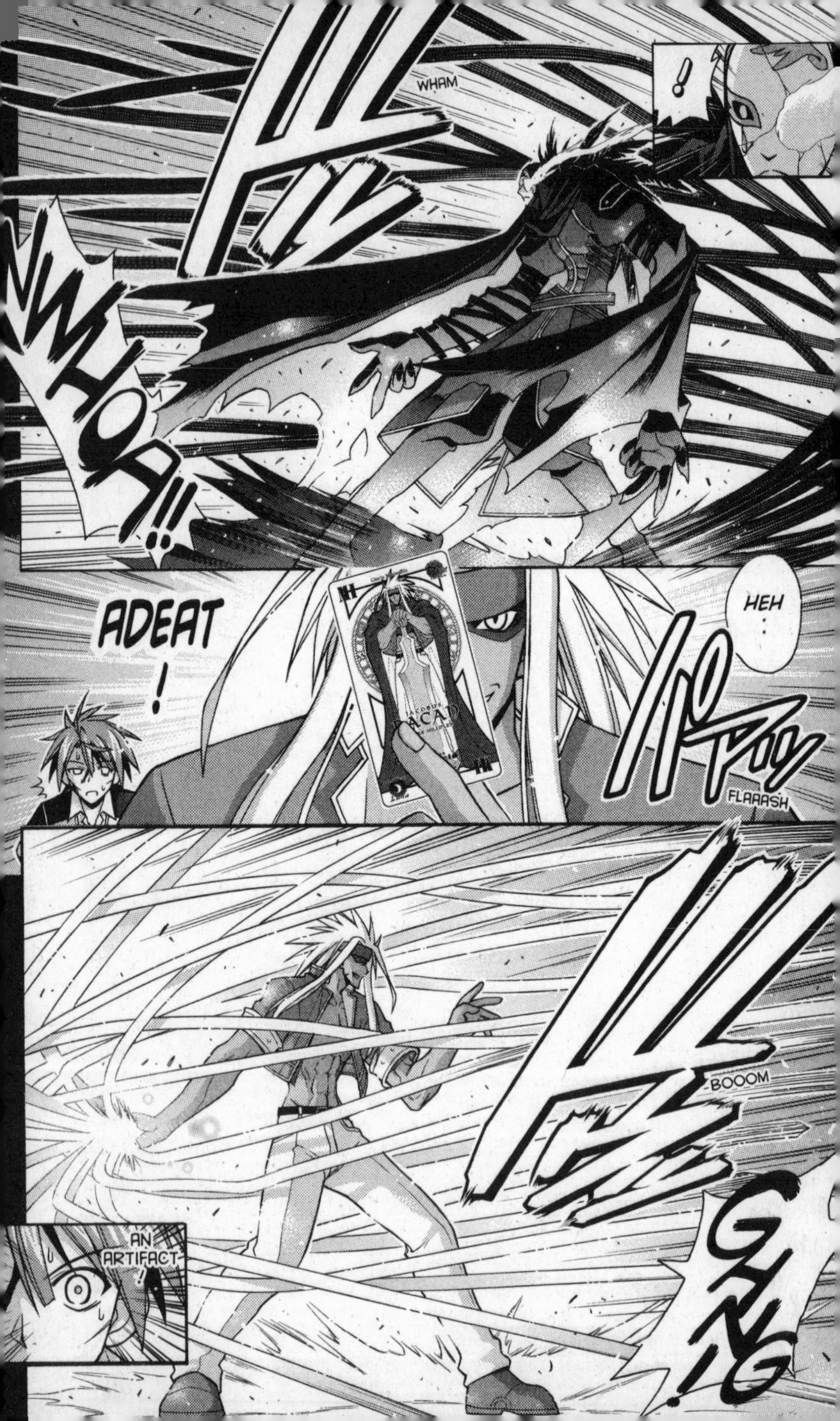
!
WHAM
WHOA!!
HEH...
FLAAASH
ADEAT!
BOOOM
GANG!
AN ARTIFACT!

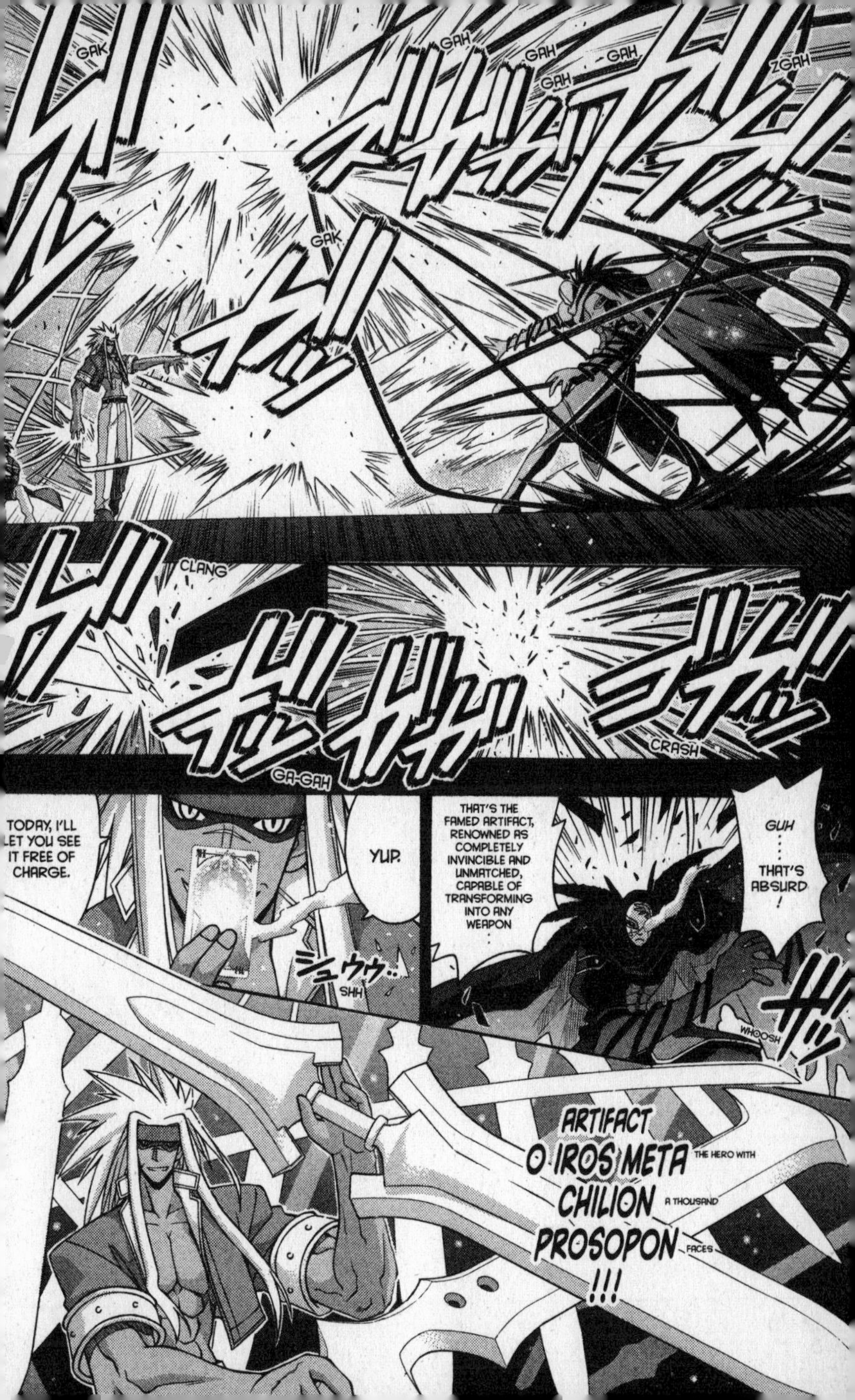
ZGAH
GAH
GAH
GAH
GAH
GAK
GAK
CRASH
GA-GAH
CLANG
GUH... THAT'S ABSURD!
THAT'S THE FAMED ARTIFACT, RENOWNED AS COMPLETELY INVINCIBLE AND UNMATCHED, CAPABLE OF TRANSFORMING INTO ANY WEAPON...
YUP.
TODAY, I'LL LET YOU SEE IT FREE OF CHARGE.
SHH
WHOOSH
ARTIFACT O IROS META CHILION PROSOPON!!!
THE HERO WITH A THOUSAND FACES

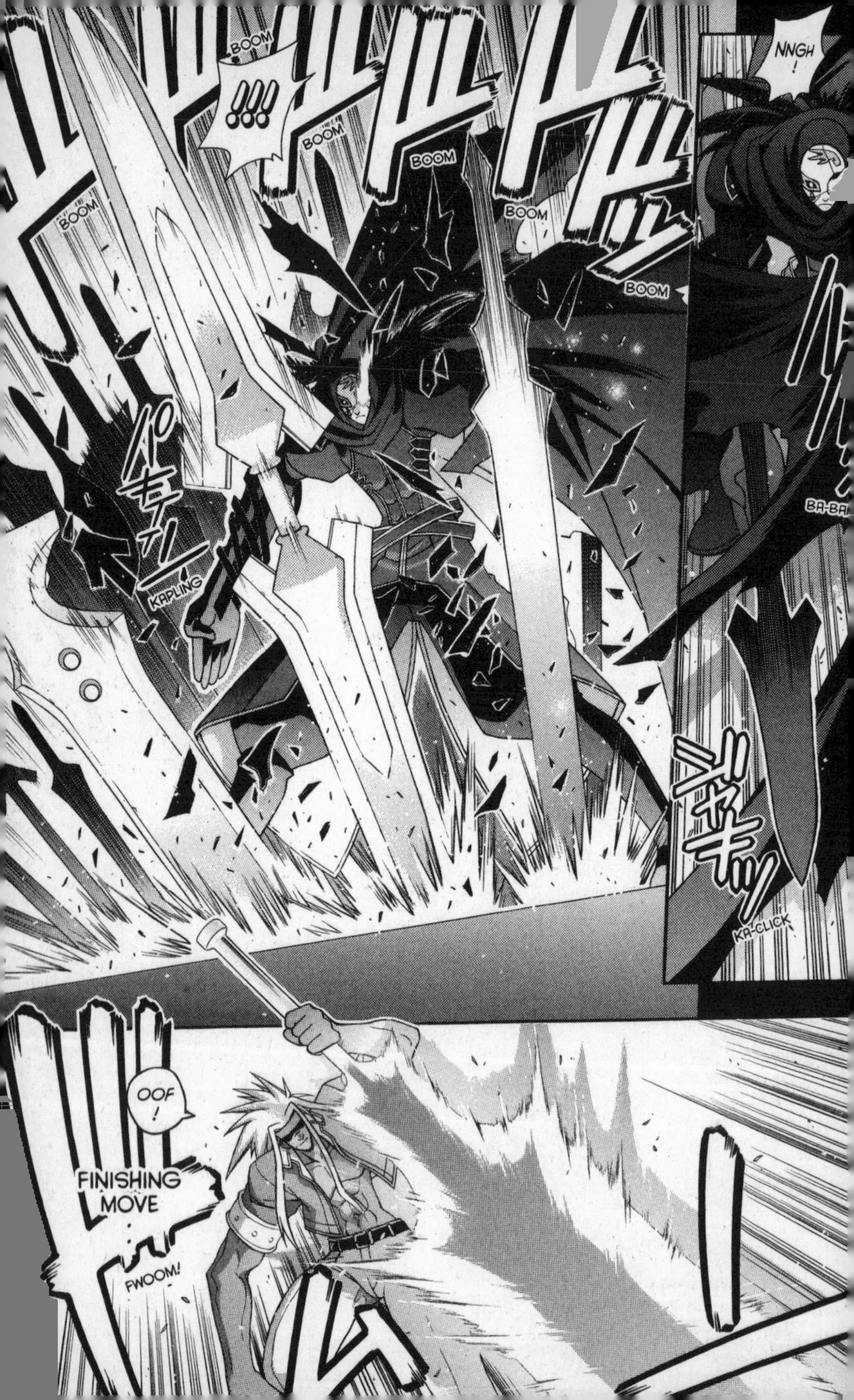
NNGH!
BA-BA
ジャキッ
KA-CLICK
BOOM
!!!
BOOM
BOOM
BOOM
BOOM
BOOM
パキィン
KAPLING
OOF!
FINISHING MOVE
FWOOM!

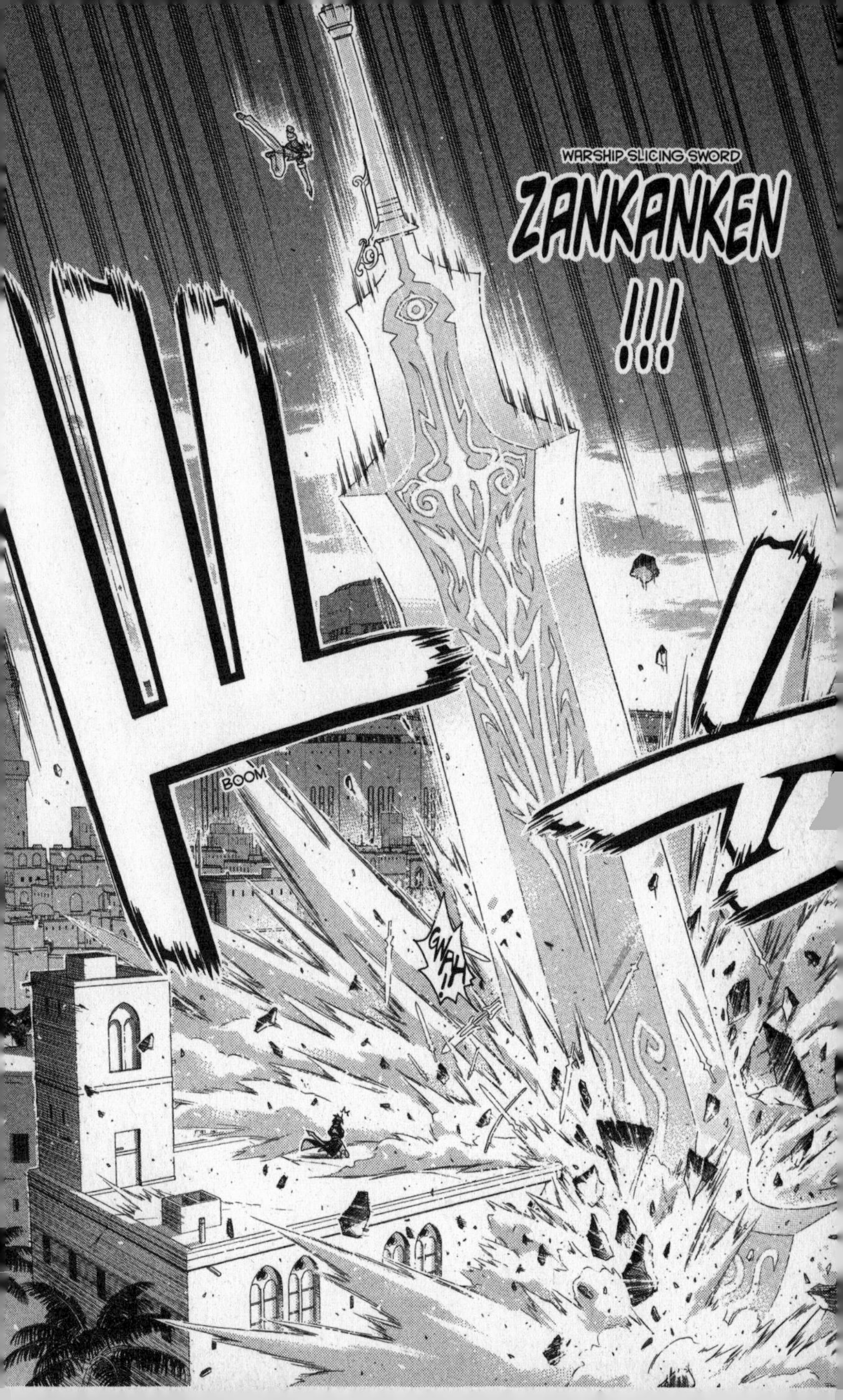
WARSHIP SLICING SWORD
ZANKANKEN !!!
BOOM
GWAH!!

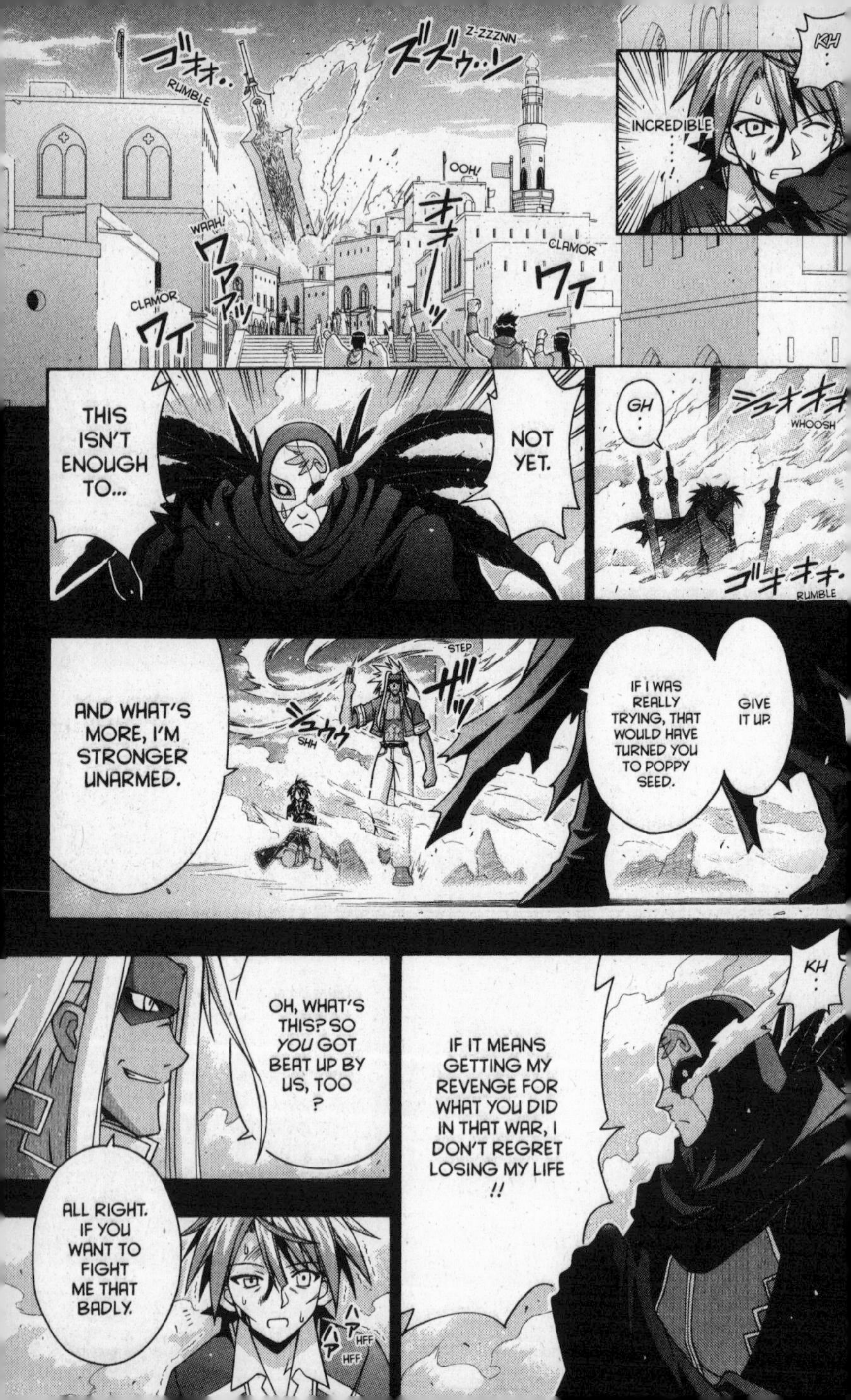
KH
INCREDIBLE
Z-ZZZNN
RUMBLE
OOH!
CLAMOR
WAAH!
CLAMOR
GH
WHOOSH
RUMBLE
NOT YET.
THIS ISN'T ENOUGH TO...
GIVE IT UP.
IF I WAS REALLY TRYING, THAT WOULD HAVE TURNED YOU TO POPPY SEED.
STEP
SHH
AND WHAT'S MORE, I'M STRONGER UNARMED.
KH
IF IT MEANS GETTING MY REVENGE FOR WHAT YOU DID IN THAT WAR, I DON'T REGRET LOSING MY LIFE!!
OH, WHAT'S THIS? SO *YOU* GOT BEAT UP BY US, TOO?
ALL RIGHT. IF YOU WANT TO FIGHT ME THAT BADLY.
HFF
HFF

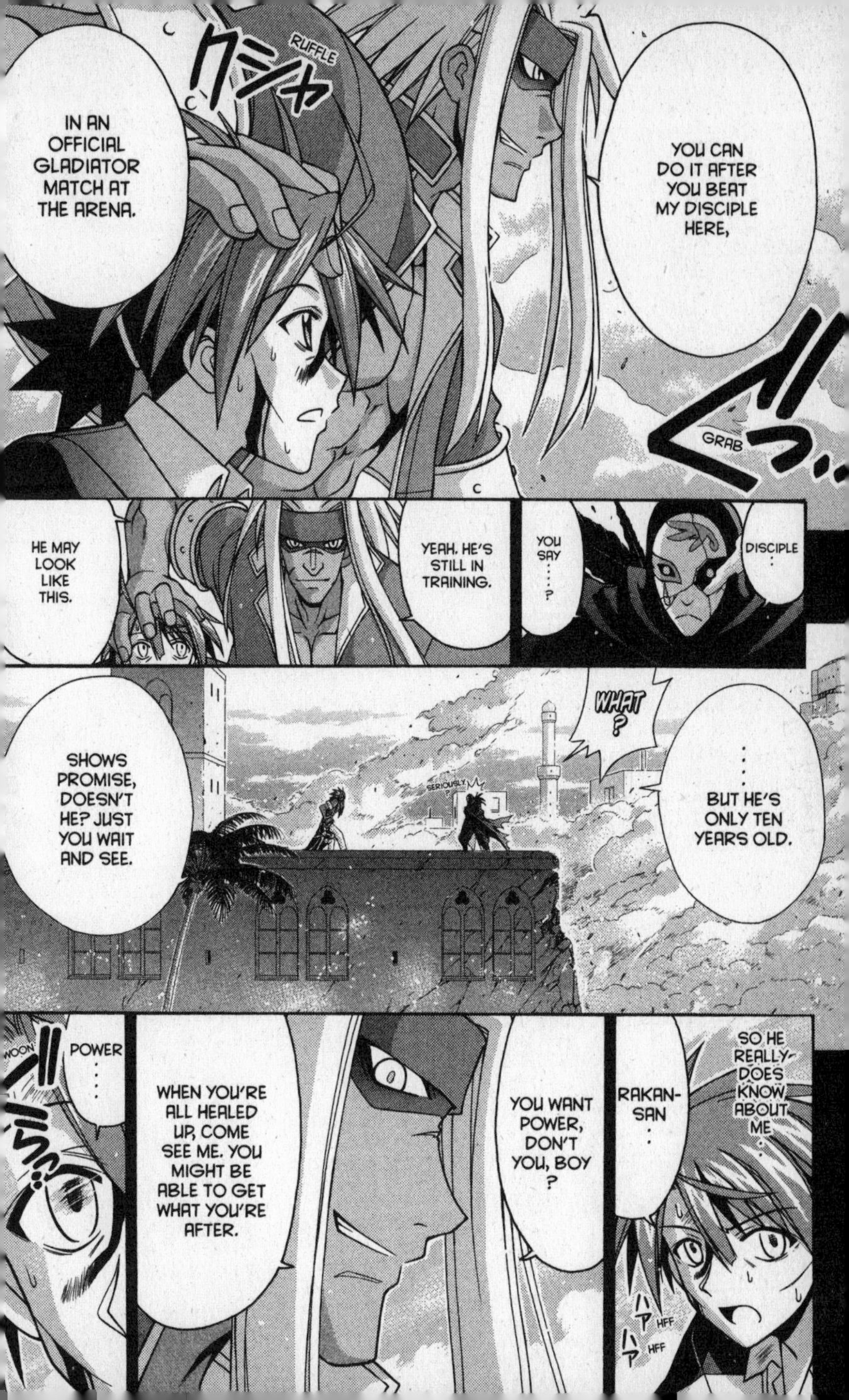
YOU CAN DO IT AFTER YOU BEAT MY DISCIPLE HERE,
GRAB
RUFFLE
IN AN OFFICIAL GLADIATOR MATCH AT THE ARENA.
DISCIPLE ...
YOU SAY ....?
YEAH. HE'S STILL IN TRAINING.
HE MAY LOOK LIKE THIS.
... BUT HE'S ONLY TEN YEARS OLD.
WHAT?
SERIOUSLY?
SHOWS PROMISE, DOESN'T HE? JUST YOU WAIT AND SEE.
SO HE REALLY DOES KNOW ABOUT ME ...
HFF
HFF
RAKAN-SAN ..
YOU WANT POWER, DON'T YOU, BOY?
WHEN YOU'RE ALL HEALED UP, COME SEE ME. YOU MIGHT BE ABLE TO GET WHAT YOU'RE AFTER.
POWER ....

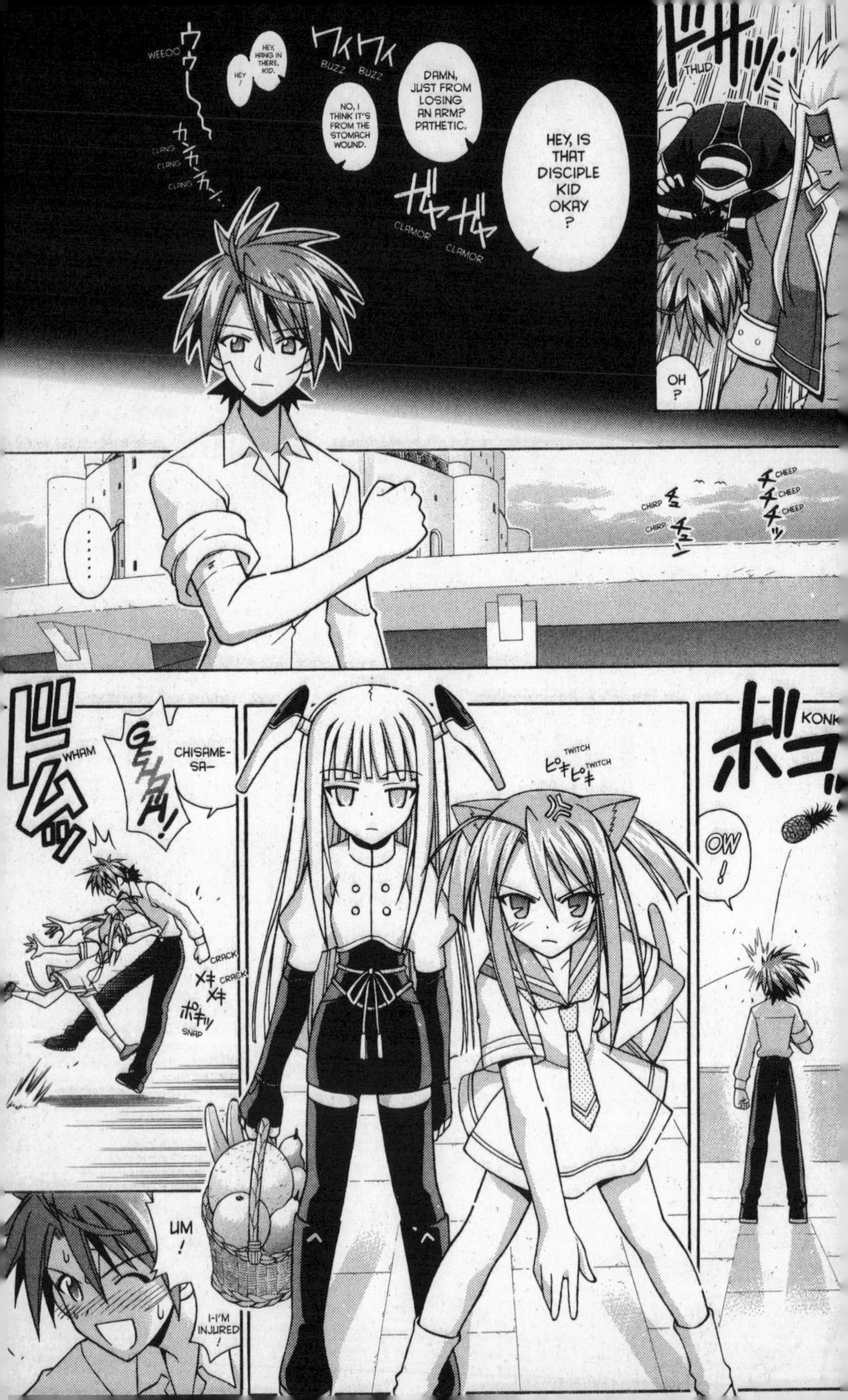
THUD
OH?
HEY, IS THAT DISCIPLE KID OKAY?
DAMN, JUST FROM LOSING AN ARM? PATHETIC.
CLAMOR CLAMOR
NO, I THINK IT'S FROM THE STOMACH WOUND.
BUZZ BUZZ
HEY, HANG IN THERE, KID.
HEY!
WEEOO
CLANG CLANG CLANG
CHEEP CHEEP CHEEP
CHIRP CHIRP
......
KONK
OW!
TWITCH TWITCH
CHISAME-SA—
GEEZ!!
WHAM
CRACK CRACK
SNAP
UM!
I-I'M INJURED!

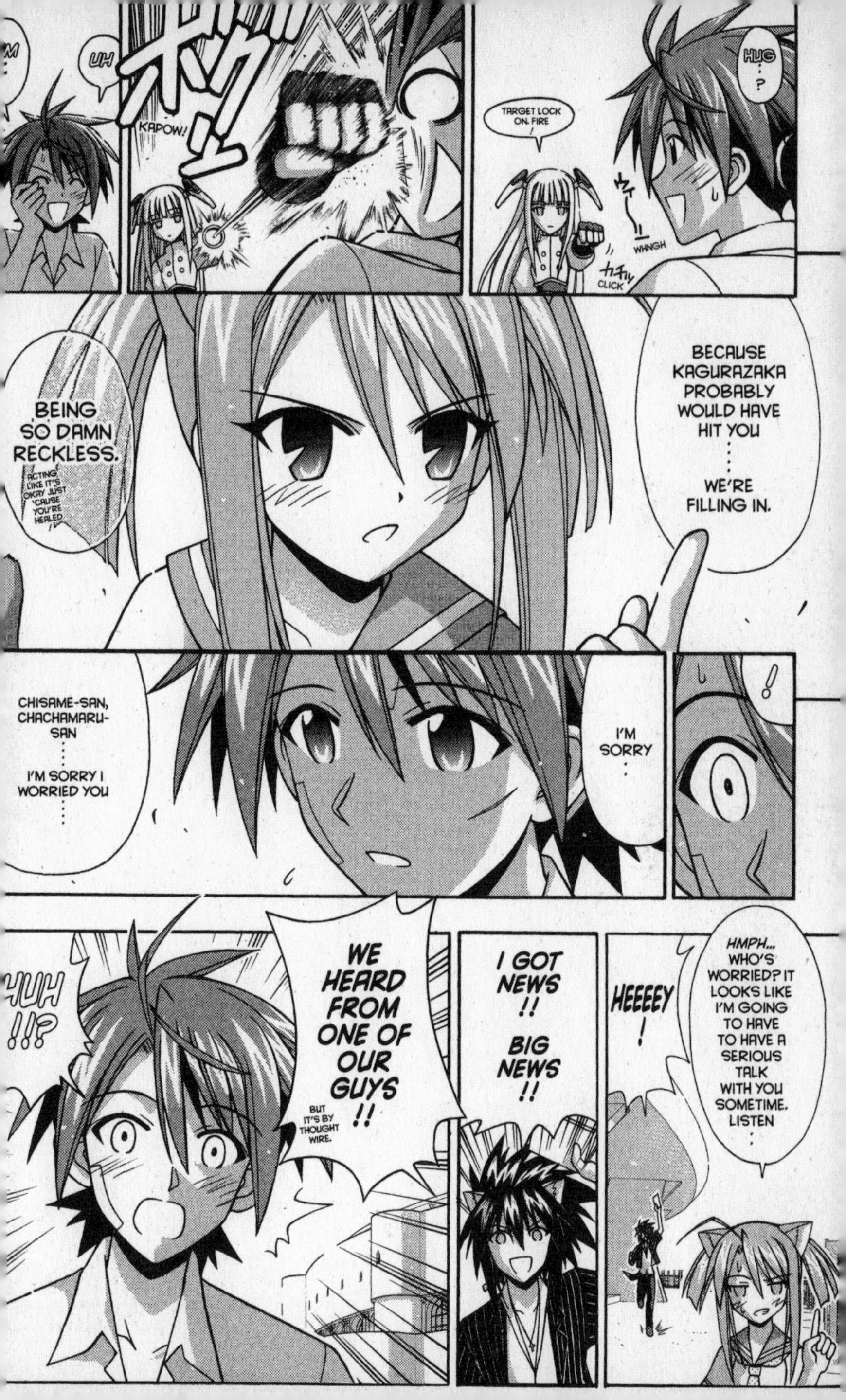

HUG...?
TARGET LOCK ON. FIRE!
WHNGH
CLICK
KAPOW!
UH
BECAUSE KAGURAZAKA PROBABLY WOULD HAVE HIT YOU... WE'RE FILLING IN.
BEING SO DAMN RECKLESS.
ACTING LIKE IT'S OKAY JUST 'CAUSE YOU'RE HEALED!
!
I'M SORRY...
CHISAME-SAN, CHACHAMARU-SAN... I'M SORRY I WORRIED YOU...
HMPH... WHO'S WORRIED? IT LOOKS LIKE I'M GOING TO HAVE TO HAVE A SERIOUS TALK WITH YOU SOMETIME. LISTEN...
HEEEEY!
I GOT NEWS!! BIG NEWS!!
WE HEARD FROM ONE OF OUR GUYS!!
BUT IT'S BY THOUGHT WIRE.
HUH!!?

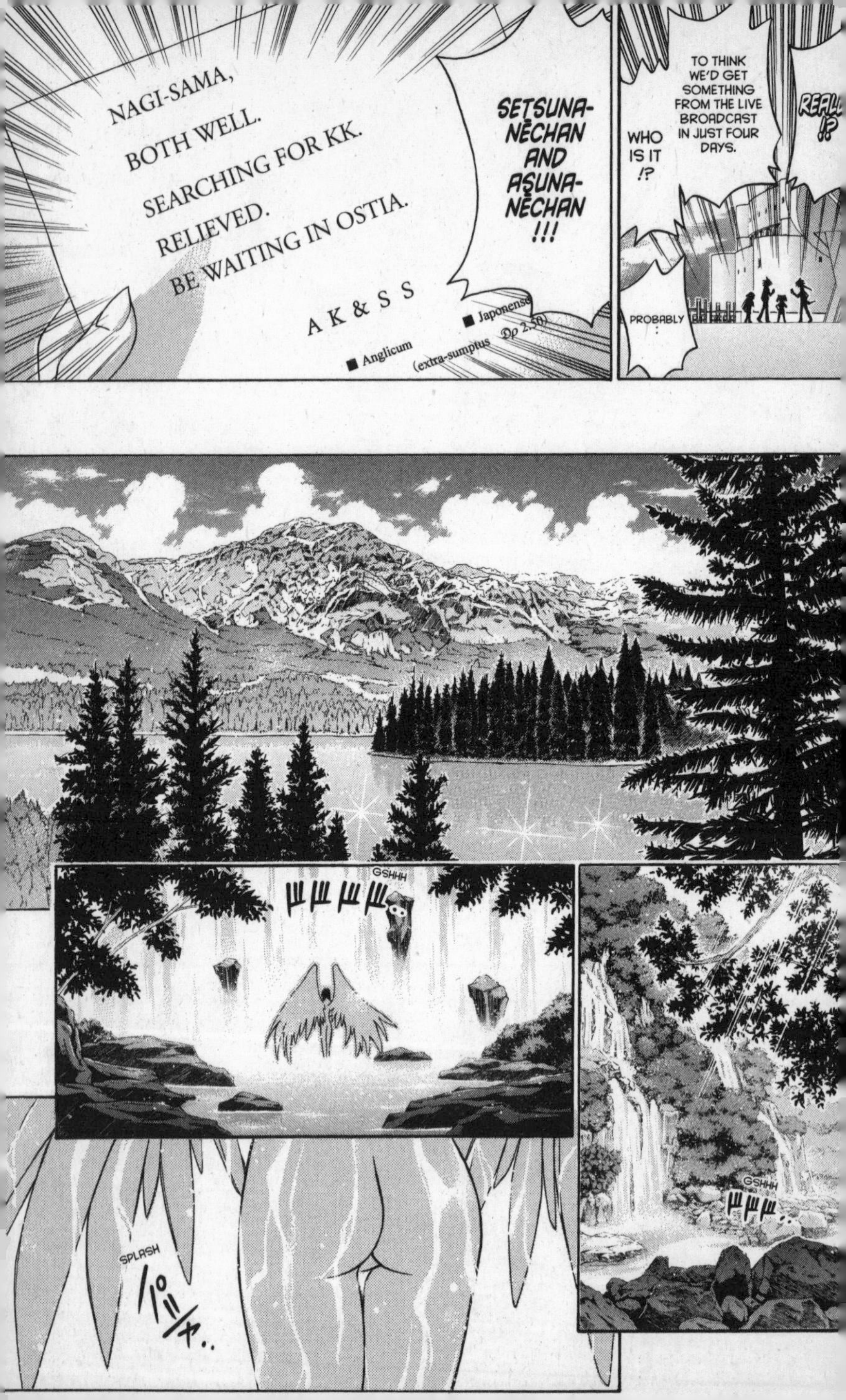
REALL !?
TO THINK WE'D GET SOMETHING FROM THE LIVE BROADCAST IN JUST FOUR DAYS.
WHO IS IT !?
PROBABLY :
SETSUNA-NĒCHAN AND ASUNA-NĒCHAN !!!
NAGI-SAMA,
BOTH WELL.
SEARCHING FOR KK.
RELIEVED.
BE WAITING IN OSTIA.
A K & S S
■ Japonense
(extra-sumptus Dp 2.50)
■ Anglicum
GSHHH
GSHHH
SPLASH
パシャ..

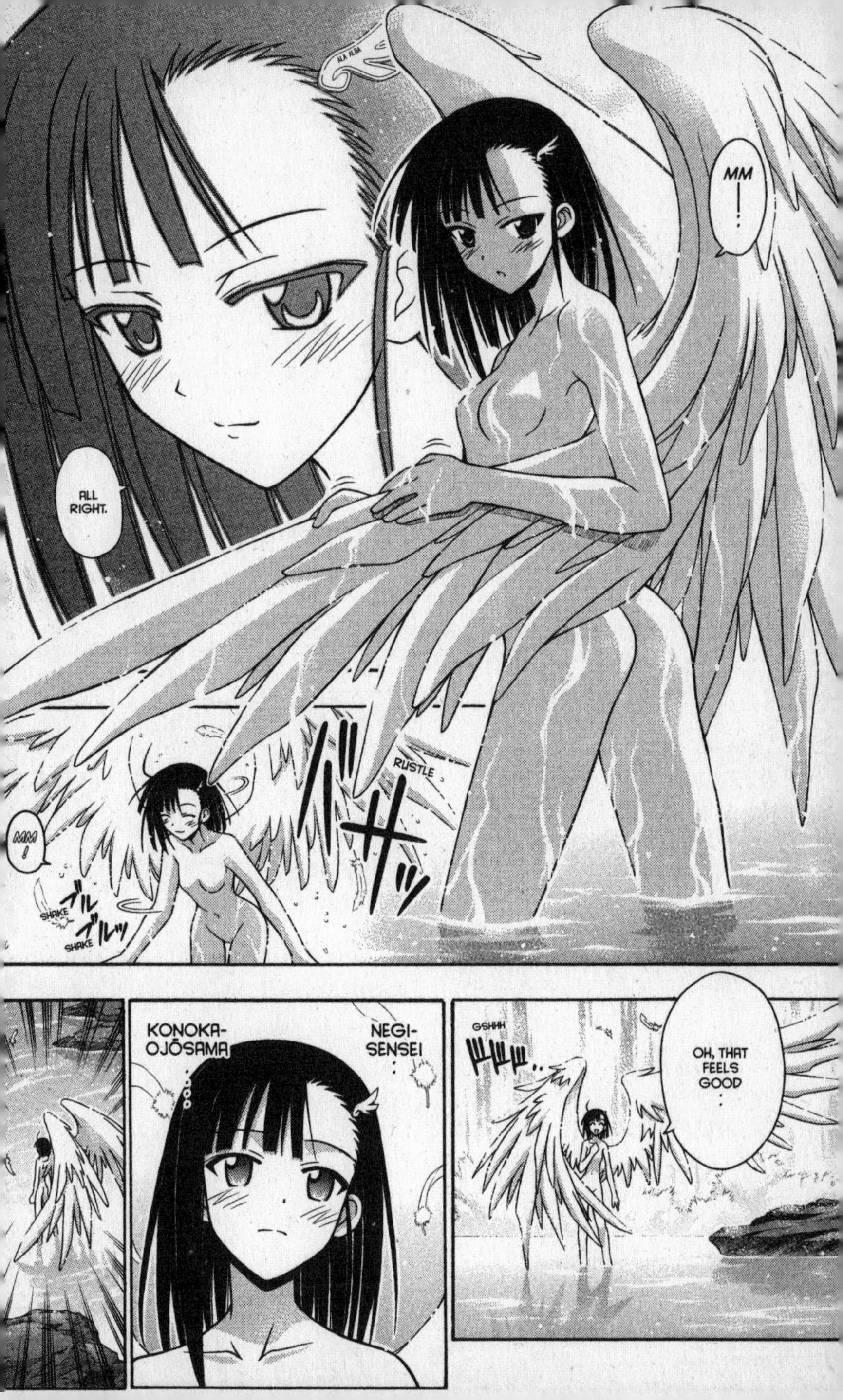
ALA ALBA
MM !
ALL RIGHT.
RUSTLE
MM !
SHAKE
SHAKE
OH, THAT FEELS GOOD ..
GSHHH
NEGI-SENSEI ..
KONOKA-OJŌSAMA ...

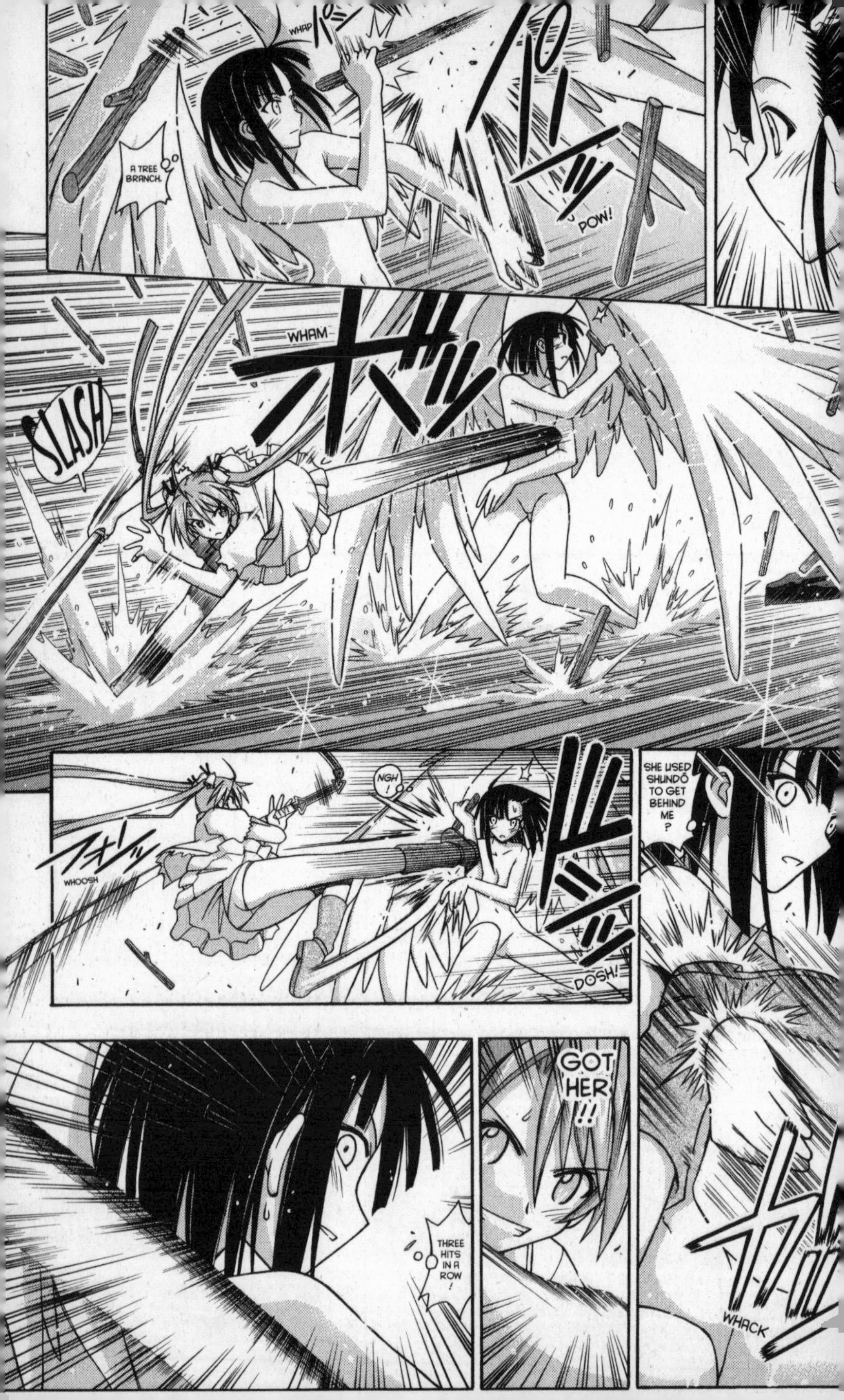
WHAP
A TREE BRANCH.
POW!
WHAM
SLASH
SHE USED SHUNDŌ TO GET BEHIND ME?
NGH!
DOSH!
WHOOSH
WHACK
GOT HER!!
THREE HITS IN A ROW!

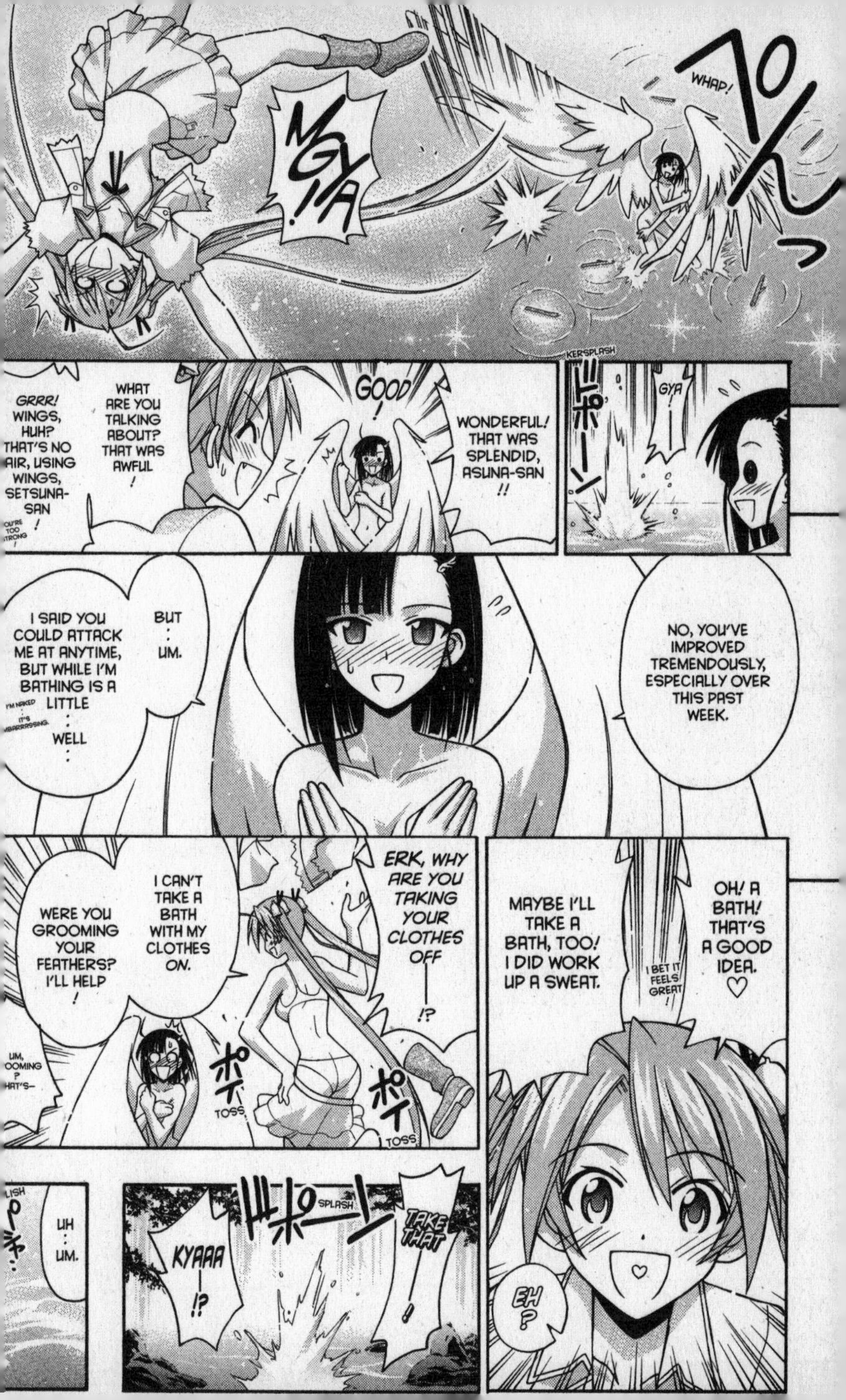

WHAP!
MGYA!
KERSPLASH
GYA!
WONDERFUL! THAT WAS SPLENDID, ASUNA-SAN!!
GOOD!
WHAT ARE YOU TALKING ABOUT? THAT WAS AWFUL!
GRRR! WINGS, HUH? THAT'S NO FAIR, USING WINGS, SETSUNA-SAN!
YOU'RE TOO STRONG!
NO, YOU'VE IMPROVED TREMENDOUSLY, ESPECIALLY OVER THIS PAST WEEK.
BUT... UM.
I SAID YOU COULD ATTACK ME AT ANYTIME, BUT WHILE I'M BATHING IS A LITTLE... WELL...
I'M NAKED
IT'S EMBARRASSING.
OH! A BATH! THAT'S A GOOD IDEA. ♡
I BET IT FEELS GREAT!
MAYBE I'LL TAKE A BATH, TOO! I DID WORK UP A SWEAT.
EH?
ERK, WHY ARE YOU TAKING YOUR CLOTHES OFF—!?
I CAN'T TAKE A BATH WITH MY CLOTHES ON.
WERE YOU GROOMING YOUR FEATHERS? I'LL HELP!
TOSS
TOSS
UM, GROOMING? THAT'S—
TAKE THAT!
SPLASH
KYAAA!?
UH... UM.

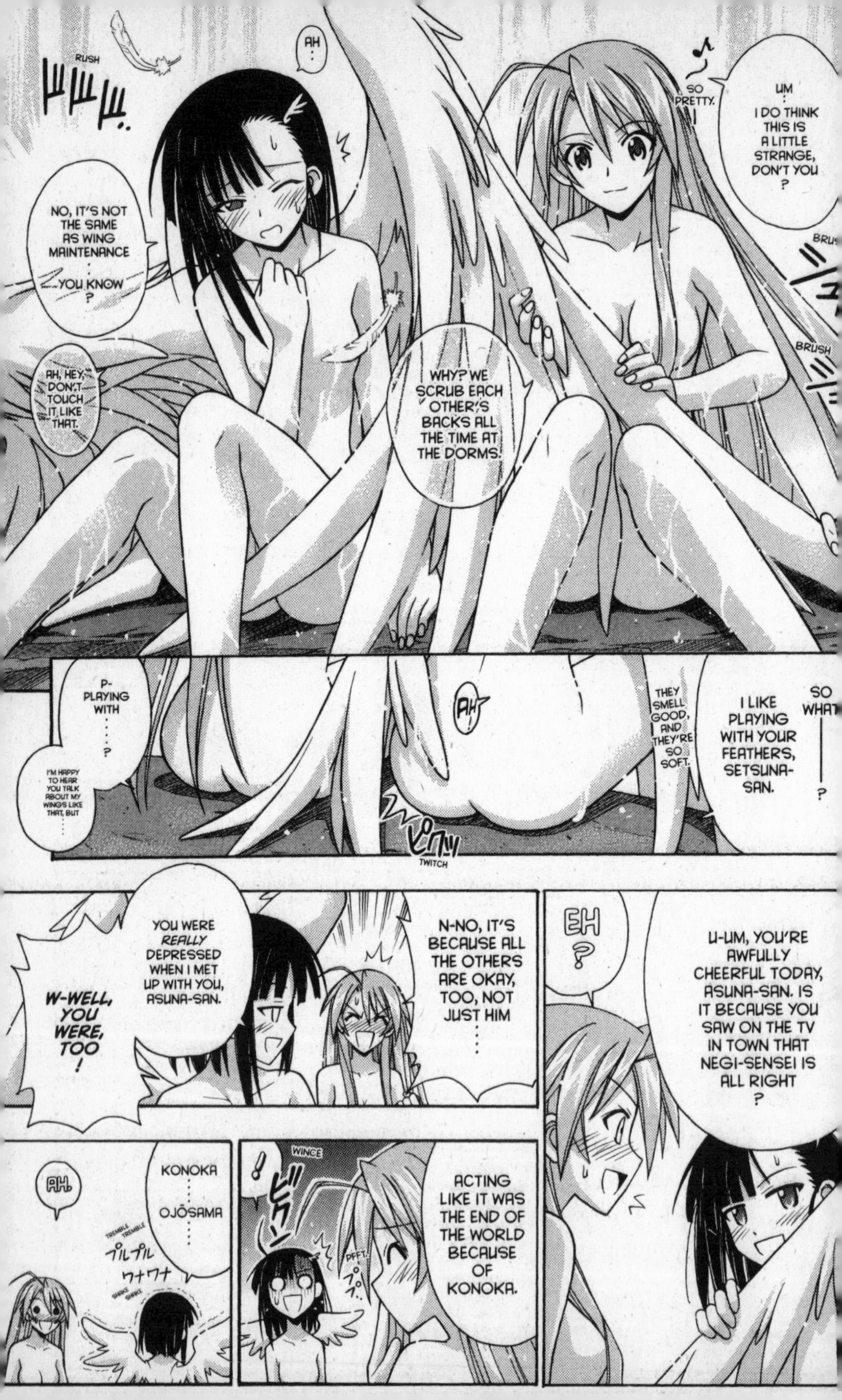
UM... I DO THINK THIS IS A LITTLE STRANGE, DON'T YOU?
SO PRETTY.
BRUSH
BRUSH
AH...
RUSH
NO, IT'S NOT THE SAME AS WING MAINTENANCE... YOU KNOW?
WHY? WE SCRUB EACH OTHER'S BACKS ALL THE TIME AT THE DORMS.
AH, HEY, DON'T TOUCH IT LIKE THAT.
SO WHAT—?
I LIKE PLAYING WITH YOUR FEATHERS, SETSUNA-SAN.
THEY SMELL GOOD, AND THEY'RE SO SOFT.
AH!
TWITCH
P-PLAYING WITH...?
I'M HAPPY TO HEAR YOU TALK ABOUT MY WINGS LIKE THAT, BUT...
U-UM, YOU'RE AWFULLY CHEERFUL TODAY, ASUNA-SAN. IS IT BECAUSE YOU SAW ON THE TV IN TOWN THAT NEGI-SENSEI IS ALL RIGHT?
EH?
N-NO, IT'S BECAUSE ALL THE OTHERS ARE OKAY, TOO, NOT JUST HIM...
YOU WERE *REALLY* DEPRESSED WHEN I MET UP WITH YOU, ASUNA-SAN.
W-WELL, YOU WERE, TOO!
ACTING LIKE IT WAS THE END OF THE WORLD BECAUSE OF KONOKA.
PFFT
WINCE
!
KONOKA... OJŌSAMA...
AH.
TREMBLE TREMBLE
プルプル
ワナワナ
SHAKE SHAKE

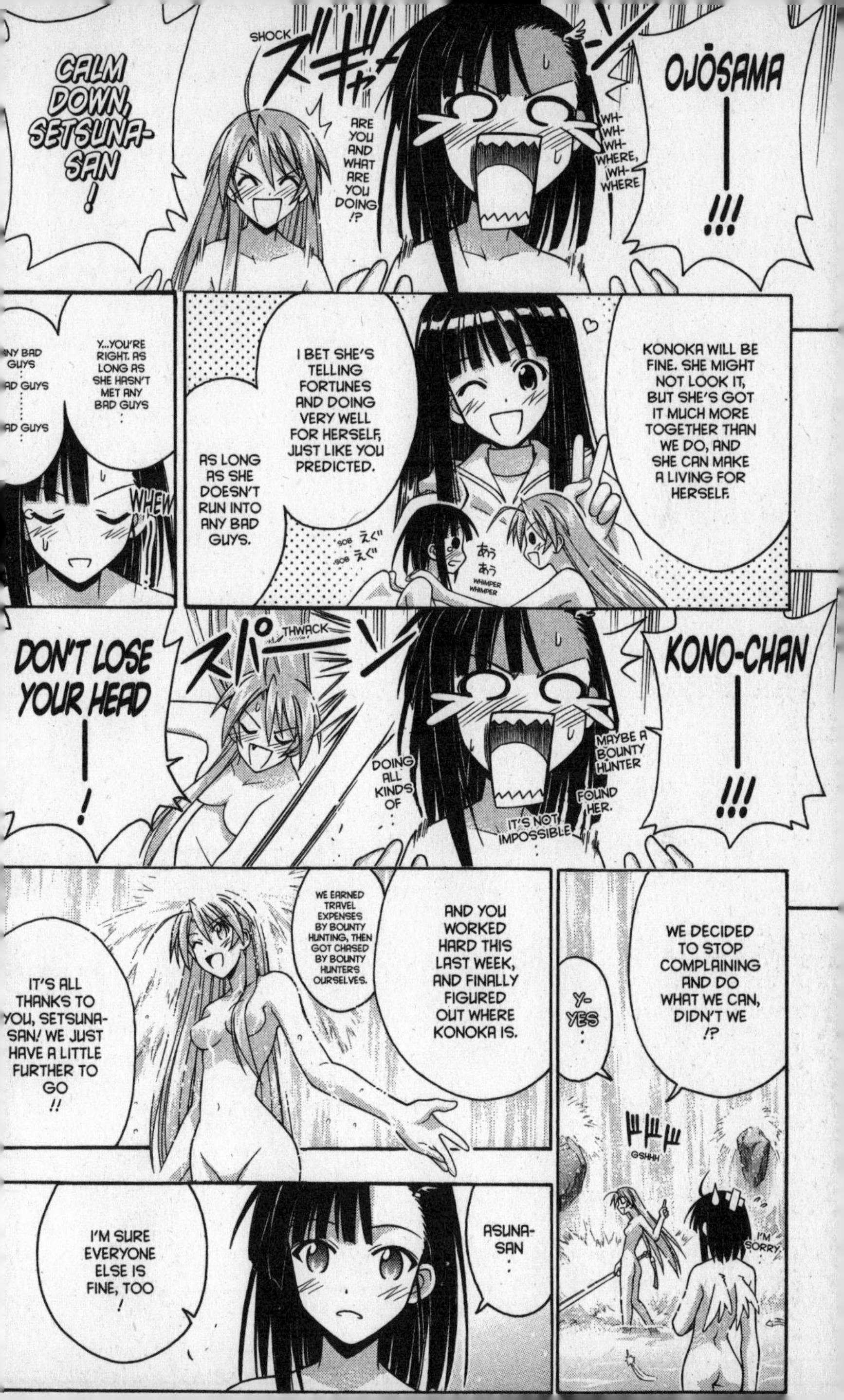
OJŌSAMA — !!!
WH-WH-WH-WHERE, WH-WHERE
ARE YOU AND WHAT ARE YOU DOING!?
SHOCK
CALM DOWN, SETSUNA-SAN!
KONOKA WILL BE FINE. SHE MIGHT NOT LOOK IT, BUT SHE'S GOT IT MUCH MORE TOGETHER THAN WE DO, AND SHE CAN MAKE A LIVING FOR HERSELF.
I BET SHE'S TELLING FORTUNES AND DOING VERY WELL FOR HERSELF, JUST LIKE YOU PREDICTED.
AS LONG AS SHE DOESN'T RUN INTO ANY BAD GUYS.
SOB SOB
WHIMPER WHIMPER
Y...YOU'RE RIGHT. AS LONG AS SHE HASN'T MET ANY BAD GUYS...
NY BAD GUYS... AD GUYS... AD GUYS...
WHEW
KONO-CHAN — !!!
MAYBE A BOUNTY HUNTER FOUND HER.
IT'S NOT IMPOSSIBLE
DOING ALL KINDS OF...
THWACK
DON'T LOSE YOUR HEAD — !
WE DECIDED TO STOP COMPLAINING AND DO WHAT WE CAN, DIDN'T WE!?
Y-YES...
GSHHH
I'M SORRY
AND YOU WORKED HARD THIS LAST WEEK, AND FINALLY FIGURED OUT WHERE KONOKA IS.
WE EARNED TRAVEL EXPENSES BY BOUNTY HUNTING, THEN GOT CHASED BY BOUNTY HUNTERS OURSELVES.
IT'S ALL THANKS TO YOU, SETSUNA-SAN! WE JUST HAVE A LITTLE FURTHER TO GO!!
ASUNA-SAN...
I'M SURE EVERYONE ELSE IS FINE, TOO!

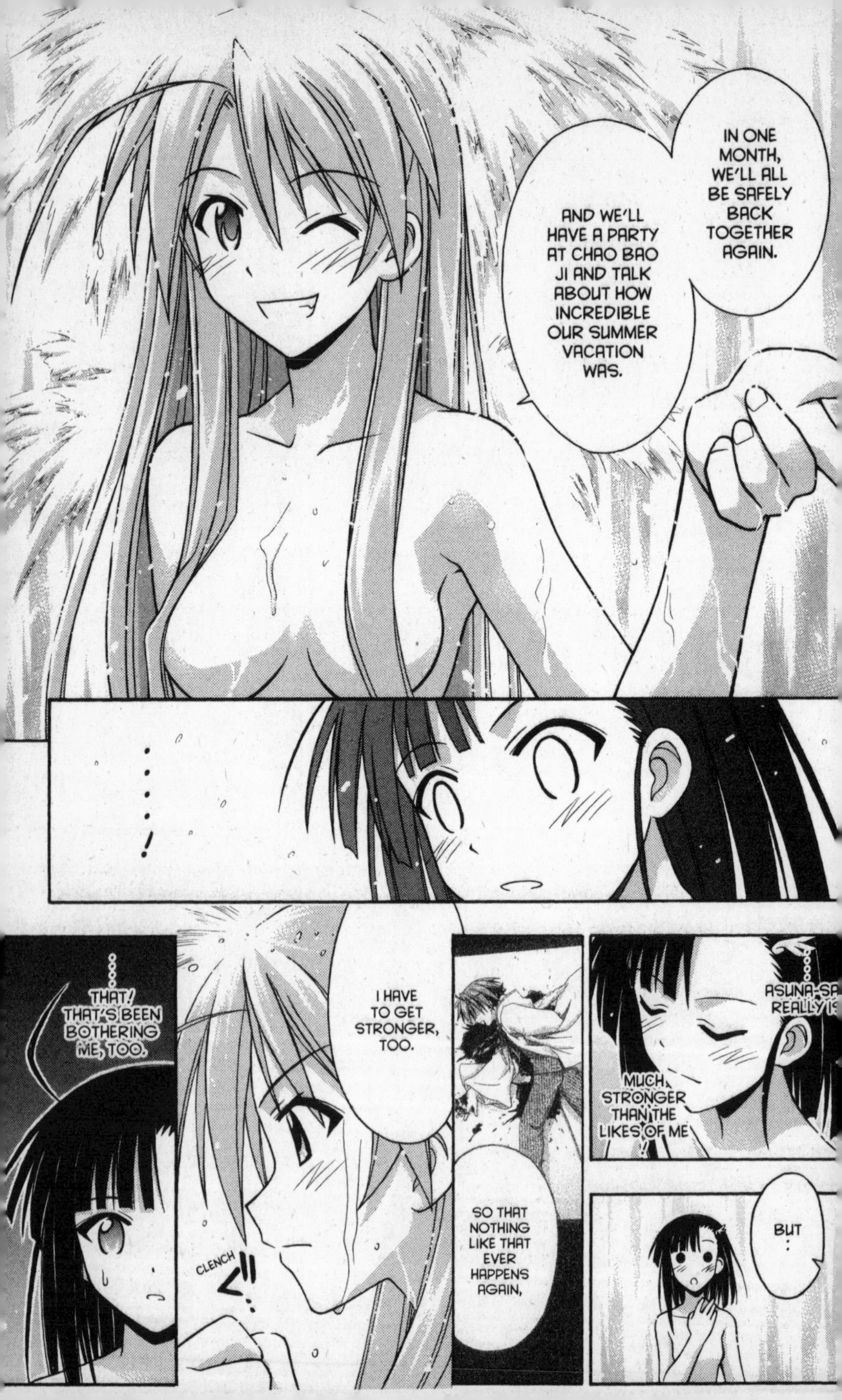
IN ONE MONTH, WE'LL ALL BE SAFELY BACK TOGETHER AGAIN.
AND WE'LL HAVE A PARTY AT CHAO BAO JI AND TALK ABOUT HOW INCREDIBLE OUR SUMMER VACATION WAS.
......!
ASUNA-SA REALLY IS
MUCH STRONGER THAN THE LIKES OF ME
BUT...
I HAVE TO GET STRONGER, TOO.
SO THAT NOTHING LIKE THAT EVER HAPPENS AGAIN,
CLENCH
.....THAT! THAT'S BEEN BOTHERING ME, TOO.

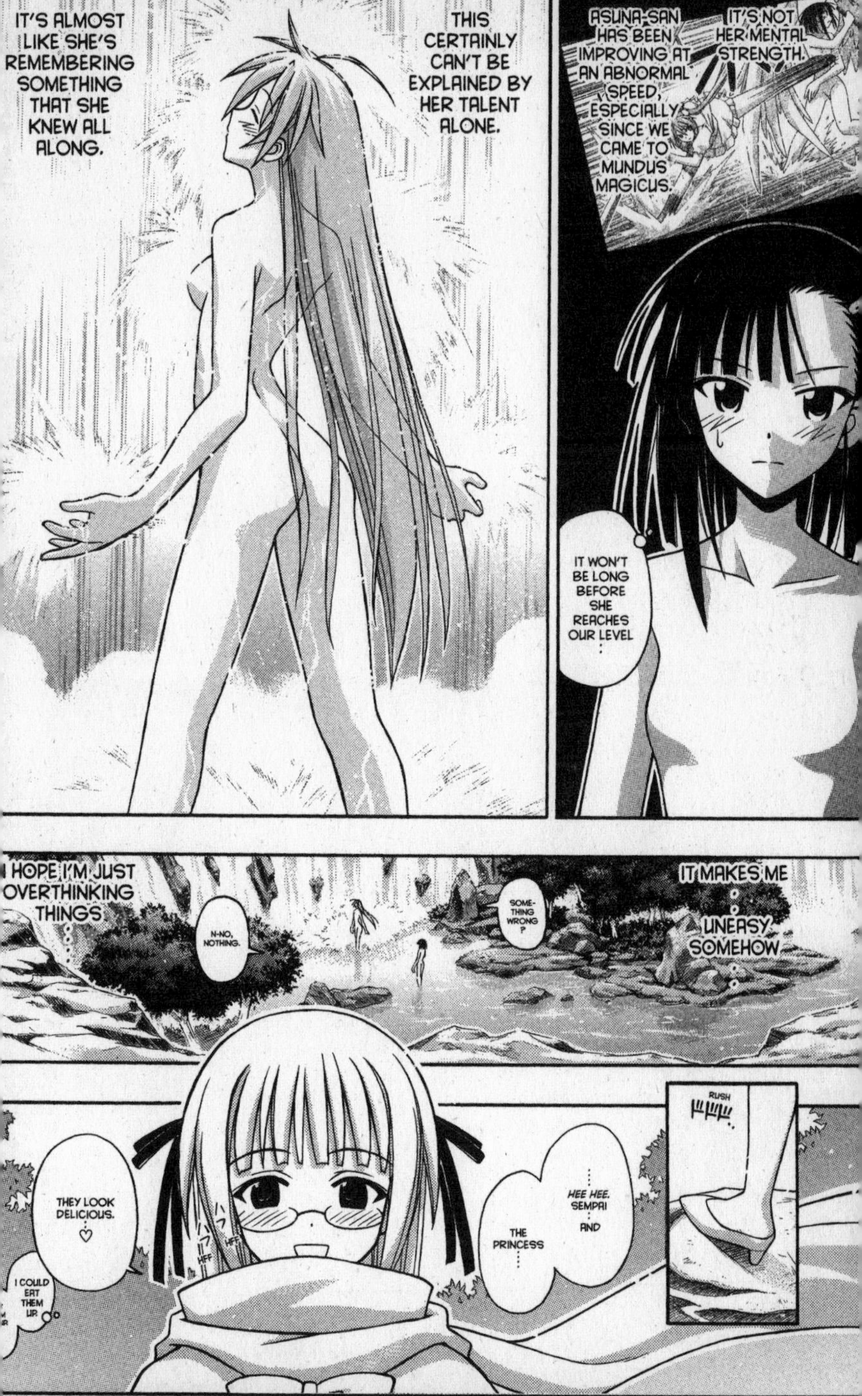
IT'S NOT HER MENTAL STRENGTH.
ASUNA-SAN HAS BEEN IMPROVING AT AN ABNORMAL SPEED, ESPECIALLY SINCE WE CAME TO MUNDUS MAGICUS.
IT WON'T BE LONG BEFORE SHE REACHES OUR LEVEL...
THIS CERTAINLY CAN'T BE EXPLAINED BY HER TALENT ALONE.
IT'S ALMOST LIKE SHE'S REMEMBERING SOMETHING THAT SHE KNEW ALL ALONG.
IT MAKES ME... UNEASY SOMEHOW...
SOME-THING WRONG?
N-NO, NOTHING.
I HOPE I'M JUST OVERTHINKING THINGS...
RUSH
...HEE HEE. SEMPAI... AND
THE PRINCESS...
HFF HFF
THEY LOOK DELICIOUS. ♡
I COULD EAT THEM UP.

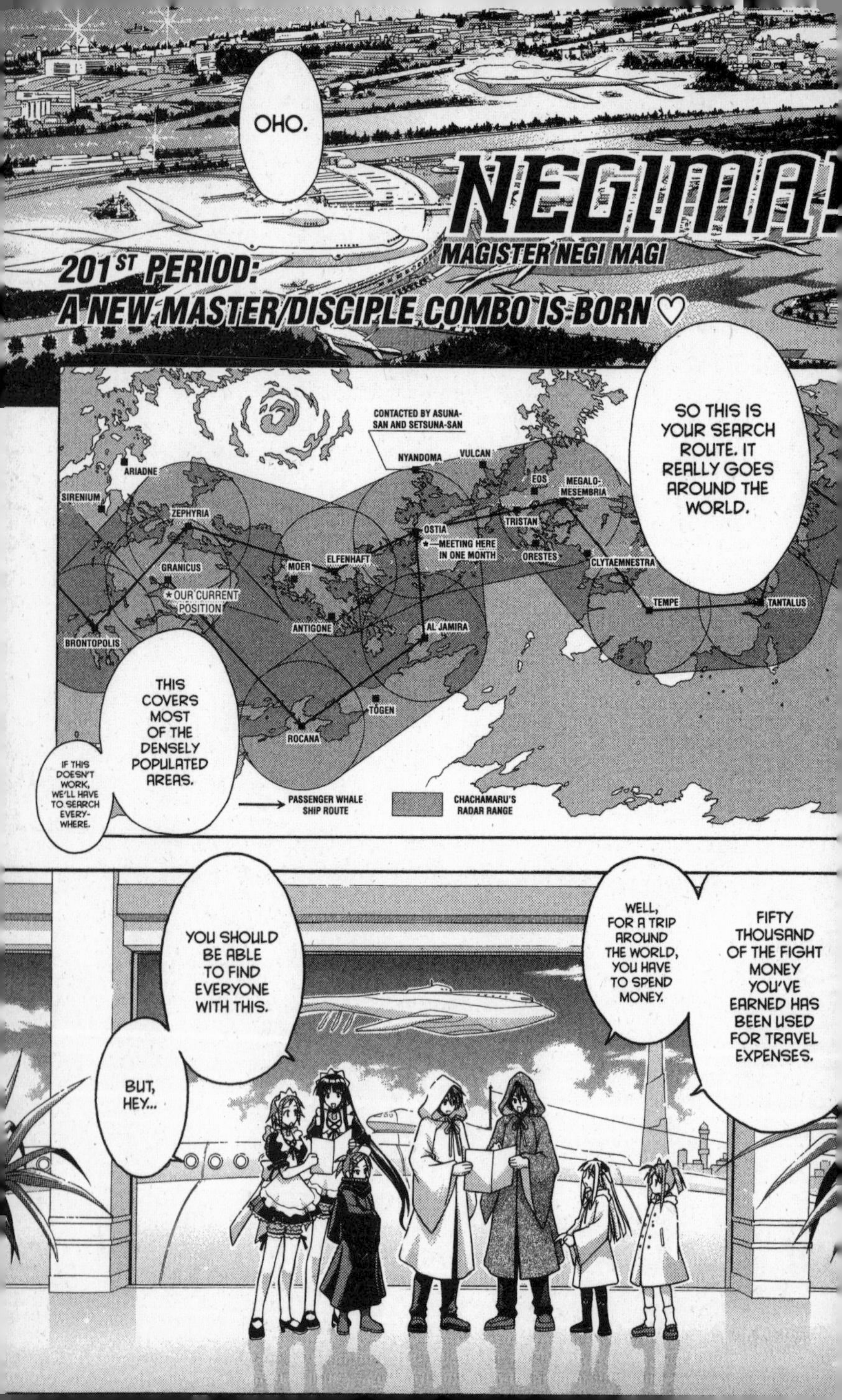
OHO.
NEGIMA!
MAGISTER NEGI MAGI
201ST PERIOD: A NEW MASTER/DISCIPLE COMBO IS BORN ♡
SO THIS IS YOUR SEARCH ROUTE. IT REALLY GOES AROUND THE WORLD.
CONTACTED BY ASUNA-SAN AND SETSUNA-SAN
NYANDOMA
VULCAN
EOS
MEGALO-MESEMBRIA
ARIADNE
SIRENIUM
ZEPHYRIA
OSTIA
★—MEETING HERE IN ONE MONTH
TRISTAN
ORESTES
CLYTAEMNESTRA
ELFENHAFT
MOER
GRANICUS
★OUR CURRENT POSITION
TEMPE
TANTALUS
ANTIGONE
AL JAMIRA
BRONTOPOLIS
TŌGEN
ROCANA
PASSENGER WHALE SHIP ROUTE
CHACHAMARU'S RADAR RANGE
THIS COVERS MOST OF THE DENSELY POPULATED AREAS.
IF THIS DOESN'T WORK, WE'LL HAVE TO SEARCH EVERY-WHERE.
FIFTY THOUSAND OF THE FIGHT MONEY YOU'VE EARNED HAS BEEN USED FOR TRAVEL EXPENSES.
WELL, FOR A TRIP AROUND THE WORLD, YOU HAVE TO SPEND MONEY.
YOU SHOULD BE ABLE TO FIND EVERYONE WITH THIS.
BUT, HEY...

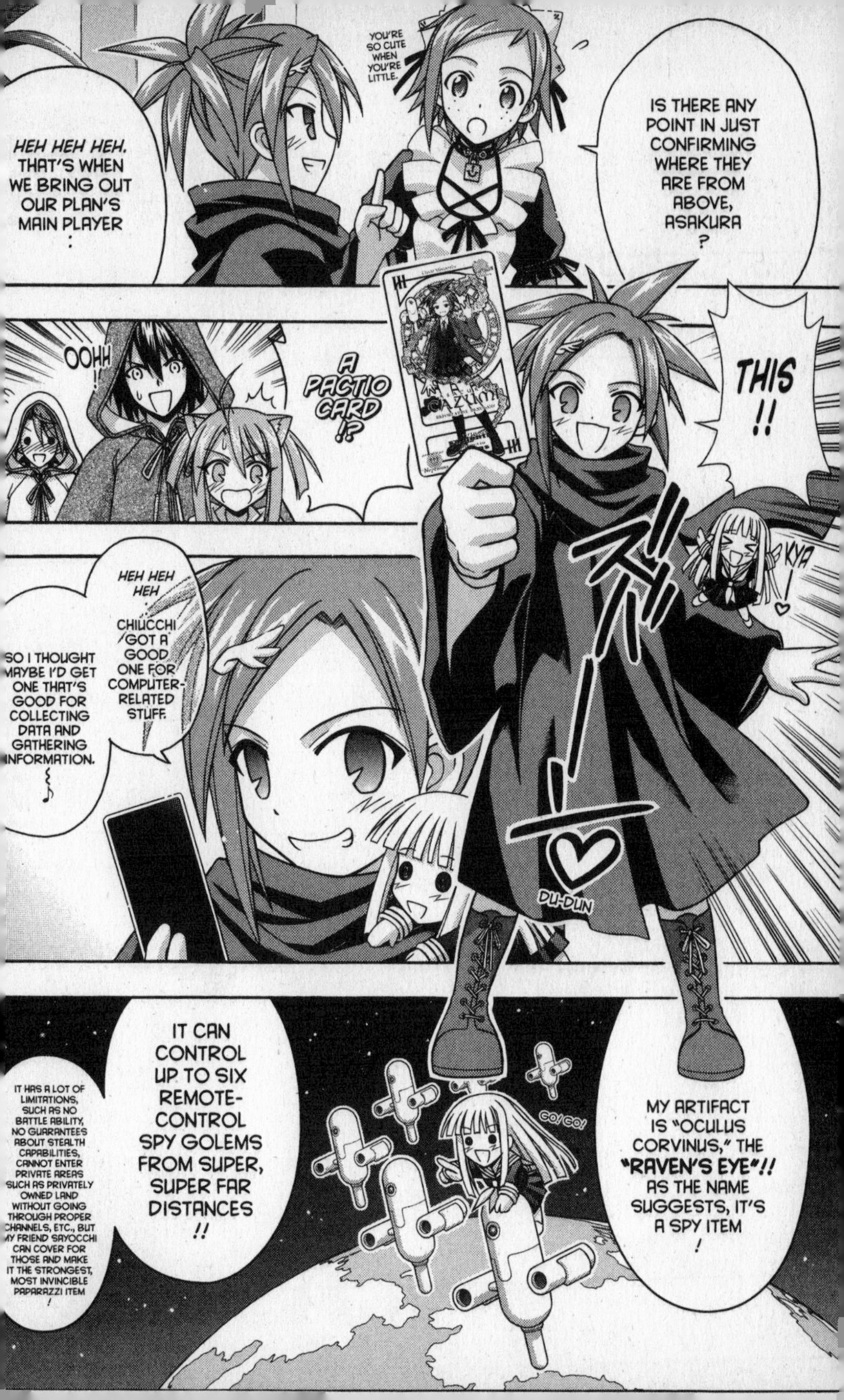
IS THERE ANY POINT IN JUST CONFIRMING WHERE THEY ARE FROM ABOVE, ASAKURA?
YOU'RE SO CUTE WHEN YOU'RE LITTLE.
HEH HEH HEH. THAT'S WHEN WE BRING OUT OUR PLAN'S MAIN PLAYER:
THIS!!
A PACTIO CARD!?
OOHH!!
KYA!
DU-DUN
HEH HEH HEH.
CHIUCCHI GOT A GOOD ONE FOR COMPUTER-RELATED STUFF.
SO I THOUGHT MAYBE I'D GET ONE THAT'S GOOD FOR COLLECTING DATA AND GATHERING INFORMATION. ♪
MY ARTIFACT IS "OCULUS CORVINUS," THE **"RAVEN'S EYE"!!** AS THE NAME SUGGESTS, IT'S A SPY ITEM!
GO! GO!
IT CAN CONTROL UP TO SIX REMOTE-CONTROL SPY GOLEMS FROM SUPER, SUPER FAR DISTANCES!!
IT HAS A LOT OF LIMITATIONS, SUCH AS NO BATTLE ABILITY, NO GUARANTEES ABOUT STEALTH CAPABILITIES, CANNOT ENTER PRIVATE AREAS SUCH AS PRIVATELY OWNED LAND WITHOUT GOING THROUGH PROPER CHANNELS, ETC., BUT MY FRIEND SAYOCCHI CAN COVER FOR THOSE AND MAKE IT THE STRONGEST, MOST INVINCIBLE PAPARAZZI ITEM!

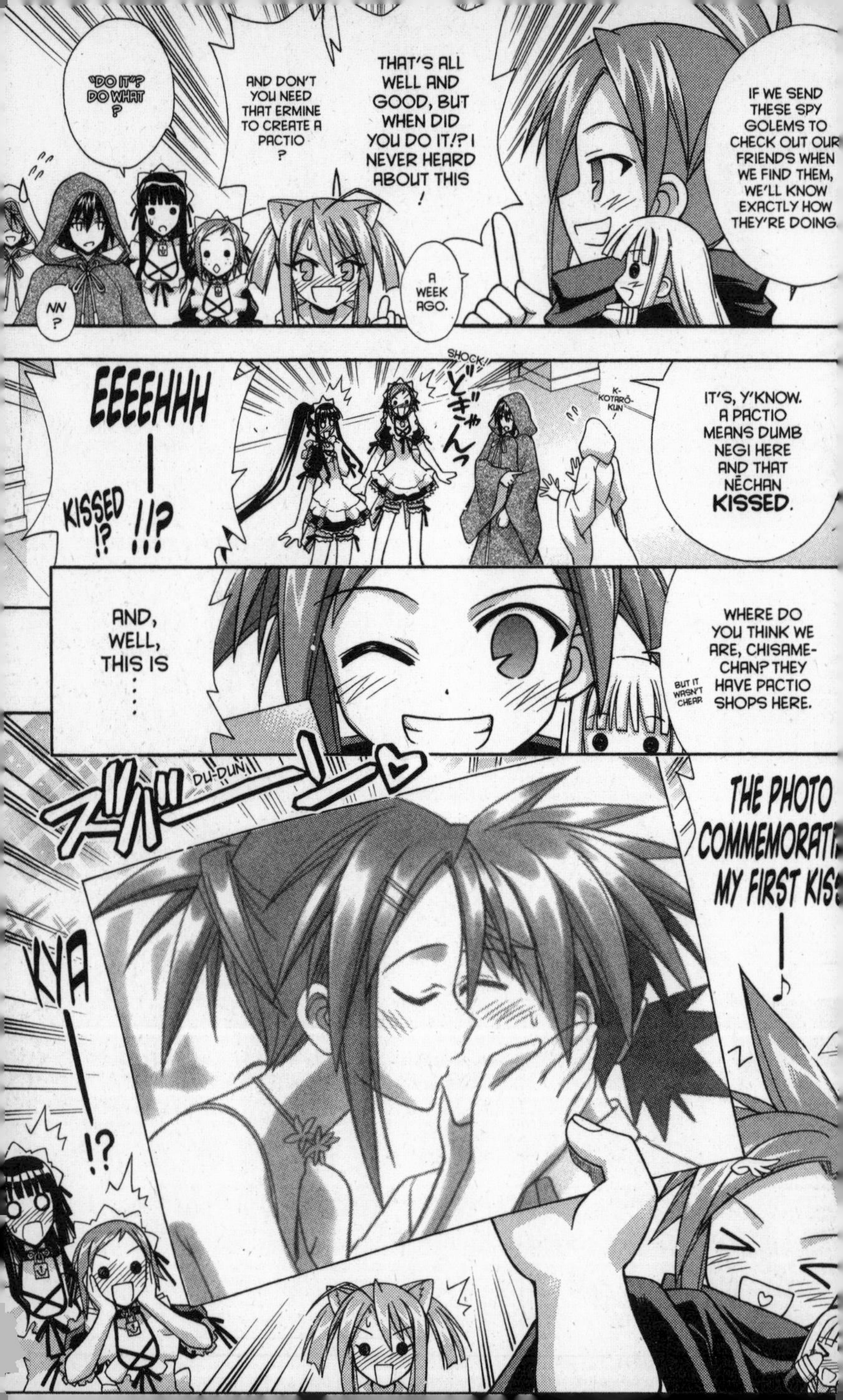
IF WE SEND THESE SPY GOLEMS TO CHECK OUT OUR FRIENDS WHEN WE FIND THEM, WE'LL KNOW EXACTLY HOW THEY'RE DOING.
THAT'S ALL WELL AND GOOD, BUT WHEN DID YOU DO IT!? I NEVER HEARD ABOUT THIS!
AND DON'T YOU NEED THAT ERMINE TO CREATE A PACTIO?
A WEEK AGO.
"DO IT"? DO WHAT?
NN?
IT'S, Y'KNOW. A PACTIO MEANS DUMB NEGI HERE AND THAT NĒCHAN KISSED.
K-KOTARŌ-KUN!
SHOCK!
どぎゃんっ
EEEEHHH—!!?
KISSED!?
WHERE DO YOU THINK WE ARE, CHISAME-CHAN? THEY HAVE PACTIO SHOPS HERE.
BUT IT WASN'T CHEAP.
AND, WELL, THIS IS......
DU-DUN
ズバーン♥
THE PHOTO COMMEMORATI
MY FIRST KIS
—♪
KYA—!?

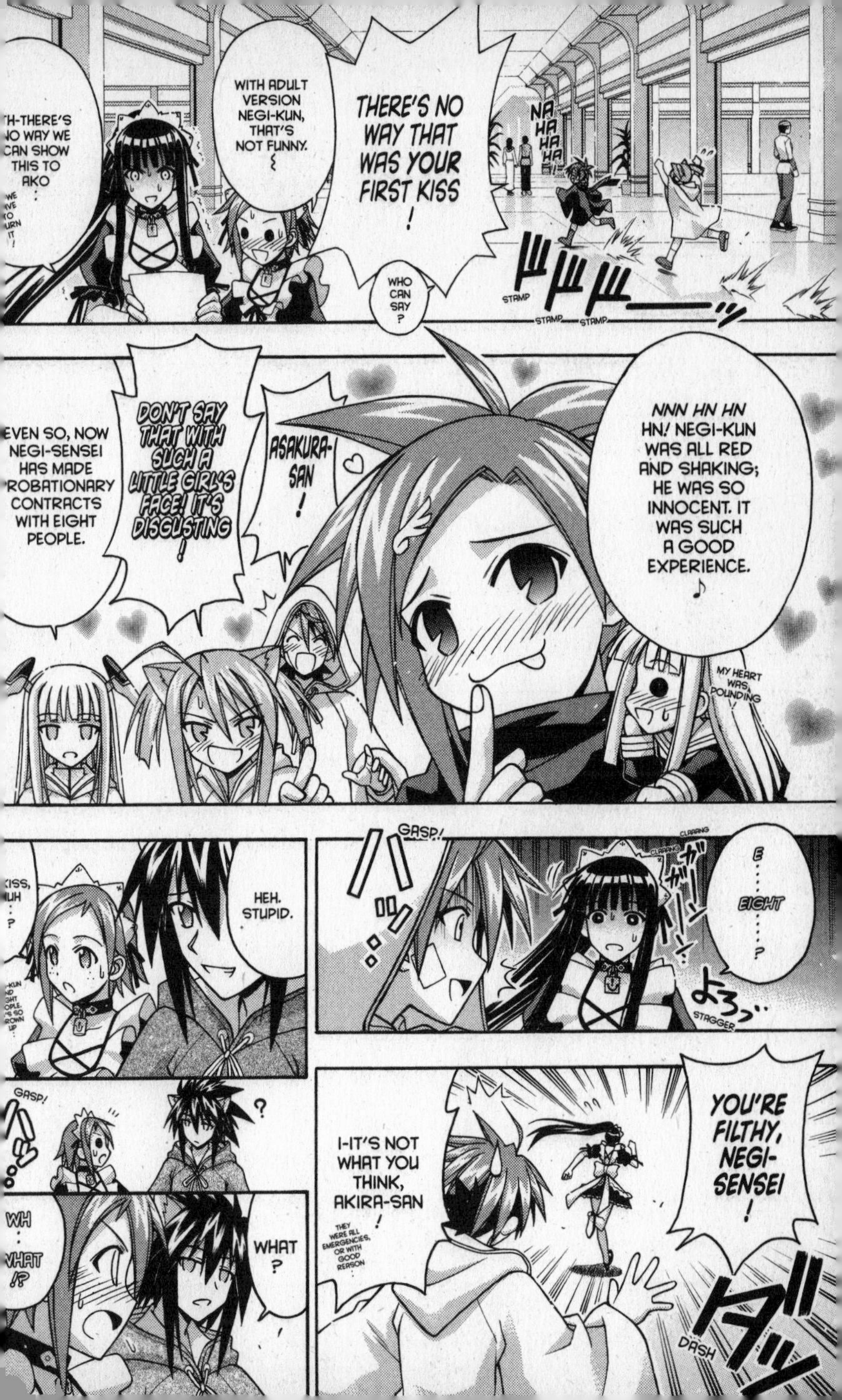
NA HA HA HA!
STAMP STAMP STAMP
THERE'S NO WAY THAT WAS YOUR FIRST KISS!
WHO CAN SAY?
WITH ADULT VERSION NEGI-KUN, THAT'S NOT FUNNY.
TH-THERE'S NO WAY WE CAN SHOW THIS TO AKO
NNN HN HN HN! NEGI-KUN WAS ALL RED AND SHAKING; HE WAS SO INNOCENT. IT WAS SUCH A GOOD EXPERIENCE. ♪
MY HEART WAS POUNDING!
ASAKURA-SAN!
DON'T SAY THAT WITH SUCH A LITTLE GIRL'S FACE! IT'S DISGUSTING!
EVEN SO, NOW NEGI-SENSEI HAS MADE PROBATIONARY CONTRACTS WITH EIGHT PEOPLE.
E... EIGHT...?
GASP!
CLAANG CLAANG
STAGGER
HEH. STUPID.
KISS, HUH...?
YOU'RE FILTHY, NEGI-SENSEI!
I-IT'S NOT WHAT YOU THINK, AKIRA-SAN!
THEY WERE ALL EMERGENCIES, OR WITH GOOD REASON
DASH
GASP!
?
WH... WHAT!?
WHAT?

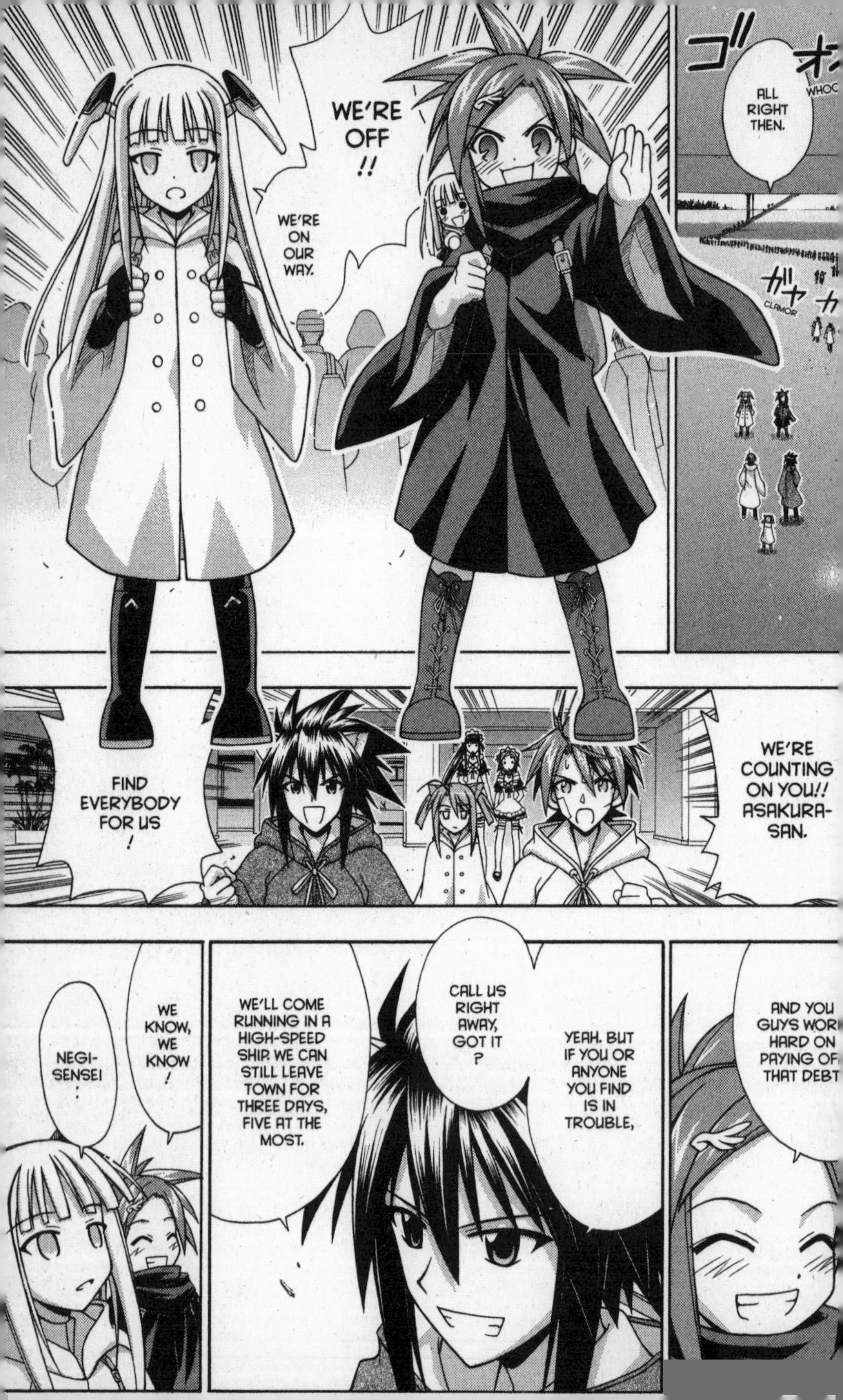
ALL RIGHT THEN.
CLAMOR
WE'RE OFF!!
WE'RE ON OUR WAY.
WE'RE COUNTING ON YOU!! ASAKURA-SAN.
FIND EVERYBODY FOR US!
AND YOU GUYS WOR HARD ON PAYING OF THAT DEBT
YEAH. BUT IF YOU OR ANYONE YOU FIND IS IN TROUBLE,
CALL US RIGHT AWAY, GOT IT?
WE'LL COME RUNNING IN A HIGH-SPEED SHIP. WE CAN STILL LEAVE TOWN FOR THREE DAYS, FIVE AT THE MOST.
WE KNOW, WE KNOW!
NEGI-SENSEI...

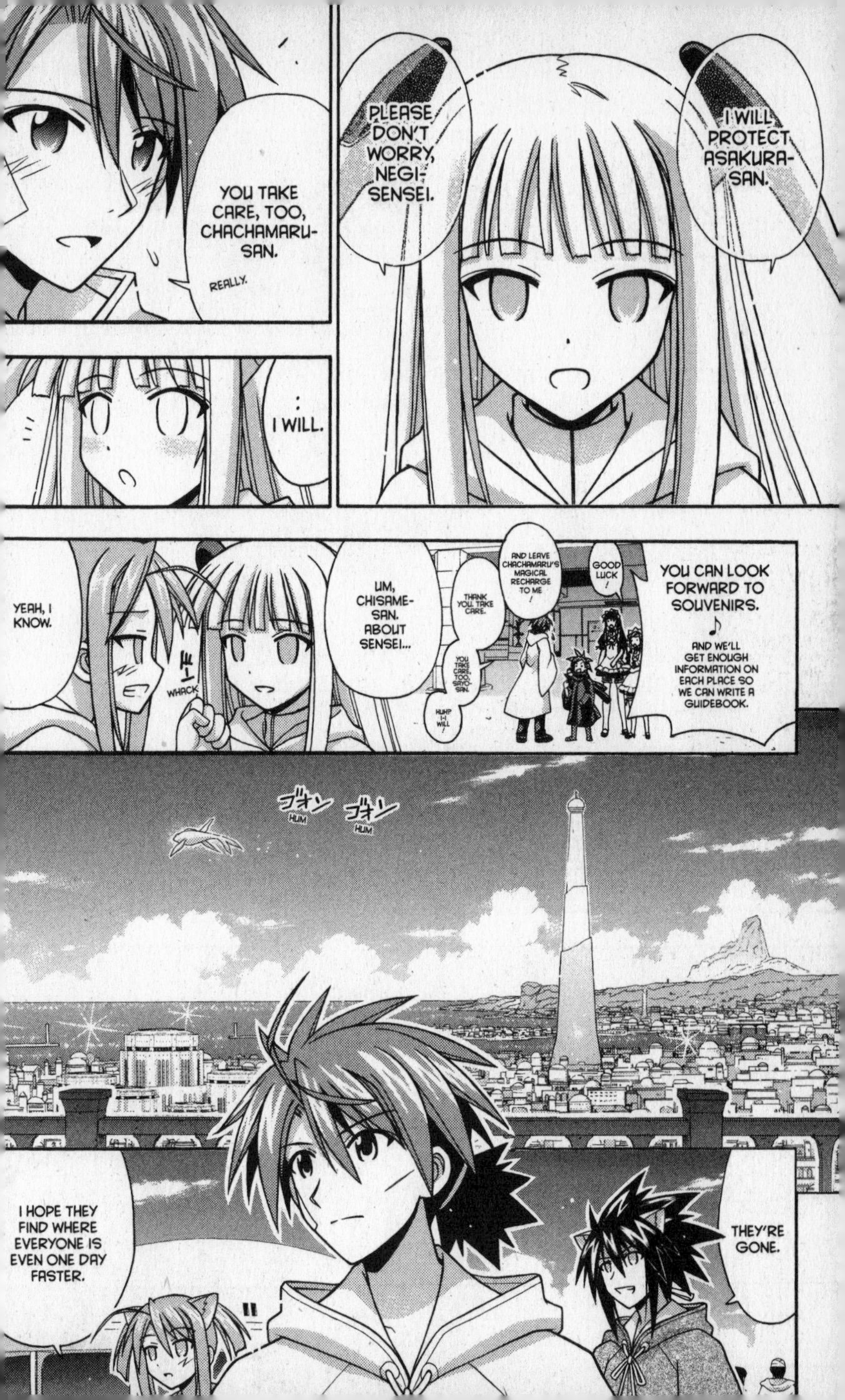
I WILL PROTECT ASAKURA-SAN.
PLEASE DON'T WORRY, NEGI-SENSEI.
YOU TAKE CARE, TOO, CHACHAMARU-SAN.
REALLY.
: I WILL.
YOU CAN LOOK FORWARD TO SOUVENIRS. ♪
AND WE'LL GET ENOUGH INFORMATION ON EACH PLACE SO WE CAN WRITE A GUIDEBOOK.
GOOD LUCK!
AND LEAVE CHACHAMARU'S MAGICAL RECHARGE TO ME!
THANK YOU. TAKE CARE.
YOU TAKE CARE, TOO, SAYO-SAN.
HUH? I-I WILL!
UM, CHISAME-SAN. ABOUT SENSEI...
WHACK
YEAH, I KNOW.
HUM
HUM
THEY'RE GONE.
I HOPE THEY FIND WHERE EVERYONE IS EVEN ONE DAY FASTER.

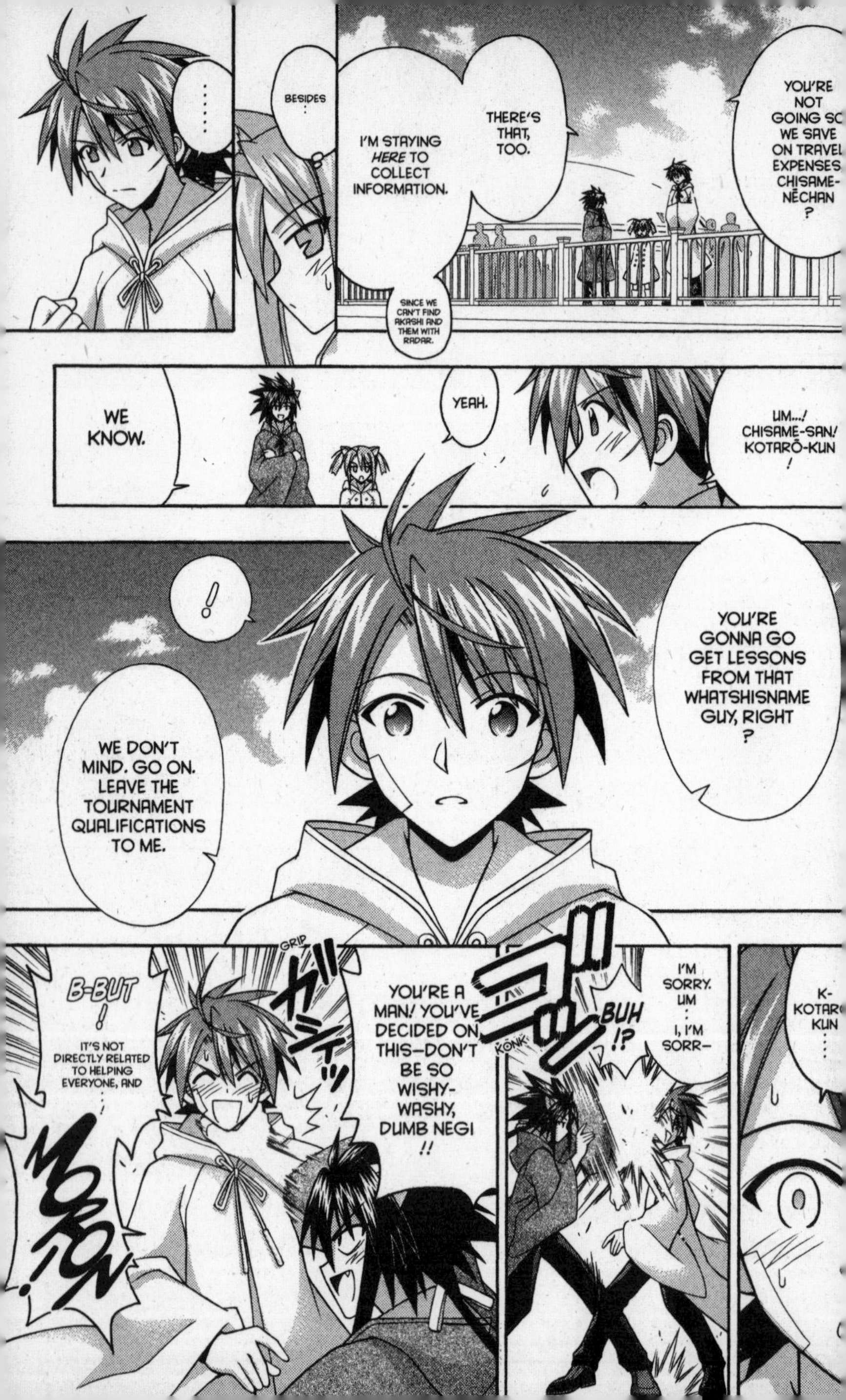
YOU'RE NOT GOING SO WE SAVE ON TRAVEL EXPENSES, CHISAME-NĒCHAN?
THERE'S THAT, TOO.
BESIDES...
I'M STAYING *HERE* TO COLLECT INFORMATION.
SINCE WE CAN'T FIND AKASHI AND THEM WITH RADAR.
......
UM...! CHISAME-SAN! KOTARŌ-KUN!
YEAH.
WE KNOW.
YOU'RE GONNA GO GET LESSONS FROM THAT WHATSHISNAME GUY, RIGHT?
!
WE DON'T MIND. GO ON. LEAVE THE TOURNAMENT QUALIFICATIONS TO ME.
K-KOTARŌ-KUN...
I'M SORRY. UM... I, I'M SORR—
BUH!?
KONK
YOU'RE A MAN! YOU'VE DECIDED ON THIS—DON'T BE SO WISHY-WASHY, DUMB NEGI!!
GRIP
B-BUT!
IT'S NOT DIRECTLY RELATED TO HELPING EVERYONE, AND...
MORON!!

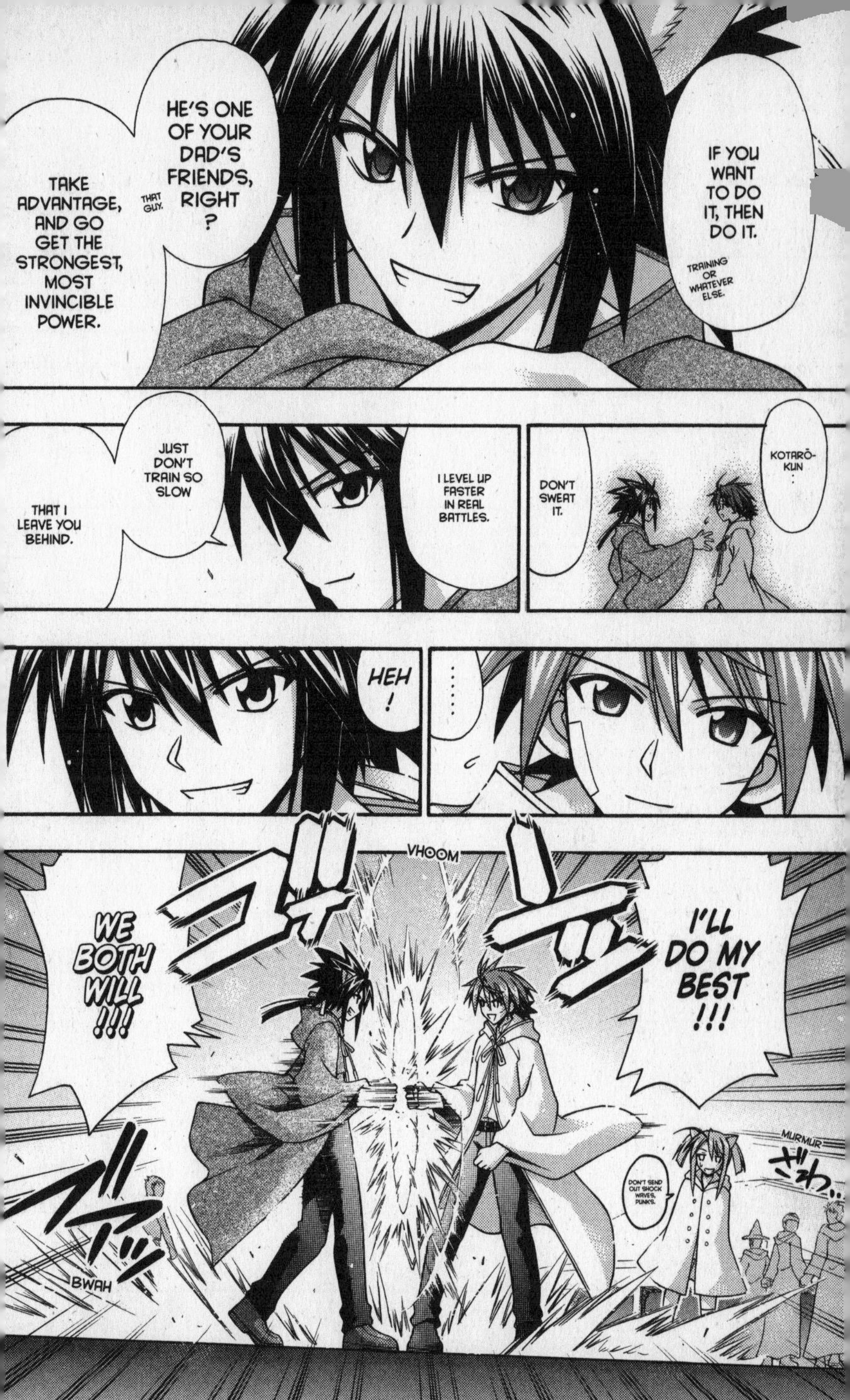
IF YOU WANT TO DO IT, THEN DO IT.
TRAINING OR WHATEVER ELSE.
HE'S ONE OF YOUR DAD'S FRIENDS, RIGHT?
THAT GUY.
TAKE ADVANTAGE, AND GO GET THE STRONGEST, MOST INVINCIBLE POWER.
KOTARŌ-KUN...
DON'T SWEAT IT.
I LEVEL UP FASTER IN REAL BATTLES.
JUST DON'T TRAIN SO SLOW
THAT I LEAVE YOU BEHIND.
......
HEH!
VHOOM
I'LL DO MY BEST!!!
WE BOTH WILL!!!
MURMUR
DON'T SEND OUT SHOCK WAVES, PUNKS.
BWAH

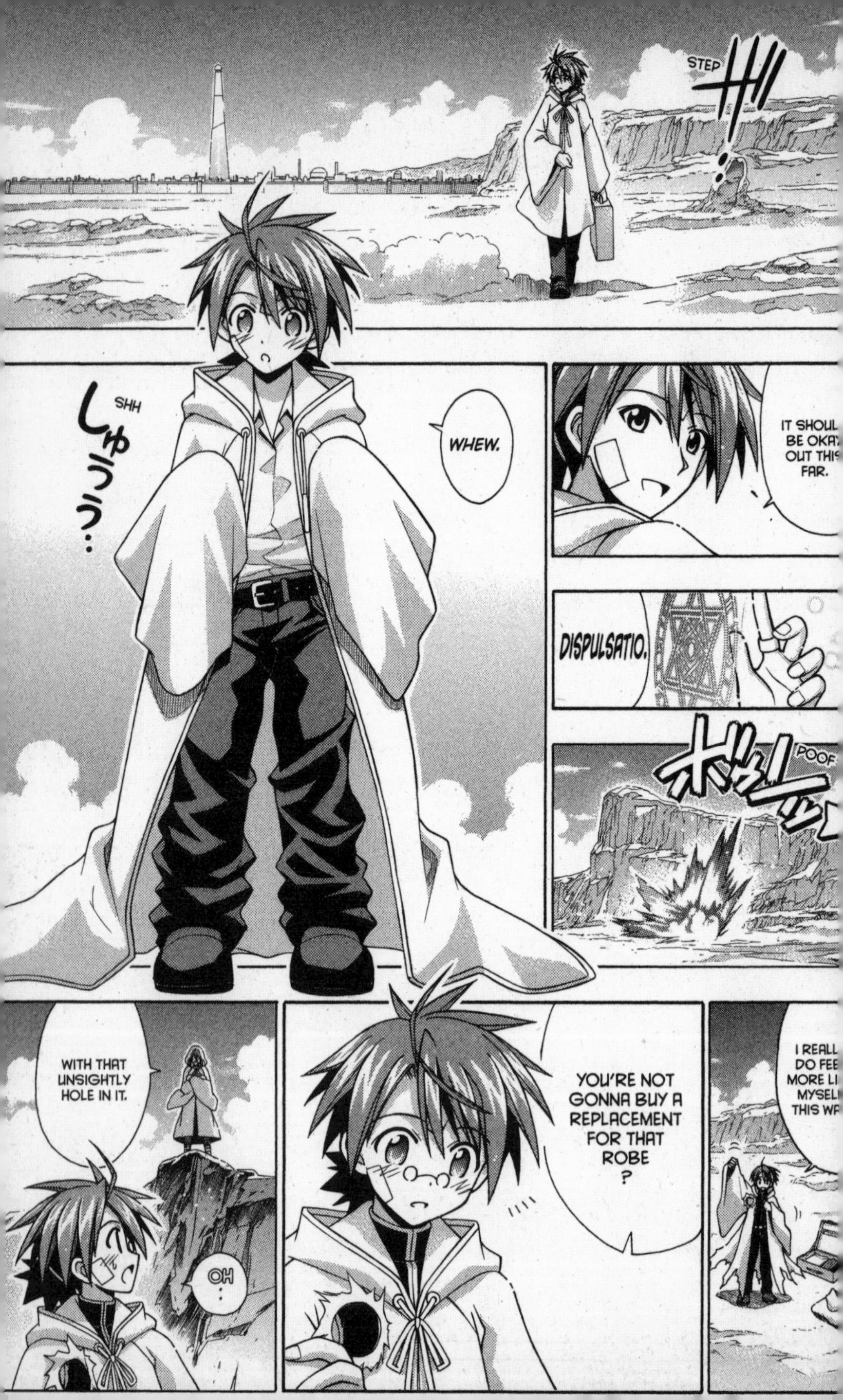

STEP
IT SHOUL
BE OKA
OUT THIS
FAR.
DISPULSATIO.
POOF
SHH
WHEW.
I REALL
DO FEE
MORE LI
MYSEL
THIS WA
YOU'RE NOT GONNA BUY A REPLACEMENT FOR THAT ROBE ?
WITH THAT UNSIGHTLY HOLE IN IT.
OH . .

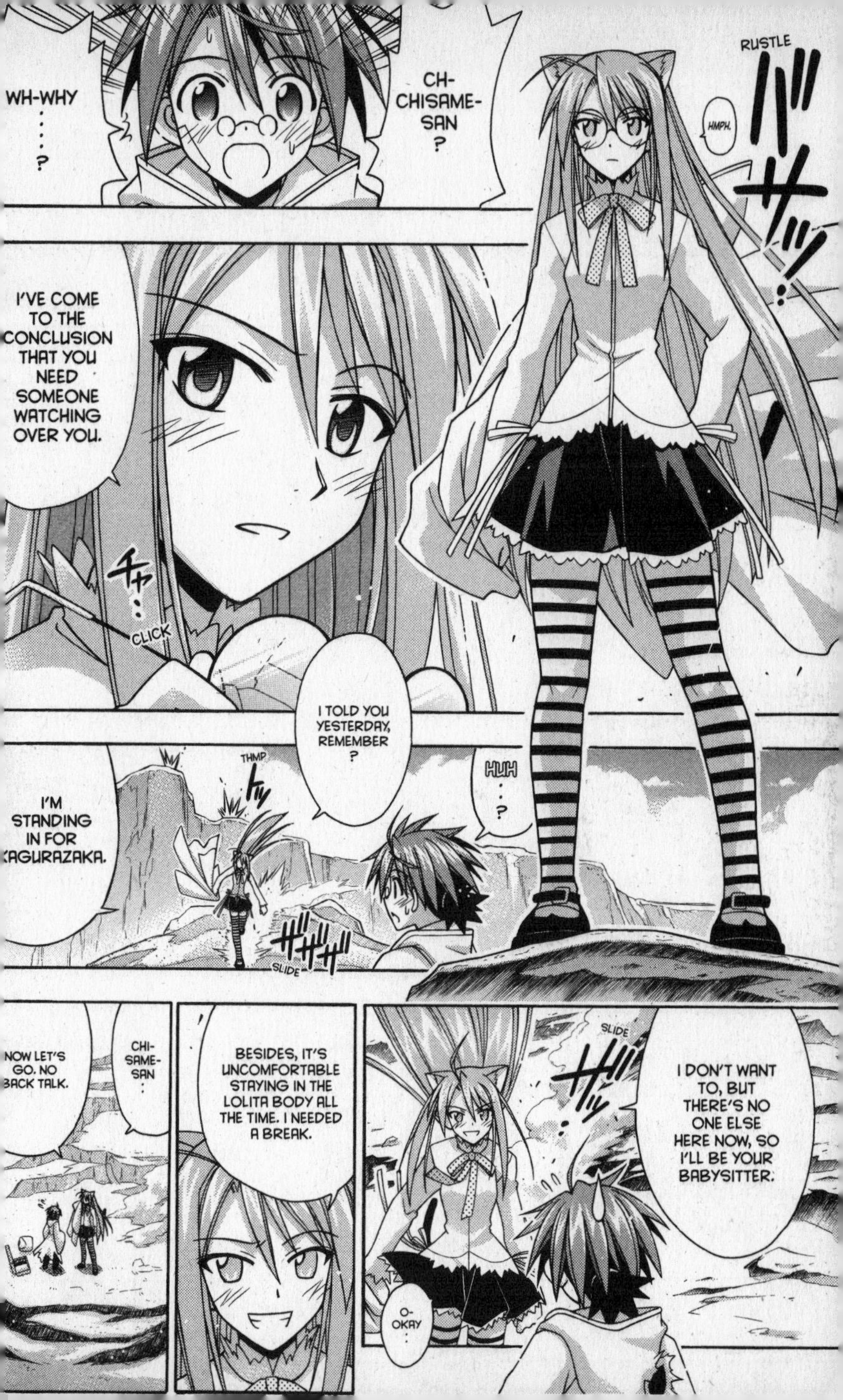
RUSTLE
HMPH.
CH-CHISAME-SAN?
WH-WHY...?
I'VE COME TO THE CONCLUSION THAT YOU NEED SOMEONE WATCHING OVER YOU.
CLICK
I TOLD YOU YESTERDAY, REMEMBER?
HUH...?
THMP
I'M STANDING IN FOR KAGURAZAKA.
SLIDE
SLIDE
I DON'T WANT TO, BUT THERE'S NO ONE ELSE HERE NOW, SO I'LL BE YOUR BABYSITTER.
O-OKAY...
BESIDES, IT'S UNCOMFORTABLE STAYING IN THE LOLITA BODY ALL THE TIME. I NEEDED A BREAK.
CHI-SAME-SAN...
NOW LET'S GO. NO BACK TALK.

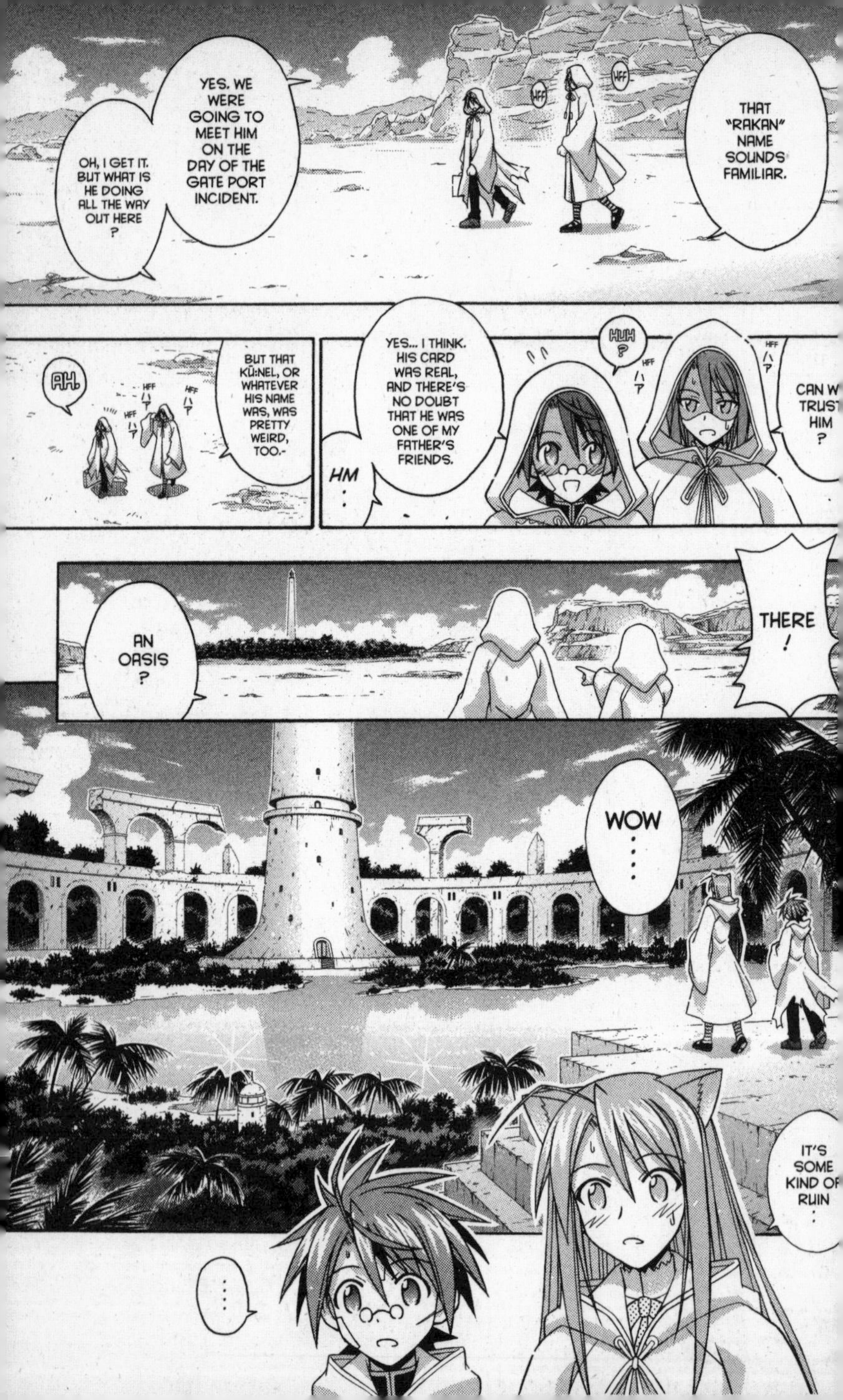

THAT "RAKAN" NAME SOUNDS FAMILIAR.
HFF
HFF
YES. WE WERE GOING TO MEET HIM ON THE DAY OF THE GATE PORT INCIDENT.
OH, I GET IT. BUT WHAT IS HE DOING ALL THE WAY OUT HERE?
CAN W TRUST HIM?
HFF
HUH?
HFF
YES... I THINK. HIS CARD WAS REAL, AND THERE'S NO DOUBT THAT HE WAS ONE OF MY FATHER'S FRIENDS.
HM...
BUT THAT KŪ:NEL, OR WHATEVER HIS NAME WAS, WAS PRETTY WEIRD, TOO.-
HFF
HFF
HFF
AH.
THERE!
AN OASIS?
WOW....
IT'S SOME KIND OF RUIN...
....

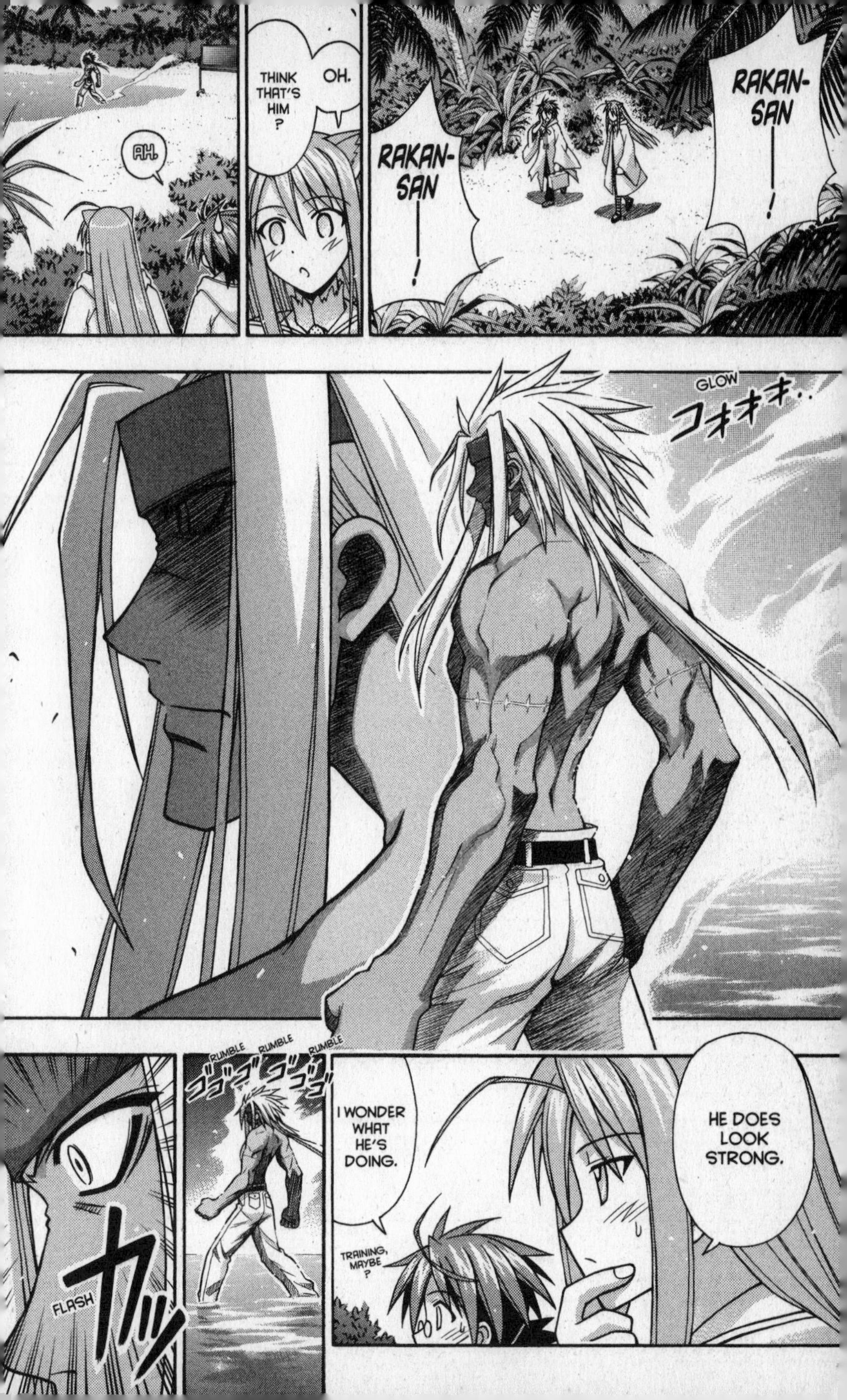
RAKAN-SAN—!
RAKAN-SAN—!
OH.
THINK THAT'S HIM?
AH.
GLOW
コォォォ..
HE DOES LOOK STRONG.
I WONDER WHAT HE'S DOING.
TRAINING, MAYBE?
RUMBLE RUMBLE RUMBLE
ゴゴゴゴゴ
FLASH
カッ

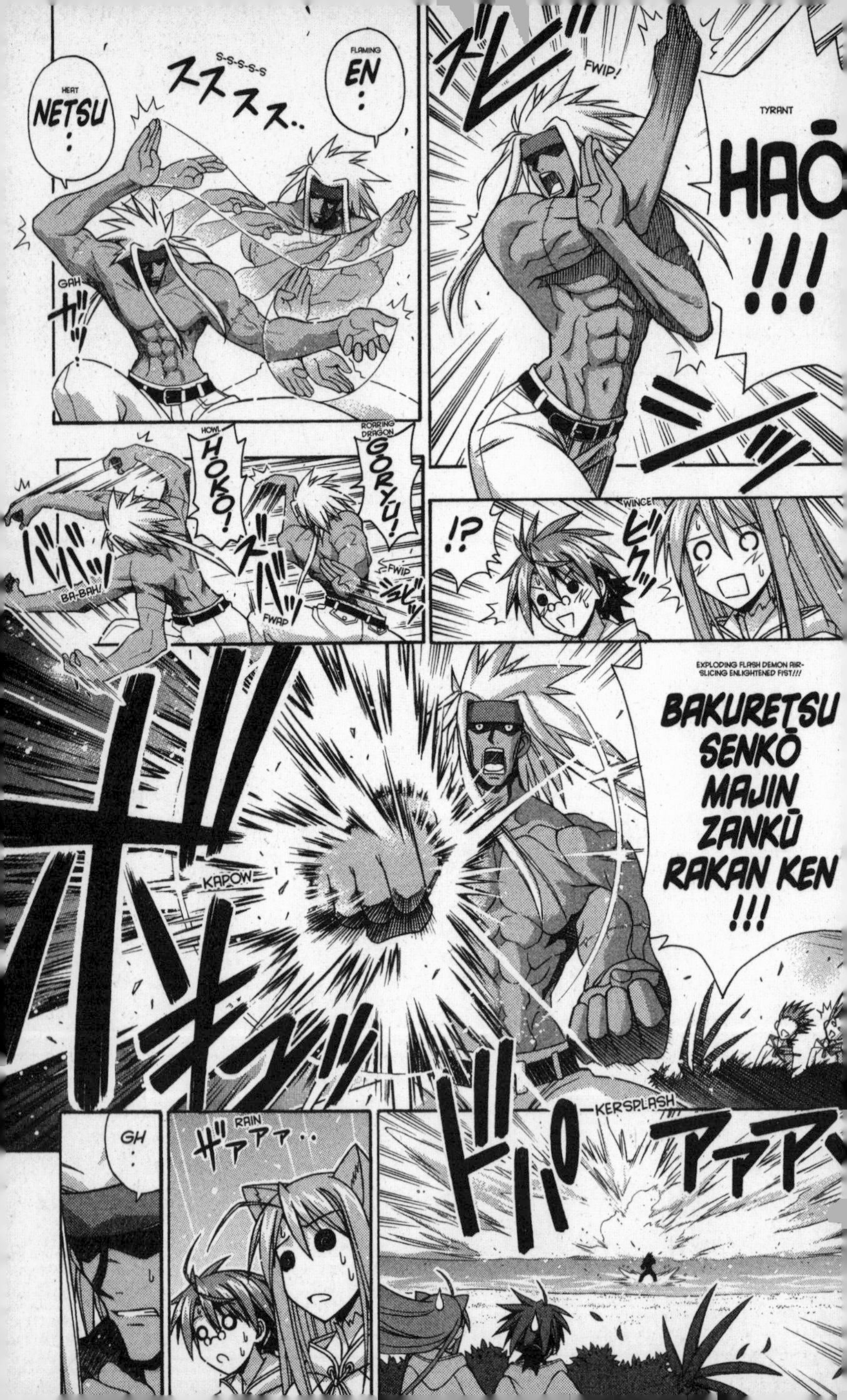

FWIP!
TYRANT
HAŌ
!!!
FLAMING
EN
:
S-S-S-S-S
ススススス..
HEAT
NETSU
:
GAH
WINCE
!?
ROARING DRAGON
GŌRYŪ!
HOWL
HŌKŌ!
FWIP
FWAP
BA-BAH!
EXPLODING FLASH DEMON AIR-SLICING ENLIGHTENED FIST!!!
BAKURETSU SENKŌ MAJIN ZANKŪ RAKAN KEN !!!
KAPOW
KERSPLASH
RAIN
ザァァァ..
GH
:

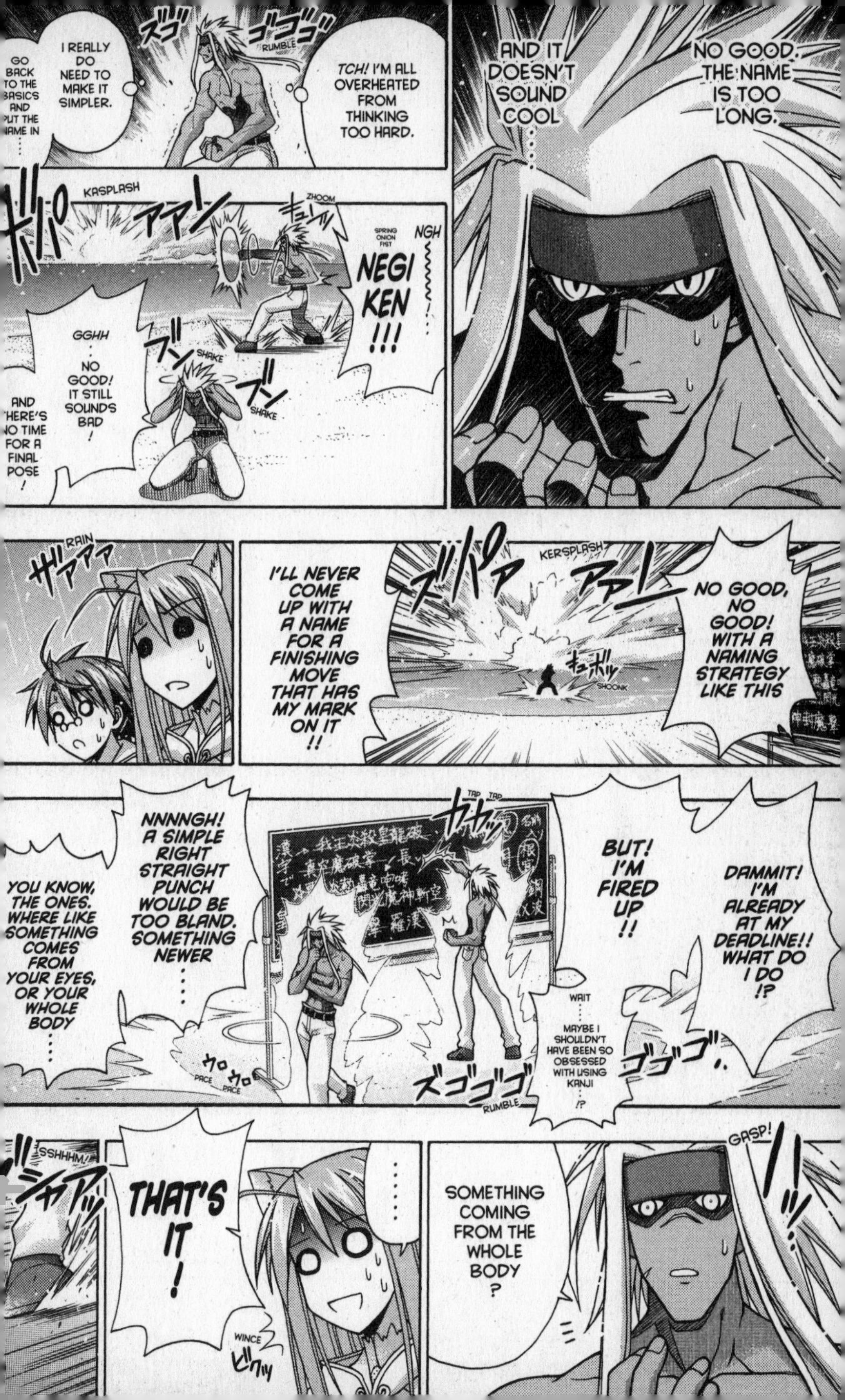

NO GOOD. THE NAME IS TOO LONG.
AND IT DOESN'T SOUND COOL...
TCH! I'M ALL OVERHEATED FROM THINKING TOO HARD.
RUMBLE
I REALLY DO NEED TO MAKE IT SIMPLER.
GO BACK TO THE BASICS AND PUT THE NAME IN...
ZHOOM
KASPLASH
SPRING ONION FIST
NEGI KEN!!!
NGH...!
GGHH... NO GOOD! IT STILL SOUNDS BAD!
SHAKE
SHAKE
AND THERE'S NO TIME FOR A FINAL POSE!
NO GOOD, NO GOOD! WITH A NAMING STRATEGY LIKE THIS
KERSPLASH
SHOONK
I'LL NEVER COME UP WITH A NAME FOR A FINISHING MOVE THAT HAS MY MARK ON IT!!
RAIN
DAMMIT! I'M ALREADY AT MY DEADLINE!! WHAT DO I DO!?
BUT! I'M FIRED UP!!
WAIT... MAYBE I SHOULDN'T HAVE BEEN SO OBSESSED WITH USING KANJI...!?
RUMBLE
TAP TAP
NNNNGH! A SIMPLE RIGHT STRAIGHT PUNCH WOULD BE TOO BLAND. SOMETHING NEWER...
PACE PACE
YOU KNOW, THE ONES. WHERE LIKE SOMETHING COMES FROM YOUR EYES, OR YOUR WHOLE BODY...
GASP!
SOMETHING COMING FROM THE WHOLE BODY?
......
WINCE
THAT'S IT!
SSHHHM!

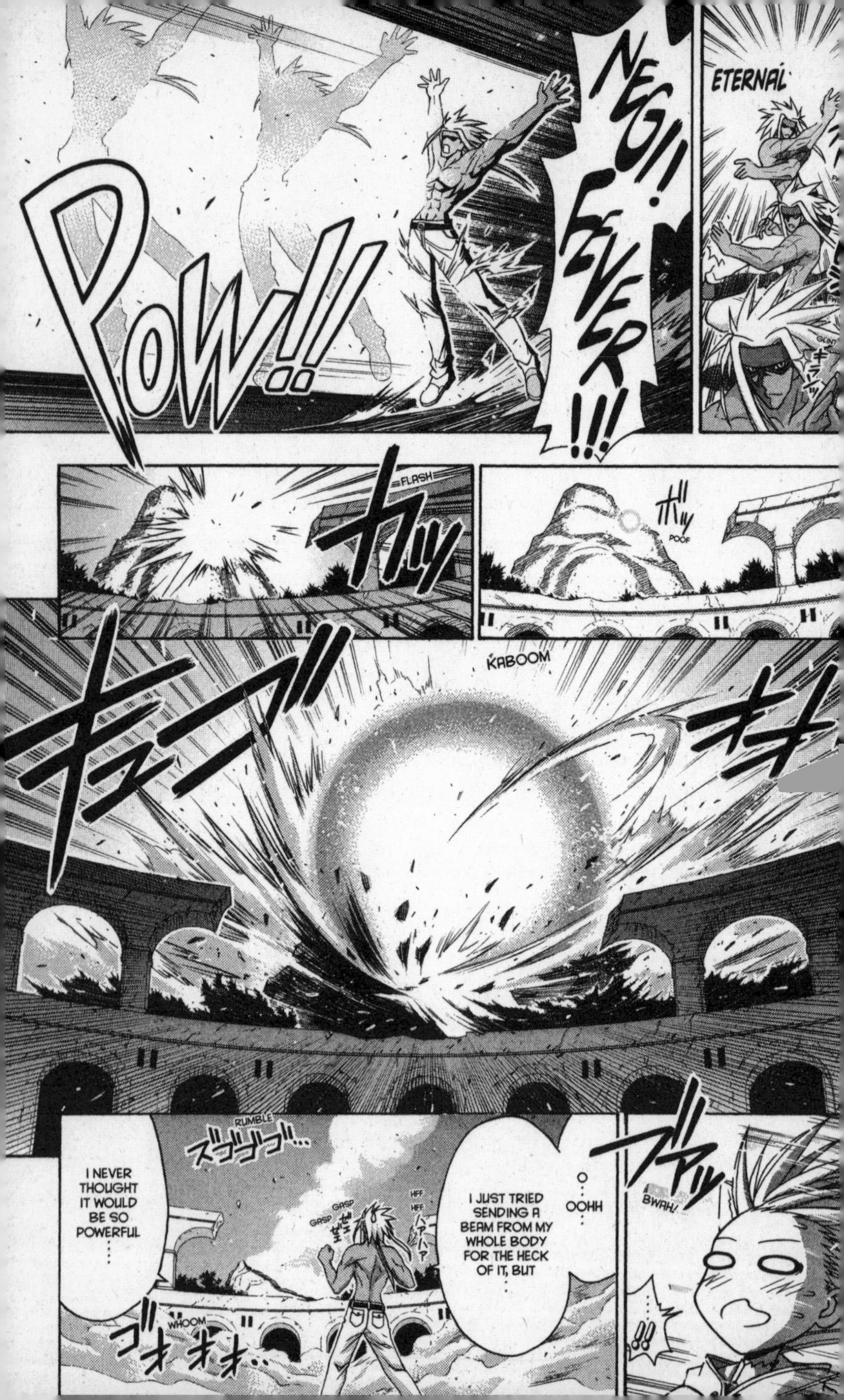

ETERNAL
GLINT
NEGI!! FEVER!!!
POW!!
POOF
FLASH
KABOOM
BWAH!
......!!
O... OOHH
I JUST TRIED SENDING A BEAM FROM MY WHOLE BODY FOR THE HECK OF IT, BUT...
HFF HFF
GASP GASP
RUMBLE
I NEVER THOUGHT IT WOULD BE SO POWERFUL...
WHOOM

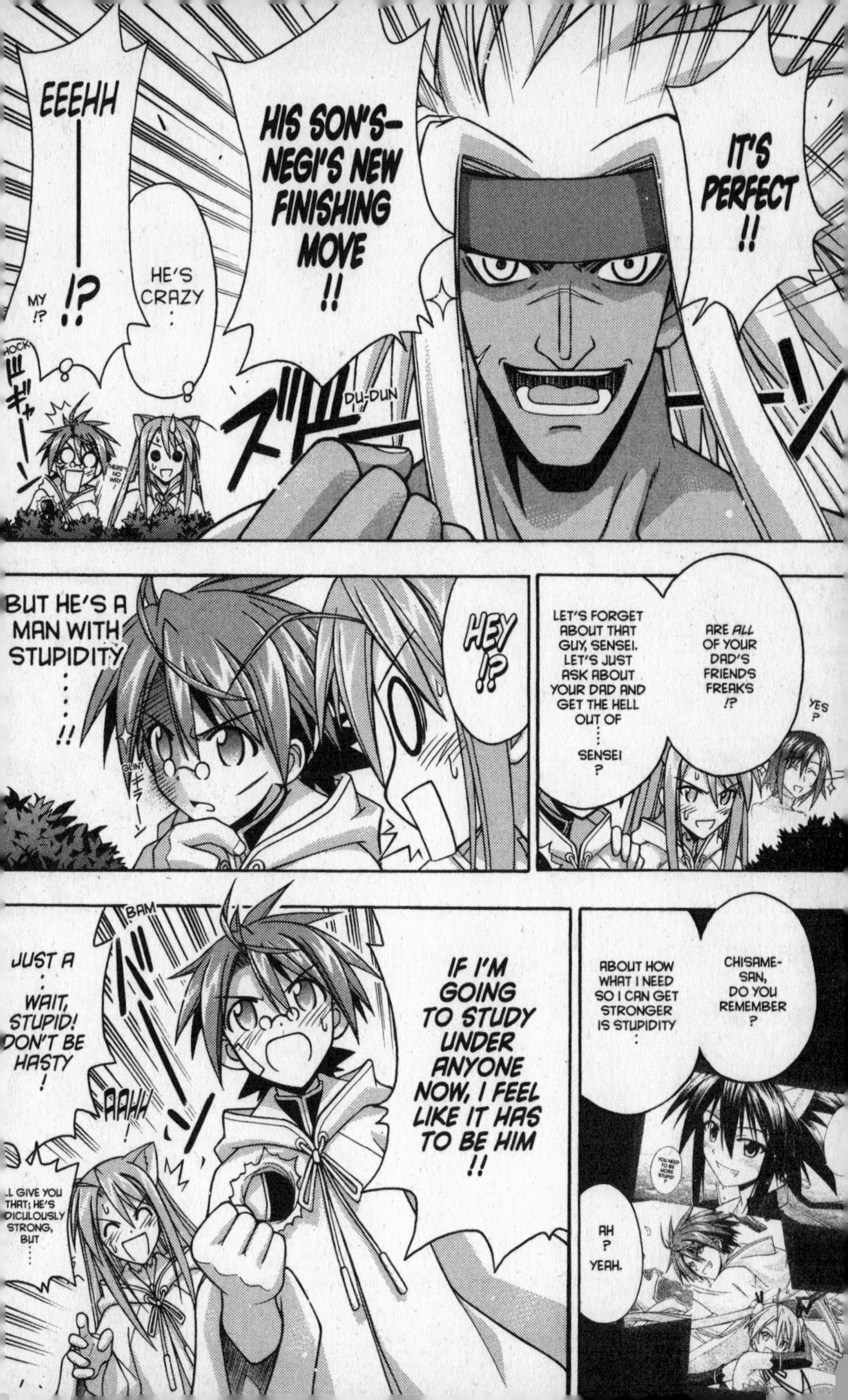
IT'S PERFECT !!
HIS SON'S—NEGI'S NEW FINISHING MOVE !!
DU-DUN
HE'S CRAZY ...
EEEHH——!?
MY !?
HOCK
THERE'S NO WAY !
ARE ALL OF YOUR DAD'S FRIENDS FREAKS !?
YES ?
LET'S FORGET ABOUT THAT GUY, SENSEI. LET'S JUST ASK ABOUT YOUR DAD AND GET THE HELL OUT OF ... SENSEI ?
HEY !?
BUT HE'S A MAN WITH STUPIDITY ......!!
GLINT
CHISAME-SAN, DO YOU REMEMBER ?
ABOUT HOW WHAT I NEED SO I CAN GET STRONGER IS STUPIDITY ...
YOU NEED TO BE MORE STUPID ?
AH ? YEAH.
IF I'M GOING TO STUDY UNDER ANYONE NOW, I FEEL LIKE IT HAS TO BE HIM !!
BAM
JUST A ... WAIT, STUPID! DON'T BE HASTY !
AAHH !
LL GIVE YOU THAT; HE'S DICULOUSLY STRONG, BUT ...

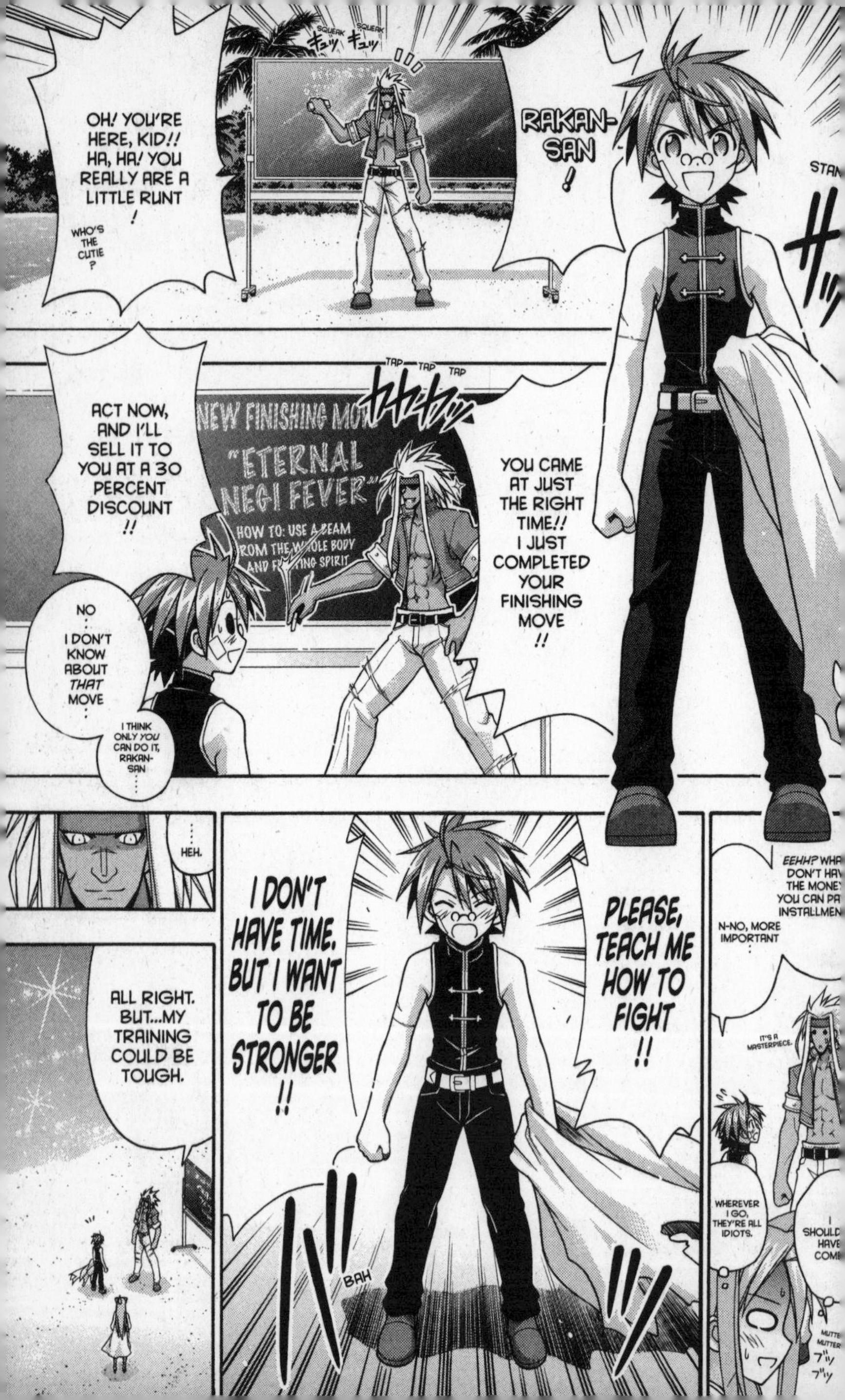
RAKAN-SAN!
STAN
SQUEAK SQUEAK
OH! YOU'RE HERE, KID!! HA, HA! YOU REALLY ARE A LITTLE RUNT!
WHO'S THE CUTIE?
TAP TAP TAP
YOU CAME AT JUST THE RIGHT TIME!! I JUST COMPLETED YOUR FINISHING MOVE!!
ACT NOW, AND I'LL SELL IT TO YOU AT A 30 PERCENT DISCOUNT!!
NEW FINISHING MOV
"ETERNAL NEGI FEVER"
HOW TO: USE A BEAM
ROM THE WHOLE BODY
AND FI TING SPIRIT
NO... I DON'T KNOW ABOUT THAT MOVE...
I THINK ONLY YOU CAN DO IT, RAKAN-SAN...
EEHH? WHA DON'T HAV THE MONEY YOU CAN PA INSTALLMEN
N-NO, MORE IMPORTANT...
IT'S A MASTERPIECE.
I SHOULD HAVE COM
WHEREVER I GO, THEY'RE ALL IDIOTS.
MUTTER MUTTER
PLEASE, TEACH ME HOW TO FIGHT!!
I DON'T HAVE TIME. BUT I WANT TO BE STRONGER!!
BAH
...HEH.
ALL RIGHT. BUT...MY TRAINING COULD BE TOUGH.

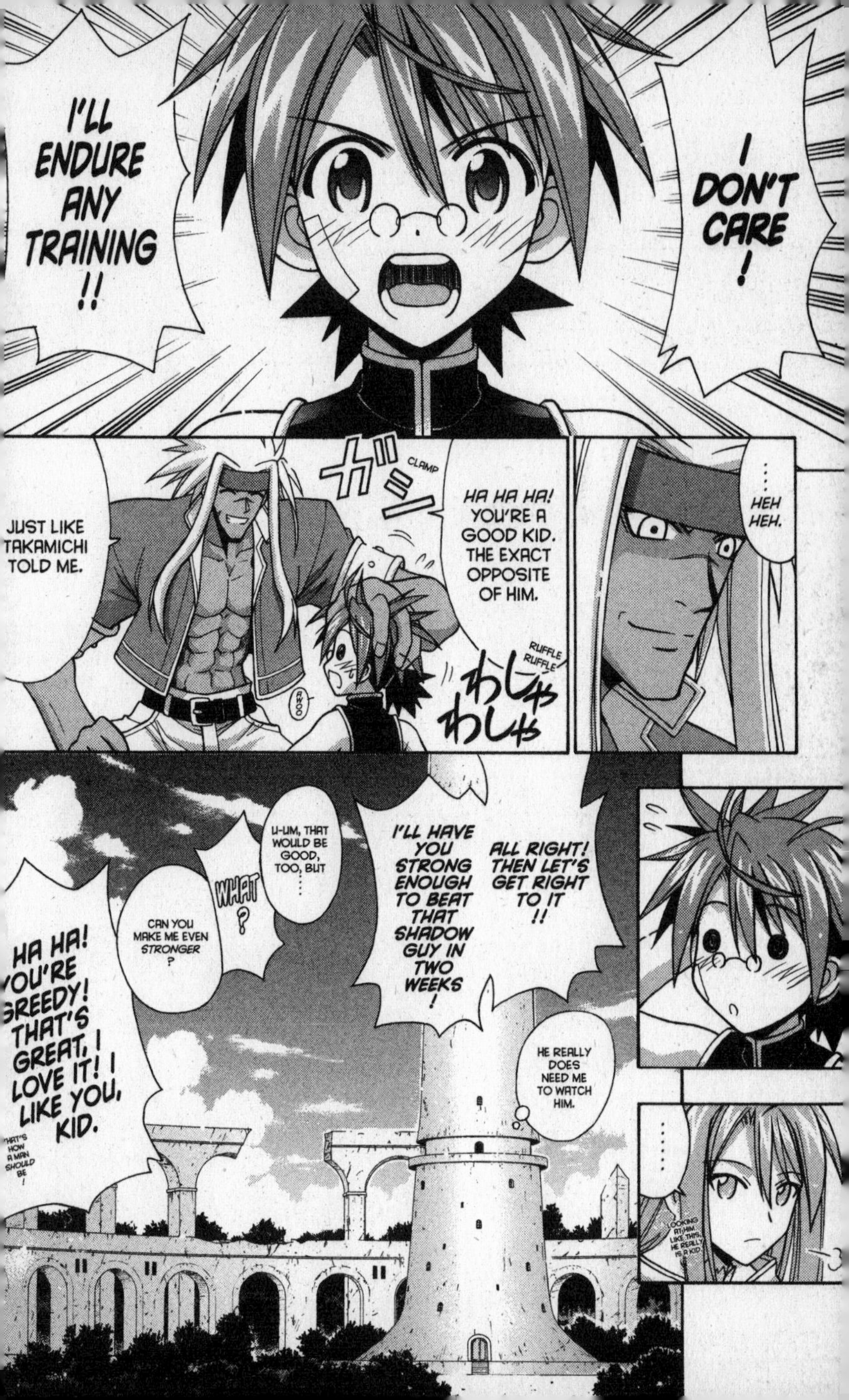
I DON'T CARE!
I'LL ENDURE ANY TRAINING!!
......HEH HEH.
CLAMP
HA HA HA! YOU'RE A GOOD KID. THE EXACT OPPOSITE OF HIM.
JUST LIKE TAKAMICHI TOLD ME.
RUFFLE RUFFLE
わしゃわしゃ
......
LOOKING AT HIM LIKE THIS, HE REALLY IS A KID
ALL RIGHT! THEN LET'S GET RIGHT TO IT!!
I'LL HAVE YOU STRONG ENOUGH TO BEAT THAT SHADOW GUY IN TWO WEEKS!
U-UM, THAT WOULD BE GOOD, TOO, BUT......
WHAT?
CAN YOU MAKE ME EVEN STRONGER?
HA HA! YOU'RE GREEDY! THAT'S GREAT, I LOVE IT! I LIKE YOU, KID.
THAT'S HOW A MAN SHOULD BE!
HE REALLY DOES NEED ME TO WATCH HIM.

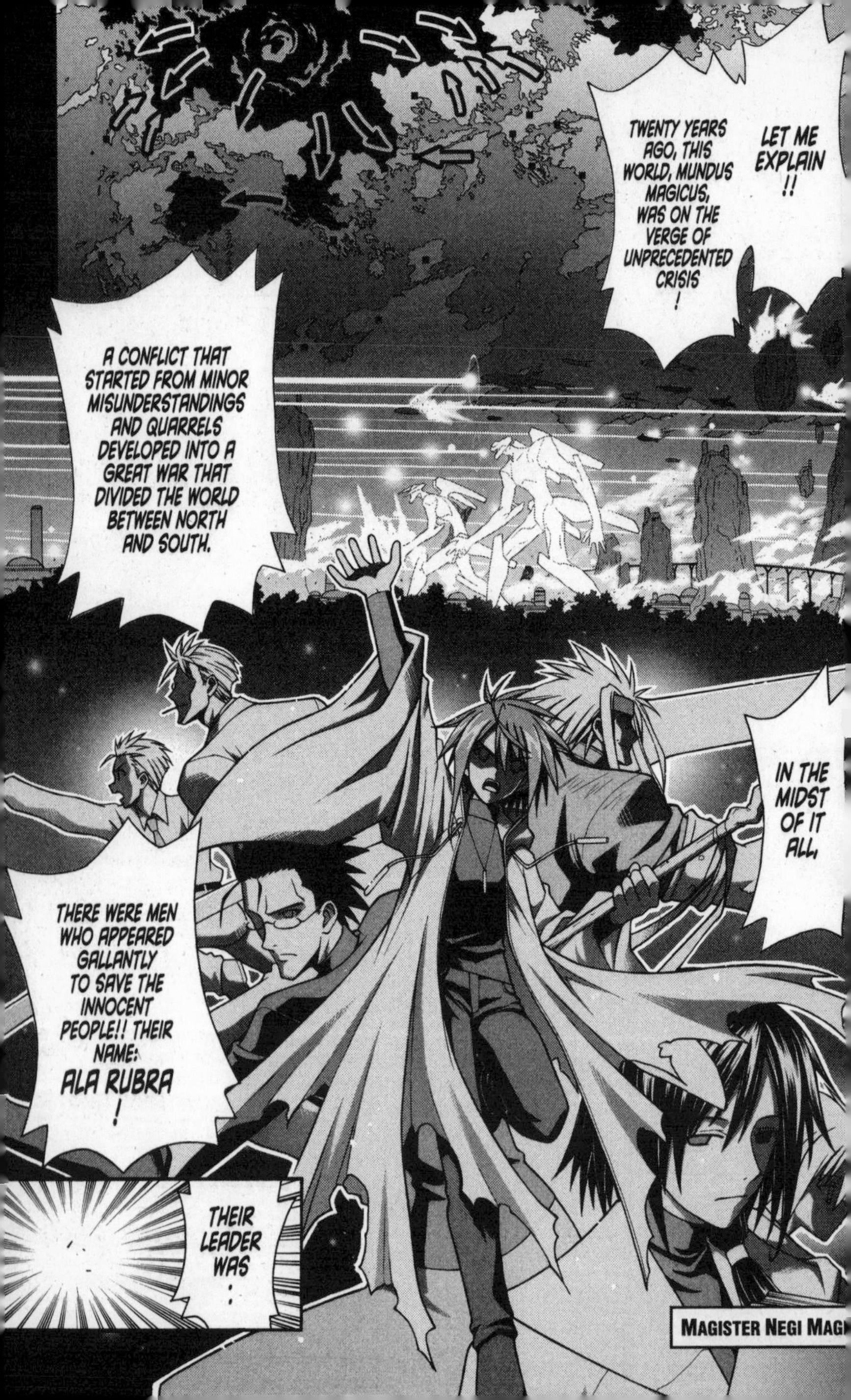
LET ME EXPLAIN !!
TWENTY YEARS AGO, THIS WORLD, MUNDUS MAGICUS, WAS ON THE VERGE OF UNPRECEDENTED CRISIS !
A CONFLICT THAT STARTED FROM MINOR MISUNDERSTANDINGS AND QUARRELS DEVELOPED INTO A GREAT WAR THAT DIVIDED THE WORLD BETWEEN NORTH AND SOUTH.
IN THE MIDST OF IT ALL,
THERE WERE MEN WHO APPEARED GALLANTLY TO SAVE THE INNOCENT PEOPLE!! THEIR NAME: ALA RUBRA !
THEIR LEADER WAS . . .

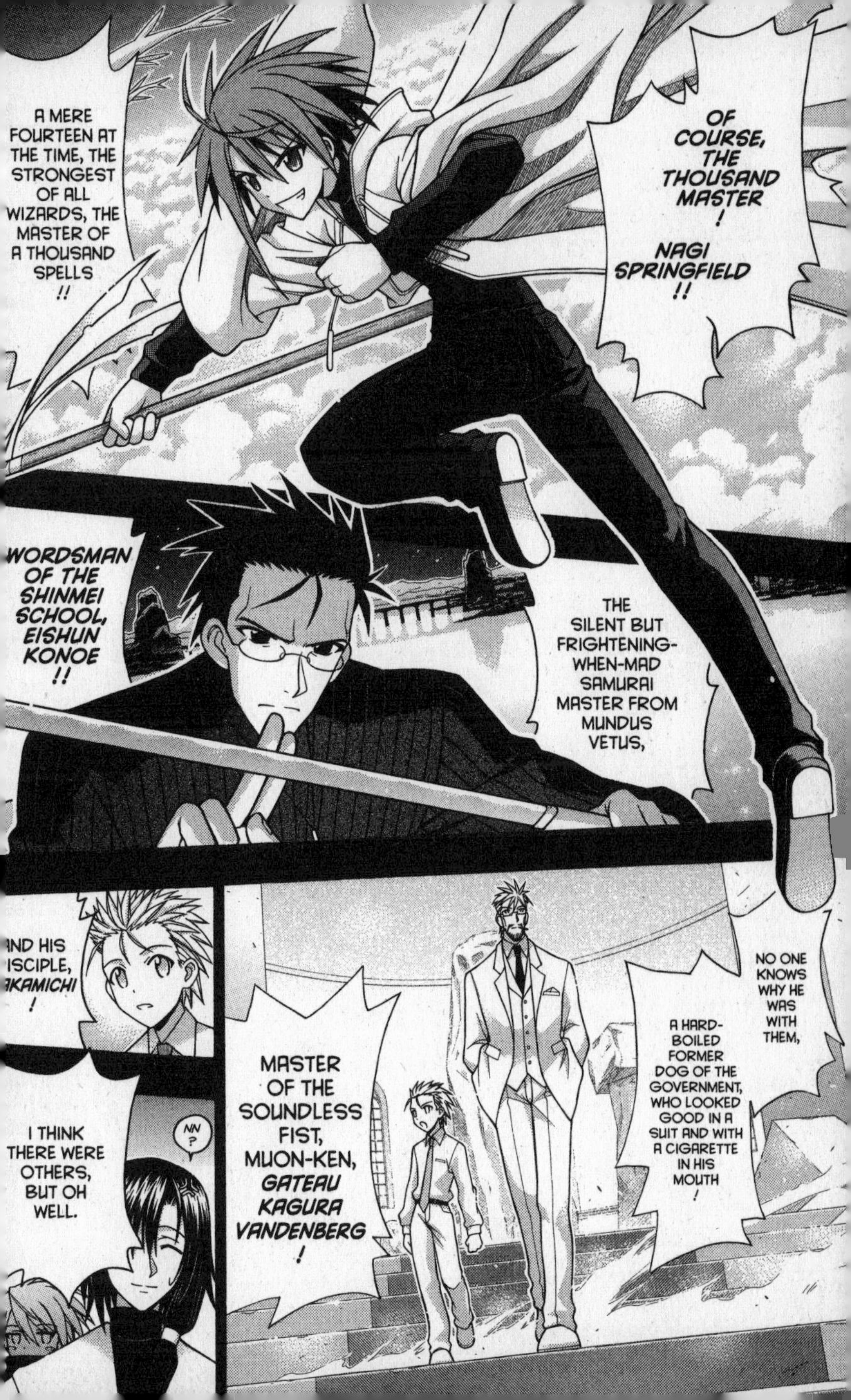
OF COURSE, THE THOUSAND MASTER! NAGI SPRINGFIELD!!
A MERE FOURTEEN AT THE TIME, THE STRONGEST OF ALL WIZARDS, THE MASTER OF A THOUSAND SPELLS!!
THE SILENT BUT FRIGHTENING-WHEN-MAD SAMURAI MASTER FROM MUNDUS VETUS,
WORDSMAN OF THE SHINMEI SCHOOL, EISHUN KONOE!!
NO ONE KNOWS WHY HE WAS WITH THEM,
A HARD-BOILED FORMER DOG OF THE GOVERNMENT, WHO LOOKED GOOD IN A SUIT AND WITH A CIGARETTE IN HIS MOUTH!
MASTER OF THE SOUNDLESS FIST, MUON-KEN, GATEAU KAGURA VANDENBERG!
ND HIS ISCIPLE, KAMICHI!
NN?
I THINK THERE WERE OTHERS, BUT OH WELL.

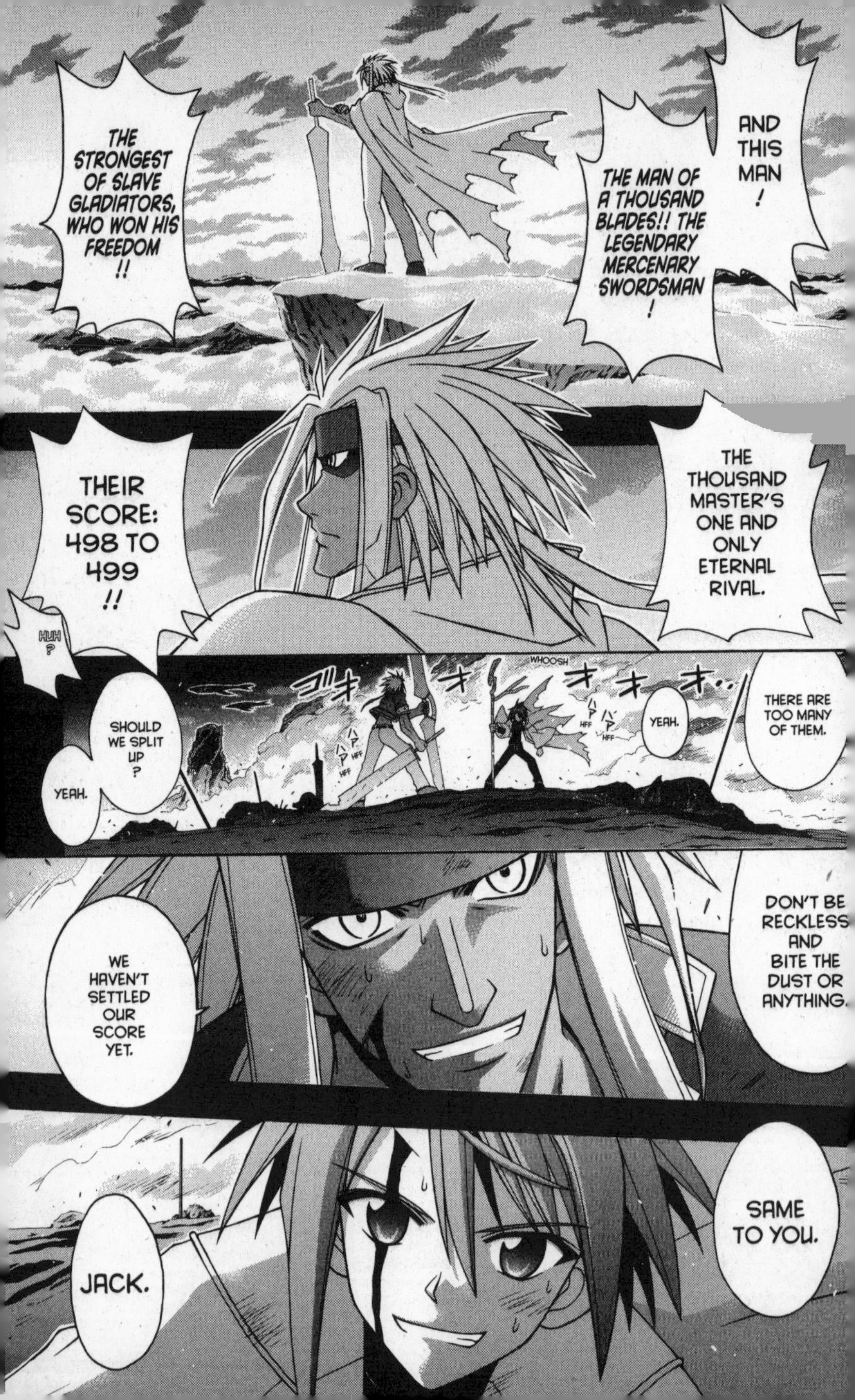
AND THIS MAN!
THE MAN OF A THOUSAND BLADES!! THE LEGENDARY MERCENARY SWORDSMAN!
THE STRONGEST OF SLAVE GLADIATORS, WHO WON HIS FREEDOM!!
THE THOUSAND MASTER'S ONE AND ONLY ETERNAL RIVAL.
THEIR SCORE: 498 TO 499!!
HUH?
THERE ARE TOO MANY OF THEM.
YEAH.
WHOOSH
HFF HFF
HFF HFF
SHOULD WE SPLIT UP?
YEAH.
DON'T BE RECKLESS AND BITE THE DUST OR ANYTHING.
WE HAVEN'T SETTLED OUR SCORE YET.
SAME TO YOU.
JACK.

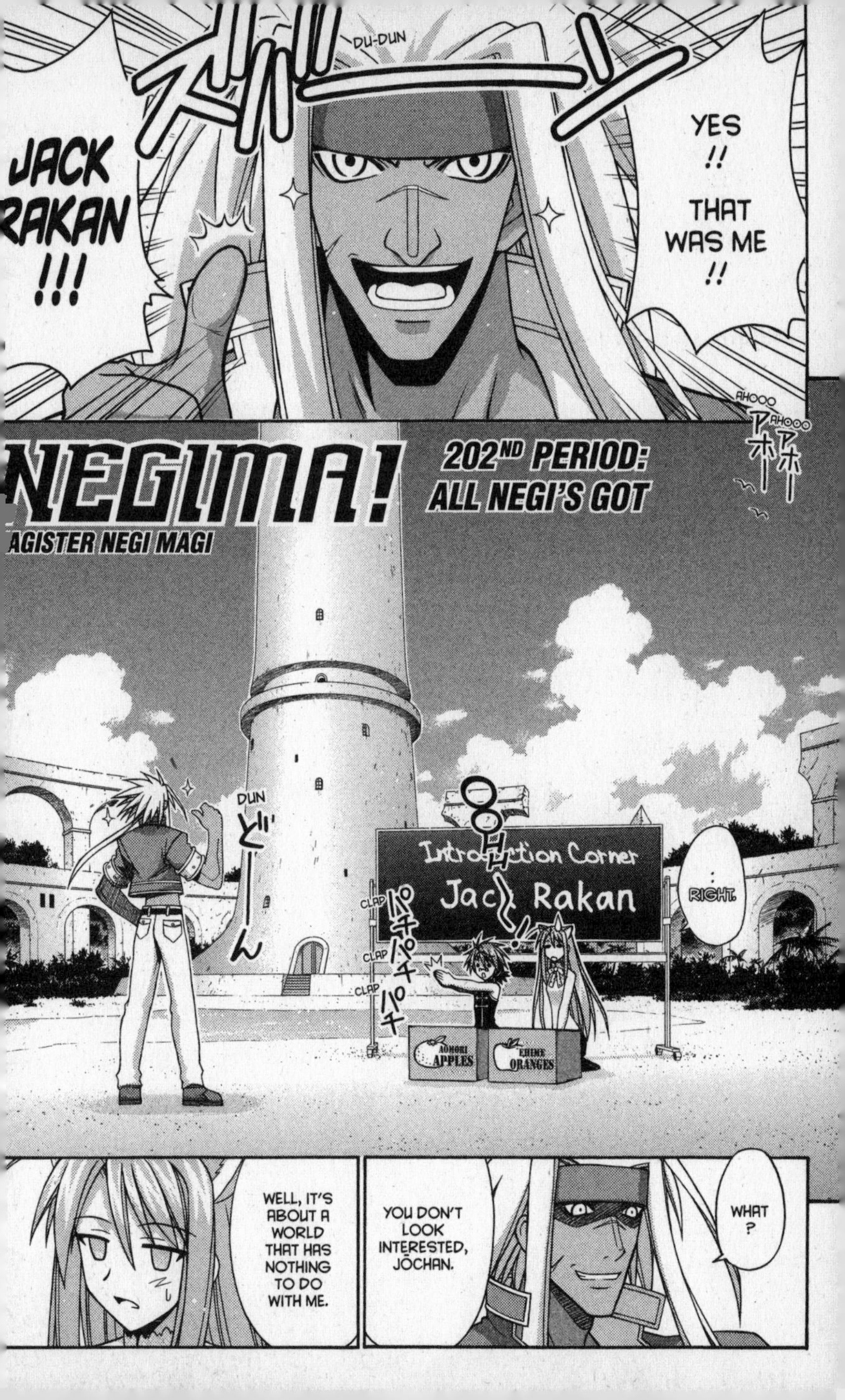
DU-DUN
YES!! THAT WAS ME!!
JACK RAKAN!!!
AHOOO
AHOOO
202ND PERIOD: ALL NEGI'S GOT
NEGIMA!
AGISTER NEGI MAGI
...RIGHT.
Introduction Corner
Jack Rakan
CLAP
CLAP
CLAP
AOMORI APPLES
EHIME ORANGES
DUN
WHAT?
YOU DON'T LOOK INTERESTED, JŌCHAN.
WELL, IT'S ABOUT A WORLD THAT HAS NOTHING TO DO WITH ME.

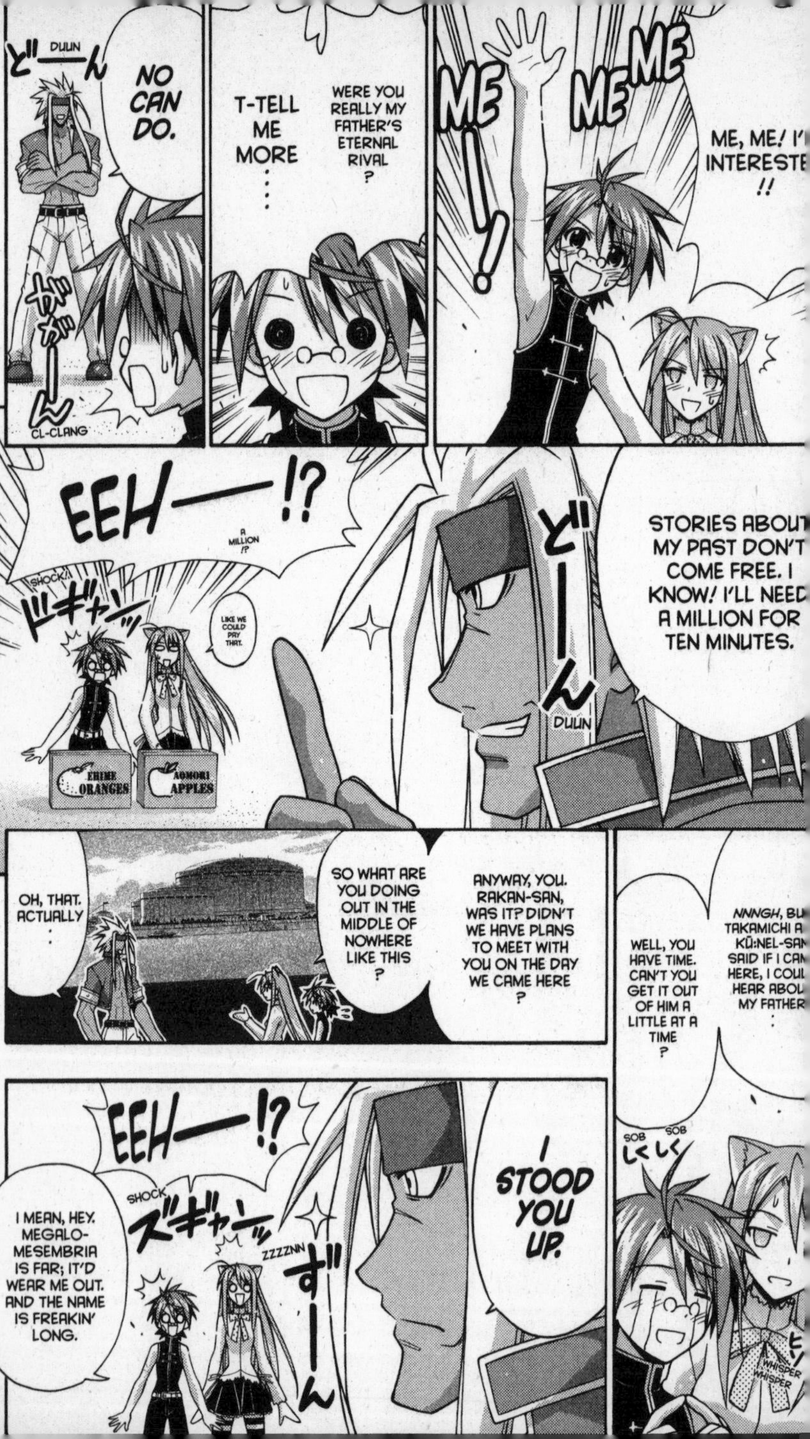
ME, ME! I'
INTERESTE
!!
ME
ME
ME
ME
!!
WERE YOU REALLY MY FATHER'S ETERNAL RIVAL?
T-TELL ME MORE......
NO CAN DO.
DUUN
CL-CLANG
STORIES ABOUT MY PAST DON'T COME FREE. I KNOW! I'LL NEED A MILLION FOR TEN MINUTES.
DUUN
EEH—!?
A MILLION!?
SHOCK
LIKE WE COULD PAY THAT.
EHIME ORANGES
AOMORI APPLES
NNNGH, BU TAKAMICHI A KŪ:NEL-SAN SAID IF I CAM HERE, I COUL HEAR ABOU MY FATHER...
WELL, YOU HAVE TIME. CAN'T YOU GET IT OUT OF HIM A LITTLE AT A TIME?
ANYWAY, YOU. RAKAN-SAN, WAS IT? DIDN'T WE HAVE PLANS TO MEET WITH YOU ON THE DAY WE CAME HERE?
SO WHAT ARE YOU DOING OUT IN THE MIDDLE OF NOWHERE LIKE THIS?
OH, THAT. ACTUALLY...
SOB
SOB
WHISPER
WHISPER
I STOOD YOU UP.
EEH—!?
SHOCK
ZZZZNN
I MEAN, HEY. MEGALO-MESEMBRIA IS FAR; IT'D WEAR ME OUT. AND THE NAME IS FREAKIN' LONG.

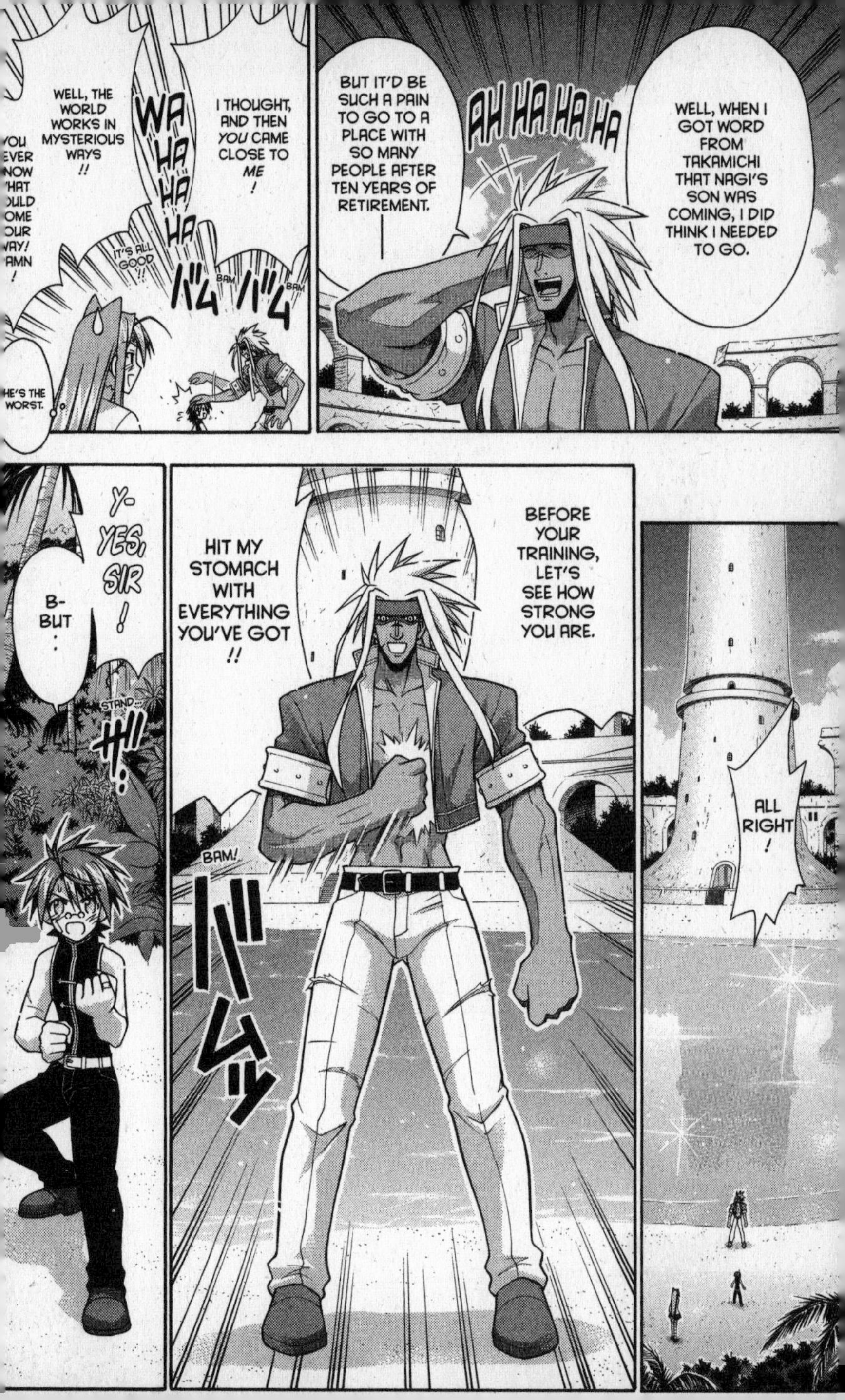

WELL, WHEN I GOT WORD FROM TAKAMICHI THAT NAGI'S SON WAS COMING, I DID THINK I NEEDED TO GO.
AH HA HA HA HA
BUT IT'D BE SUCH A PAIN TO GO TO A PLACE WITH SO MANY PEOPLE AFTER TEN YEARS OF RETIREMENT.
I THOUGHT, AND THEN YOU CAME CLOSE TO ME!
WA HA HA HA
WELL, THE WORLD WORKS IN MYSTERIOUS WAYS!!
IT'S ALL GOOD!!
BAM
BAM
HE'S THE WORST.
ALL RIGHT!
BEFORE YOUR TRAINING, LET'S SEE HOW STRONG YOU ARE.
HIT MY STOMACH WITH EVERYTHING YOU'VE GOT!!
BAM!
Y-YES, SIR!
B-BUT...
STAND...

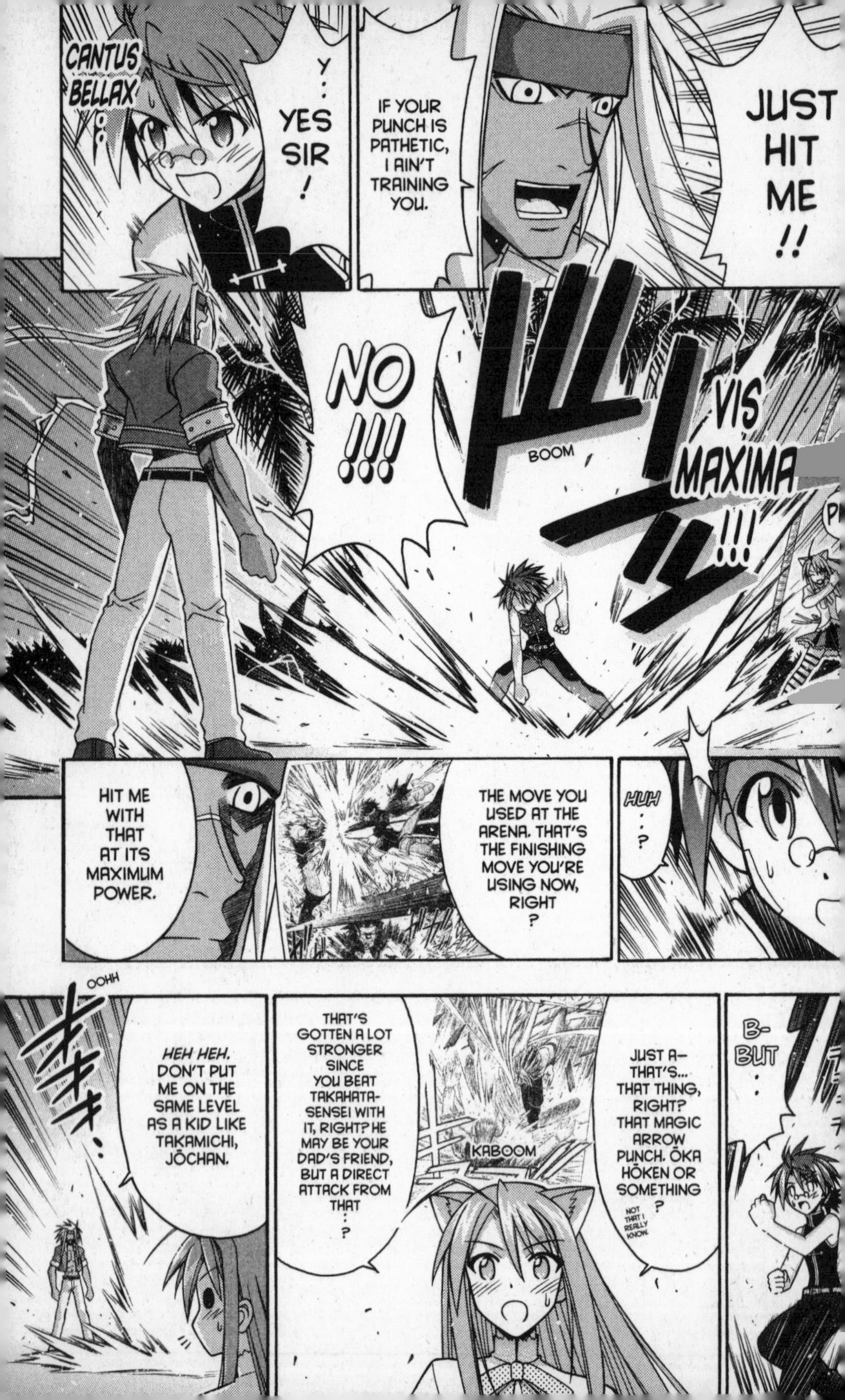
JUST HIT ME!!
IF YOUR PUNCH IS PATHETIC, I AIN'T TRAINING YOU.
Y... YES SIR!
CANTUS BELLAX...
VIS MAXIMA!!!
BOOM
NO!!!!
HUH...?
THE MOVE YOU USED AT THE ARENA. THAT'S THE FINISHING MOVE YOU'RE USING NOW, RIGHT?
HIT ME WITH THAT AT ITS MAXIMUM POWER.
B-BUT...
JUST A— THAT'S... THAT THING, RIGHT? THAT MAGIC ARROW PUNCH. ŌKA HŌKEN OR SOMETHING?
NOT THAT I REALLY KNOW.
KABOOM
THAT'S GOTTEN A LOT STRONGER SINCE YOU BEAT TAKAHATA-SENSEI WITH IT, RIGHT? HE MAY BE YOUR DAD'S FRIEND, BUT A DIRECT ATTACK FROM THAT...?
HEH HEH. DON'T PUT ME ON THE SAME LEVEL AS A KID LIKE TAKAMICHI, JŌCHAN.
OOHH

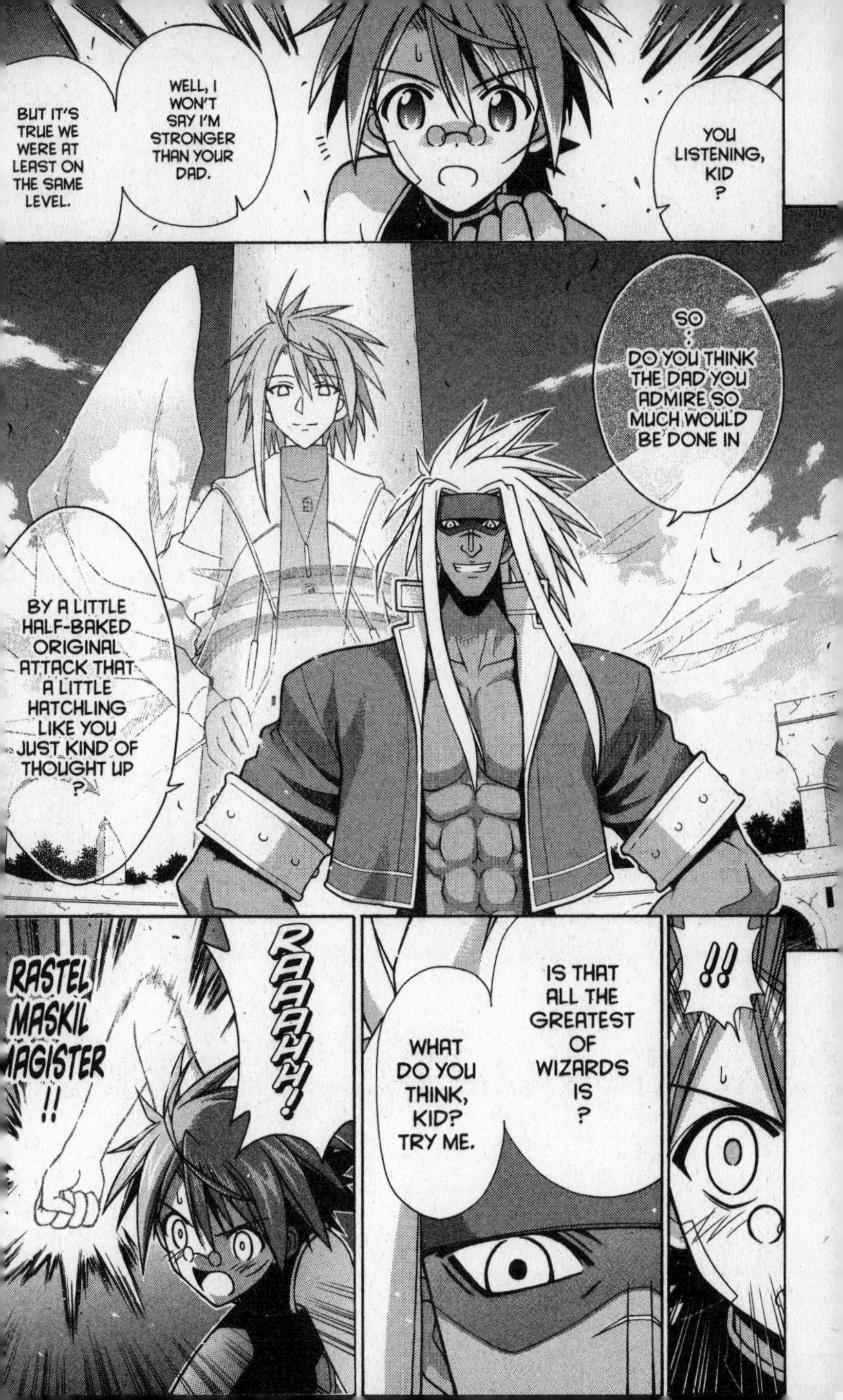
YOU LISTENING, KID?
WELL, I WON'T SAY I'M STRONGER THAN YOUR DAD.
BUT IT'S TRUE WE WERE AT LEAST ON THE SAME LEVEL.
SO... DO YOU THINK THE DAD YOU ADMIRE SO MUCH WOULD BE DONE IN
BY A LITTLE HALF-BAKED ORIGINAL ATTACK THAT A LITTLE HATCHLING LIKE YOU JUST KIND OF THOUGHT UP?
!!
IS THAT ALL THE GREATEST OF WIZARDS IS?
WHAT DO YOU THINK, KID? TRY ME.
RAAAAHH!
RASTEL MASKIL MAGISTER!!

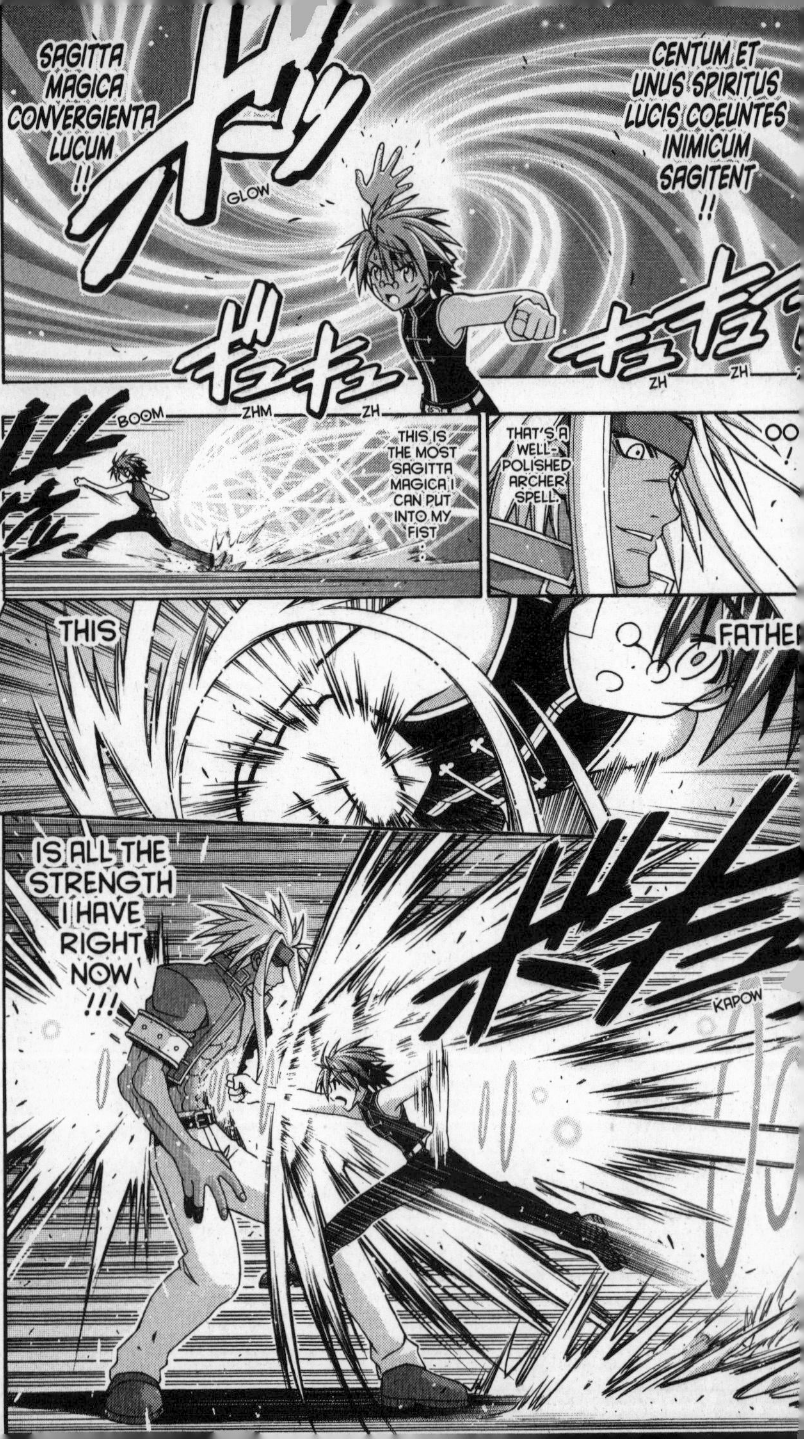

CENTUM ET UNUS SPIRITUS LUCIS COEUNTES INIMICUM SAGITENT !!
SAGITTA MAGICA CONVERGIENTA LUCUM !!
GLOW
ZH
ZH
ZH
ZHM
OO !
THAT'S A WELL-POLISHED ARCHER SPELL.
BOOM
THIS IS THE MOST SAGITTA MAGICA I CAN PUT INTO MY FIST...
FATHE
THIS
IS ALL THE STRENGTH I HAVE RIGHT NOW !!!
KAPOW

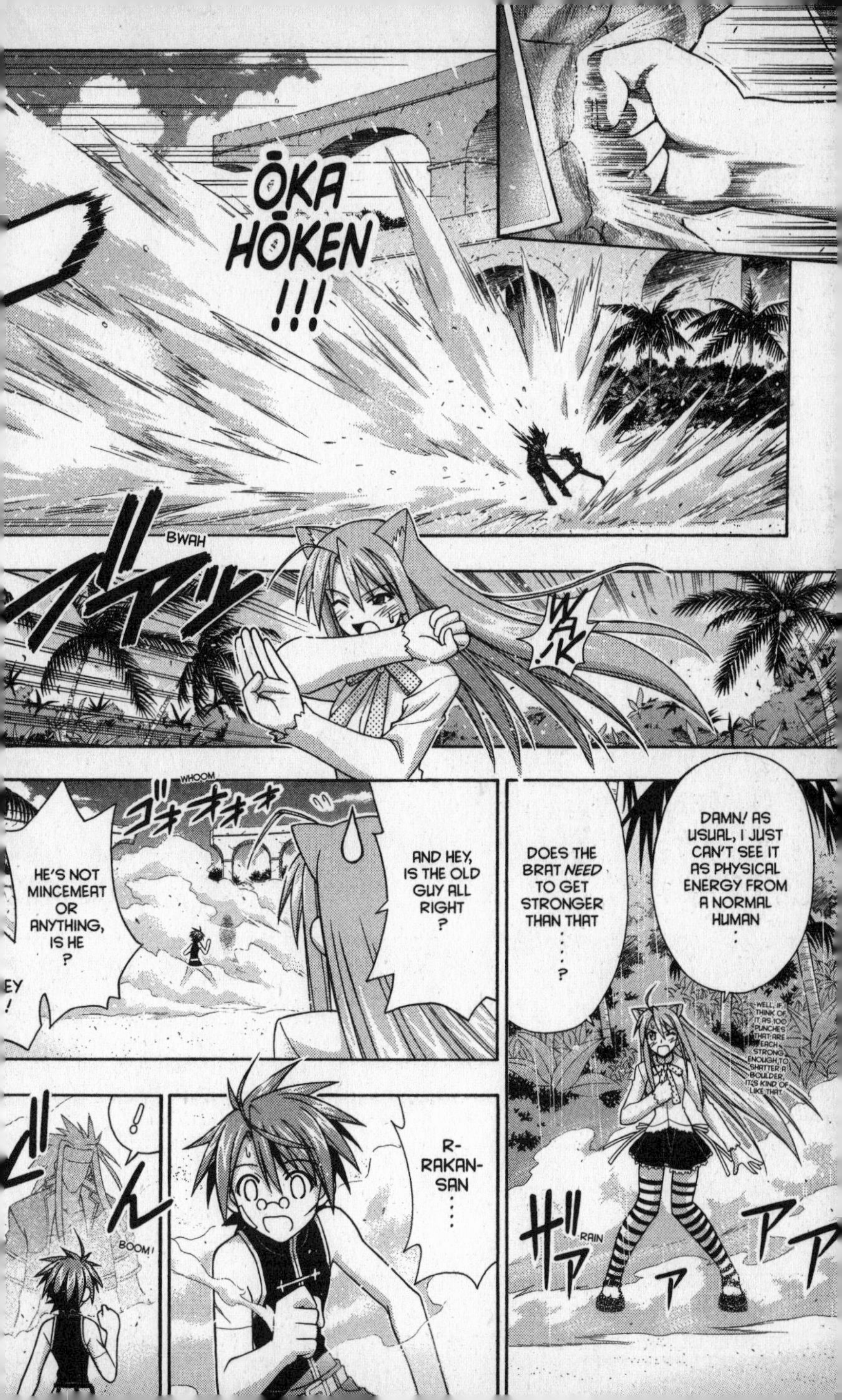
ŌKA HŌKEN !!!
BWAH
WAK!
DAMN! AS USUAL, I JUST CAN'T SEE IT AS PHYSICAL ENERGY FROM A NORMAL HUMAN.
WELL, IF I THINK OF IT AS 100 PUNCHES THAT ARE EACH STRONG ENOUGH TO SHATTER A BOULDER, IT'S KIND OF LIKE THAT.
DOES THE BRAT NEED TO GET STRONGER THAN THAT....?
RAIN
WHOOM
AND HEY, IS THE OLD GUY ALL RIGHT?
HE'S NOT MINCEMEAT OR ANYTHING, IS HE?
R-RAKAN-SAN....
!
BOOM!

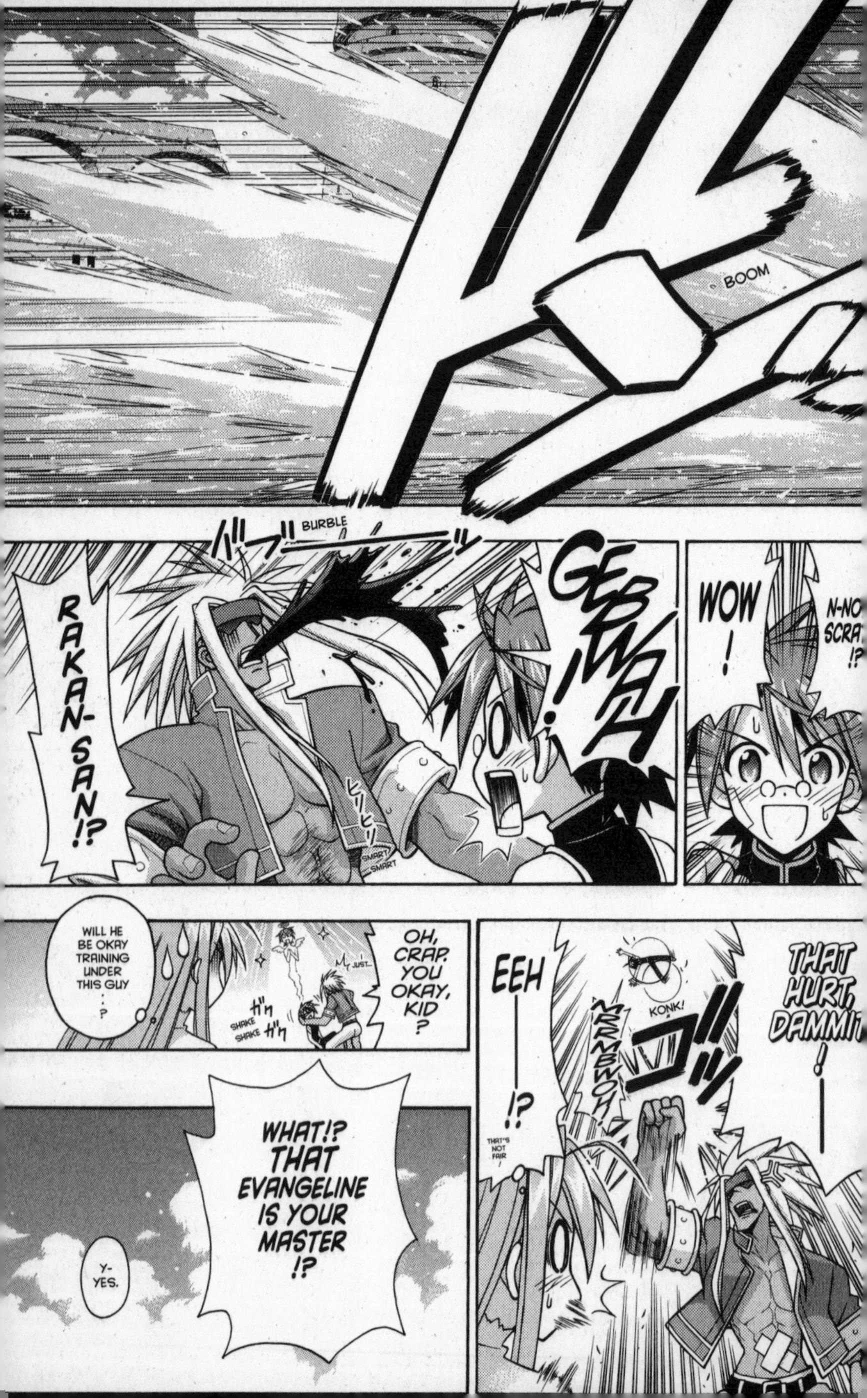

BOOM
WOW!
N-NO SCRA... !?
GEBWAH!!
BURBLE
RAKAN-SAN!?
SMART SMART
THAT HURT, DAMMIT!
KONK!
EEH—!?
MRRMBWOH!
THAT'S NOT FAIR!
OH, CRAP. YOU OKAY, KID?
JUST...
SHAKE SHAKE
WILL HE BE OKAY TRAINING UNDER THIS GUY...?
WHAT!? THAT EVANGELINE IS YOUR MASTER!?
Y-YES.

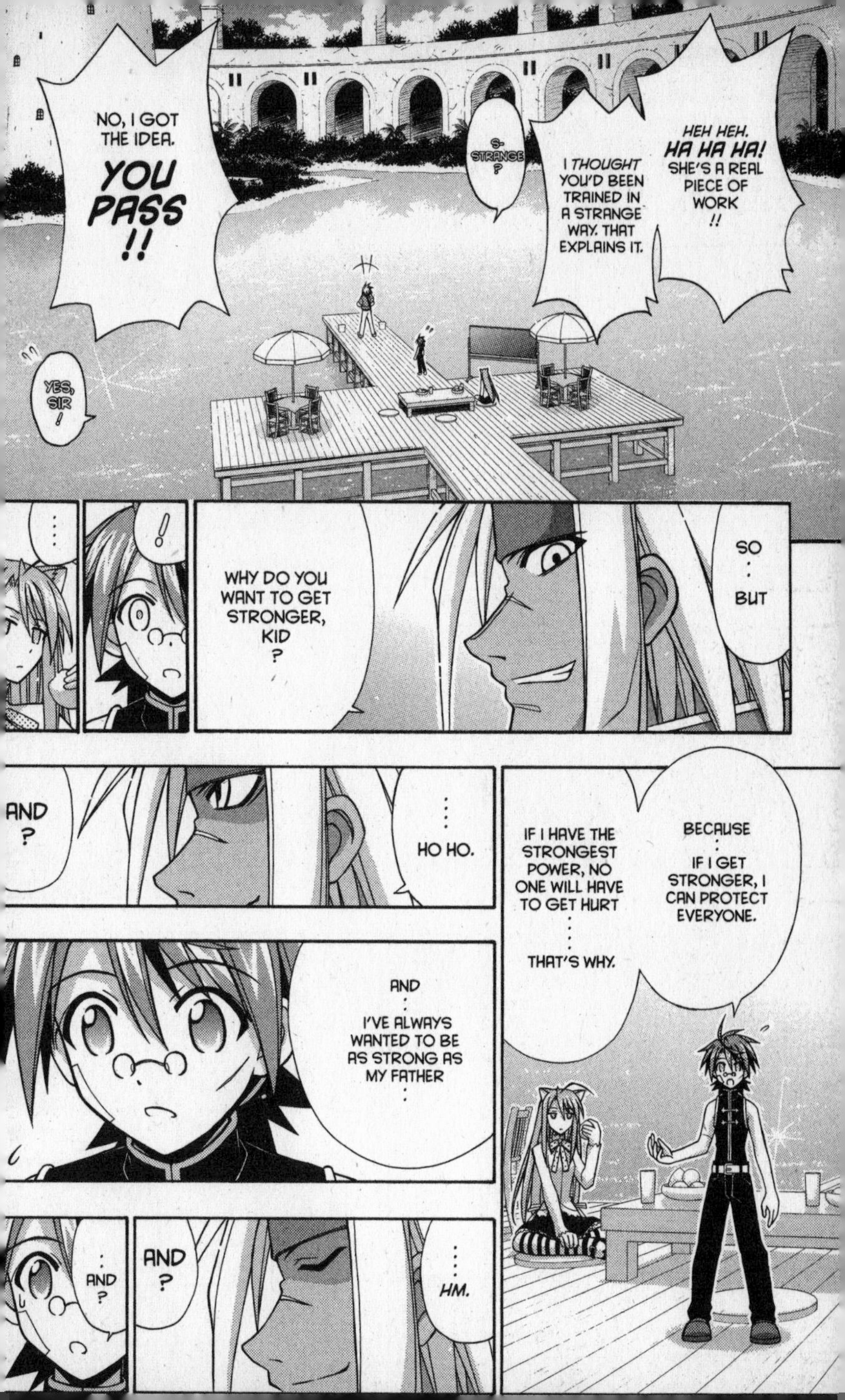
HEH HEH. HA HA HA! SHE'S A REAL PIECE OF WORK !!
I *THOUGHT* YOU'D BEEN TRAINED IN A STRANGE WAY. THAT EXPLAINS IT.
S-STRANGE ?
NO, I GOT THE IDEA. **YOU PASS !!**
YES, SIR !
SO . . . BUT
WHY DO YOU WANT TO GET STRONGER, KID ?
!
. . . .
BECAUSE . . . IF I GET STRONGER, I CAN PROTECT EVERYONE.
IF I HAVE THE STRONGEST POWER, NO ONE WILL HAVE TO GET HURT . . . THAT'S WHY.
. . . . HO HO.
AND ?
AND . . . I'VE ALWAYS WANTED TO BE AS STRONG AS MY FATHER . . .
. . . . HM.
AND ?
. . AND ?

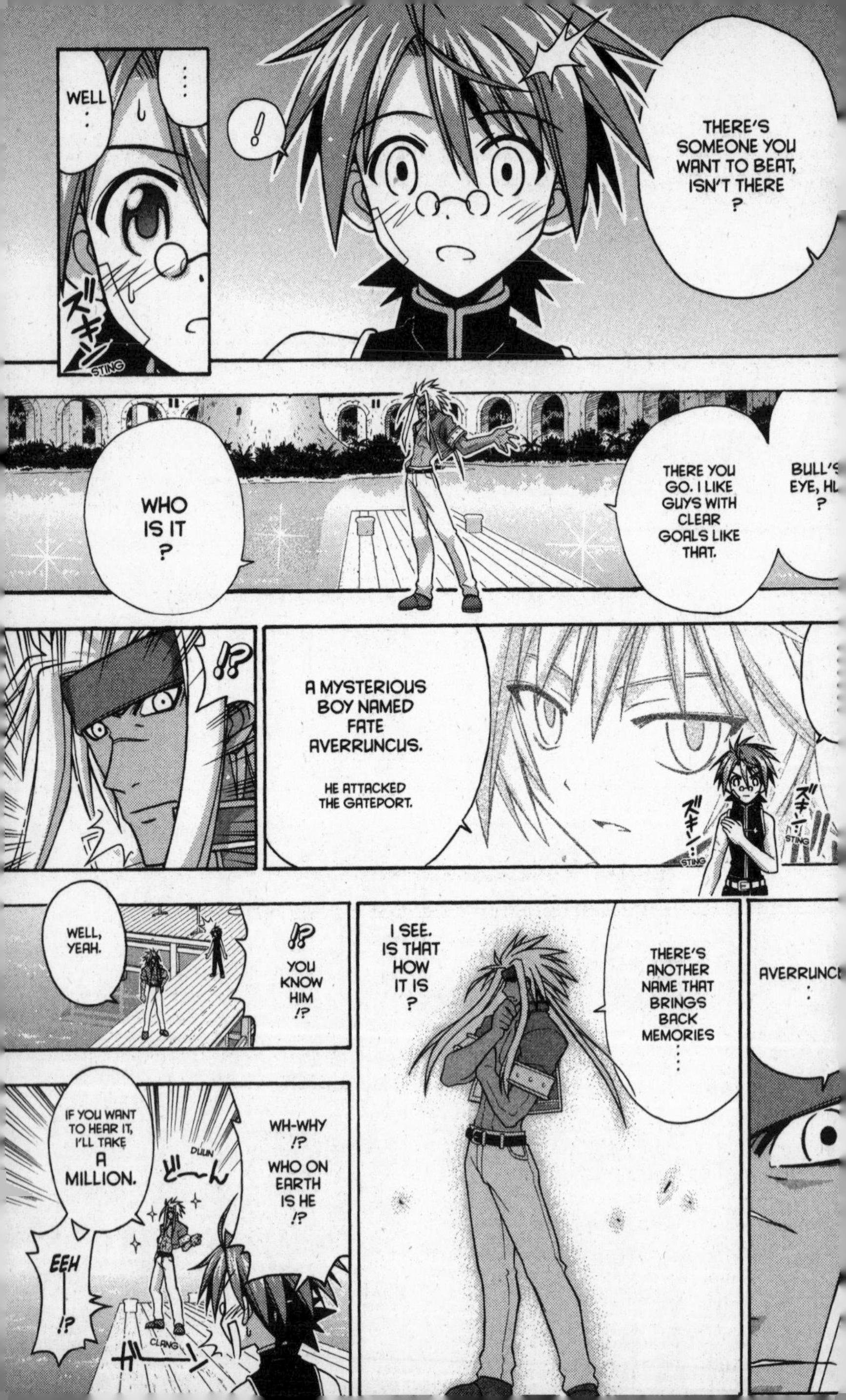

!
THERE'S SOMEONE YOU WANT TO BEAT, ISN'T THERE ?
WELL . .
. . . .
STING
BULL'S EYE, HU ?
THERE YOU GO. I LIKE GUYS WITH CLEAR GOALS LIKE THAT.
WHO IS IT ?
A MYSTERIOUS BOY NAMED FATE AVERRUNCUS.
HE ATTACKED THE GATEPORT.
STING
STING
!?
AVERRUNC :
THERE'S ANOTHER NAME THAT BRINGS BACK MEMORIES . . . .
I SEE. IS THAT HOW IT IS ?
!? YOU KNOW HIM !?
WELL, YEAH.
WH-WHY !? WHO ON EARTH IS HE !?
IF YOU WANT TO HEAR IT, I'LL TAKE A MILLION.
DUUN
EEH — !?
CLANG

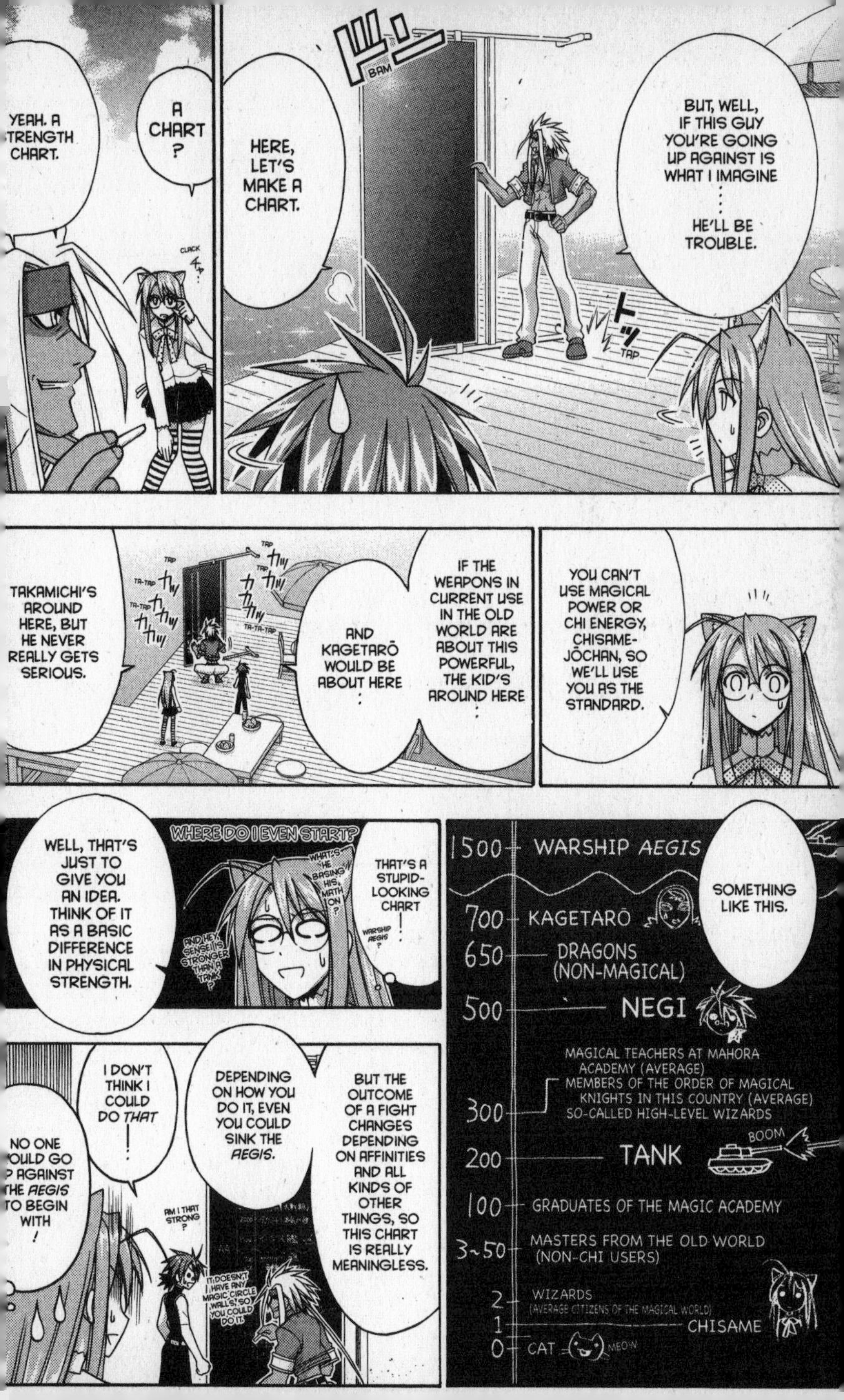
BUT, WELL, IF THIS GUY YOU'RE GOING UP AGAINST IS WHAT I IMAGINE... HE'LL BE TROUBLE.
TAP
BAM
HERE, LET'S MAKE A CHART.
A CHART?
CLACK
YEAH. A TRENGTH CHART.
YOU CAN'T USE MAGICAL POWER OR CHI ENERGY, CHISAME-JŌCHAN, SO WE'LL USE YOU AS THE STANDARD.
IF THE WEAPONS IN CURRENT USE IN THE OLD WORLD ARE ABOUT THIS POWERFUL, THE KID'S AROUND HERE...
AND KAGETARŌ WOULD BE ABOUT HERE...
TAP
TA-TAP
TA-TAP
TA-TA-TAP
TAKAMICHI'S AROUND HERE, BUT HE NEVER REALLY GETS SERIOUS.
SOMETHING LIKE THIS.
1500 WARSHIP *AEGIS*
700 KAGETARŌ
650 DRAGONS (NON-MAGICAL)
500 NEGI
MAGICAL TEACHERS AT MAHORA ACADEMY (AVERAGE)
MEMBERS OF THE ORDER OF MAGICAL KNIGHTS IN THIS COUNTRY (AVERAGE)
300 SO-CALLED HIGH-LEVEL WIZARDS
200 TANK
BOOM
100 GRADUATES OF THE MAGIC ACADEMY
3~50 MASTERS FROM THE OLD WORLD (NON-CHI USERS)
2 WIZARDS (AVERAGE CITIZENS OF THE MAGICAL WORLD)
1 CHISAME
0 CAT
MEOW
WHERE DO I EVEN START?
THAT'S A STUPID-LOOKING CHART!
WHAT'S HE BASING HIS MATH ON?
WARSHIP AEGIS?
AND HEY, SENSEI IS STRONGER THAN A TANK?
WELL, THAT'S JUST TO GIVE YOU AN IDEA. THINK OF IT AS A BASIC DIFFERENCE IN PHYSICAL STRENGTH.
BUT THE OUTCOME OF A FIGHT CHANGES DEPENDING ON AFFINITIES AND ALL KINDS OF OTHER THINGS, SO THIS CHART IS REALLY MEANINGLESS.
DEPENDING ON HOW YOU DO IT, EVEN YOU COULD SINK THE *AEGIS*.
I DON'T THINK I COULD DO *THAT*!
NO ONE OULD GO P AGAINST THE *AEGIS* TO BEGIN WITH!
AM I THAT STRONG?
IT DOESN'T HAVE ANY MAGIC CIRCLE WALLS, SO YOU COULD DO IT.

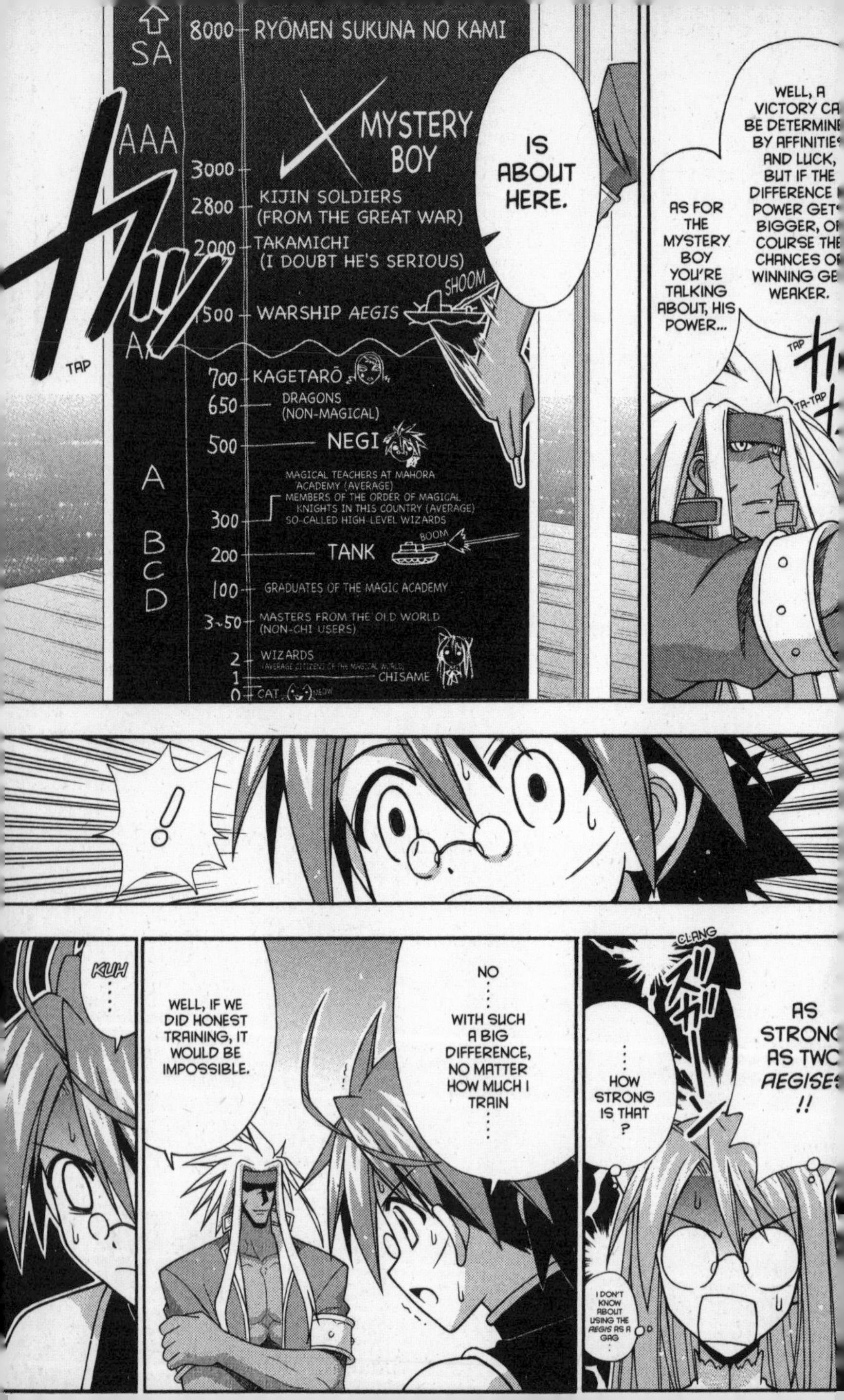
WELL, A VICTORY CA BE DETERMINE BY AFFINITIE AND LUCK, BUT IF THE DIFFERENCE I POWER GET BIGGER, OF COURSE THE CHANCES OF WINNING GE WEAKER.
AS FOR THE MYSTERY BOY YOU'RE TALKING ABOUT, HIS POWER...
TAP
TA-TAP
8000 RYŌMEN SUKUNA NO KAMI
SA
AAA
MYSTERY BOY
3000
2800 KIJIN SOLDIERS (FROM THE GREAT WAR)
2000 TAKAMICHI (I DOUBT HE'S SERIOUS)
1500 WARSHIP AEGIS
SHOOM
AA
700 KAGETARŌ
650 DRAGONS (NON-MAGICAL)
500 NEGI
A
MAGICAL TEACHERS AT MAHORA ACADEMY (AVERAGE)
MEMBERS OF THE ORDER OF MAGICAL KNIGHTS IN THIS COUNTRY (AVERAGE)
300 SO-CALLED HIGH-LEVEL WIZARDS
B
200 TANK
BOOM
C
100 GRADUATES OF THE MAGIC ACADEMY
D
3~50 MASTERS FROM THE OLD WORLD (NON-CHI USERS)
2 WIZARDS (AVERAGE CITIZENS OF THE MAGICAL WORLD)
1 CHISAME
0 CAT
MEOW
IS ABOUT HERE.
TAP
!
CLANG
AS STRONC AS TWC AEGISE !!
...HOW STRONG IS THAT?
I DON'T KNOW ABOUT USING THE AEGIS AS A GAG...
NO... WITH SUCH A BIG DIFFERENCE, NO MATTER HOW MUCH I TRAIN....
WELL, IF WE DID HONEST TRAINING, IT WOULD BE IMPOSSIBLE.
KUH...

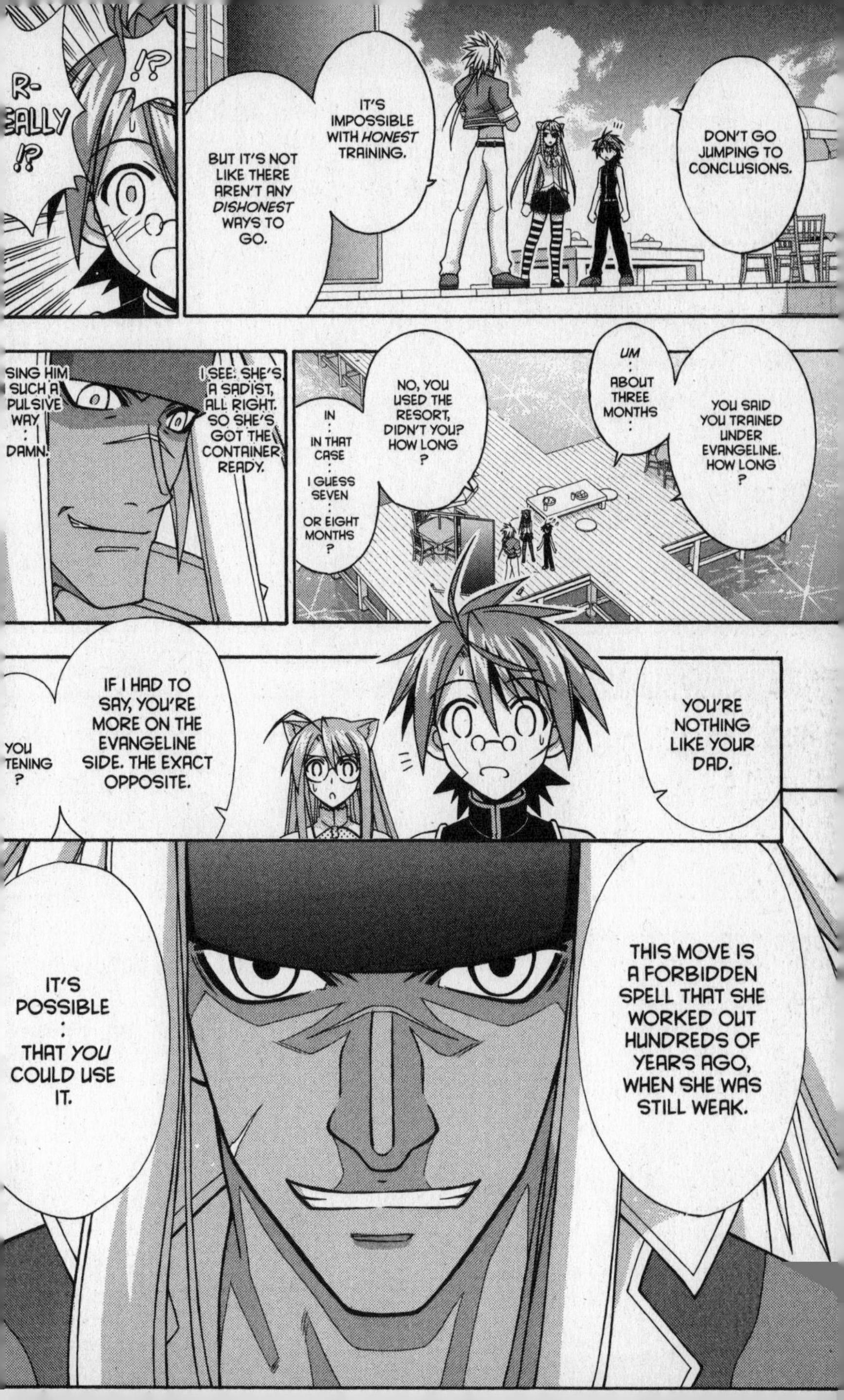
DON'T GO JUMPING TO CONCLUSIONS.
IT'S IMPOSSIBLE WITH *HONEST* TRAINING.
BUT IT'S NOT LIKE THERE AREN'T ANY *DISHONEST* WAYS TO GO.
!?
R-EALLY !?
YOU SAID YOU TRAINED UNDER EVANGELINE. HOW LONG ?
UM : ABOUT THREE MONTHS :
NO, YOU USED THE RESORT, DIDN'T YOU? HOW LONG ?
IN : IN THAT CASE : I GUESS SEVEN : OR EIGHT MONTHS ?
I SEE. SHE'S A SADIST, ALL RIGHT. SO SHE'S GOT THE CONTAINER READY.
SING HIM SUCH A PULSIVE WAY : DAMN.
YOU'RE NOTHING LIKE YOUR DAD.
IF I HAD TO SAY, YOU'RE MORE ON THE EVANGELINE SIDE. THE EXACT OPPOSITE.
YOU TENING ?
THIS MOVE IS A FORBIDDEN SPELL THAT SHE WORKED OUT HUNDREDS OF YEARS AGO, WHEN SHE WAS STILL WEAK.
IT'S POSSIBLE : THAT *YOU* COULD USE IT.

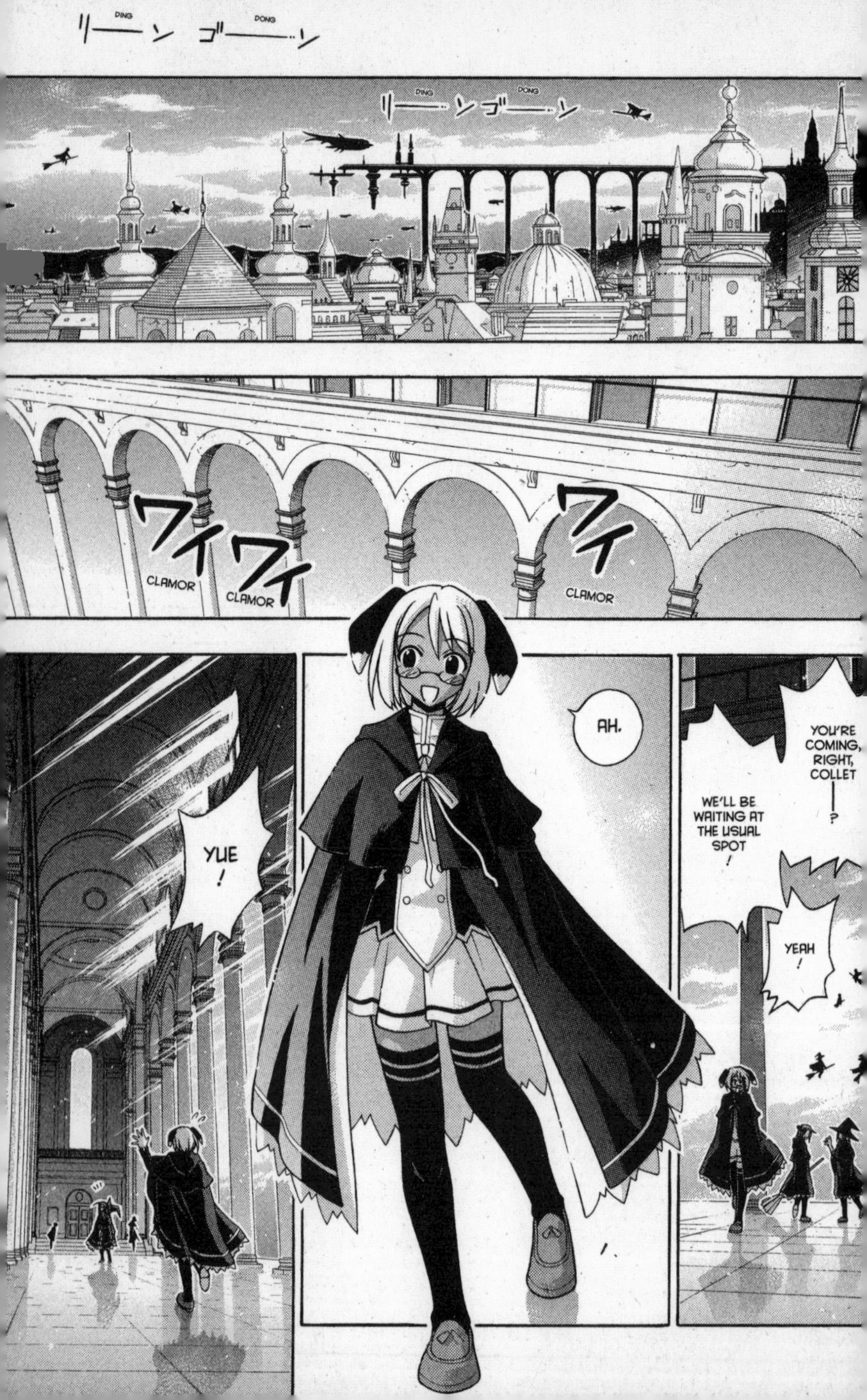

DING DONG
リーン ゴーン
DING DONG
リーンゴーン
ワイ
CLAMOR
ワイワイ
CLAMOR
CLAMOR
YOU'RE COMING, RIGHT, COLLET—?
WE'LL BE WAITING AT THE USUAL SPOT!
YEAH!
AH.
YUE!

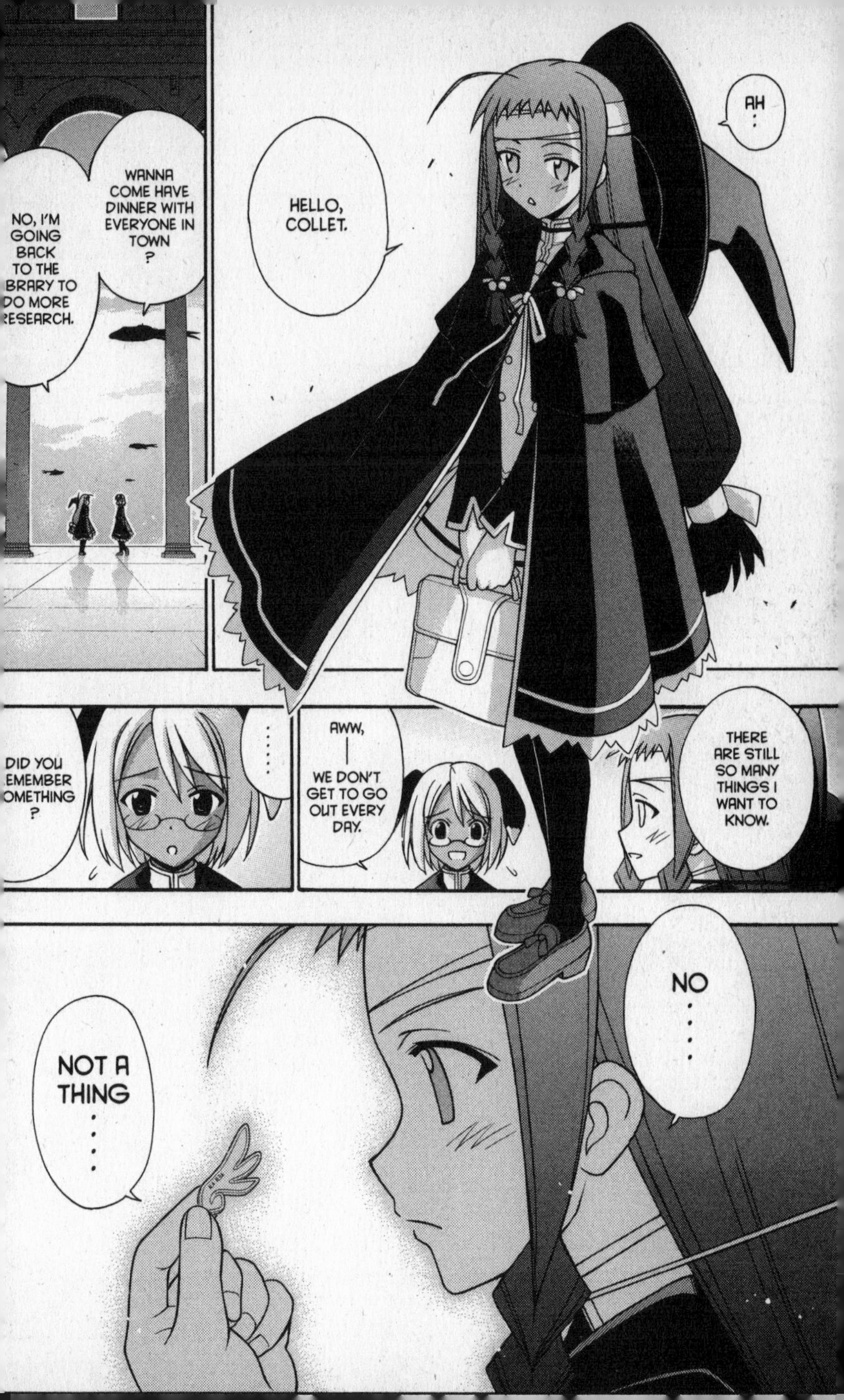
AH...
HELLO, COLLET.
WANNA COME HAVE DINNER WITH EVERYONE IN TOWN?
NO, I'M GOING BACK TO THE BRARY TO DO MORE ESEARCH.
THERE ARE STILL SO MANY THINGS I WANT TO KNOW.
AWW, — WE DON'T GET TO GO OUT EVERY DAY.
......
DID YOU EMEMBER OMETHING?
NO.....
NOT A THING.....

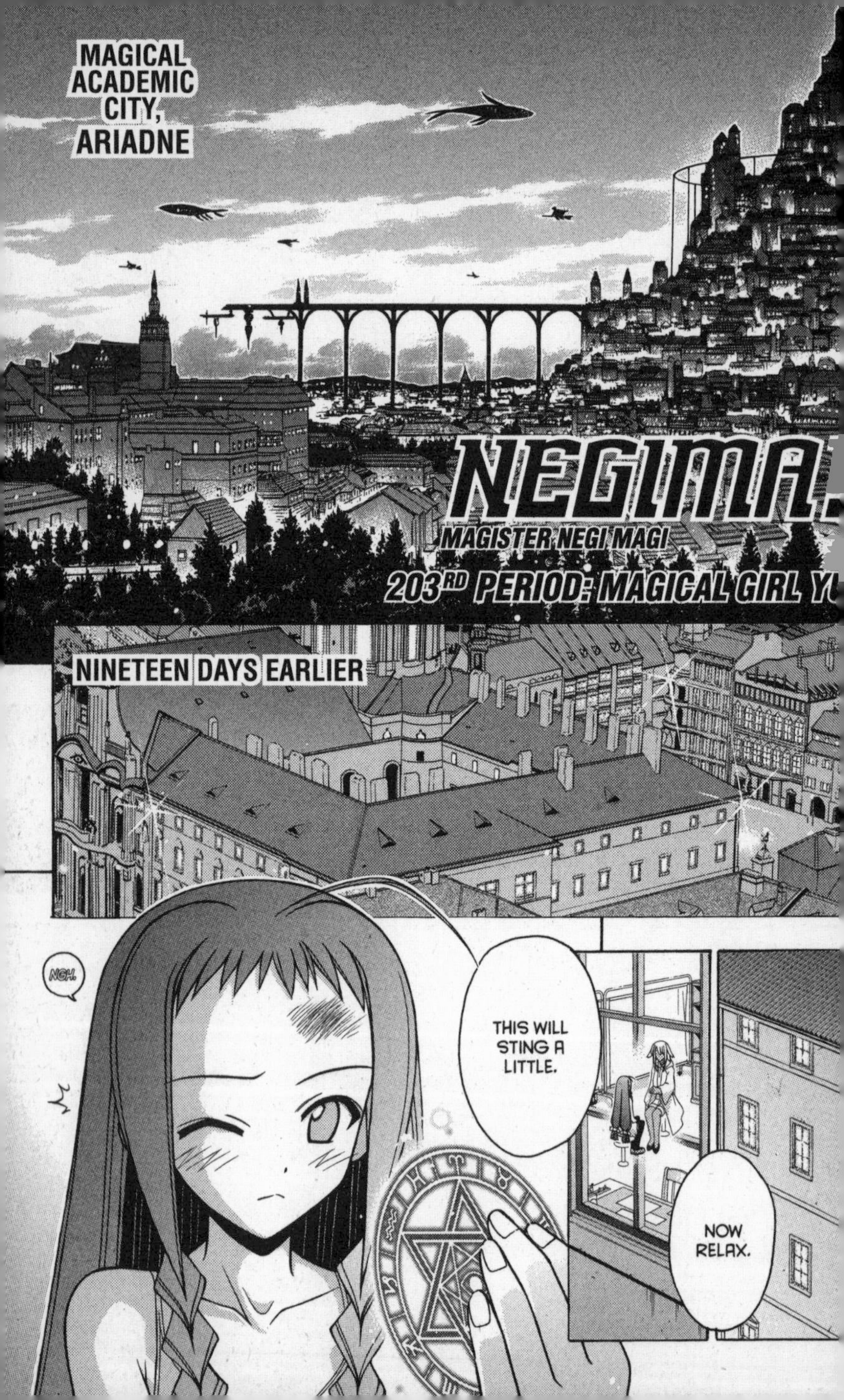
MAGICAL ACADEMIC CITY, ARIADNE
NEGIMA
MAGISTER NEGI MAGI
203RD PERIOD: MAGICAL GIRL YU
NINETEEN DAYS EARLIER
THIS WILL STING A LITTLE.
NOW RELAX.
NGH.

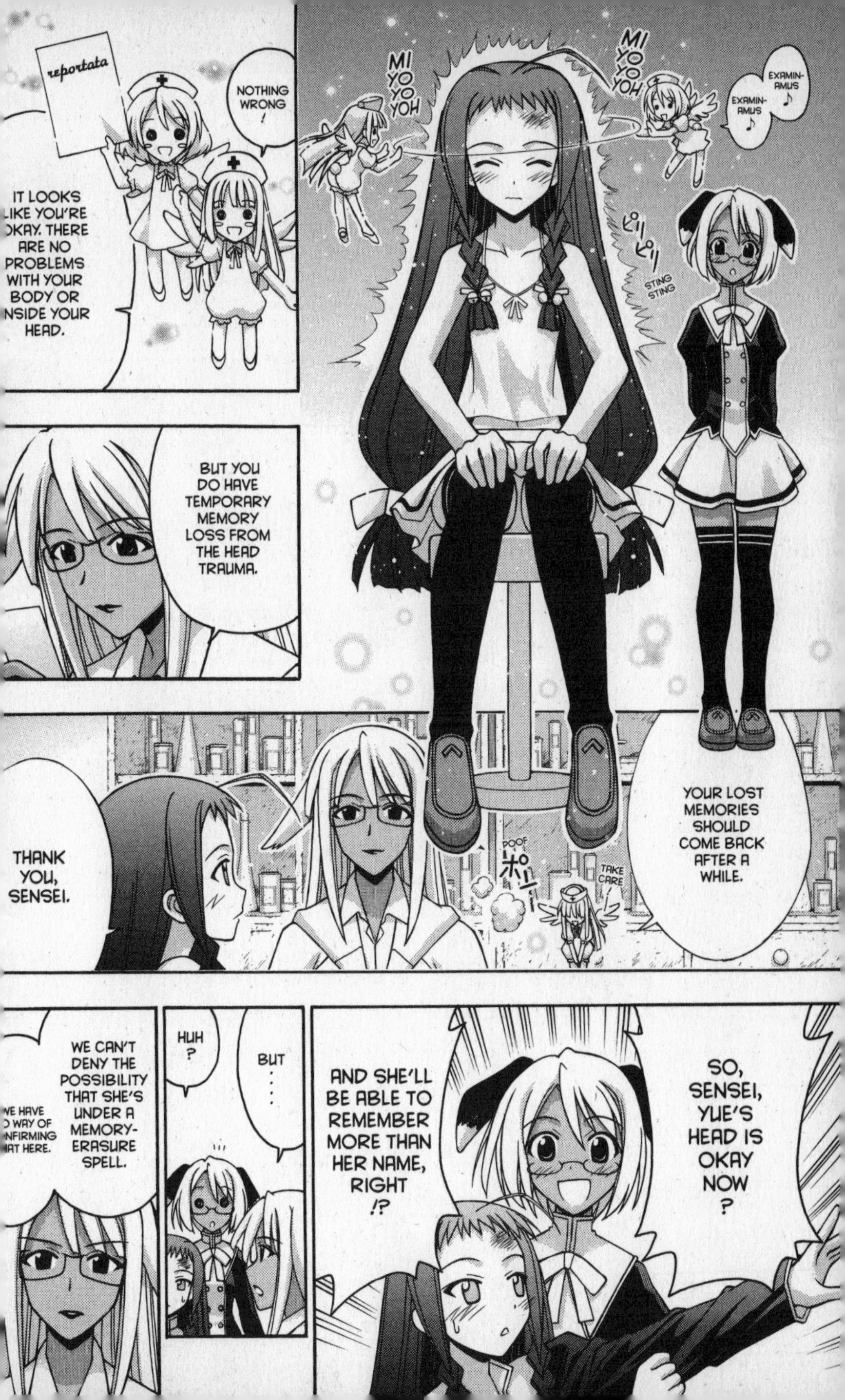
MI YO YO YOH
EXAMIN-AMUS ♪
EXAMIN-AMUS ♪
MI YO YO YOH
ピリ ピリ
STING STING
reportata
NOTHING WRONG!
IT LOOKS IKE YOU'RE OKAY. THERE ARE NO PROBLEMS WITH YOUR BODY OR NSIDE YOUR HEAD.
BUT YOU DO HAVE TEMPORARY MEMORY LOSS FROM THE HEAD TRAUMA.
YOUR LOST MEMORIES SHOULD COME BACK AFTER A WHILE.
POOF
ポン
TAKE CARE!
THANK YOU, SENSEI.
SO, SENSEI, YUE'S HEAD IS OKAY NOW?
AND SHE'LL BE ABLE TO REMEMBER MORE THAN HER NAME, RIGHT!?
BUT...
HUH?
WE CAN'T DENY THE POSSIBILITY THAT SHE'S UNDER A MEMORY-ERASURE SPELL.
E HAVE O WAY OF NFIRMING AT HERE.

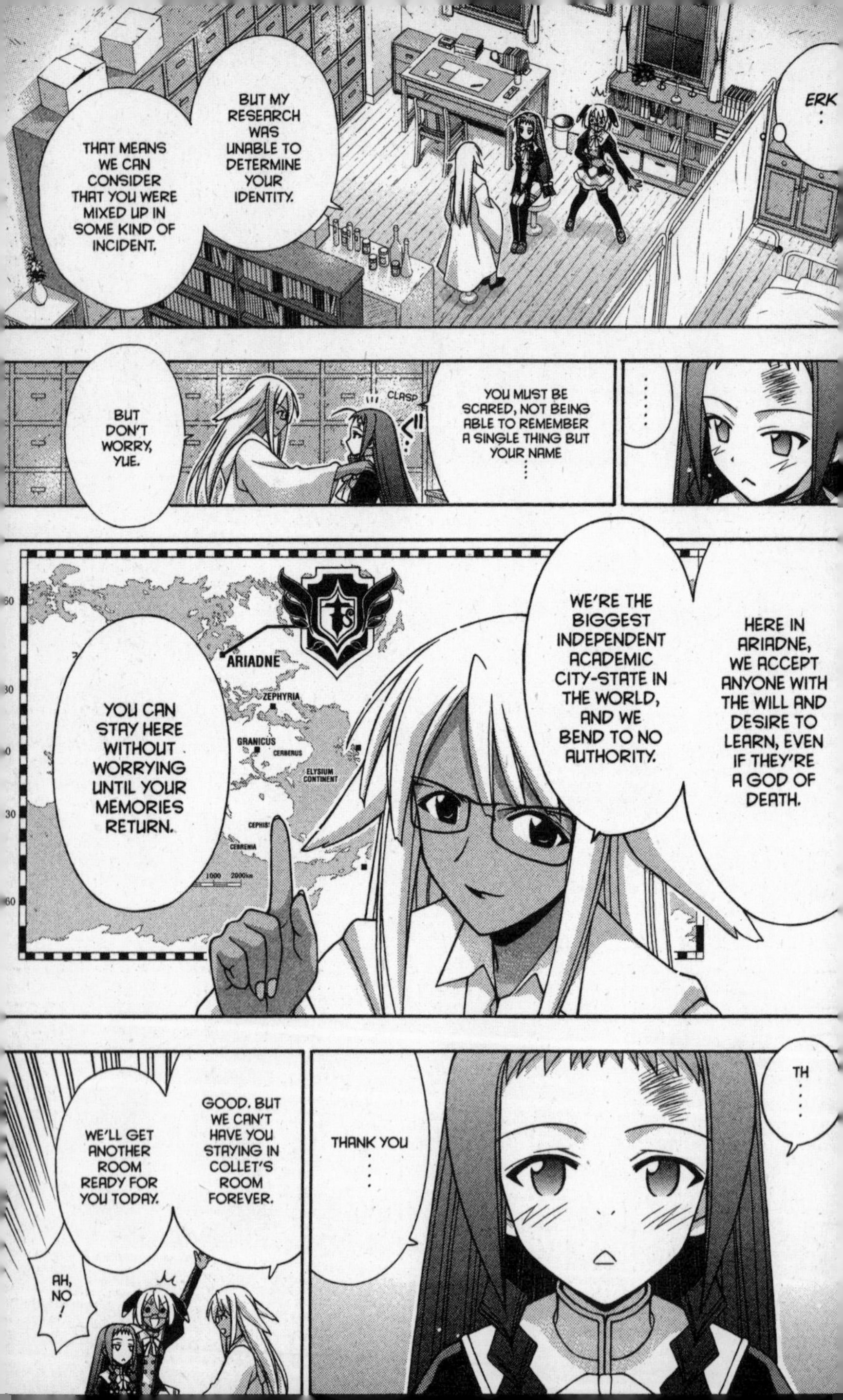
ERK
...
BUT MY RESEARCH WAS UNABLE TO DETERMINE YOUR IDENTITY.
THAT MEANS WE CAN CONSIDER THAT YOU WERE MIXED UP IN SOME KIND OF INCIDENT.
......
YOU MUST BE SCARED, NOT BEING ABLE TO REMEMBER A SINGLE THING BUT YOUR NAME ...
CLASP
BUT DON'T WORRY, YUE.
HERE IN ARIADNE, WE ACCEPT ANYONE WITH THE WILL AND DESIRE TO LEARN, EVEN IF THEY'RE A GOD OF DEATH.
WE'RE THE BIGGEST INDEPENDENT ACADEMIC CITY-STATE IN THE WORLD, AND WE BEND TO NO AUTHORITY.
ARIADNE
ZEPHYRIA
GRANICUS
CERBERUS
ELYSIUM CONTINENT
CEBRENIA
1000 2000km
YOU CAN STAY HERE WITHOUT WORRYING UNTIL YOUR MEMORIES RETURN.
TH ...
THANK YOU ...
GOOD. BUT WE CAN'T HAVE YOU STAYING IN COLLET'S ROOM FOREVER.
WE'LL GET ANOTHER ROOM READY FOR YOU TODAY.
AH, NO!

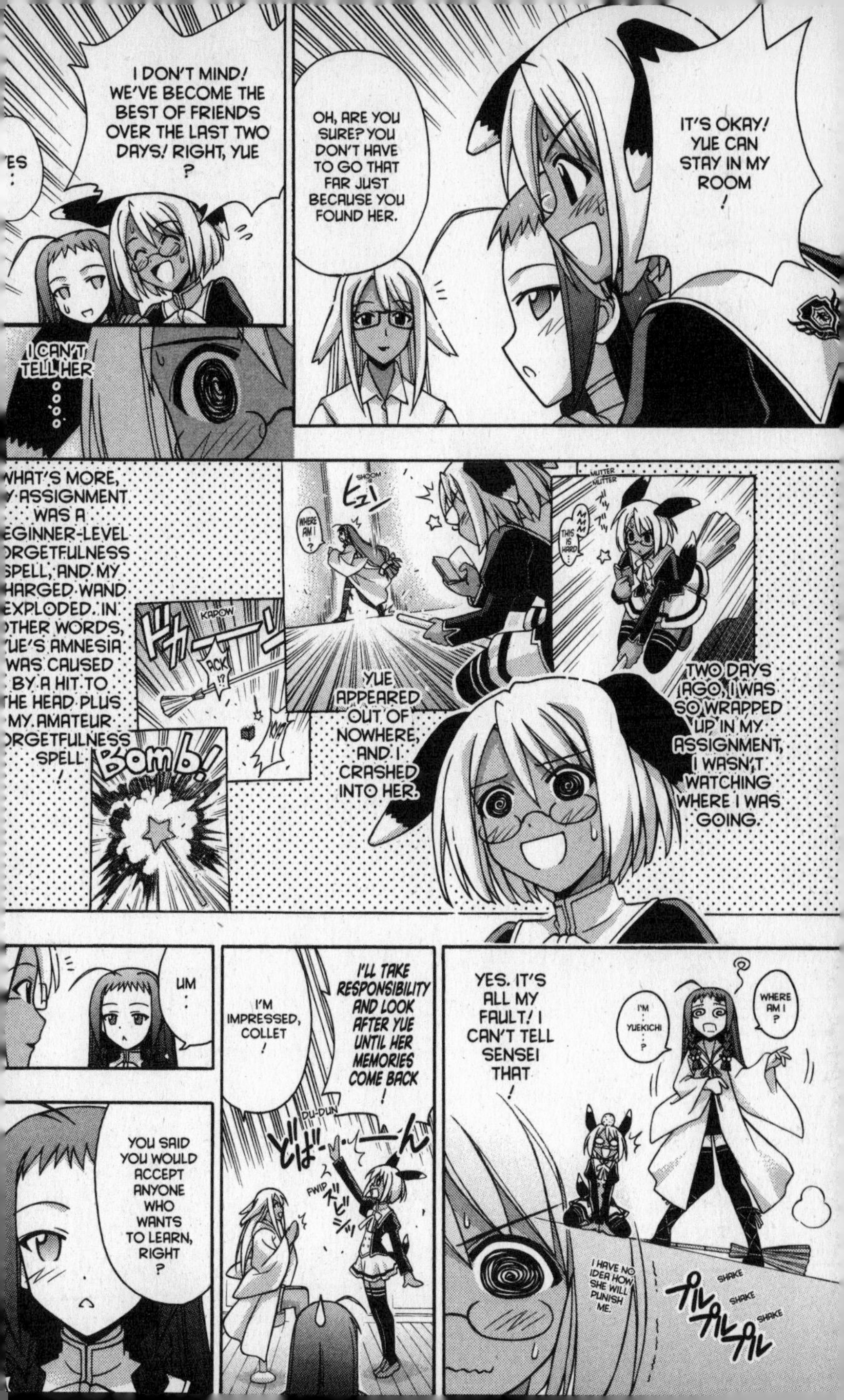
IT'S OKAY! YUE CAN STAY IN MY ROOM!
OH, ARE YOU SURE? YOU DON'T HAVE TO GO THAT FAR JUST BECAUSE YOU FOUND HER.
I DON'T MIND! WE'VE BECOME THE BEST OF FRIENDS OVER THE LAST TWO DAYS! RIGHT, YUE?
YES...
I CAN'T TELL HER....
TWO DAYS AGO, I WAS SO WRAPPED UP IN MY ASSIGNMENT, I WASN'T WATCHING WHERE I WAS GOING.
MUTTER MUTTER
THIS IS HARD...
SHOOM
WHERE AM I?
YUE APPEARED OUT OF NOWHERE, AND I CRASHED INTO HER.
KAPOW
ACK!?
Bomb!
WHAT'S MORE, Y ASSIGNMENT WAS A EGINNER-LEVEL ORGETFULNESS SPELL, AND MY HARGED WAND EXPLODED. IN OTHER WORDS, YUE'S AMNESIA WAS CAUSED BY A HIT TO THE HEAD PLUS MY AMATEUR ORGETFULNESS SPELL!
WHERE AM I?
I'M YUEKICHI...?
YES. IT'S ALL MY FAULT! I CAN'T TELL SENSEI THAT!
I HAVE NO IDEA HOW SHE WILL PUNISH ME.
SHAKE SHAKE SHAKE
I'LL TAKE RESPONSIBILITY AND LOOK AFTER YUE UNTIL HER MEMORIES COME BACK!
I'M IMPRESSED, COLLET!
DU-DUN
FWIP
UM...
YOU SAID YOU WOULD ACCEPT ANYONE WHO WANTS TO LEARN, RIGHT?

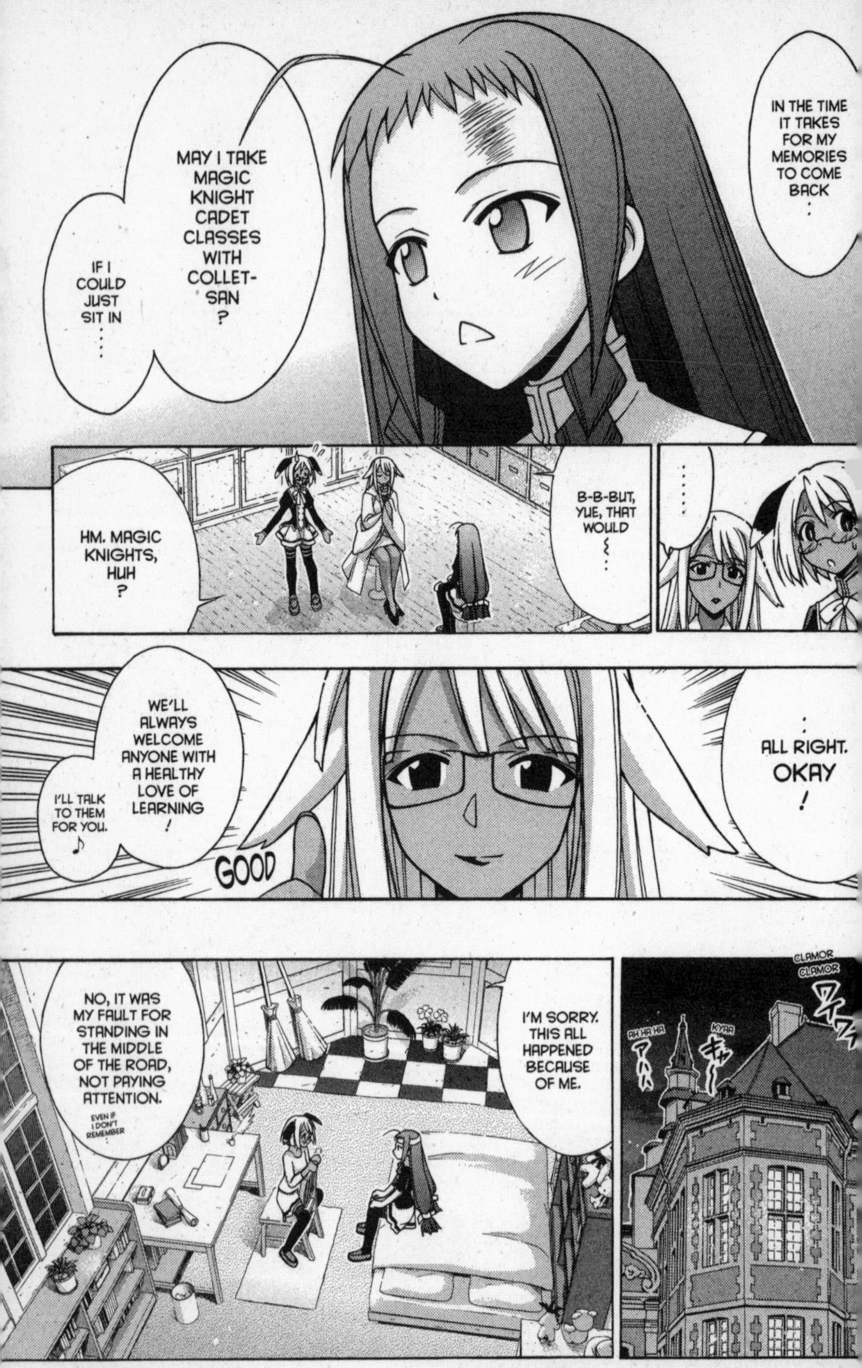
IN THE TIME IT TAKES FOR MY MEMORIES TO COME BACK :
MAY I TAKE MAGIC KNIGHT CADET CLASSES WITH COLLET-SAN ?
IF I COULD JUST SIT IN . . . .
. . . . . .
B-B-BUT, YUE, THAT WOULD ~ . . .
HM. MAGIC KNIGHTS, HUH ?
: ALL RIGHT. OKAY !
WE'LL ALWAYS WELCOME ANYONE WITH A HEALTHY LOVE OF LEARNING !
I'LL TALK TO THEM FOR YOU. ♪
GOOD
CLAMOR CLAMOR
KYAA
AH HA HA
I'M SORRY. THIS ALL HAPPENED BECAUSE OF ME.
NO, IT WAS MY FAULT FOR STANDING IN THE MIDDLE OF THE ROAD, NOT PAYING ATTENTION.
EVEN IF I DON'T REMEMBER :

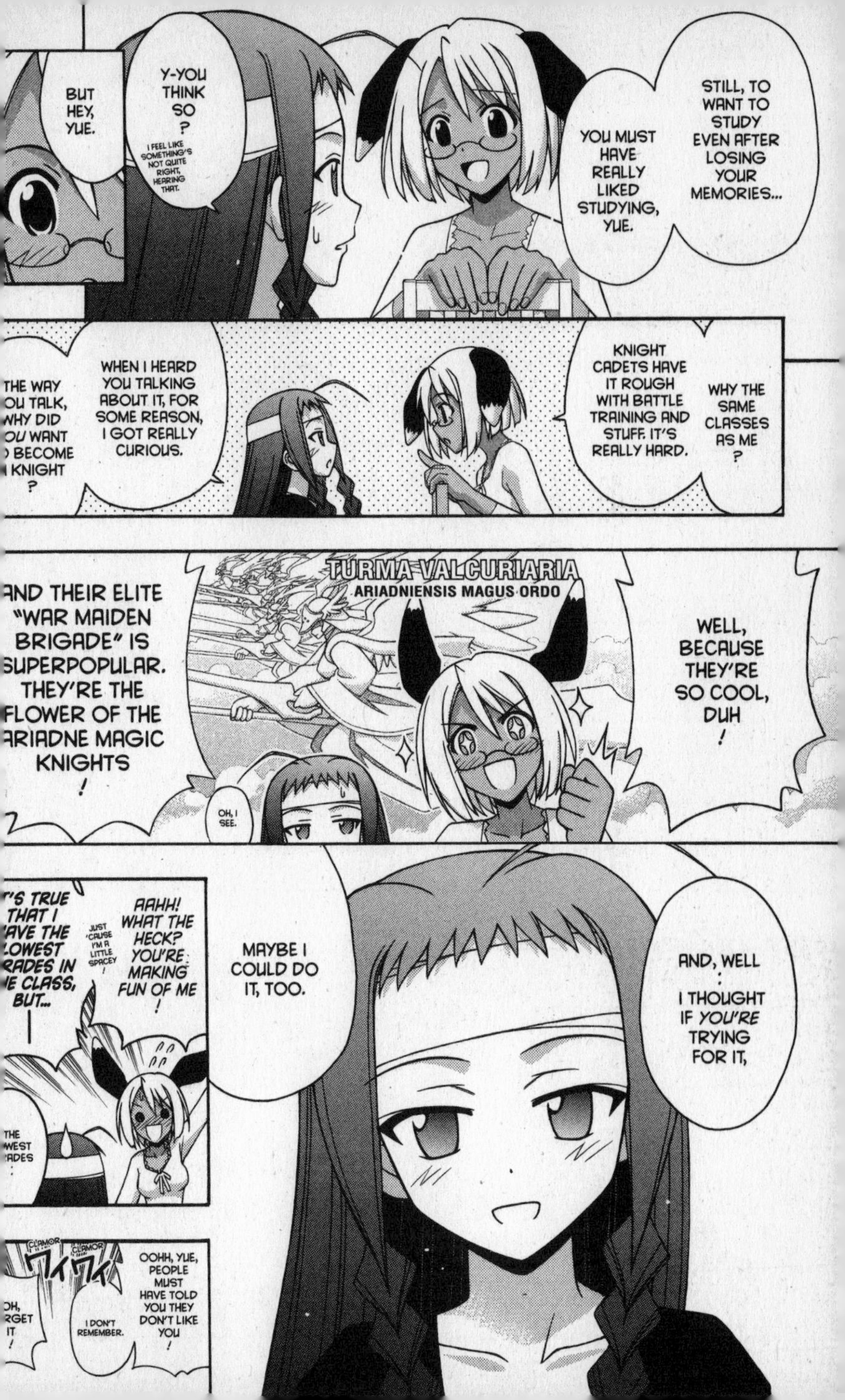
STILL, TO WANT TO STUDY EVEN AFTER LOSING YOUR MEMORIES...
YOU MUST HAVE REALLY LIKED STUDYING, YUE.
Y-YOU THINK SO?
I FEEL LIKE SOMETHING'S NOT QUITE RIGHT, HEARING THAT.
BUT HEY, YUE.
WHY THE SAME CLASSES AS ME?
KNIGHT CADETS HAVE IT ROUGH WITH BATTLE TRAINING AND STUFF. IT'S REALLY HARD.
WHEN I HEARD YOU TALKING ABOUT IT, FOR SOME REASON, I GOT REALLY CURIOUS.
THE WAY OU TALK, WHY DID OU WANT BECOME KNIGHT?
WELL, BECAUSE THEY'RE SO COOL, DUH!
TURMA VALCURIARIA
ARIADNIENSIS MAGUS ORDO
ND THEIR ELITE "WAR MAIDEN BRIGADE" IS UPERPOPULAR. THEY'RE THE FLOWER OF THE RIADNE MAGIC KNIGHTS!
OH, I SEE.
AND, WELL: I THOUGHT IF YOU'RE TRYING FOR IT,
MAYBE I COULD DO IT, TOO.
AAHH! WHAT THE HECK? YOU'RE MAKING FUN OF ME!
JUST 'CAUSE I'M A LITTLE SPACEY!
'S TRUE THAT I AVE THE LOWEST RADES IN E CLASS, BUT...
THE WEST ADES
CLAMOR
CLAMOR
OOHH, YUE, PEOPLE MUST HAVE TOLD YOU THEY DON'T LIKE YOU!
I DON'T REMEMBER.
OH, RGET IT!

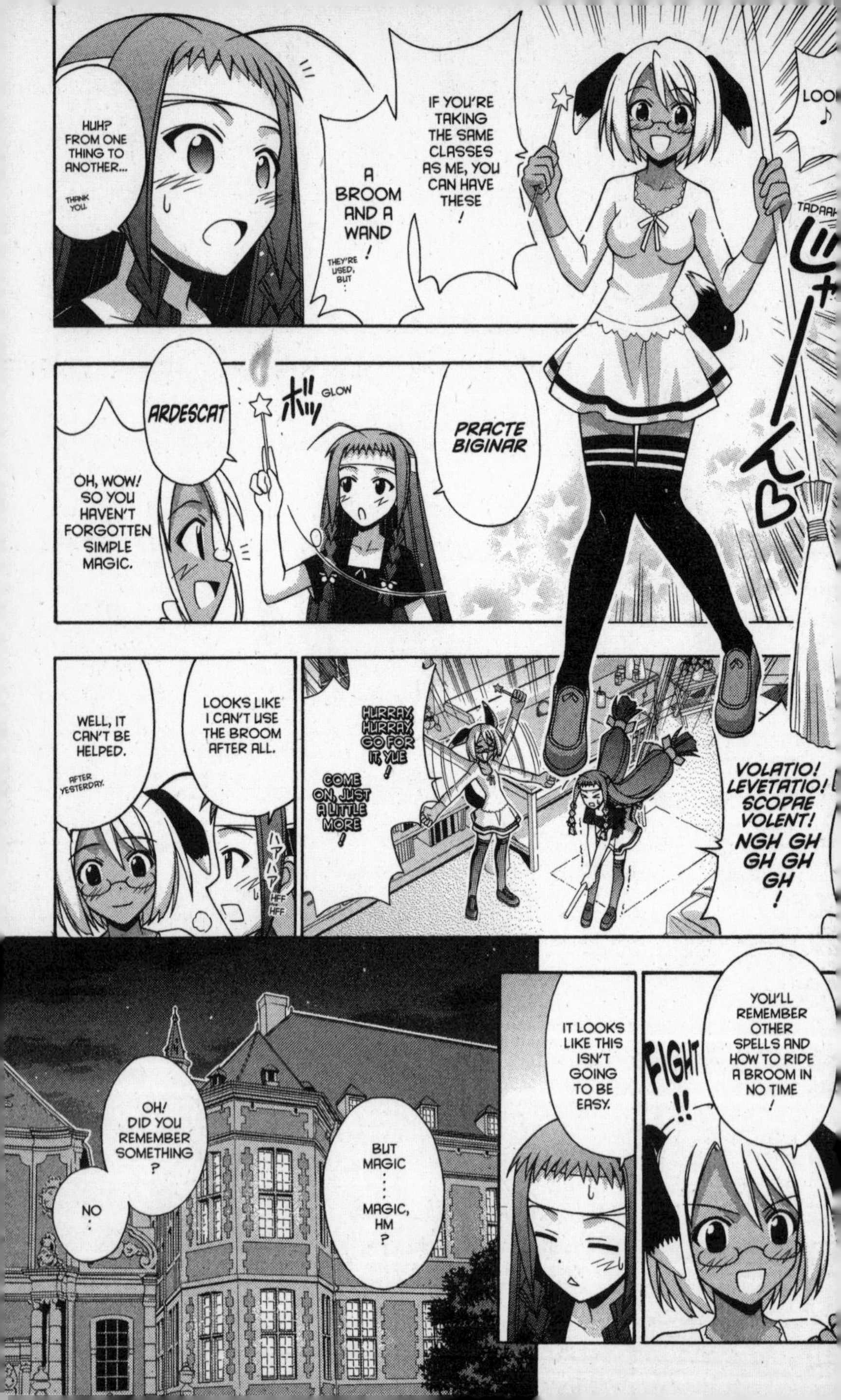
LOO ♪
TADAAH
IF YOU'RE TAKING THE SAME CLASSES AS ME, YOU CAN HAVE THESE!
A BROOM AND A WAND!
THEY'RE USED, BUT.
HUH? FROM ONE THING TO ANOTHER...
THANK YOU.
PRACTE BIGINAR
ボッ
GLOW
ARDESCAT
OH, WOW! SO YOU HAVEN'T FORGOTTEN SIMPLE MAGIC.
VOLATIO! LEVETATIO! SCOPAE VOLENT! NGH GH GH GH GH!
HURRAY, HURRAY, GO FOR IT, YUE!
COME ON, JUST A LITTLE MORE!
LOOKS LIKE I CAN'T USE THE BROOM AFTER ALL.
ハァハァ
HFF HFF
WELL, IT CAN'T BE HELPED.
AFTER YESTERDAY.
YOU'LL REMEMBER OTHER SPELLS AND HOW TO RIDE A BROOM IN NO TIME!
FIGHT!!
IT LOOKS LIKE THIS ISN'T GOING TO BE EASY.
BUT MAGIC... MAGIC, HM?
OH! DID YOU REMEMBER SOMETHING?
NO...

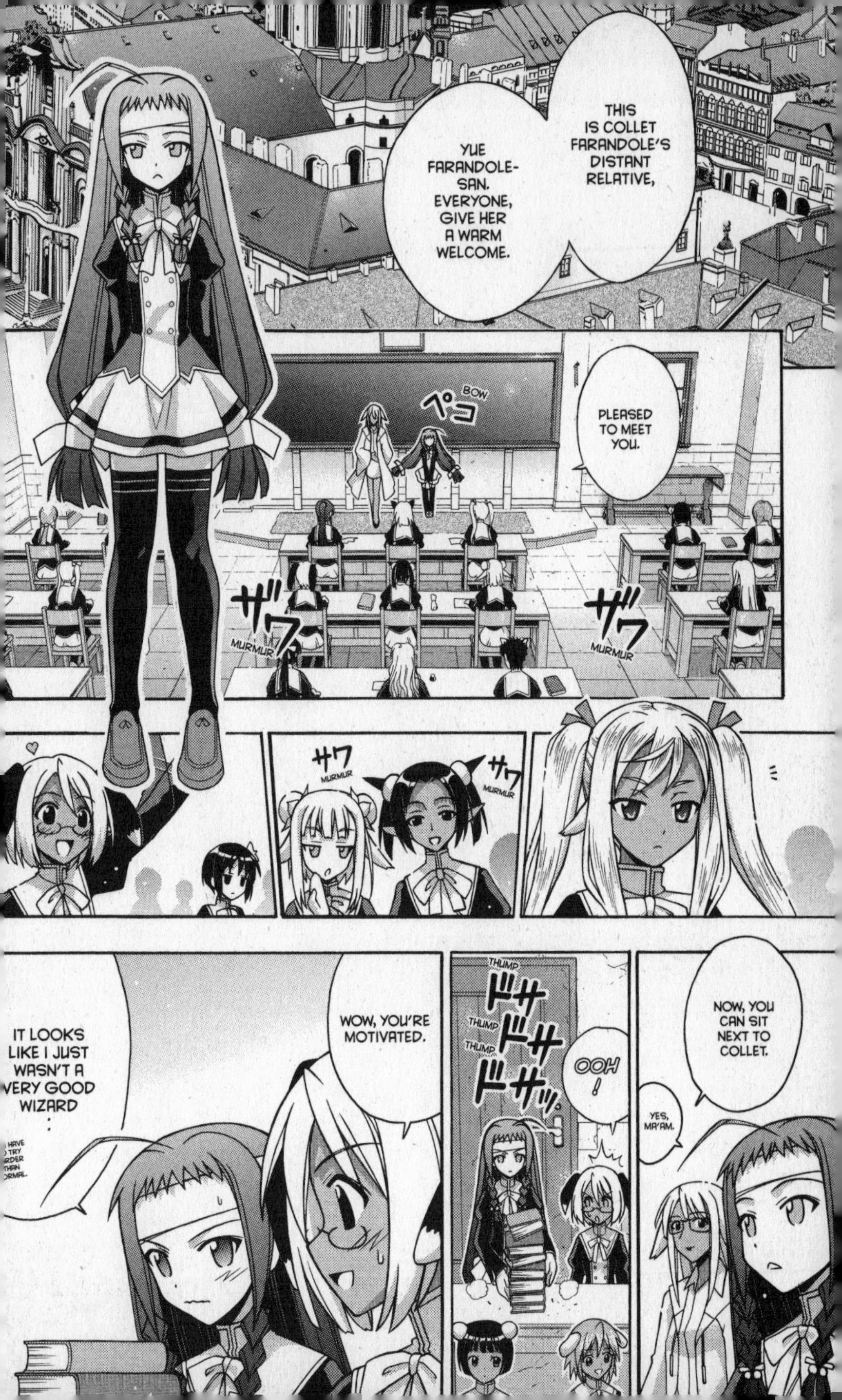
THIS IS COLLET FARANDOLE'S DISTANT RELATIVE,
YUE FARANDOLE-SAN. EVERYONE, GIVE HER A WARM WELCOME.
PLEASED TO MEET YOU.
ペコ
BOW
ザワ
MURMUR
ザワ
MURMUR
サワ
MURMUR
サワ
MURMUR
NOW, YOU CAN SIT NEXT TO COLLET.
YES, MA'AM.
ドサ
THUMP
ドサ
THUMP
ドサッ
THUMP
OOH!
WOW, YOU'RE MOTIVATED.
IT LOOKS LIKE I JUST WASN'T A VERY GOOD WIZARD
:

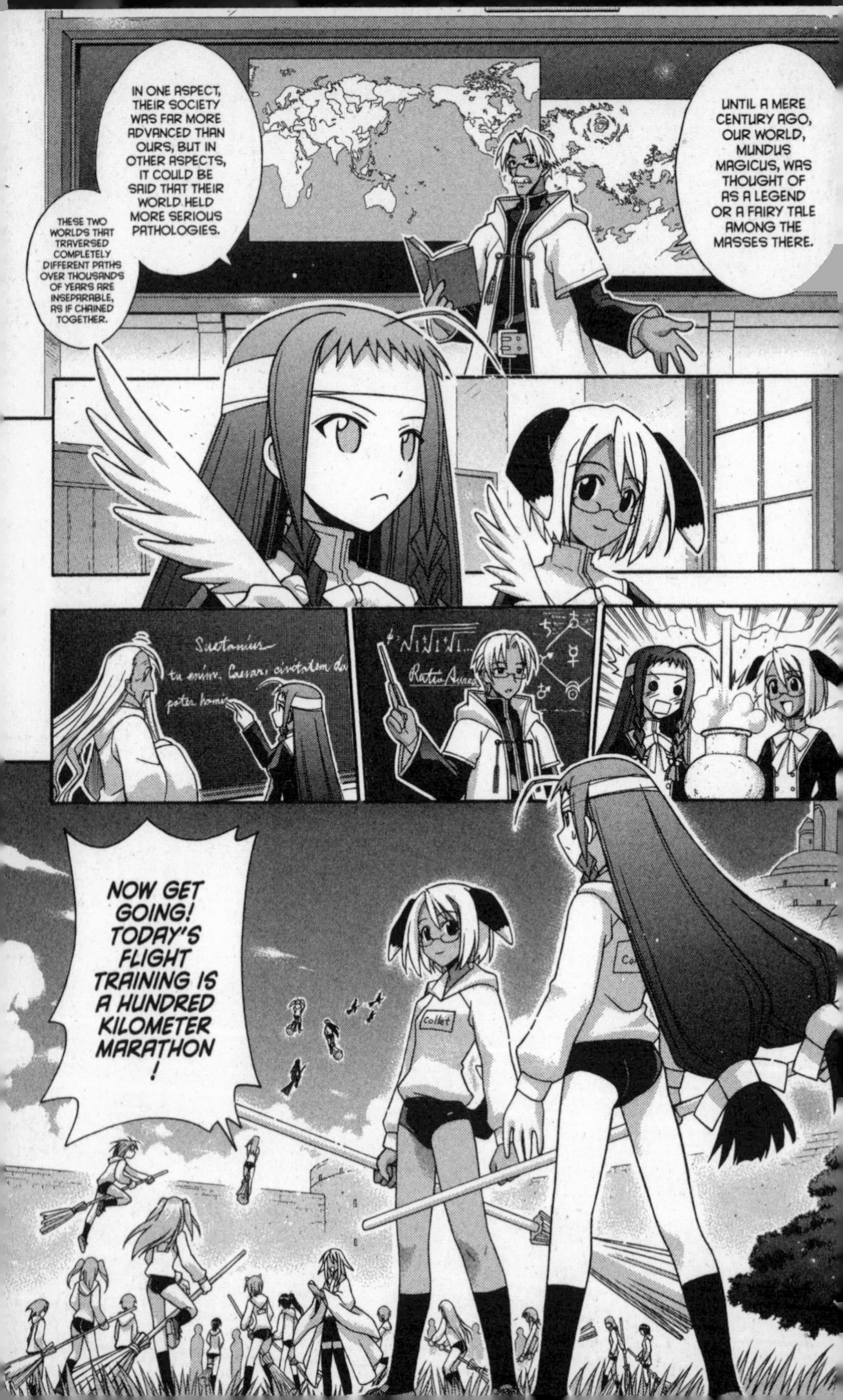
UNTIL A MERE CENTURY AGO, OUR WORLD, MUNDUS MAGICUS, WAS THOUGHT OF AS A LEGEND OR A FAIRY TALE AMONG THE MASSES THERE.
IN ONE ASPECT, THEIR SOCIETY WAS FAR MORE ADVANCED THAN OURS, BUT IN OTHER ASPECTS, IT COULD BE SAID THAT THEIR WORLD HELD MORE SERIOUS PATHOLOGIES.
THESE TWO WORLDS THAT TRAVERSED COMPLETELY DIFFERENT PATHS OVER THOUSANDS OF YEARS ARE INSEPARABLE, AS IF CHAINED TOGETHER.
NOW GET GOING! TODAY'S FLIGHT TRAINING IS A HUNDRED KILOMETER MARATHON!

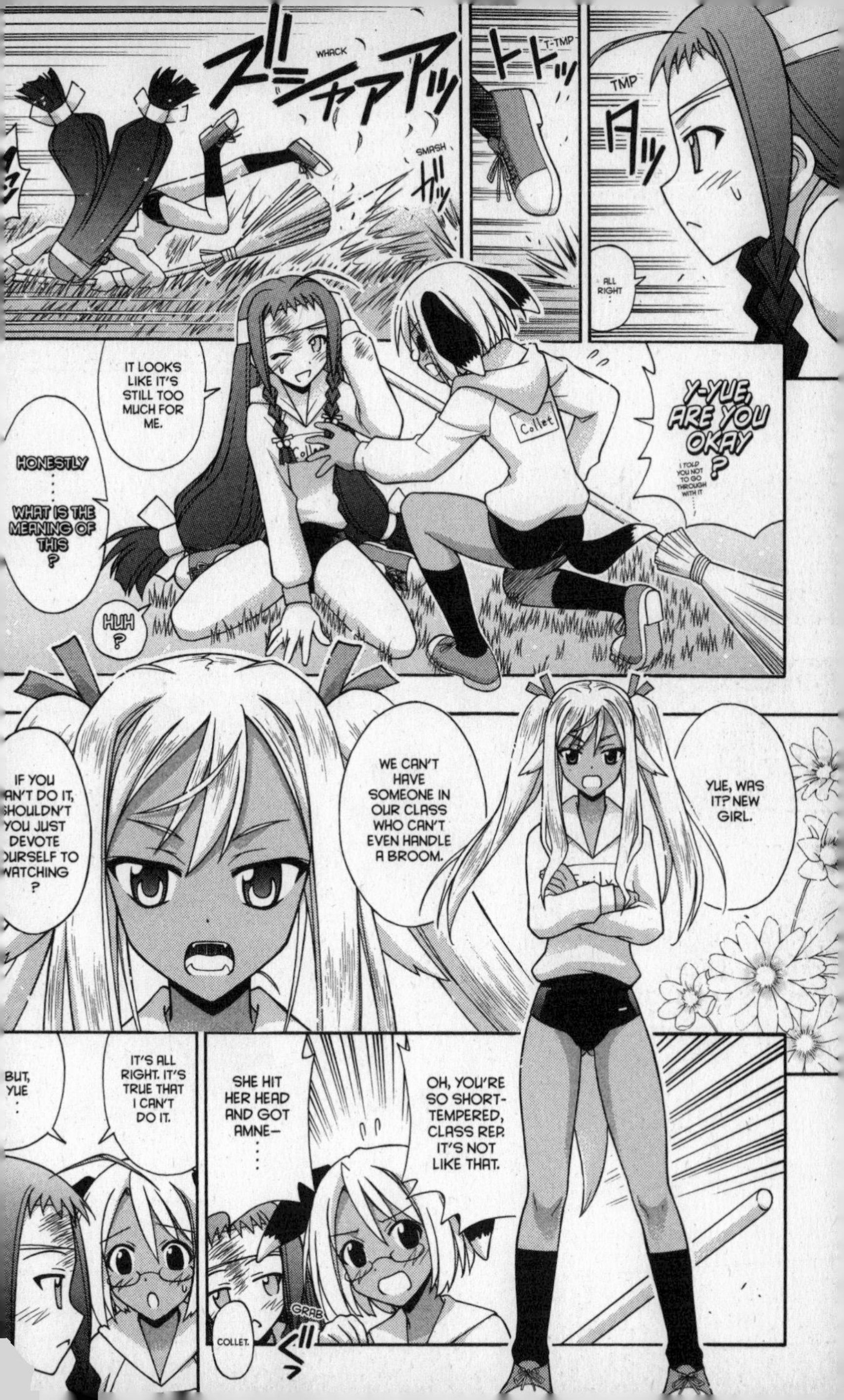

TMP
ALL RIGHT . . .
T-TMP
WHACK
SMASH
Y-YUE, ARE YOU OKAY?
I TOLD YOU NOT TO GO THROUGH WITH IT . . .
IT LOOKS LIKE IT'S STILL TOO MUCH FOR ME.
HONESTLY . . . WHAT IS THE MEANING OF THIS?
HUH?
YUE, WAS IT? NEW GIRL.
WE CAN'T HAVE SOMEONE IN OUR CLASS WHO CAN'T EVEN HANDLE A BROOM.
IF YOU AN'T DO IT, SHOULDN'T YOU JUST DEVOTE OURSELF TO WATCHING?
OH, YOU'RE SO SHORT-TEMPERED, CLASS REP. IT'S NOT LIKE THAT.
SHE HIT HER HEAD AND GOT AMNE- . . .
GRAB
COLLET.
IT'S ALL RIGHT. IT'S TRUE THAT I CAN'T DO IT.
BUT, YUE . . .

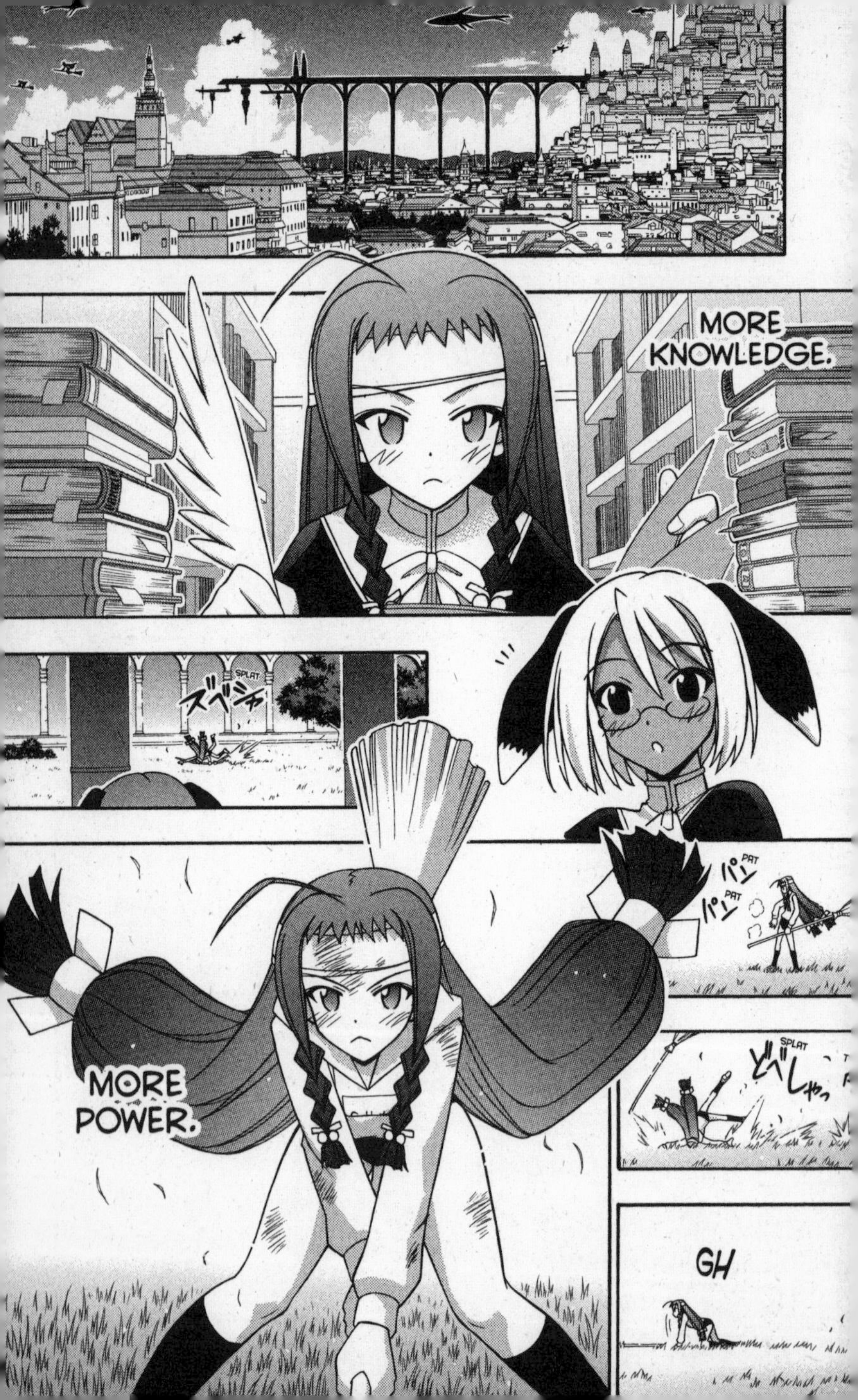
MORE KNOWLEDGE.
SPLAT
ズベシャ
PAT
パン
PAT
パン
SPLAT
どべしゃっ
GH
MORE POWER.

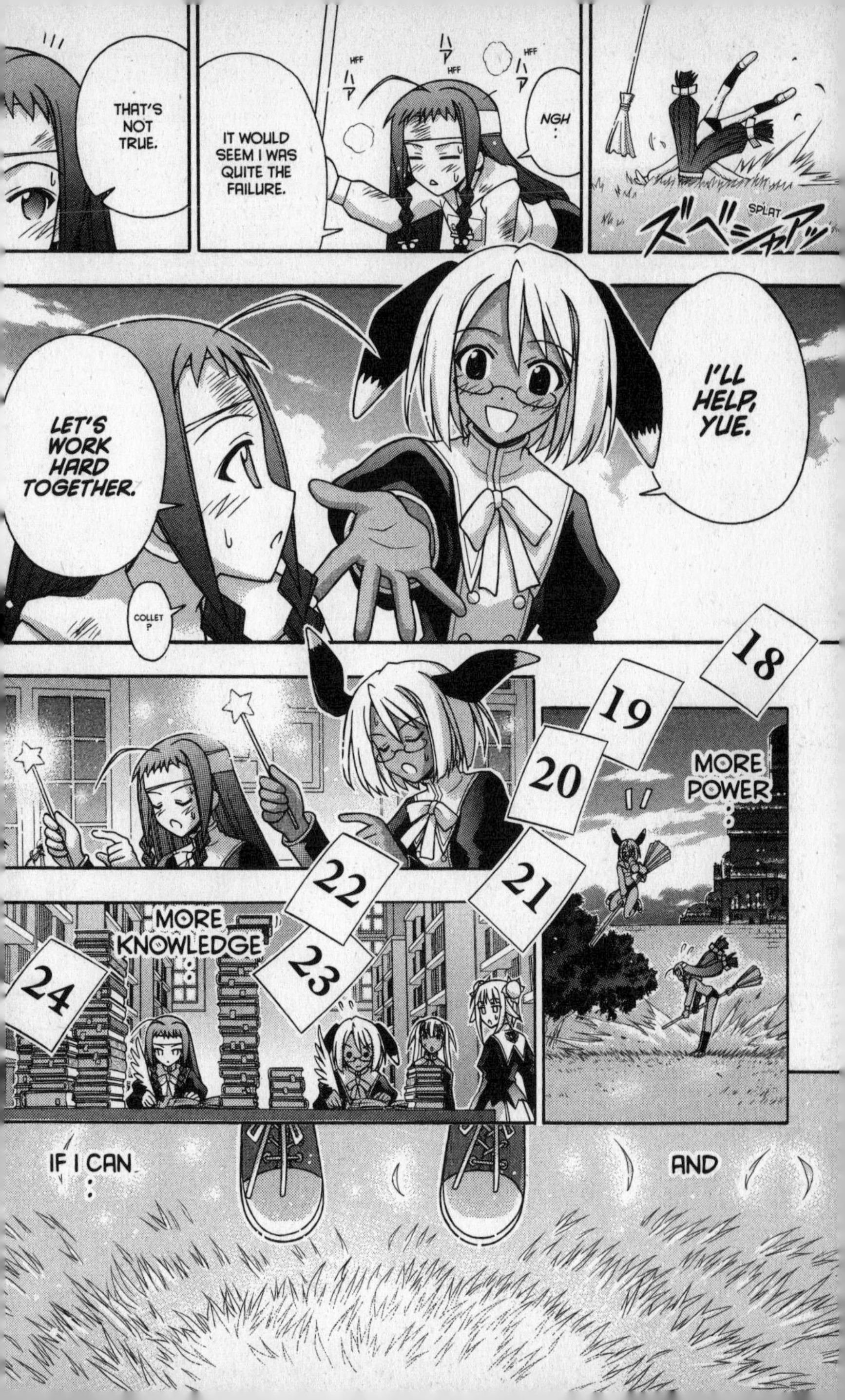
ズベシャアッ
SPLAT
NGH...
HFF
HFF
HFF
IT WOULD SEEM I WAS QUITE THE FAILURE.
THAT'S NOT TRUE.
I'LL HELP, YUE.
LET'S WORK HARD TOGETHER.
COLLET?
18
19
20
21
MORE POWER...
22
23
MORE KNOWLEDGE...
24
IF I CAN...
AND

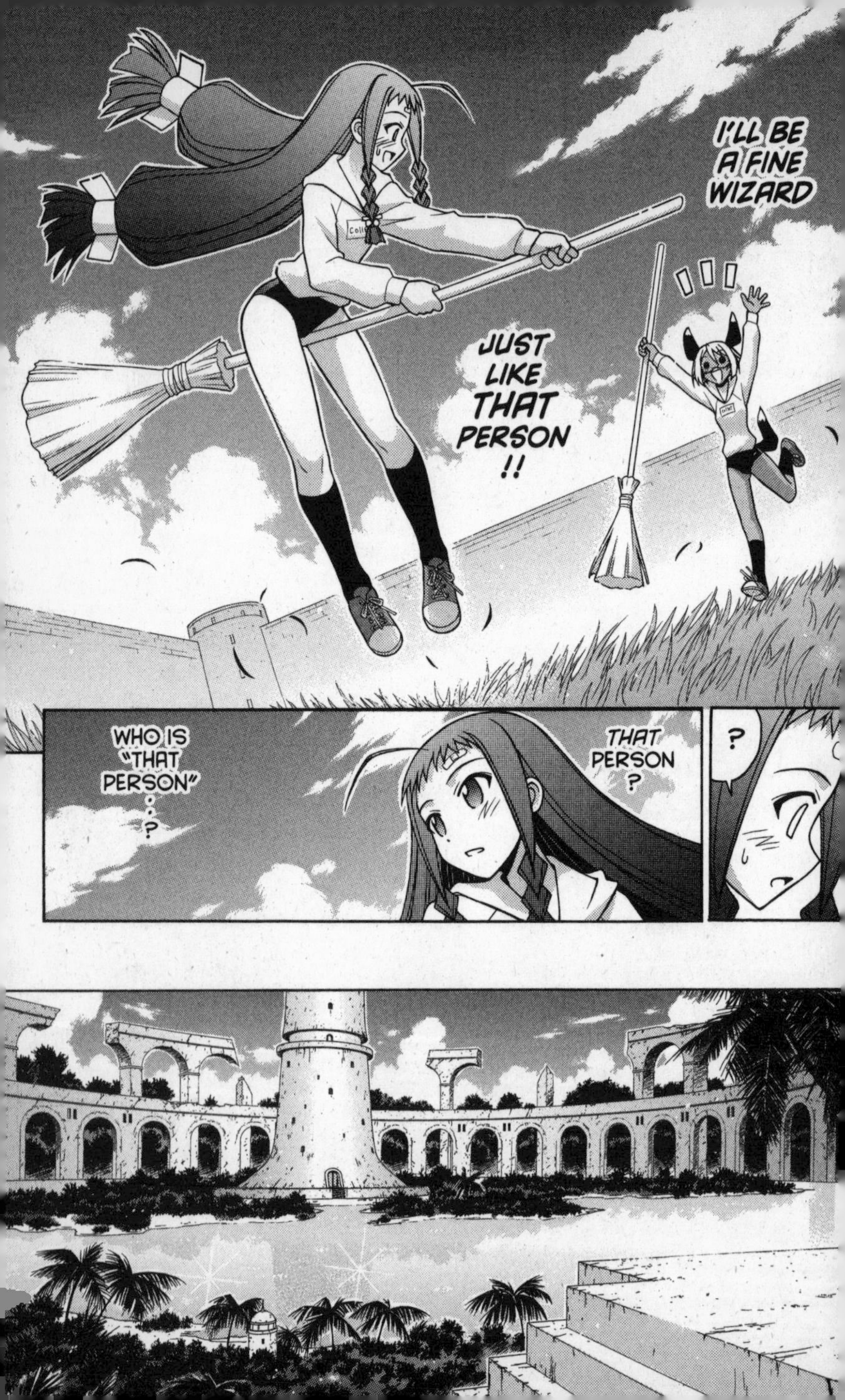
I'LL BE A FINE WIZARD
JUST LIKE THAT PERSON !!
?
THAT PERSON ?
WHO IS "THAT PERSON" ...?

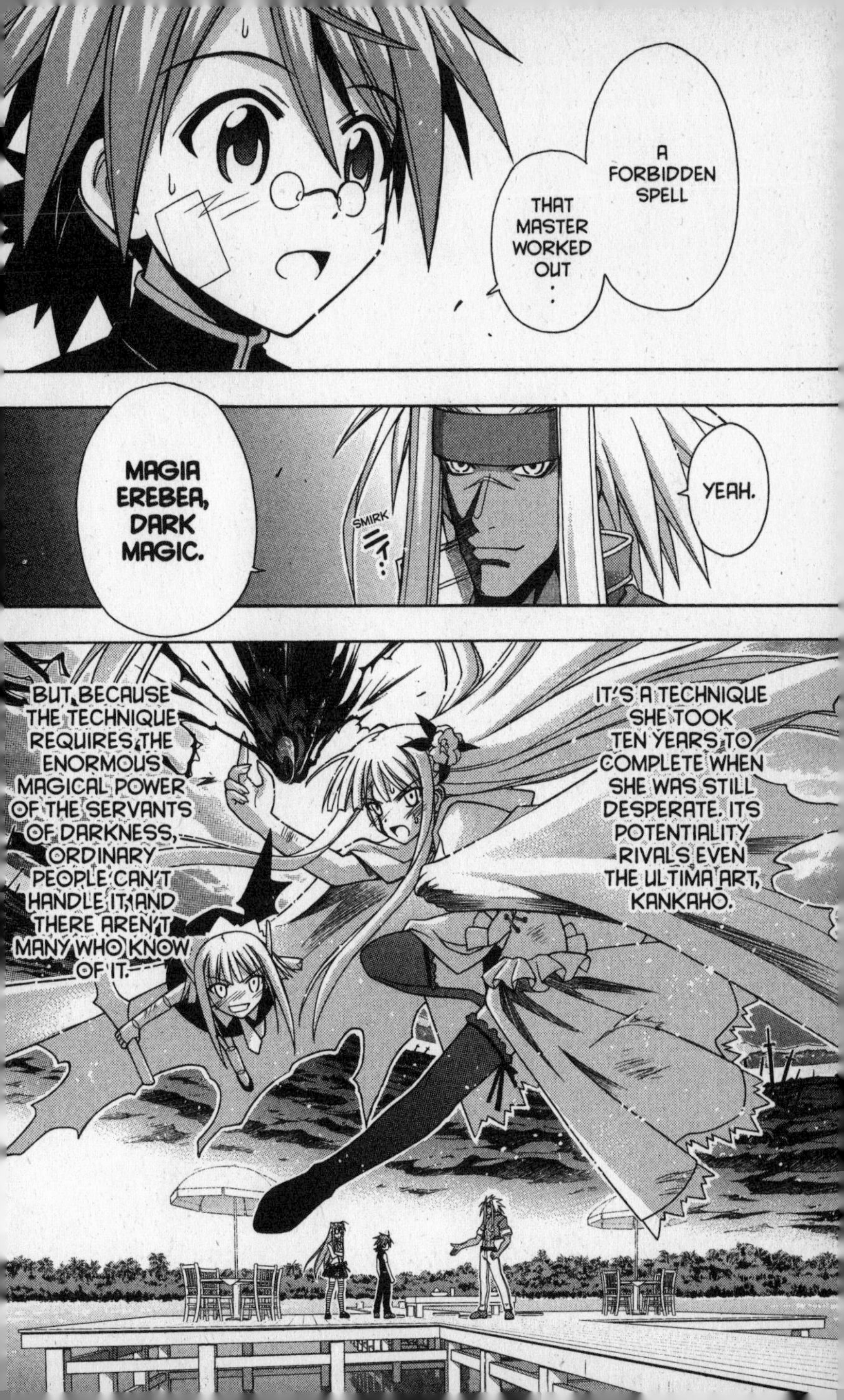
A FORBIDDEN SPELL
THAT MASTER WORKED OUT ...
YEAH.
SMIRK
MAGIA EREBEA, DARK MAGIC.
IT'S A TECHNIQUE SHE TOOK TEN YEARS TO COMPLETE WHEN SHE WAS STILL DESPERATE. ITS POTENTIALITY RIVALS EVEN THE ULTIMA ART, KANKAHŌ.
BUT BECAUSE THE TECHNIQUE REQUIRES THE ENORMOUS MAGICAL POWER OF THE SERVANTS OF DARKNESS, ORDINARY PEOPLE CAN'T HANDLE IT, AND THERE AREN'T MANY WHO KNOW OF IT.

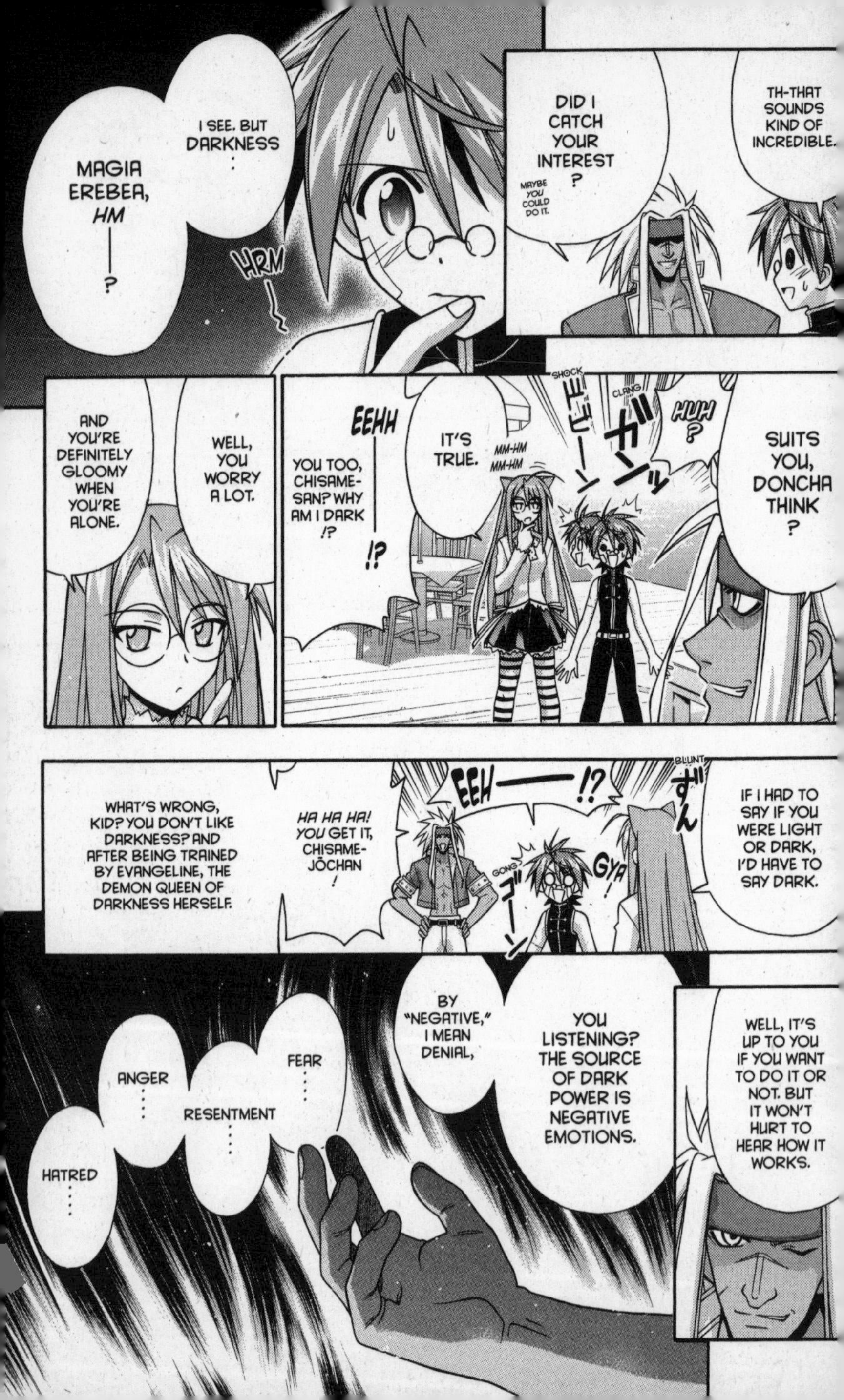
TH-THAT SOUNDS KIND OF INCREDIBLE.
DID I CATCH YOUR INTEREST?
MAYBE YOU COULD DO IT.
I SEE. BUT DARKNESS...
HRM
MAGIA EREBEA, HM—?
SUITS YOU, DONCHA THINK?
HUH?
CLANG
SHOCK
IT'S TRUE.
MM-HM MM-HM
EEHH—!?
YOU TOO, CHISAME-SAN? WHY AM I DARK!?
WELL, YOU WORRY A LOT.
AND YOU'RE DEFINITELY GLOOMY WHEN YOU'RE ALONE.
IF I HAD TO SAY IF YOU WERE LIGHT OR DARK, I'D HAVE TO SAY DARK.
BLUNT
GYA!
EEH—!?
GONG
HA HA HA! YOU GET IT, CHISAME-JŌCHAN!
WHAT'S WRONG, KID? YOU DON'T LIKE DARKNESS? AND AFTER BEING TRAINED BY EVANGELINE, THE DEMON QUEEN OF DARKNESS HERSELF.
WELL, IT'S UP TO YOU IF YOU WANT TO DO IT OR NOT. BUT IT WON'T HURT TO HEAR HOW IT WORKS.
YOU LISTENING? THE SOURCE OF DARK POWER IS NEGATIVE EMOTIONS.
BY "NEGATIVE," I MEAN DENIAL,
FEAR...
RESENTMENT...
ANGER...
HATRED...

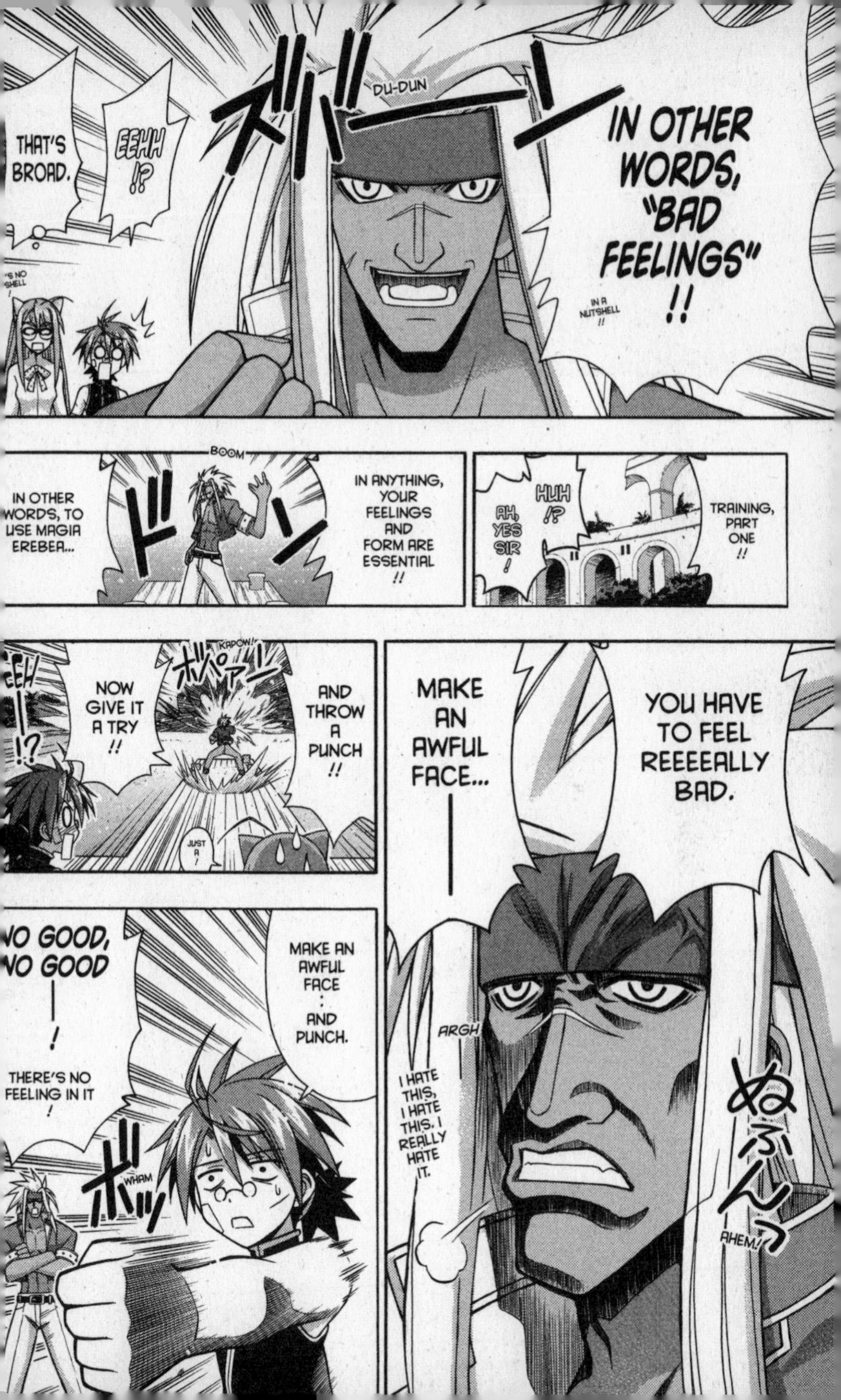
IN OTHER WORDS, "BAD FEELINGS" !!
IN A NUTSHELL !!
DU-DUN
EEHH !?
THAT'S BROAD.
TRAINING, PART ONE !!
HUH !?
AH, YES SIR !
IN ANYTHING, YOUR FEELINGS AND FORM ARE ESSENTIAL !!
BOOM
IN OTHER WORDS, TO USE MAGIA EREBEA...
YOU HAVE TO FEEL REEEEALLY BAD.
MAKE AN AWFUL FACE...
ARGH
I HATE THIS, I HATE THIS. I REALLY HATE IT.
AHEM!
AND THROW A PUNCH !!
KAPOW!
NOW GIVE IT A TRY !!
JUST A !
MAKE AN AWFUL FACE : AND PUNCH.
NO GOOD, NO GOOD !
THERE'S NO FEELING IN IT !
WHAM

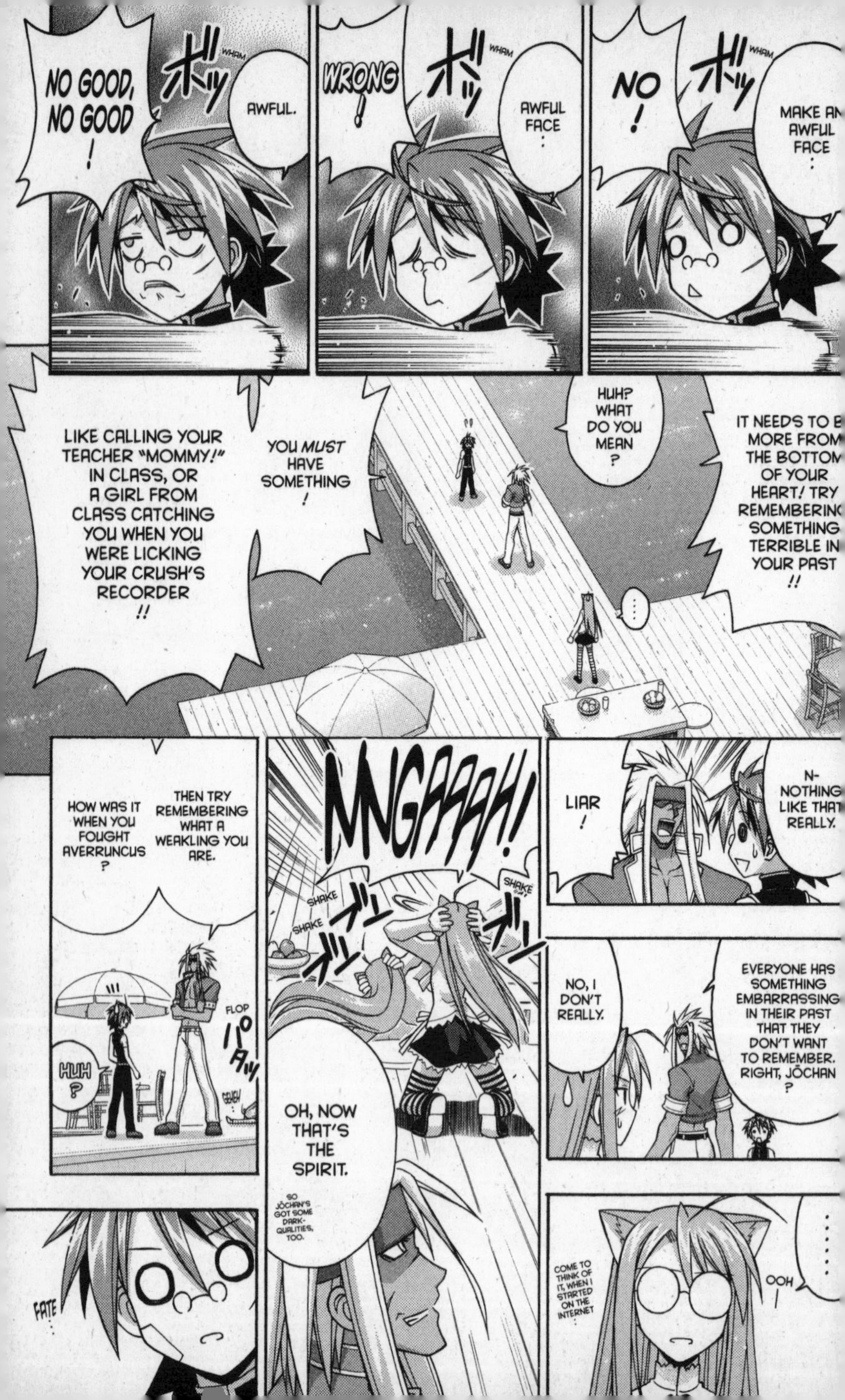
MAKE AN AWFUL FACE :
WHAM
NO !
AWFUL FACE :
WHAM
WRONG !
AWFUL.
WHAM
NO GOOD, NO GOOD !
IT NEEDS TO BE MORE FROM THE BOTTOM OF YOUR HEART! TRY REMEMBERING SOMETHING TERRIBLE IN YOUR PAST !!
HUH? WHAT DO YOU MEAN ?
. . . .
YOU MUST HAVE SOMETHING !
LIKE CALLING YOUR TEACHER "MOMMY!" IN CLASS, OR A GIRL FROM CLASS CATCHING YOU WHEN YOU WERE LICKING YOUR CRUSH'S RECORDER !!
N-NOTHING LIKE THAT REALLY.
LIAR !
EVERYONE HAS SOMETHING EMBARRASSING IN THEIR PAST THAT THEY DON'T WANT TO REMEMBER. RIGHT, JŌCHAN ?
NO, I DON'T REALLY.
MNGAAAH!
SHAKE
SHAKE
SHAKE
THEN TRY REMEMBERING WHAT A WEAKLING YOU ARE.
HOW WAS IT WHEN YOU FOUGHT AVERRUNCUS ?
FLOP
HUH ?
. . . . .
OOH !
COME TO THINK OF IT, WHEN I STARTED ON THE INTERNET :
OH, NOW THAT'S THE SPIRIT.
SO JŌCHAN'S GOT SOME DARK-QUALITIES, TOO.
FATE :

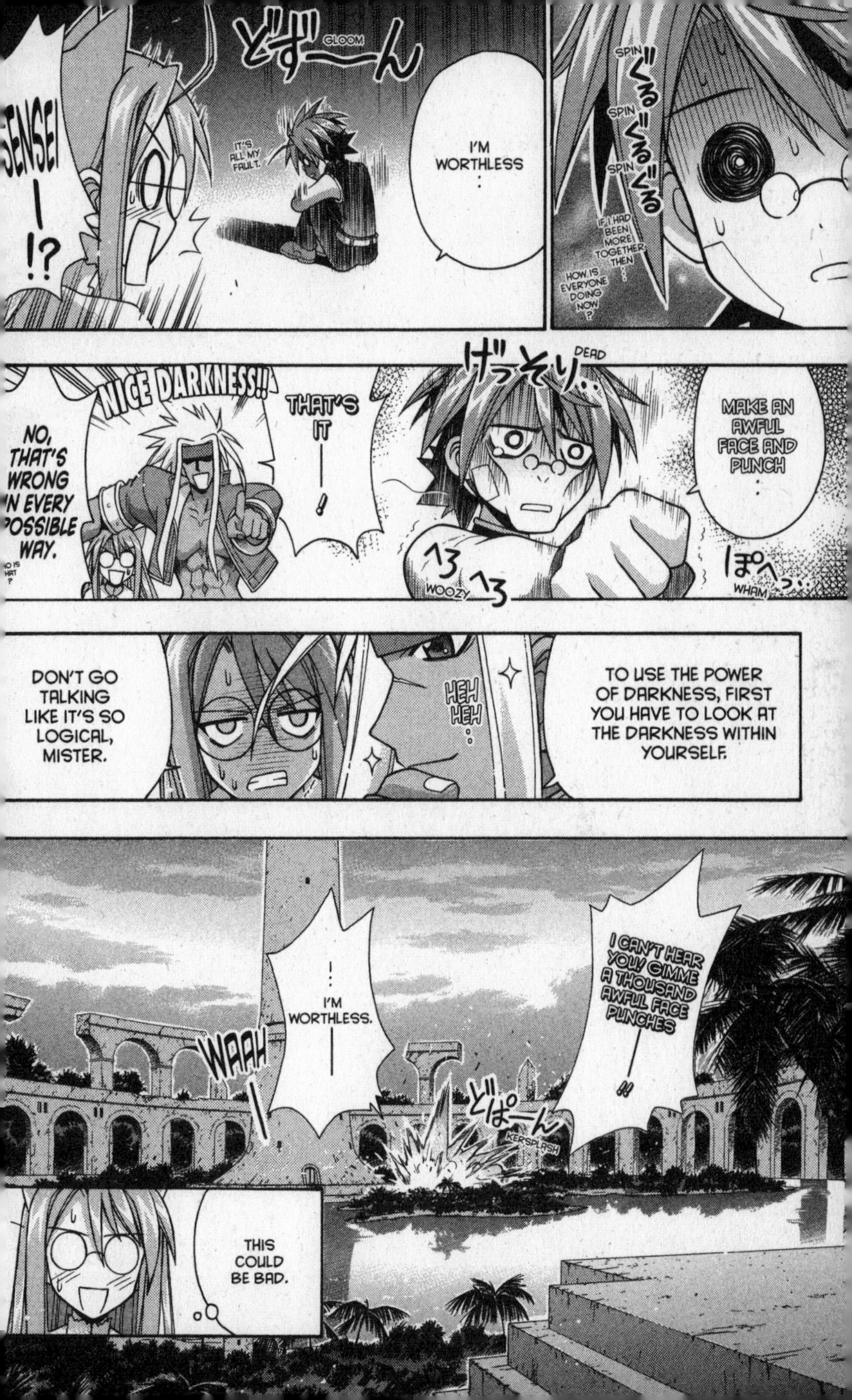

SPIN ぐる
SPIN ぐる
SPIN ぐるぐる
IF I HAD BEEN MORE TOGETHER THEN...
HOW IS EVERYONE DOING NOW?
どずーん GLOOM
IT'S ALL MY FAULT.
I'M WORTHLESS...
SENSEI—!?
MAKE AN AWFUL FACE AND PUNCH...
ぽへっ... WHAM
げっそり... DEAD
へろへろ WOOZY
THAT'S IT—!
NICE DARKNESS!!
NO, THAT'S WRONG IN EVERY POSSIBLE WAY.
TO USE THE POWER OF DARKNESS, FIRST YOU HAVE TO LOOK AT THE DARKNESS WITHIN YOURSELF.
HEH HEH...
DON'T GO TALKING LIKE IT'S SO LOGICAL, MISTER.
I CAN'T HEAR YOU! GIMME A THOUSAND AWFUL FACE PUNCHES—!!
どぱーん KERSPLASH
...I'M WORTHLESS.—
WAAH—
THIS COULD BE BAD.

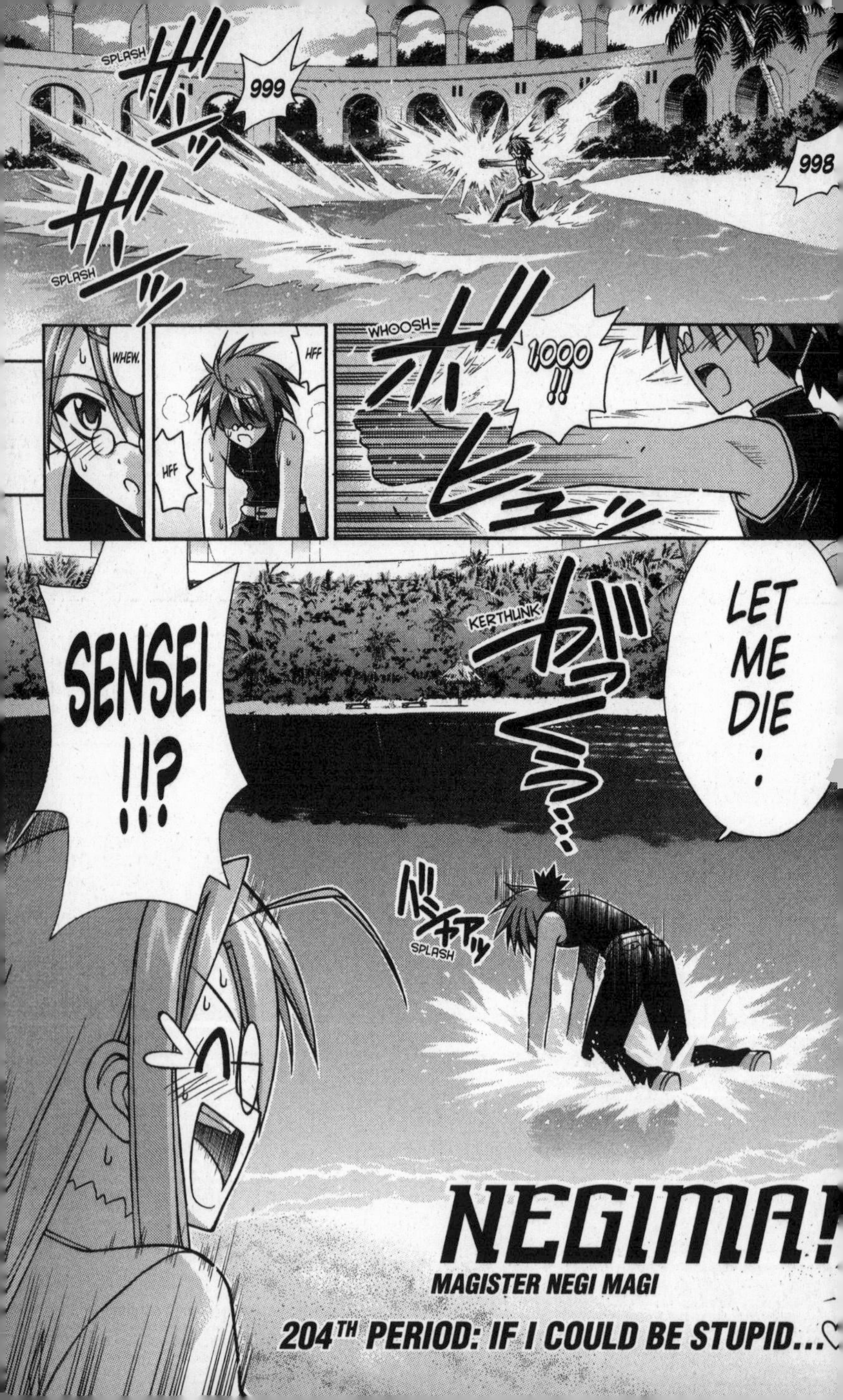
998
999
SPLASH
SPLASH
WHOOSH
1,000!!
HFF
HFF
WHEW.
LET ME DIE...
KERTHUNK
SENSEI!!?
SPLASH
NEGIMA!
MAGISTER NEGI MAGI
204TH PERIOD: IF I COULD BE STUPID...♡

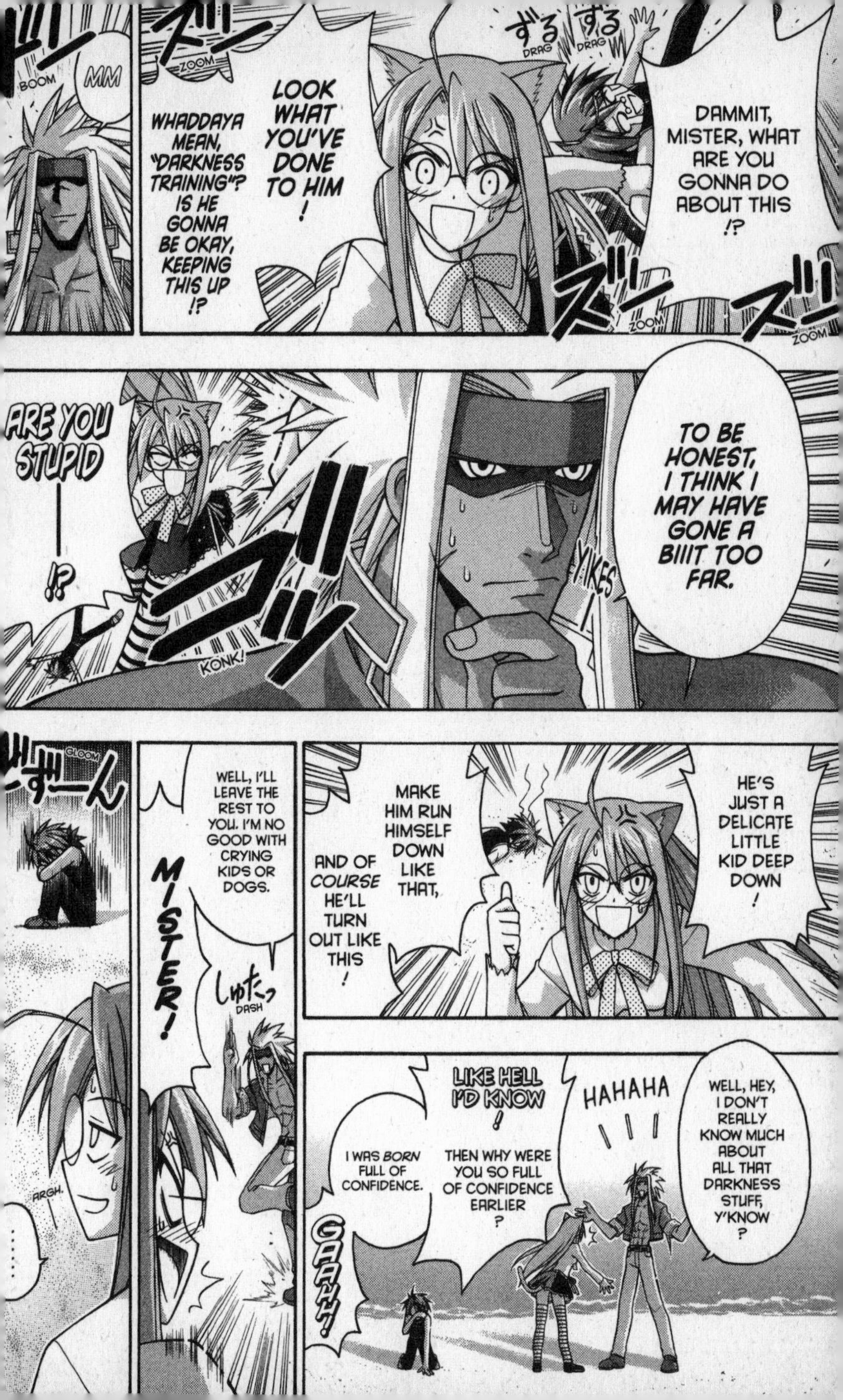
ずる
DRAG
ずる
DRAG
DAMMIT, MISTER, WHAT ARE YOU GONNA DO ABOUT THIS!?
ZOOM
ZOOM
LOOK WHAT YOU'VE DONE TO HIM!
WHADDAYA MEAN, "DARKNESS TRAINING"? IS HE GONNA BE OKAY, KEEPING THIS UP!?
ZOOM
BOOM
MM
TO BE HONEST, I THINK I MAY HAVE GONE A BIIIT TOO FAR.
YIKES!
ARE YOU STUPID—!?
KONK!
HE'S JUST A DELICATE LITTLE KID DEEP DOWN!
MAKE HIM RUN HIMSELF DOWN LIKE THAT,
AND OF COURSE HE'LL TURN OUT LIKE THIS!
WELL, HEY, I DON'T REALLY KNOW MUCH ABOUT ALL THAT DARKNESS STUFF, Y'KNOW?
HAHAHA
LIKE HELL I'D KNOW!
THEN WHY WERE YOU SO FULL OF CONFIDENCE EARLIER?
I WAS BORN FULL OF CONFIDENCE.
GAAAH!
WELL, I'LL LEAVE THE REST TO YOU. I'M NO GOOD WITH CRYING KIDS OR DOGS.
MISTER!
しゅたっ
DASH
ずーん
GLOOM
ARGH.
...

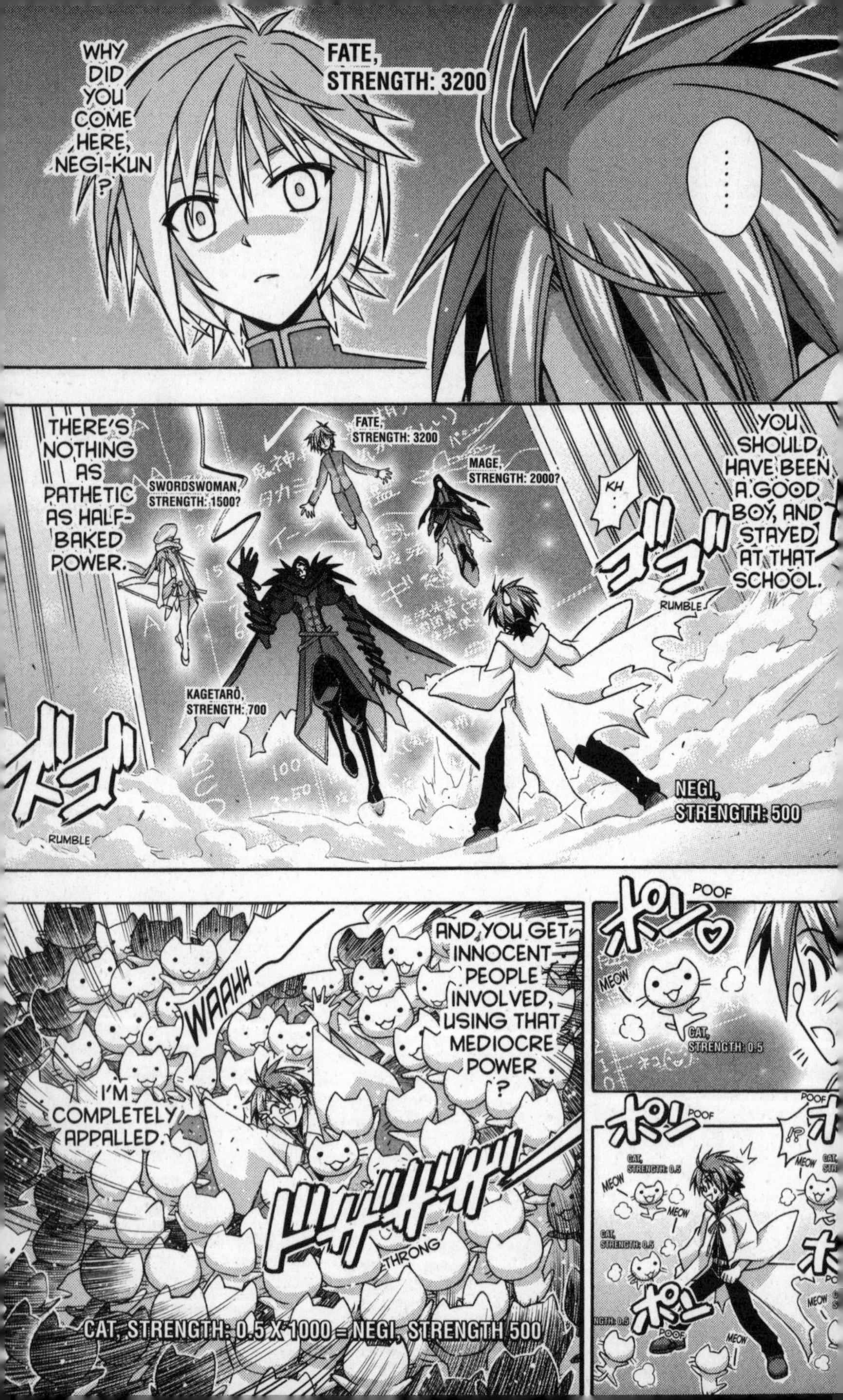
FATE,
STRENGTH: 3200
WHY DID YOU COME HERE, NEGI-KUN?
......
YOU SHOULD HAVE BEEN A GOOD BOY, AND STAYED AT THAT SCHOOL.
KH...
ゴゴ
RUMBLE
FATE,
STRENGTH: 3200
MAGE,
STRENGTH: 2000?
SWORDSWOMAN,
STRENGTH: 1500?
THERE'S NOTHING AS PATHETIC AS HALF-BAKED POWER.
KAGETARŌ,
STRENGTH: 700
NEGI,
STRENGTH: 500
ズゴ
RUMBLE
ポン♡
POOF
MEOW
CAT,
STRENGTH: 0.5
POOF
ポン
POOF
!?
CAT,
STRENGTH: 0.5
MEOW
MEOW
MEOW
CAT,
STRENGTH: 0.5
ポン
POOF
MEOW
MEOW
AND YOU GET INNOCENT PEOPLE INVOLVED, USING THAT MEDIOCRE POWER?
WAAHH
I'M COMPLETELY APPALLED.
THRONG
CAT, STRENGTH: 0.5 X 1000 = NEGI, STRENGTH 500

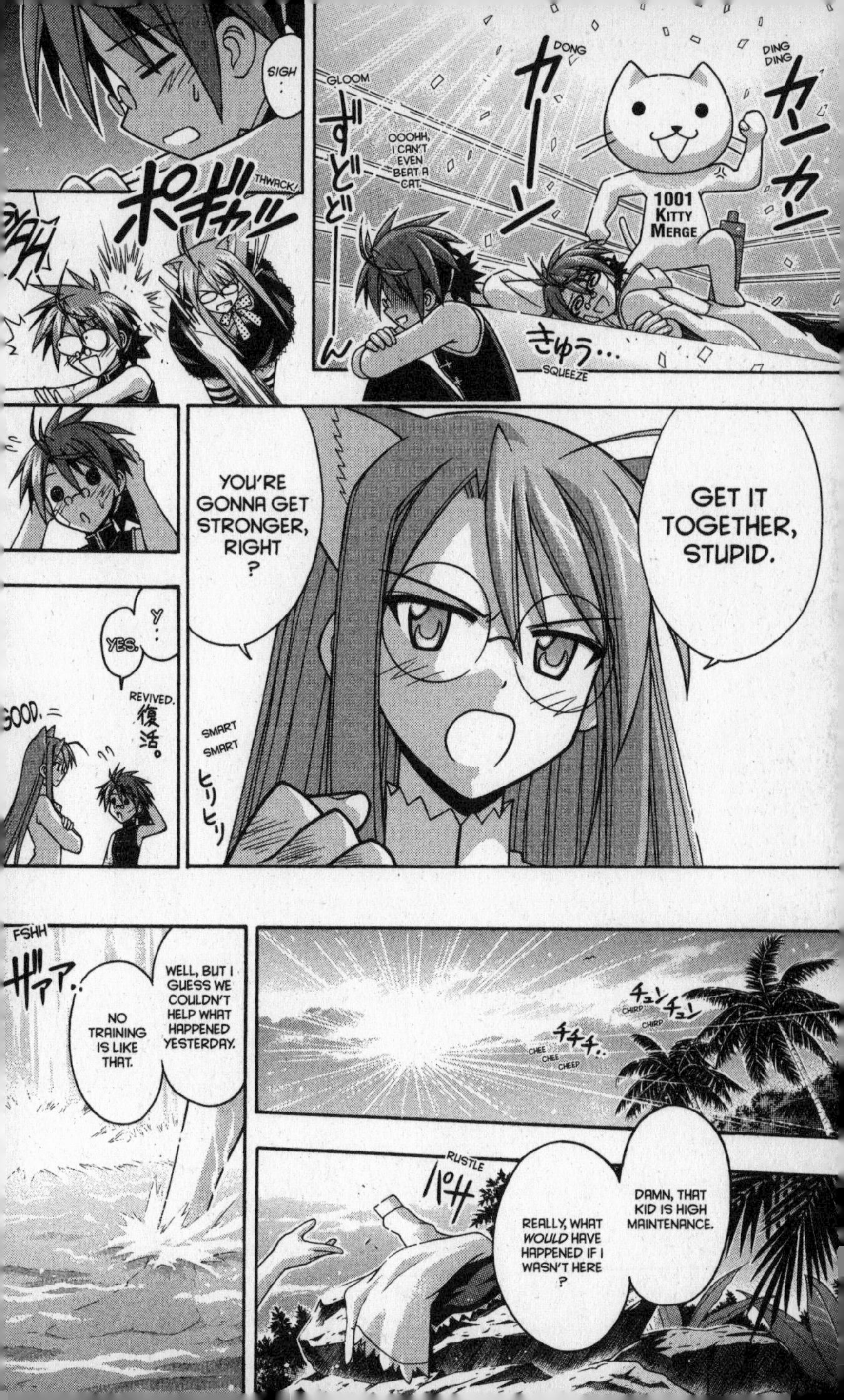
DING DING
カーンカーン
1001 Kitty Merge
DONG
カーン
GLOOM
ずどーん
OOOHH, I CAN'T EVEN BEAT A CAT.
きゅう…
SQUEEZE
SIGH…
THWACK!
ポギャッ
GET IT TOGETHER, STUPID.
YOU'RE GONNA GET STRONGER, RIGHT?
SMART SMART
ヒリヒリ
Y… YES.
REVIVED.
復活。
GOOD.
チュンチュン
CHIRP CHIRP
チチチ..
CHEE CHEE CHEEP
DAMN, THAT KID IS HIGH MAINTENANCE.
REALLY, WHAT *WOULD* HAVE HAPPENED IF I WASN'T HERE?
RUSTLE
パサ
FSHH
ザァア..
WELL, BUT I GUESS WE COULDN'T HELP WHAT HAPPENED YESTERDAY.
NO TRAINING IS LIKE THAT.

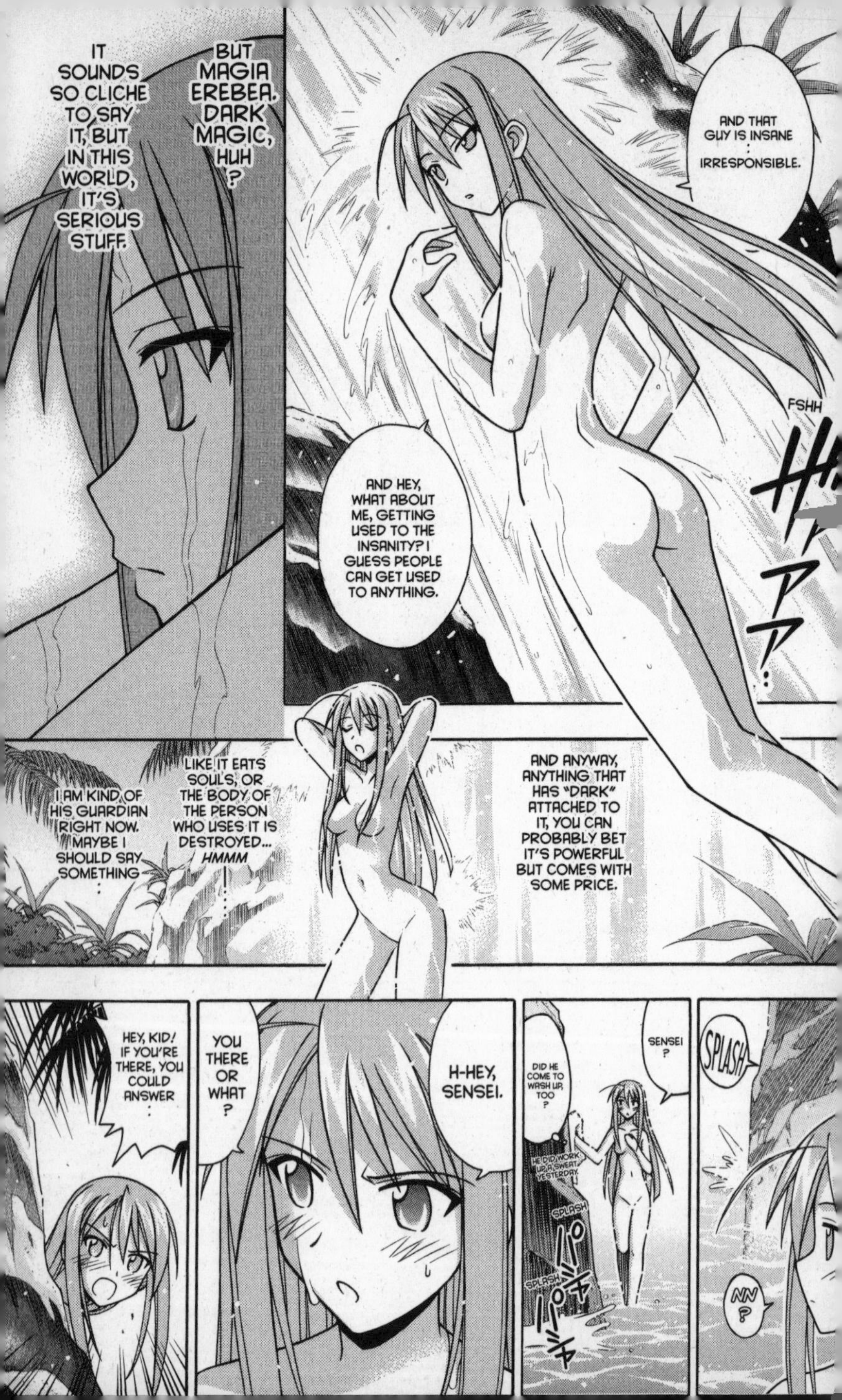
AND THAT GUY IS INSANE : IRRESPONSIBLE.
FSHH
AND HEY, WHAT ABOUT ME, GETTING USED TO THE INSANITY? I GUESS PEOPLE CAN GET USED TO ANYTHING.
BUT MAGIA EREBEA. DARK MAGIC, HUH ?
IT SOUNDS SO CLICHE TO SAY IT, BUT IN THIS WORLD, IT'S SERIOUS STUFF.
AND ANYWAY, ANYTHING THAT HAS "DARK" ATTACHED TO IT, YOU CAN PROBABLY BET IT'S POWERFUL BUT COMES WITH SOME PRICE.
LIKE IT EATS SOULS, OR THE BODY OF THE PERSON WHO USES IT IS DESTROYED... HMMM
I AM KIND OF HIS GUARDIAN RIGHT NOW. MAYBE I SHOULD SAY SOMETHING :
SPLASH
NN ?
SENSEI ?
DID HE COME TO WASH UP, TOO ?
HE DID WORK UP A SWEAT YESTERDAY.
SPLASH
SPLASH
H-HEY, SENSEI.
YOU THERE OR WHAT ?
HEY, KID! IF YOU'RE THERE, YOU COULD ANSWER :

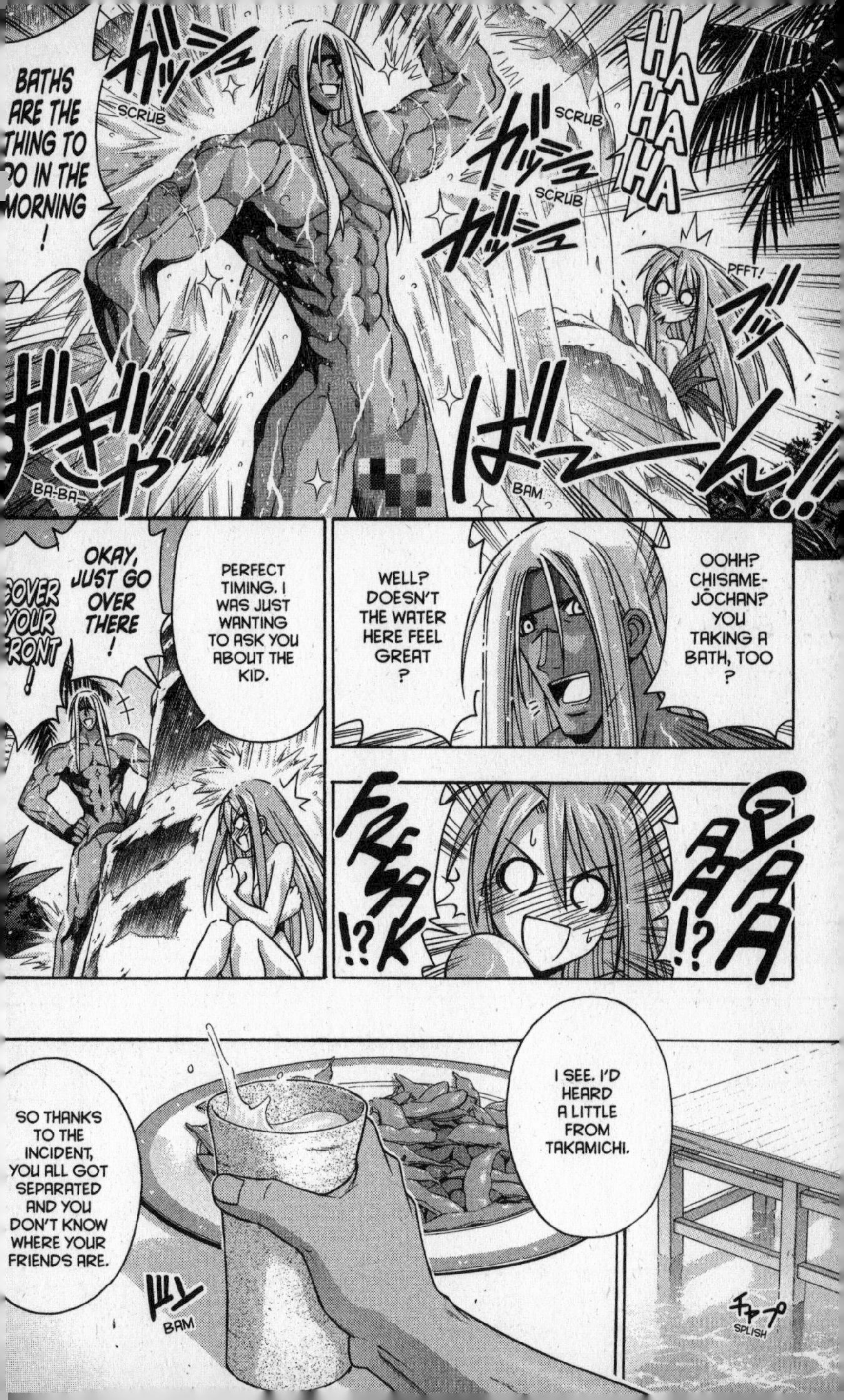
HA HA HA HA
SCRUB
SCRUB
SCRUB
BATHS ARE THE THING TO DO IN THE MORNING!
PFFT!
BAM
BA-BA-
OOHH? CHISAME-JŌCHAN? YOU TAKING A BATH, TOO?
WELL? DOESN'T THE WATER HERE FEEL GREAT?
GYAAAA!?
FREAK!?
PERFECT TIMING. I WAS JUST WANTING TO ASK YOU ABOUT THE KID.
OKAY, JUST GO OVER THERE!
COVER YOUR RONT!
I SEE. I'D HEARD A LITTLE FROM TAKAMICHI.
SO THANKS TO THE INCIDENT, YOU ALL GOT SEPARATED AND YOU DON'T KNOW WHERE YOUR FRIENDS ARE.
BAM
SPLISH

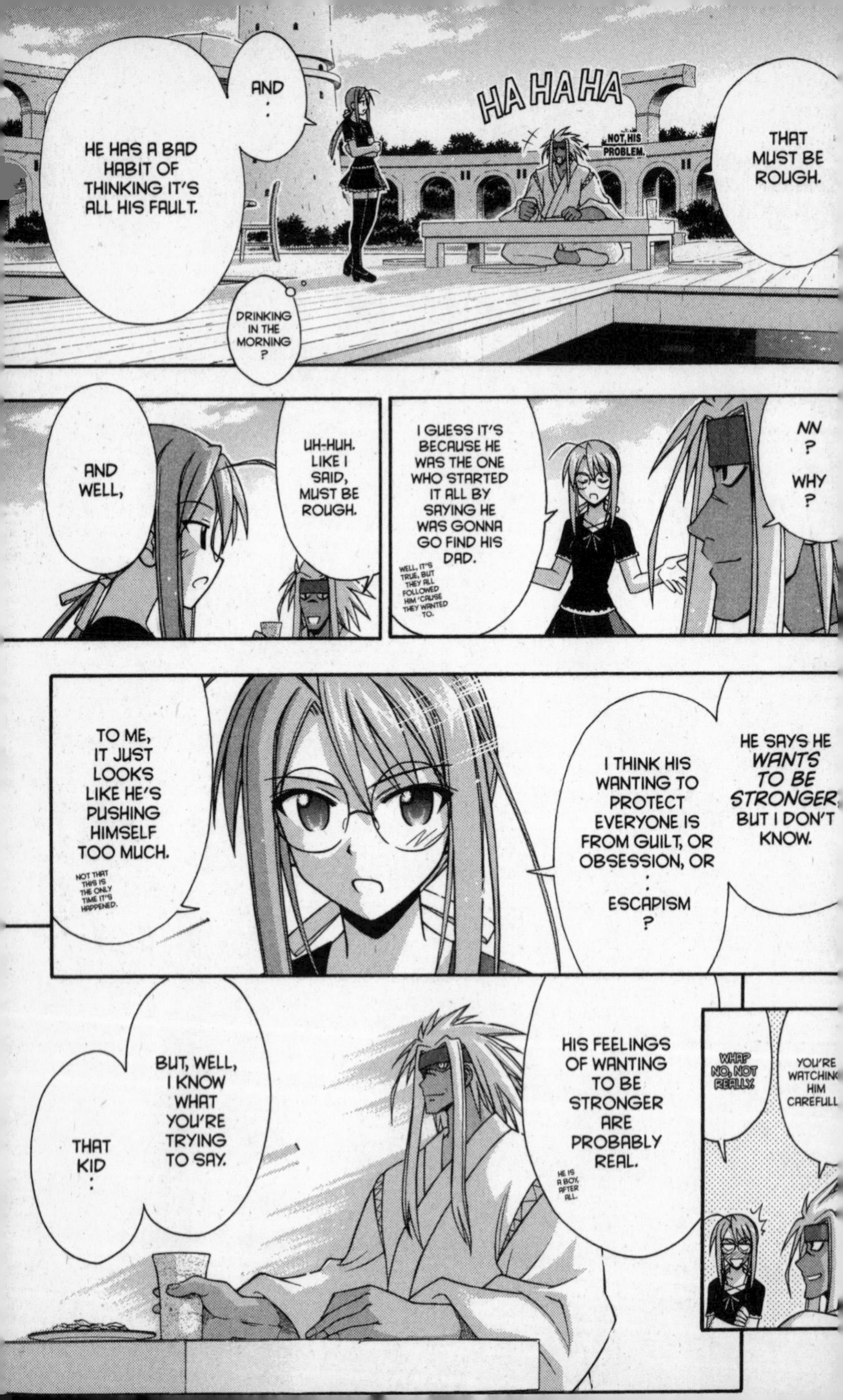
THAT MUST BE ROUGH.
HA HA HA
NOT HIS PROBLEM.
AND :
HE HAS A BAD HABIT OF THINKING IT'S ALL HIS FAULT.
DRINKING IN THE MORNING ?
NN ? WHY ?
I GUESS IT'S BECAUSE HE WAS THE ONE WHO STARTED IT ALL BY SAYING HE WAS GONNA GO FIND HIS DAD.
WELL, IT'S TRUE, BUT THEY ALL FOLLOWED HIM 'CAUSE THEY WANTED TO.
UH-HUH. LIKE I SAID, MUST BE ROUGH.
AND WELL,
HE SAYS HE WANTS TO BE STRONGER BUT I DON'T KNOW.
I THINK HIS WANTING TO PROTECT EVERYONE IS FROM GUILT, OR OBSESSION, OR : ESCAPISM ?
TO ME, IT JUST LOOKS LIKE HE'S PUSHING HIMSELF TOO MUCH.
NOT THAT THIS IS THE ONLY TIME IT'S HAPPENED.
YOU'RE WATCHING HIM CAREFULL
WHA? NO, NOT REALLY.
HIS FEELINGS OF WANTING TO BE STRONGER ARE PROBABLY REAL.
HE IS A BOY, AFTER ALL.
BUT, WELL, I KNOW WHAT YOU'RE TRYING TO SAY.
THAT KID :

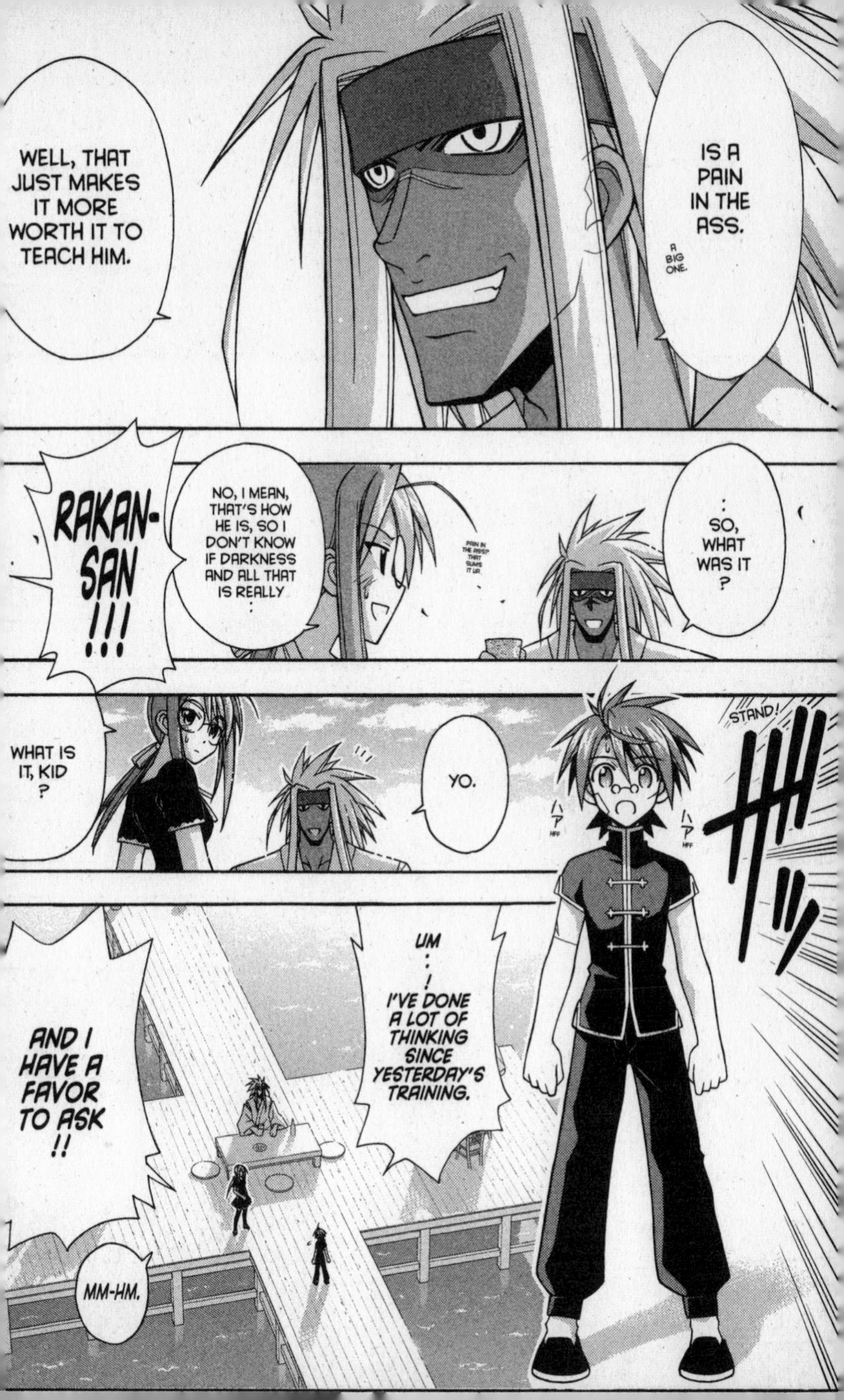
IS A PAIN IN THE ASS.
A BIG ONE.
WELL, THAT JUST MAKES IT MORE WORTH IT TO TEACH HIM.
...SO, WHAT WAS IT?
PAIN IN THE ASS? THAT SUMS IT UP.
NO, I MEAN, THAT'S HOW HE IS, SO I DON'T KNOW IF DARKNESS AND ALL THAT IS REALLY...
RAKAN-SAN!!!
STAND!
HFF
HFF
YO.
WHAT IS IT, KID?
UM...! I'VE DONE A LOT OF THINKING SINCE YESTERDAY'S TRAINING.
AND I HAVE A FAVOR TO ASK!!
MM-HM.

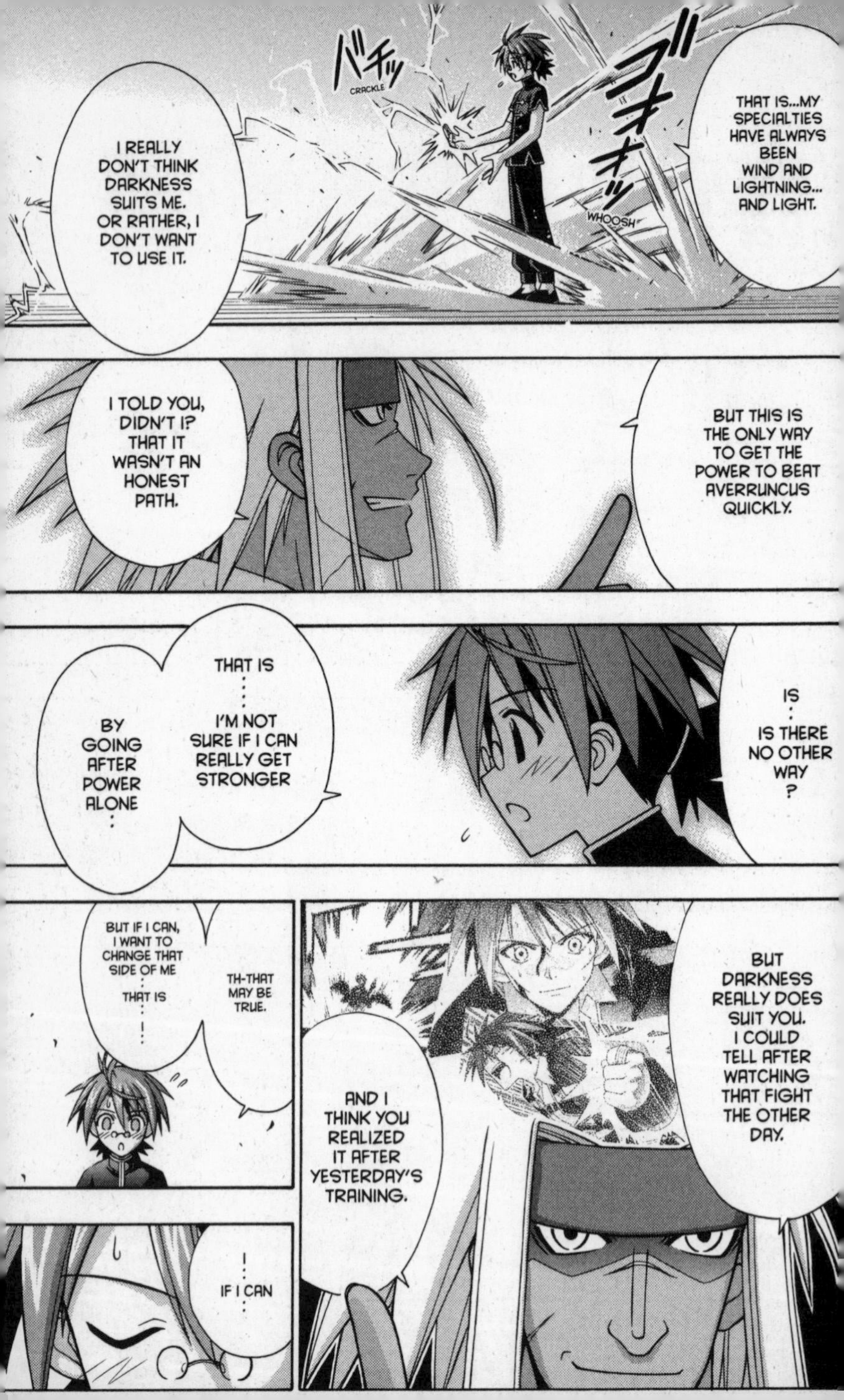
THAT IS...MY SPECIALTIES HAVE ALWAYS BEEN WIND AND LIGHTNING... AND LIGHT.
WHOOSH
CRACKLE
I REALLY DON'T THINK DARKNESS SUITS ME. OR RATHER, I DON'T WANT TO USE IT.
BUT THIS IS THE ONLY WAY TO GET THE POWER TO BEAT AVERRUNCUS QUICKLY.
I TOLD YOU, DIDN'T I? THAT IT WASN'T AN HONEST PATH.
IS... IS THERE NO OTHER WAY?
THAT IS... I'M NOT SURE IF I CAN REALLY GET STRONGER BY GOING AFTER POWER ALONE...
BUT DARKNESS REALLY DOES SUIT YOU. I COULD TELL AFTER WATCHING THAT FIGHT THE OTHER DAY.
AND I THINK YOU REALIZED IT AFTER YESTERDAY'S TRAINING.
TH-THAT MAY BE TRUE.
BUT IF I CAN, I WANT TO CHANGE THAT SIDE OF ME... THAT IS...!
...IF I CAN...

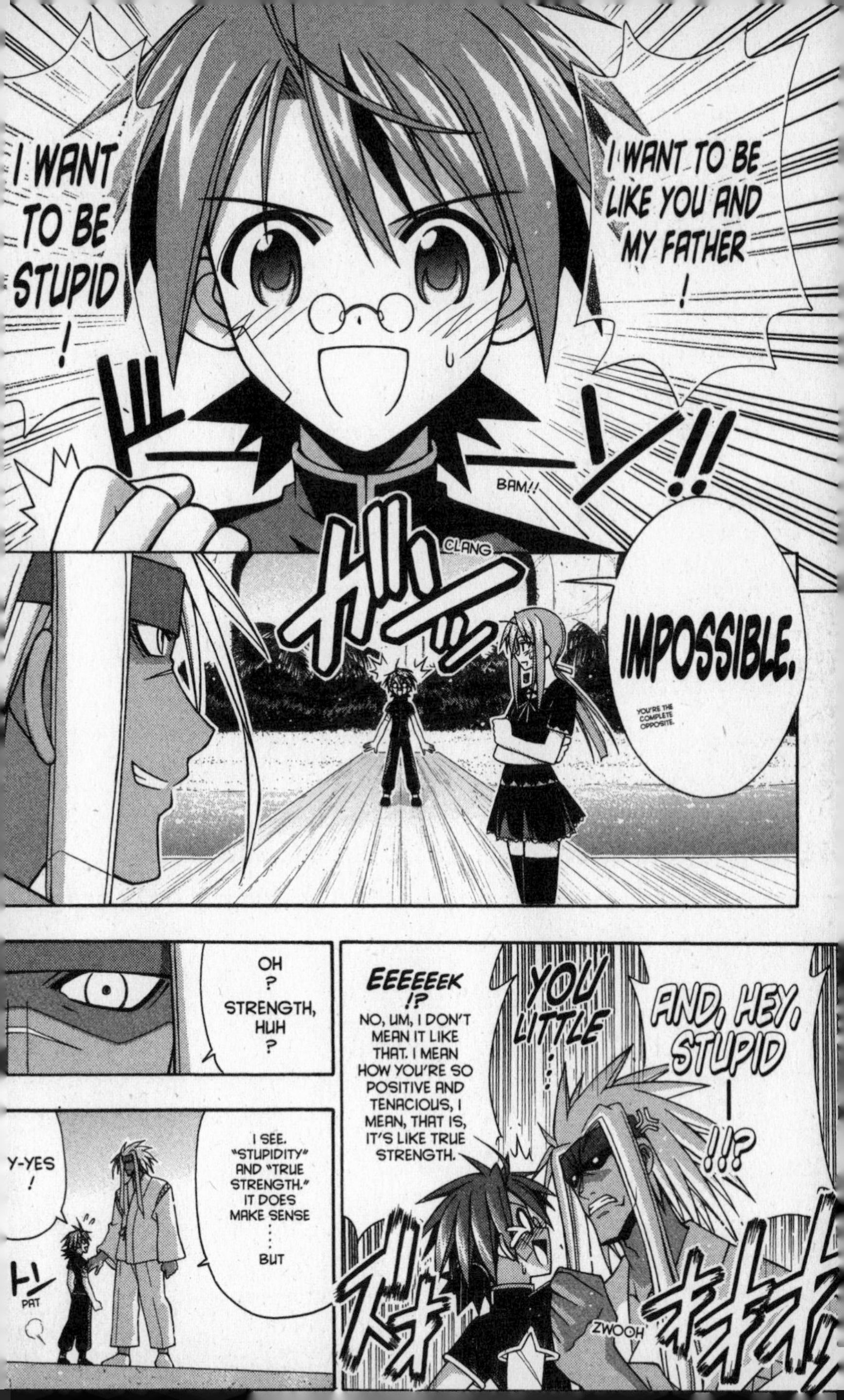

I WANT TO BE LIKE YOU AND MY FATHER!
I WANT TO BE STUPID!
BAM!!
IMPOSSIBLE.
YOU'RE THE COMPLETE OPPOSITE.
CLANG
AND, HEY, STUPID!!?
YOU LITTLE...
EEEEEEK!? NO, UM, I DON'T MEAN IT LIKE THAT. I MEAN HOW YOU'RE SO POSITIVE AND TENACIOUS, I MEAN, THAT IS, IT'S LIKE TRUE STRENGTH.
ZWOOH
OH? STRENGTH, HUH?
I SEE. "STUPIDITY" AND "TRUE STRENGTH." IT DOES MAKE SENSE... BUT
Y-YES!
PAT

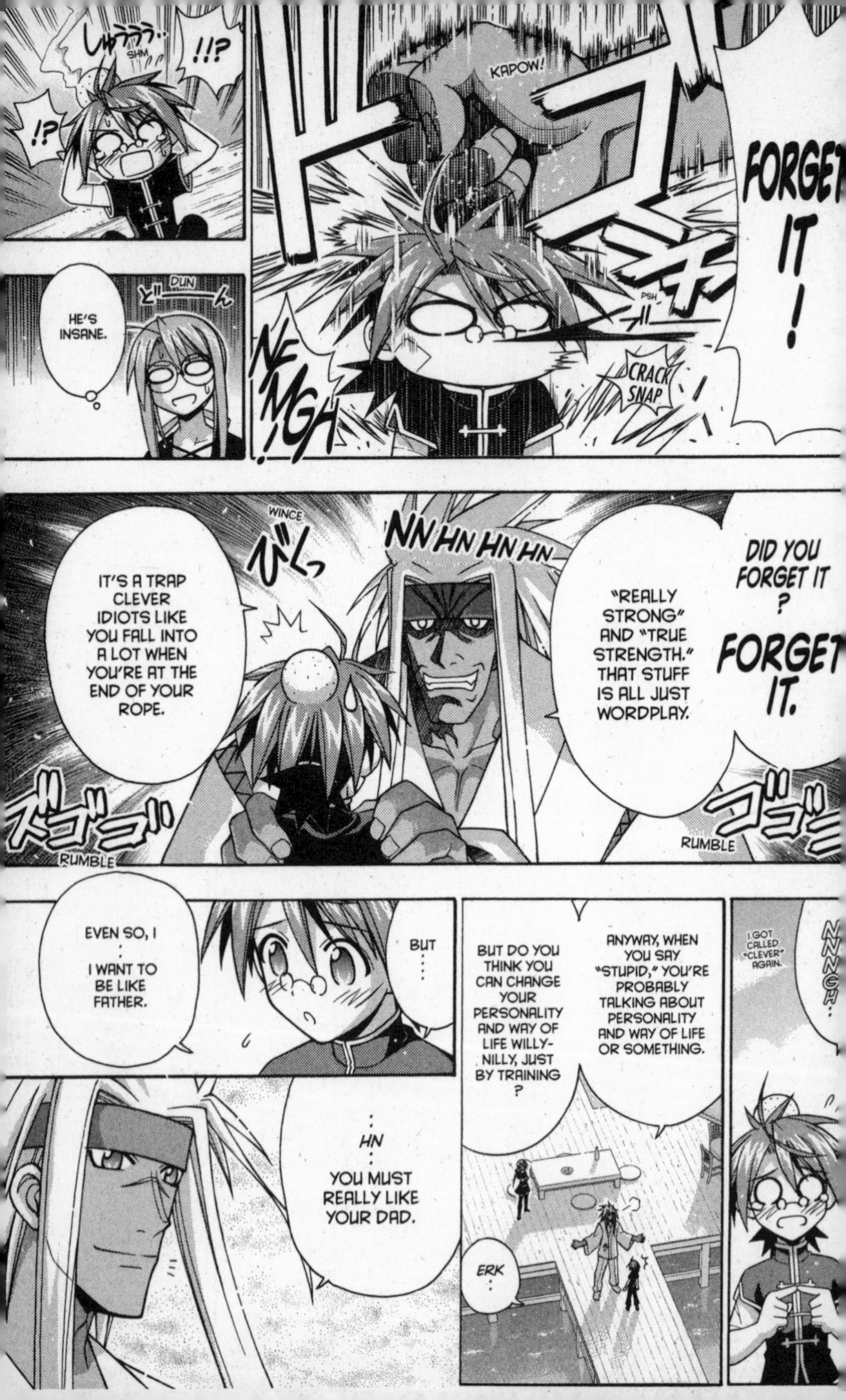
FORGET IT!
KAPOW!
PSH
CRACK SNAP
NNGH!
SHM
!!?
!?
DUN
HE'S INSANE.
DID YOU FORGET IT? FORGET IT.
"REALLY STRONG" AND "TRUE STRENGTH." THAT STUFF IS ALL JUST WORDPLAY.
NN HN HN HN
RUMBLE
WINCE
IT'S A TRAP CLEVER IDIOTS LIKE YOU FALL INTO A LOT WHEN YOU'RE AT THE END OF YOUR ROPE.
RUMBLE
NNNGH...
I GOT CALLED "CLEVER" AGAIN.
ANYWAY, WHEN YOU SAY "STUPID," YOU'RE PROBABLY TALKING ABOUT PERSONALITY AND WAY OF LIFE OR SOMETHING.
BUT DO YOU THINK YOU CAN CHANGE YOUR PERSONALITY AND WAY OF LIFE WILLY-NILLY, JUST BY TRAINING?
ERK...
BUT...
EVEN SO, I... I WANT TO BE LIKE FATHER.
...HN... YOU MUST REALLY LIKE YOUR DAD.

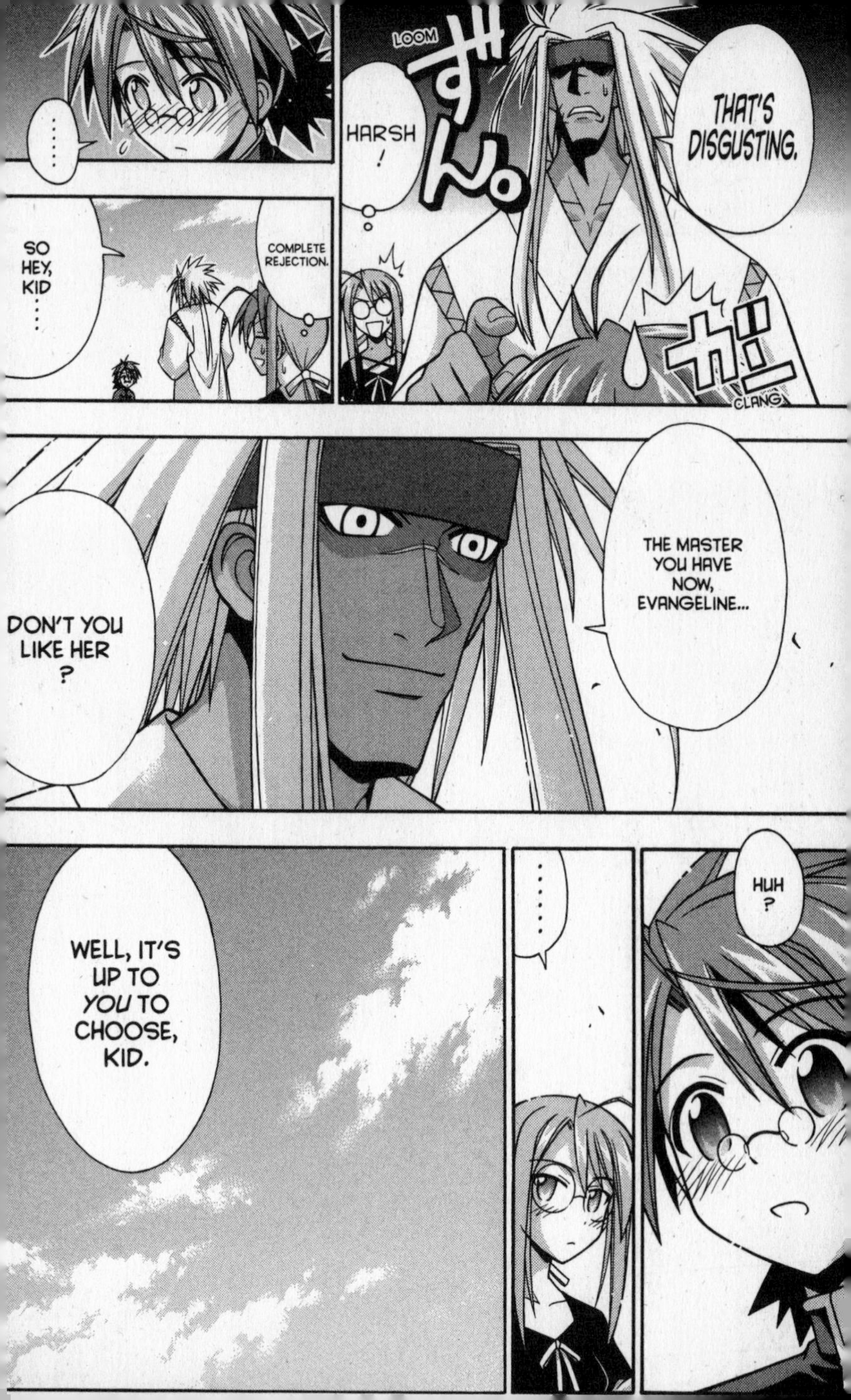
THAT'S DISGUSTING.
LOOM
HARSH!
CLANG
......
COMPLETE REJECTION.
SO HEY, KID....
THE MASTER YOU HAVE NOW, EVANGELINE...
DON'T YOU LIKE HER?
HUH?
......
WELL, IT'S UP TO *YOU* TO CHOOSE, KID.

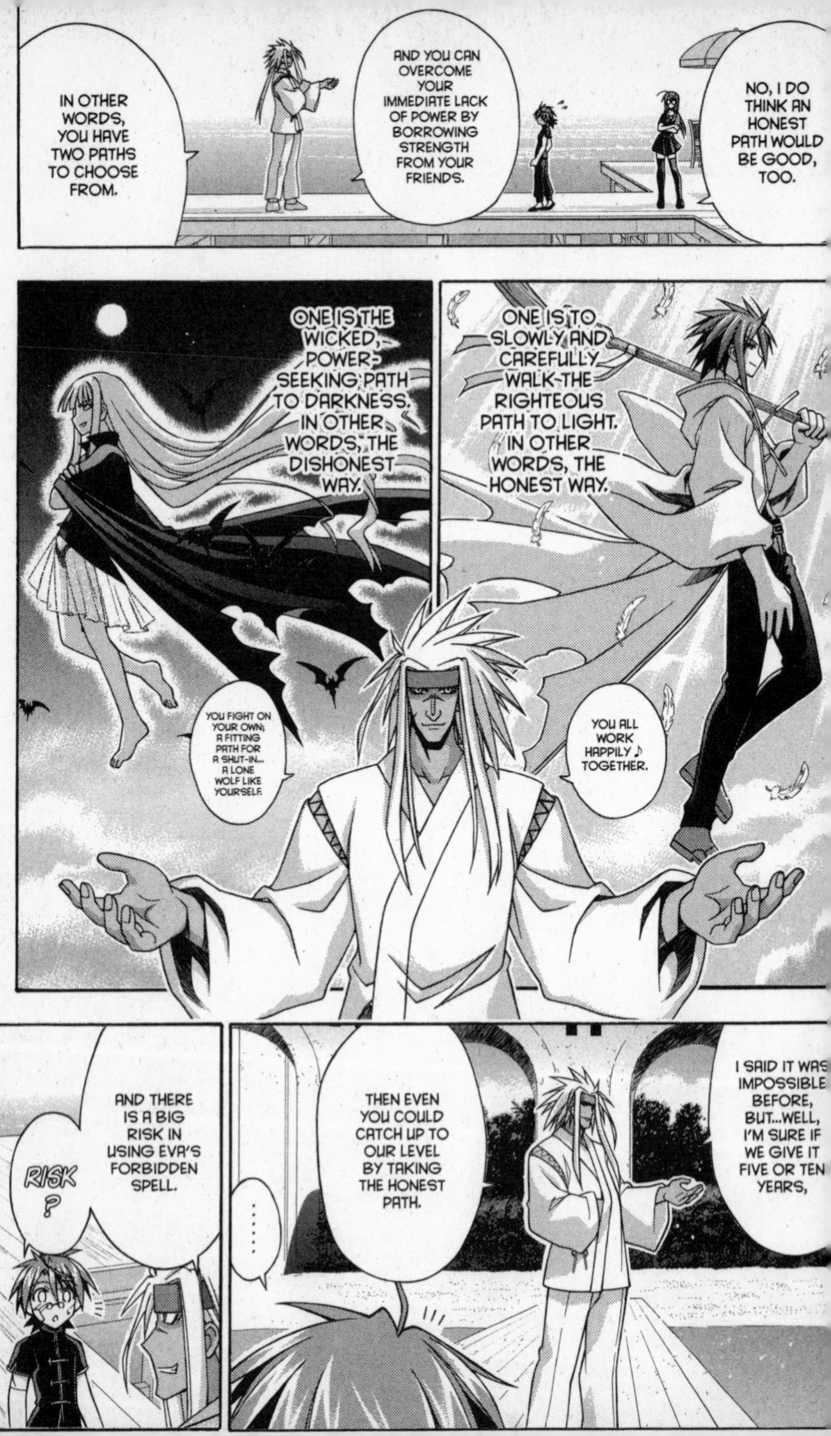
NO, I DO THINK AN HONEST PATH WOULD BE GOOD, TOO.
AND YOU CAN OVERCOME YOUR IMMEDIATE LACK OF POWER BY BORROWING STRENGTH FROM YOUR FRIENDS.
IN OTHER WORDS, YOU HAVE TWO PATHS TO CHOOSE FROM.
ONE IS TO SLOWLY AND CAREFULLY WALK THE RIGHTEOUS PATH TO LIGHT. IN OTHER WORDS, THE HONEST WAY.
ONE IS THE WICKED, POWER-SEEKING PATH TO DARKNESS. IN OTHER WORDS, THE DISHONEST WAY.
YOU ALL WORK HAPPILY♪ TOGETHER.
YOU FIGHT ON YOUR OWN; A FITTING PATH FOR A SHUT-IN... A LONE WOLF LIKE YOURSELF.
I SAID IT WAS IMPOSSIBLE BEFORE, BUT...WELL, I'M SURE IF WE GIVE IT FIVE OR TEN YEARS,
THEN EVEN YOU COULD CATCH UP TO OUR LEVEL BY TAKING THE HONEST PATH.
......
AND THERE IS A BIG RISK IN USING EVA'S FORBIDDEN SPELL.
RISK?

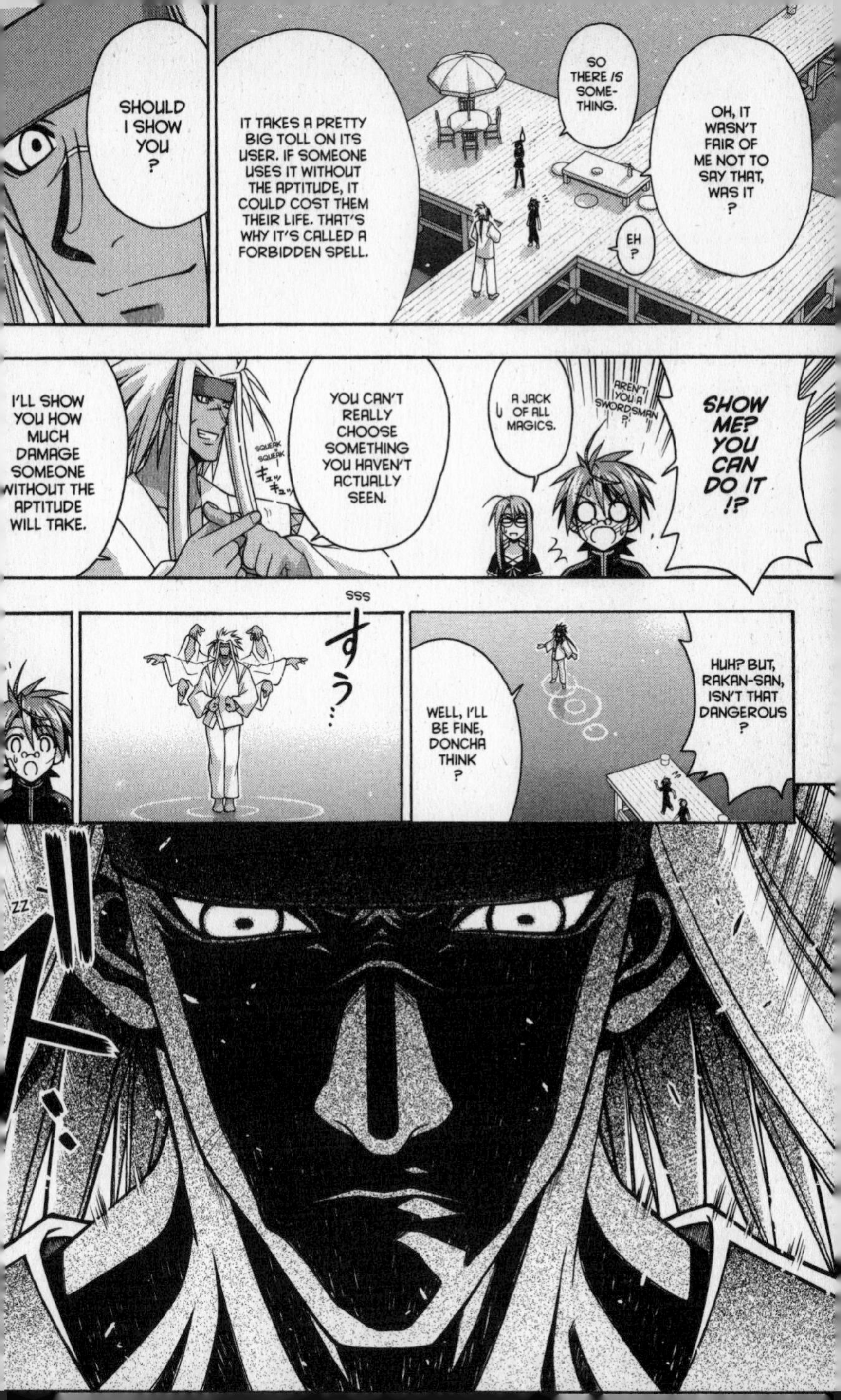

OH, IT WASN'T FAIR OF ME NOT TO SAY THAT, WAS IT?
SO THERE *IS* SOMETHING.
EH?
IT TAKES A PRETTY BIG TOLL ON ITS USER. IF SOMEONE USES IT WITHOUT THE APTITUDE, IT COULD COST THEM THEIR LIFE. THAT'S WHY IT'S CALLED A FORBIDDEN SPELL.
SHOULD I SHOW YOU?
SHOW ME? YOU CAN DO IT!?
AREN'T YOU A SWORDSMAN?!
A JACK OF ALL MAGICS.
YOU CAN'T REALLY CHOOSE SOMETHING YOU HAVEN'T ACTUALLY SEEN.
SQUEAK SQUEAK
キュッキュッ
I'LL SHOW YOU HOW MUCH DAMAGE SOMEONE WITHOUT THE APTITUDE WILL TAKE.
HUH? BUT, RAKAN-SAN, ISN'T THAT DANGEROUS?
WELL, I'LL BE FINE, DONCHA THINK?
SSS
すう…
ZZ

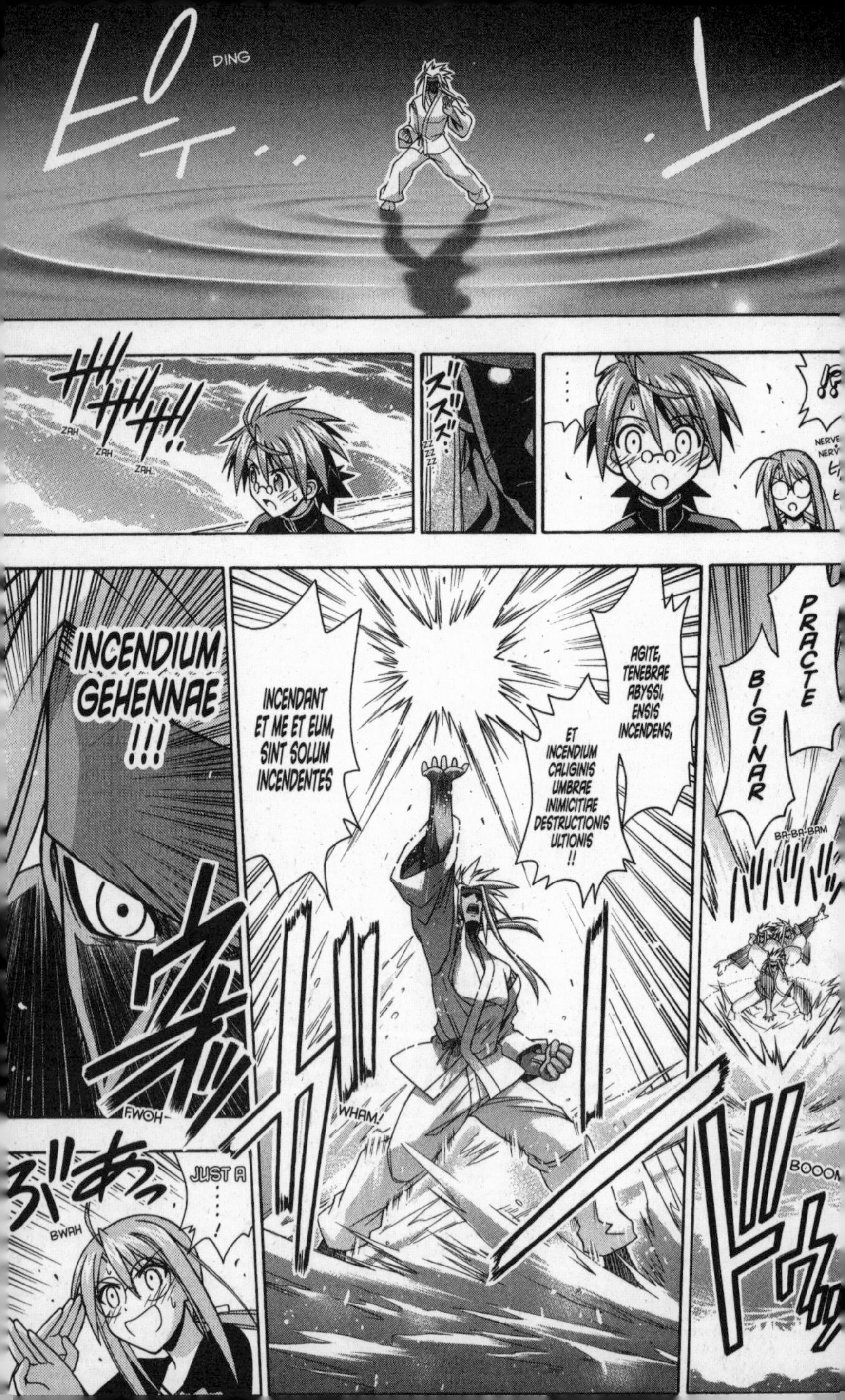
DING
!?
NERVE NERVE
ZZ ZZ ZZ
ZAH ZAH ZAH..
PRACTE BIGINAR
BA-BA-BAM
AGITE, TENEBRAE ABYSSI, ENSIS INCENDENS,
ET INCENDIUM CALIGINIS UMBRAE INIMICITIAE DESTRUCTIONIS ULTIONIS !!
INCENDANT ET ME ET EUM, SINT SOLUM INCENDENTES
INCENDIUM GEHENNAE !!!
FWOH
BOOOM
WHAM!
JUST A ......!
BWAH

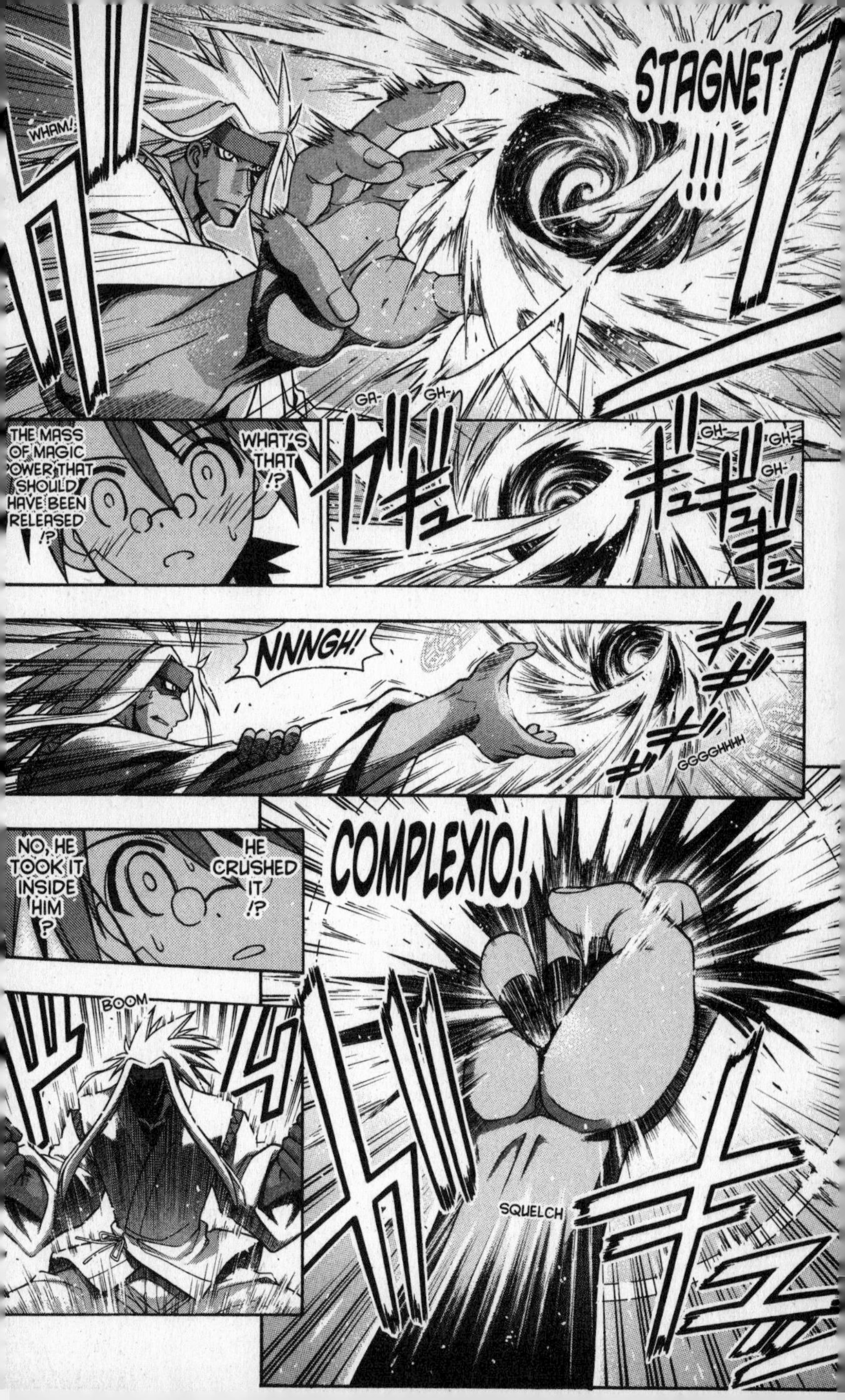

WHAM!
STAGNET!!!
GA-
GH-
GH-
GH-
GH-
WHAT'S THAT!?
THE MASS OF MAGIC POWER THAT SHOULD HAVE BEEN RELEASED!?
NNNGH!
GGGGHHHH
COMPLEXIO!
SQUELCH
HE CRUSHED IT!?
NO, HE TOOK IT INSIDE HIM?
BOOM

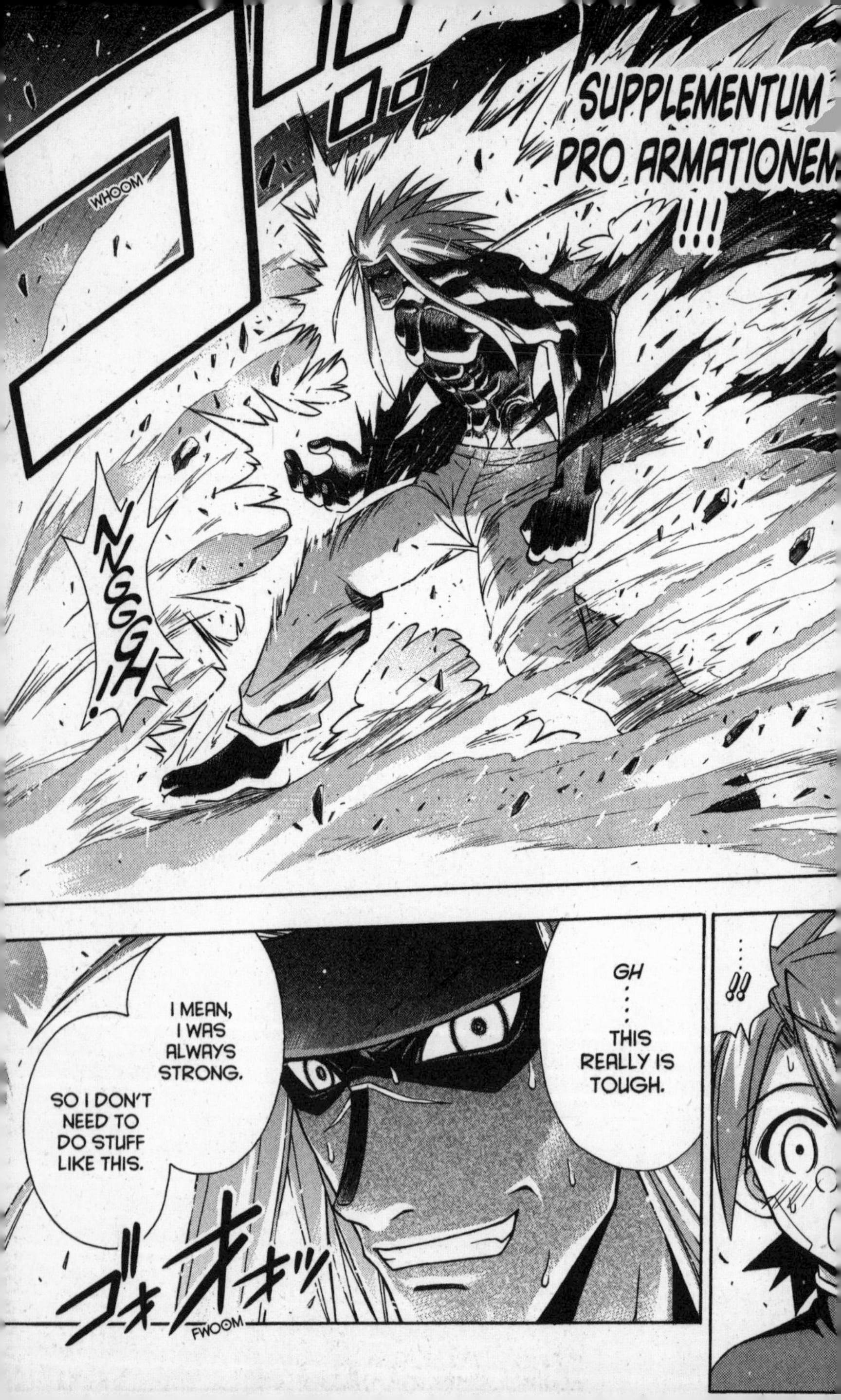
SUPPLEMENTUM PRO ARMATIONEM!!!
WHOOM
NNGGGH!!
...!!
GH... THIS REALLY IS TOUGH.
I MEAN, I WAS ALWAYS STRONG.
SO I DON'T NEED TO DO STUFF LIKE THIS.
FWOOM

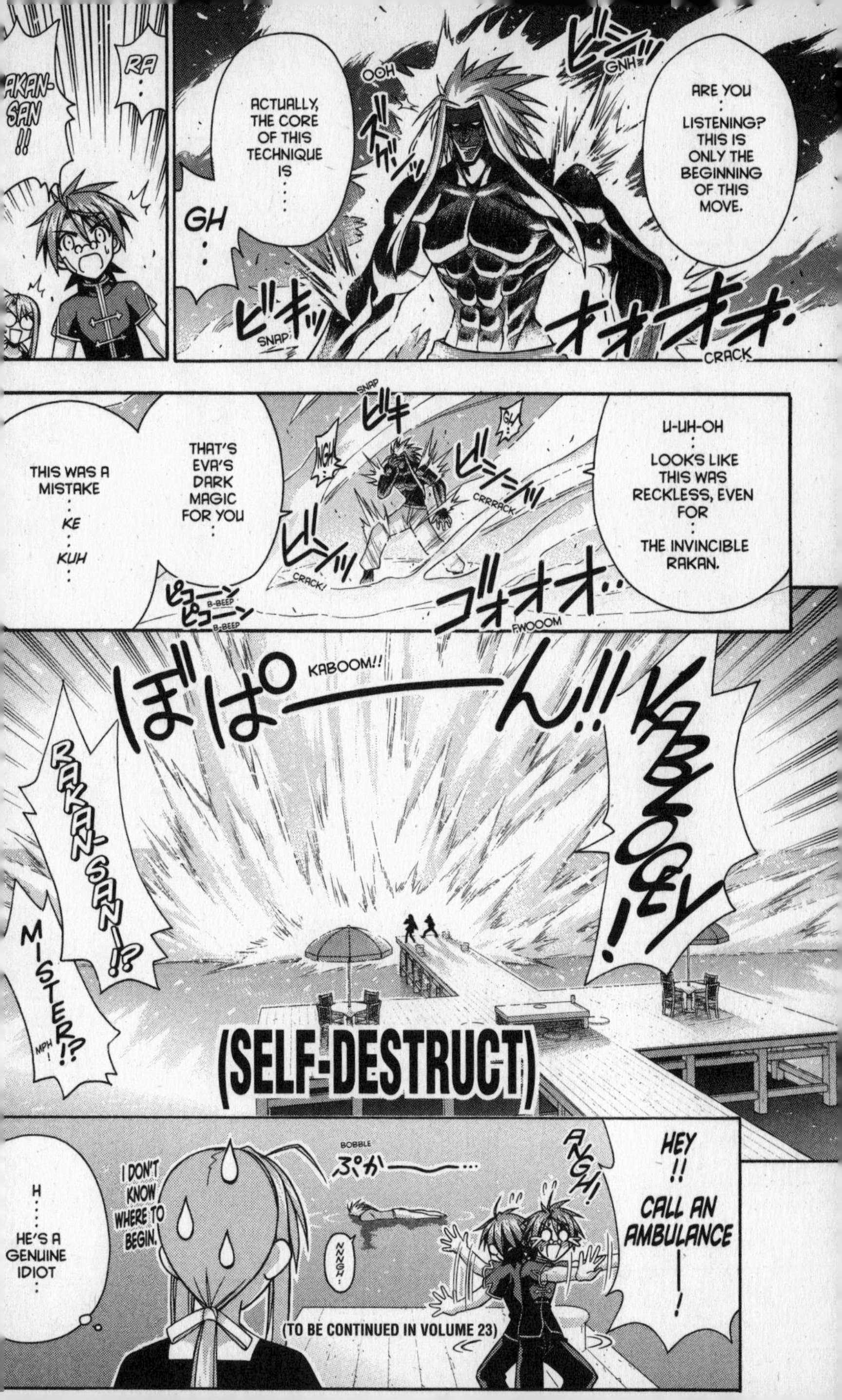
GNH
ARE YOU... LISTENING? THIS IS ONLY THE BEGINNING OF THIS MOVE.
OOH
ACTUALLY, THE CORE OF THIS TECHNIQUE IS...
GH...
SNAP
CRACK
RA...
AKAN-SAN !!
U-UH-OH... LOOKS LIKE THIS WAS RECKLESS, EVEN FOR... THE INVINCIBLE RAKAN.
SNAP
GH
NGH
CRRRACK
CRACK!
FWOOOM
THAT'S EVA'S DARK MAGIC FOR YOU...
THIS WAS A MISTAKE... KE... KUH...
B-BEEP
B-BEEP
KABLOOEY!
KABOOM!!
RAKAN-SAN!!?
MISTER!!?
MPH!
(SELF-DESTRUCT)
HEY!! CALL AN AMBULANCE—!
ANGH!
BOBBLE
NNNGH...
I DON'T KNOW WHERE TO BEGIN.
H... HE'S A GENUINE IDIOT...
(TO BE CONTINUED IN VOLUME 23)

- STAFF -

Ken Akamatsu
Takashi Takemoto
Kenichi Nakamura
Masaki Ohyama
Keiichi Yamashita
Tadashi Maki
Tohru Mitsuhashi

Thanks To

Ran Ayanaga

MAGICAL WORLD MAP & CLASSMATES

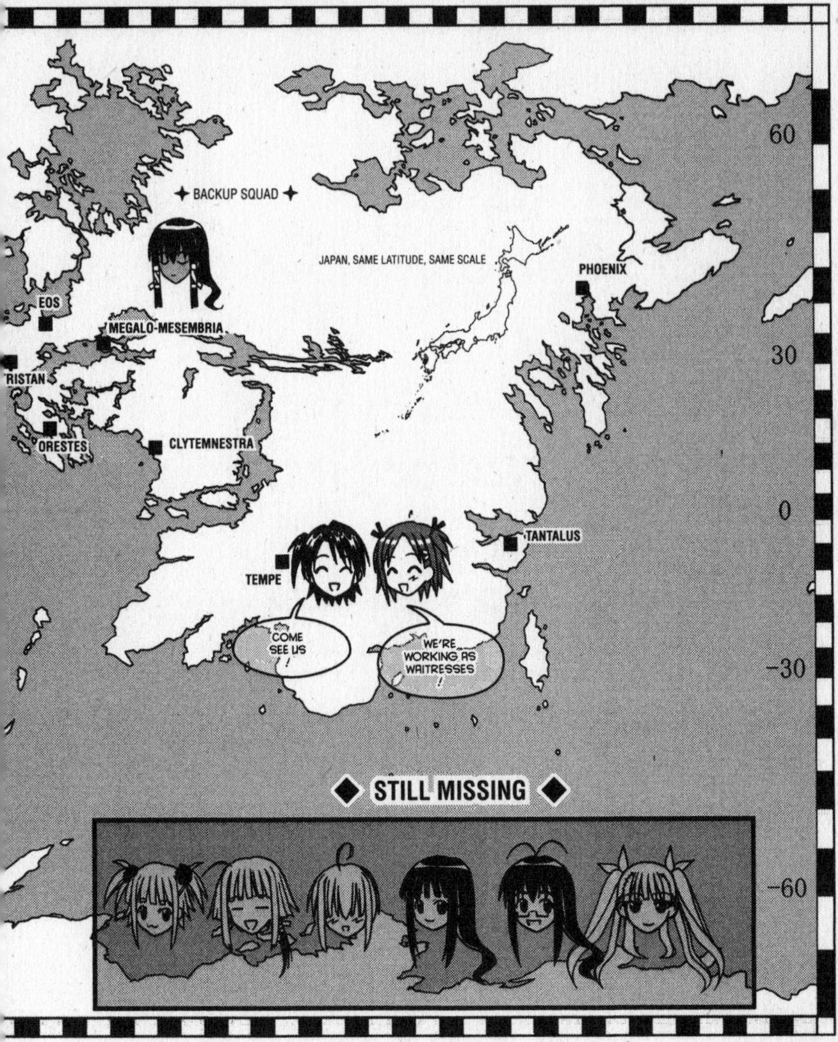

BACKUP SQUAD
JAPAN, SAME LATITUDE, SAME SCALE
PHOENIX
EOS
MEGALO-MESEMBRIA
RISTAN
ORESTES
CLYTEMNESTRA
TANTALUS
TEMPE
COME SEE US!
WE'RE WORKING AS WAITRESSES!
60
30
0
-30
-60
STILL MISSING

Tabula Mundi Magici

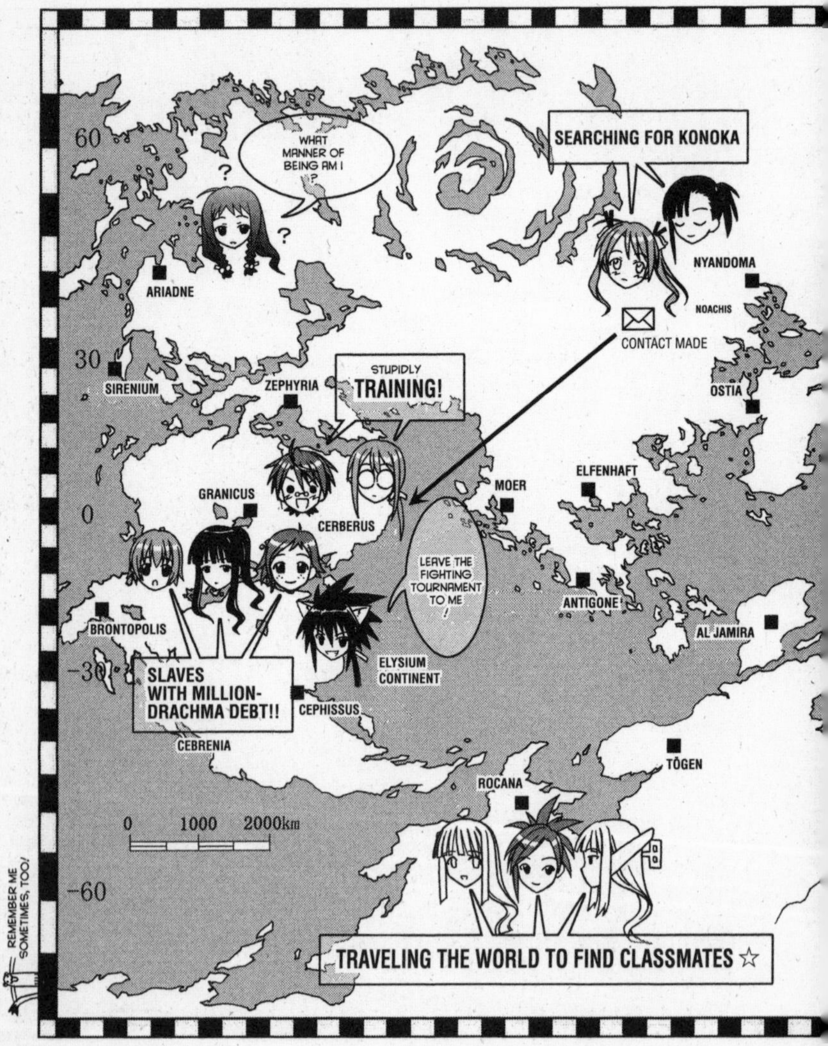

SEARCHING FOR KONOKA
WHAT MANNER OF BEING AM I ?
?
?
60
30
0
-30
-60
ARIADNE
NYANDOMA
NOACHIS
CONTACT MADE
SIRENIUM
ZEPHYRIA
STUPIDLY TRAINING!
OSTIA
ELFENHAFT
MOER
GRANICUS
CERBERUS
LEAVE THE FIGHTING TOURNAMENT TO ME !
ANTIGONE
AL JAMIRA
BRONTOPOLIS
ELYSIUM CONTINENT
SLAVES WITH MILLION-DRACHMA DEBT!!
CEPHISSUS
CEBRENIA
TŌGEN
ROCANA
0 1000 2000km
TRAVELING THE WORLD TO FIND CLASSMATES ☆
REMEMBER ME SOMETIMES, TOO!

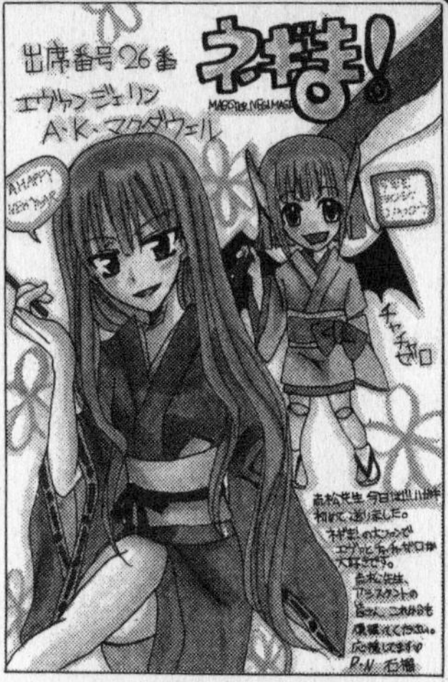
出席番号26番
ネギま!
MAGISTER NEGI MAGI
エヴァンジェリン A・K・マクダウェル

LOOKS GOOD IN JAPANESE CLOTHING, TOO. ▶

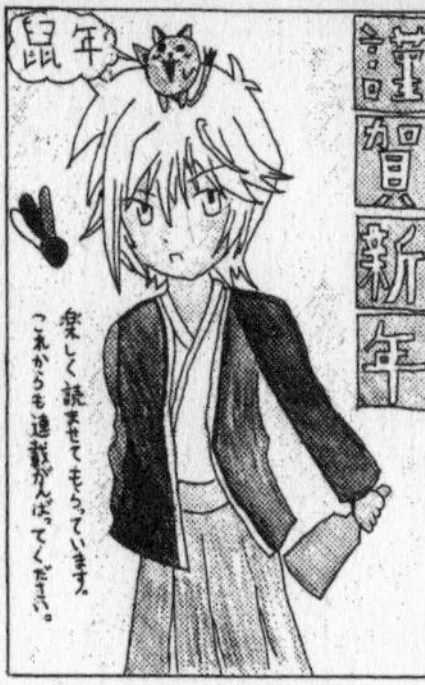
鼠年
謹賀新年
楽しく読ませてもらっています。これからも連載がんばってください。

▲ HEARTWARMING FATE

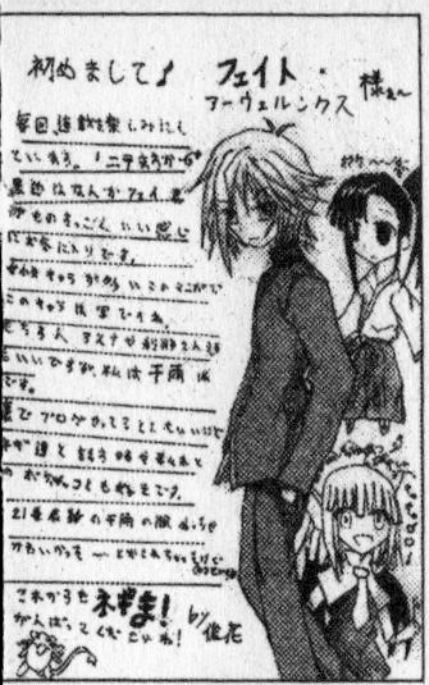
初めまして♪ フェイト・アーウェルンクス 様ぇ〜

▲ LOOKS POPULAR (LAUGH)

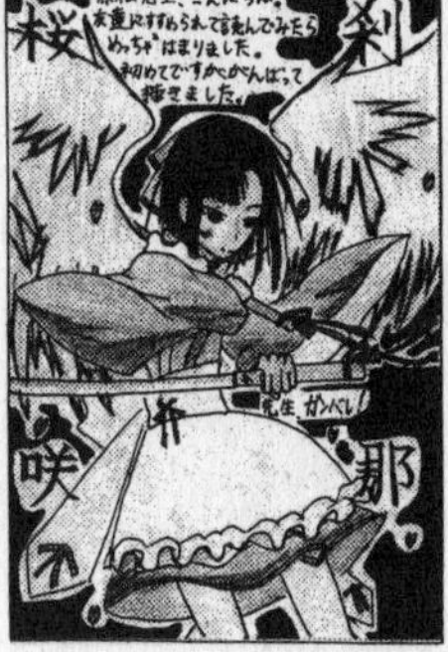
赤松先生、こんにちは。
桜
刹
咲
那

▶ COOL☆

NEGIMA!
FAN ART CORNER

I WRACKED MY BRAINS CHOOSING THESE, TOO (^^; SETSUNA, ASUNA, AND EVA HAVE ALWAYS BEEN POPULAR, BUT NOW I'M STARTING TO FEEL MORE AND MORE LOVE FOR FATE, KOTARŌ, AND ANYA ★ ANYHOW, LET'S GET STARTED (^^)

TEXT BY ASSISTANT MAX

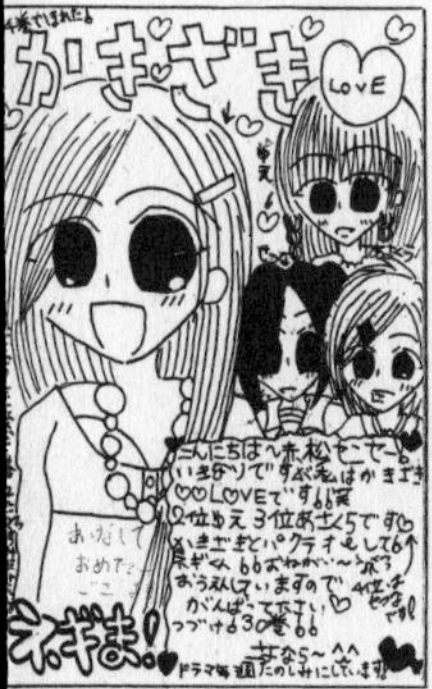
かきざき
LOVE
ネギま!

▲ OOHH! IT'S KAKIZAKI!

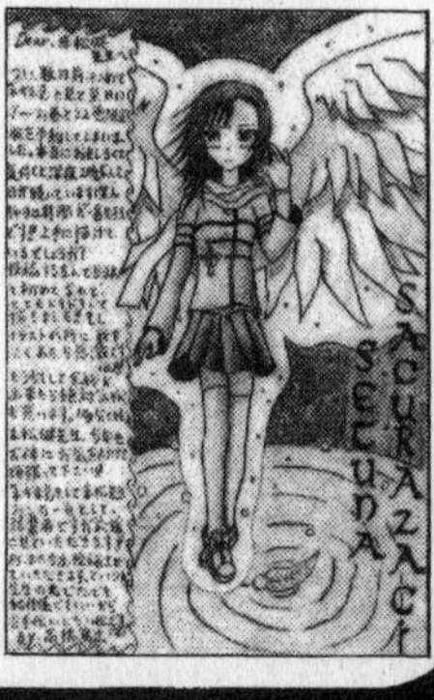
SACURAZACI
SECUNA

▶ IT'S REFRESHING TO SEE HER IN NORMAL CLOTHES.

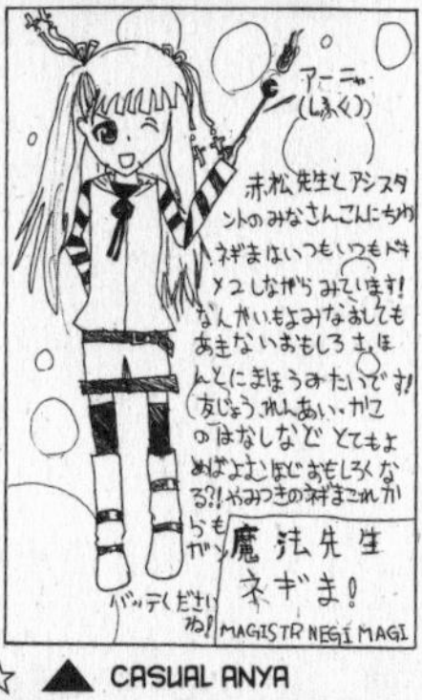
魔法先生
ネギま!
MAGISTR NEGI MAGI

▲ CASUAL ANYA

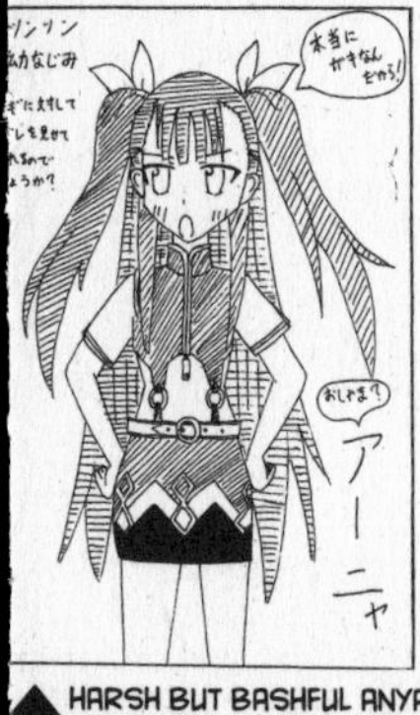
本当にガキなんだから!
おしゃま?
アーニャ

▲ HARSH BUT BASHFUL ANYA☆

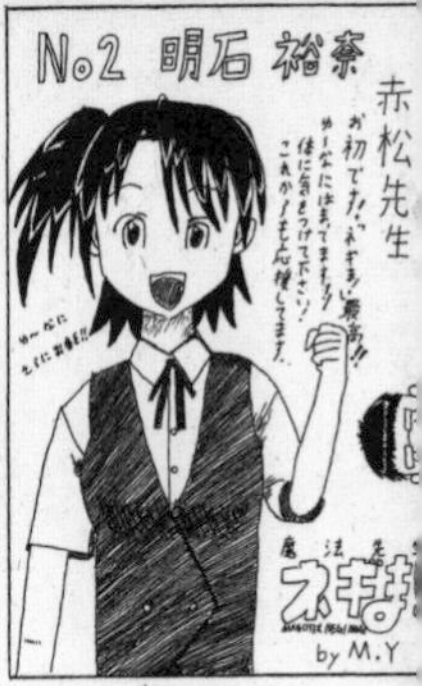
No2 明石 裕奈
赤松先生
ネギま!
by M.Y

▲ EVER-ENERGETIC YŪNA ☆

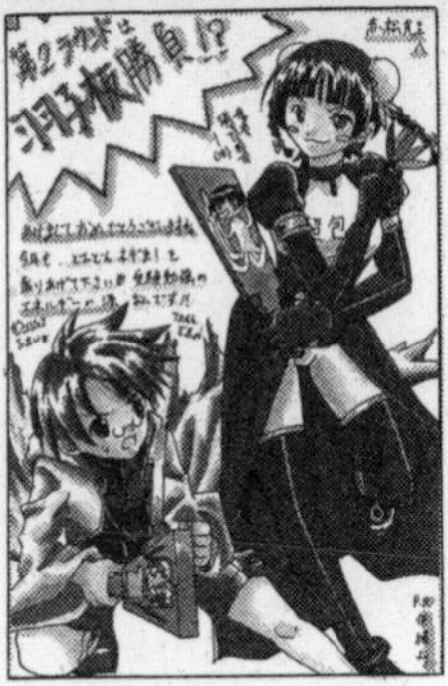
第2ラウンドは
羽子板勝負!?

▲ THE PICTURES ON THEIR PADDLES ARE FUN.

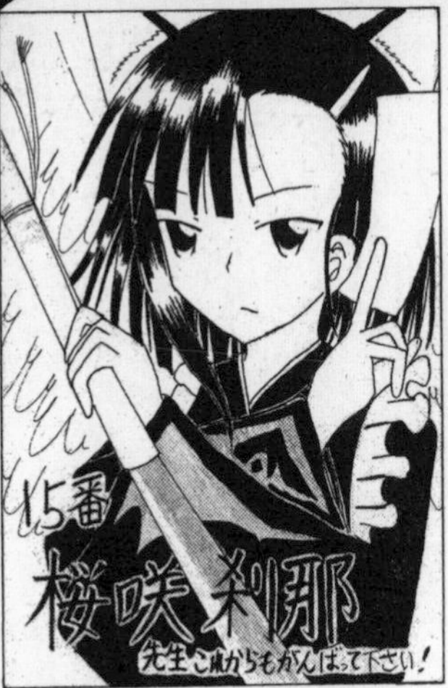
15番
桜咲刹那
先生これからもがんばって下さい!

▲ IT HAS A "FWIP!" FEELING

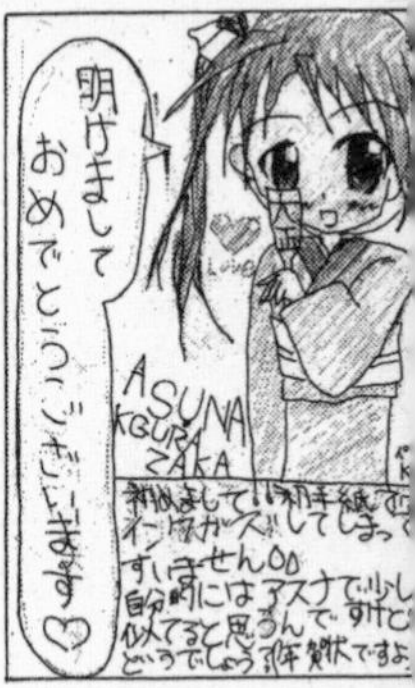
明けましておめでとうございます♡
ASUNA KGURA ZAKA

▲ IT DOES LOOK LIKE HER(^

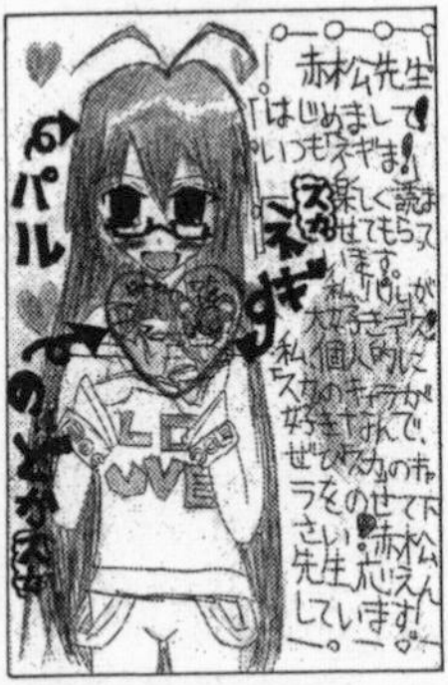
赤松先生
「はじめまして!
パル
ネギ

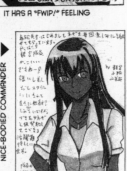

▲ YOU EVEN COLORED HER ANTENNAE ♡

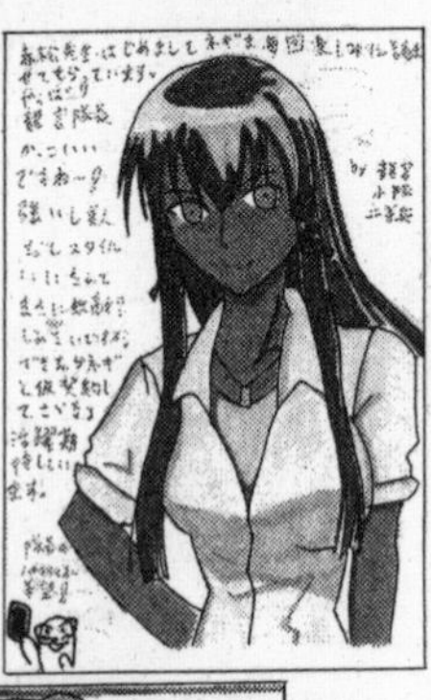

NICE-BODIED COMMANDER ▶

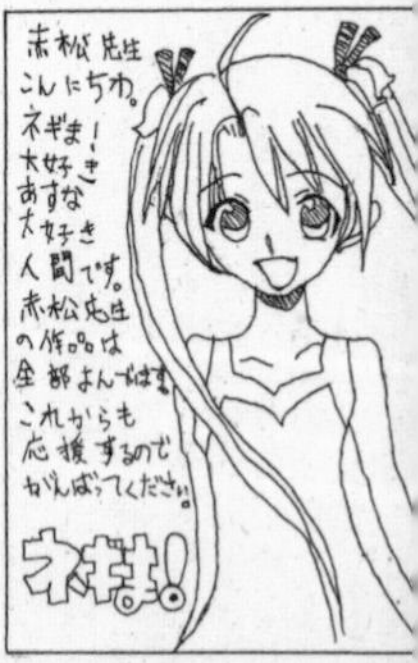
赤松先生こんにちわ。
ネギま!大好きあすな大好き人間です。
赤松先生の作品は全部よんでます。
これからも応援するのでがんばってください。
ネギま!

▲ YES☆THANK YOU FOR YOUR SUPPORT!

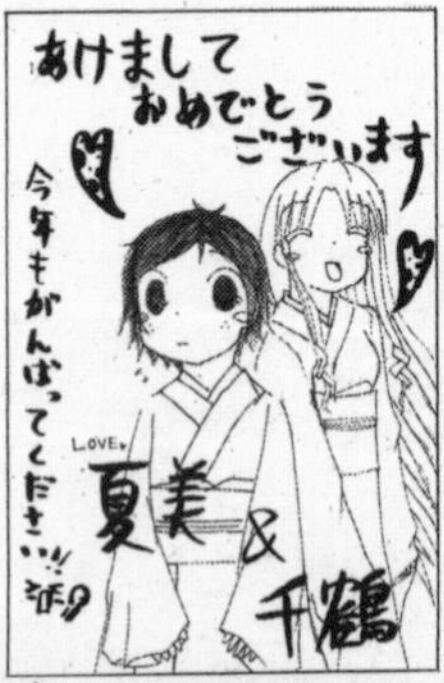
あけましておめでとうございます
今年もがんばってください!!
LOVE
夏美 & 千鶴

▲ THEY WORK WELL TOGETHER, DON'T THEY?

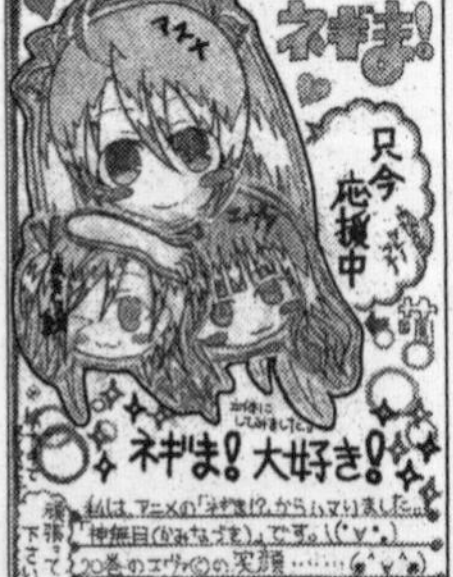
ネギま!
只今応援中
ネギま!大好き!

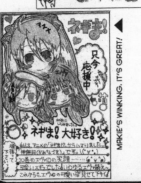

◀ MAKIE'S WINKING. IT'S GREAT!

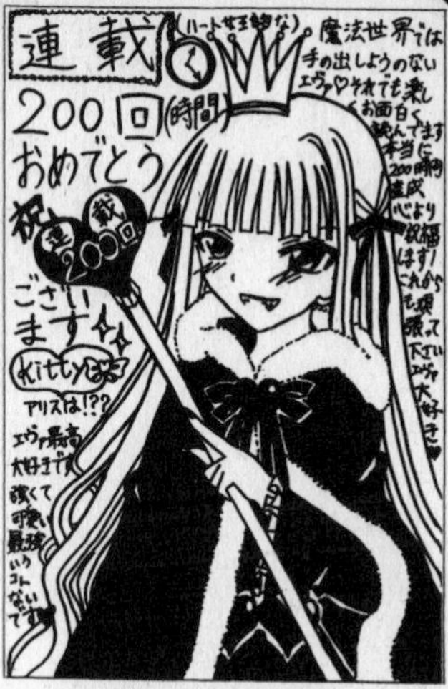
連載200回(時間)おめでとう
ございます

THE COSTUME SUITS HER (LAUGH)

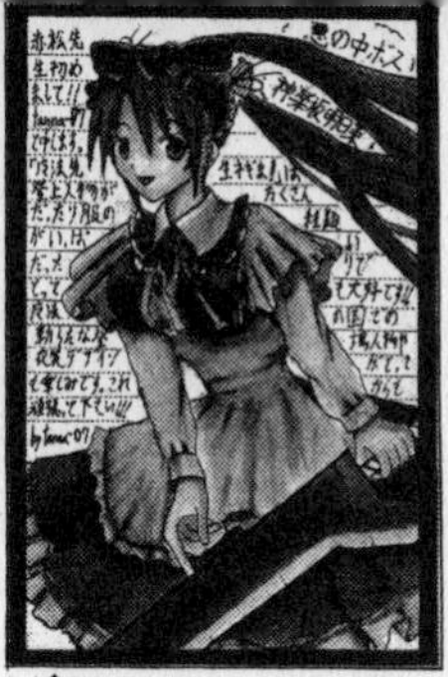

A NICE, RUGGED DESIGN.

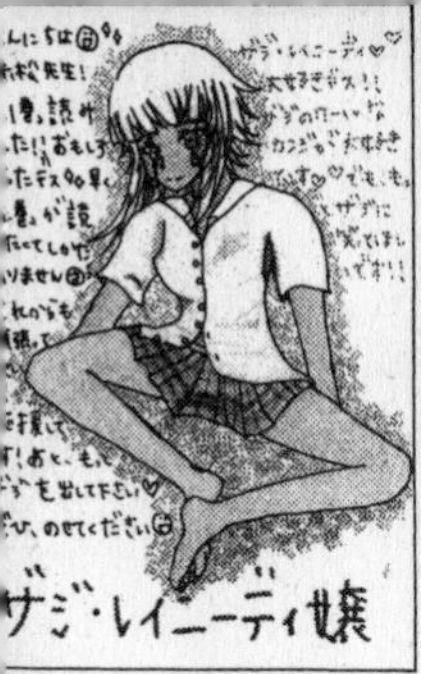
ザジ・レイニーディ嬢

I FEEL ZAZIE'S PRESENCE.

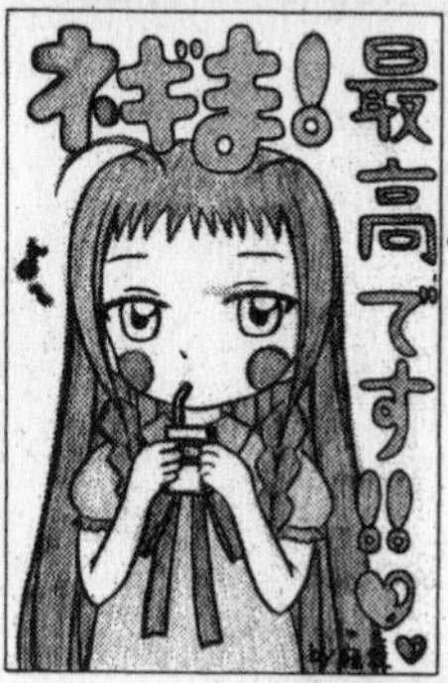
ネギま!最高です!!

WHAT JUICE IS SHE DRINKING? (LAUGH)

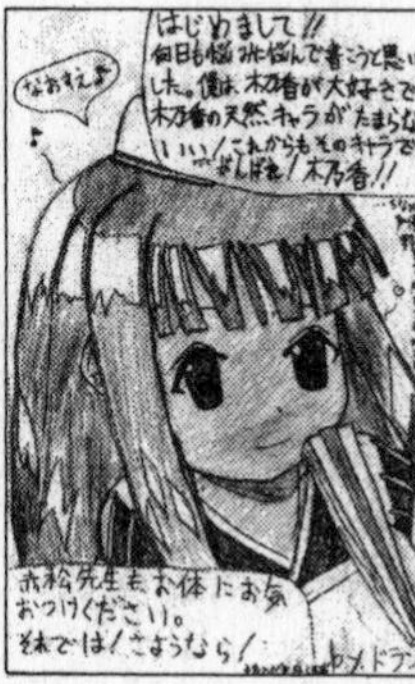
はじめまして!!

SO GENTEEL (^^)

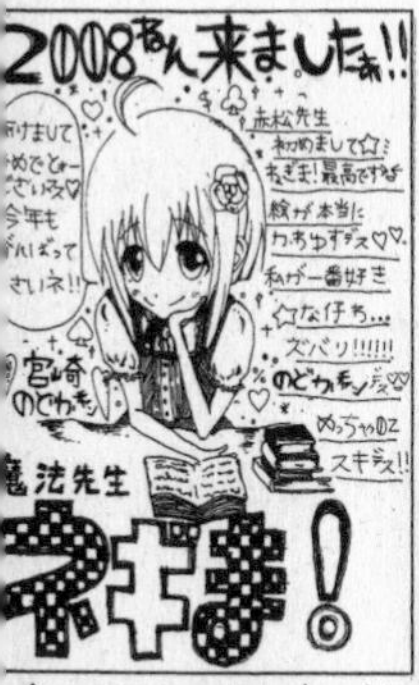
2008ねん来ましたぁ!!
魔法先生
ネギま!

EVEN HER CLOTHES ARE DETAILED (^^)

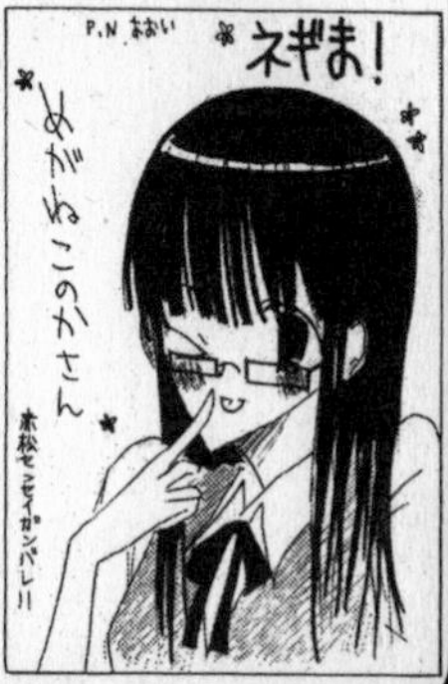
ネギま!
めがねこのかさん

SHE LOOKS GOOD IN GLASSES.

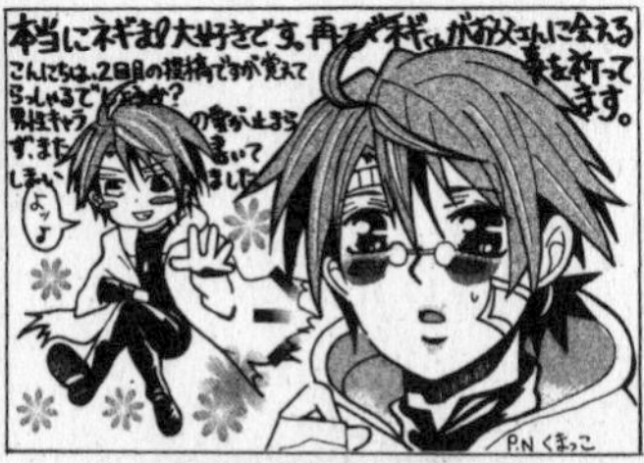
本当にネギま!大好きです。

THANKS FOR SUPPORTING OUR MALE CHARACTERS!

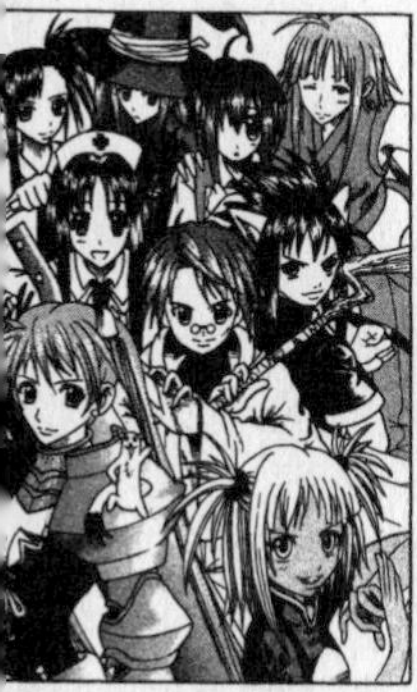

IT'S A MASTERPIECE☆

今回の FEATURED CHARACTER

KOTARŌ INUGAMI RANKING

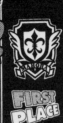

FIRST PLACE

HAPPY NEW YEAR!
毎週楽しく読んでいます。応援しています。

▲ THIS TIME, WE'RE FEATURING KOTARŌ. HE DOES APPEAR IN THE NEW ANIME! TAKAHARA-SAN IS IN FIRST PLACE; HIS USE OF BETA (BLACK) IS VERY GOOD. BLACK IS KOTARŌ'S IMAGE COLOR, AFTER ALL. (^^)

(COMMENTARY: AKAMATSU)

SECOND PLACE

コタロー

▲ WHO WILL HE END UP WITH, YOU ASK? I GUESS IT HAS TO BE KOTA X NEGI (LAUGH) MAYBE HE'LL SURPRISE US AND END UP WITH KUGIMIYA?

THIRD PLACE

KOTARŌ EVEN LOOKS GOOD IN JAPANESE CLOTHES. NOW THE GIRLS IN 3-A WON'T BE ABLE TO LEAVE HIM ALONE?! (LAUGH) ▼

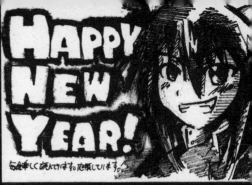

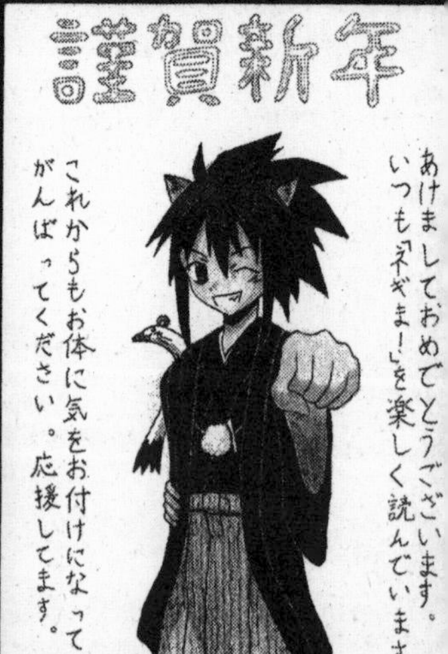

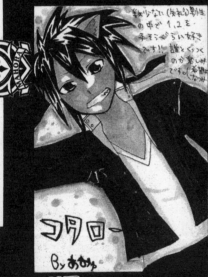

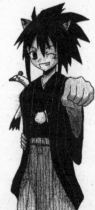

謹賀新年
あけましておめでとうございます。
いつも「ネギま!」を楽しく読んでいます。
これからもお体に気をお付けになって
がんばってください。応援してます。

NEGI MAGI MAGISTER

3-D BACKGROUNDS EXPLANATION CORNER

IT LOOKS LIKE THIS VOLUME'S MAIN FEATURE
JUST HAS TO BE THIS LARGE STRUCTURE.

• GRANICUS ARENAS

SCENE NAME: ARENA   POLYGON COUNT: 503,511

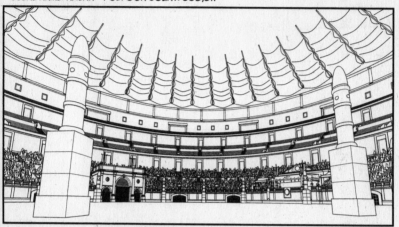

THE GIANT STRUCTURE THAT CAN BE SEEN FROM ANYWHERE IN THE CITY OF GRANICUS IS THIS SET OF ARENAS. OF THE FIVE ARENAS, THE ONE THAT NEGI AND KOTARŌ HAD THEIR MATCHES IN IS THE BIGGEST, BOASTING A DIAMETER OF 60 M, AND THE BUILDING ITSELF HAS A DIAMETER OF 200 M. IT CAN HOLD MORE THAN 50,000 PEOPLE, IS COMPLETE WITH FACILITIES LIKE CAFÉS, AND IS A BIG ENTERTAINMENT CENTER FOR THE CITIZENS.

IT GOES WITHOUT SAYING THAT IT'S MODELED AFTER THE COLISEUM IN ANCIENT ROME; THE SHAPES ARE DIFFERENT IN THAT ONE IS AN ELLIPSE AND ONE IS A CIRCLE, BUT THE ARCHITECTURAL PATTERN IS ALMOST THE SAME.

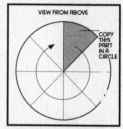

VIEW FROM ABOVE

COPY THIS PART IN A CIRCLE

FOR CYLINDRICAL OBJECTS, I MAKE ONLY ONE PART, COPY, AND ROTATE IT FOR THE REST, SO IT'S EASIER THAN IT LOOKS.

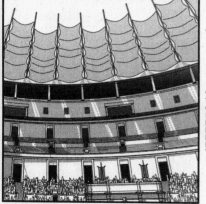

• THE ARENA'S SHADOWS

THERE ARE CANOPIES SPREAD OVER THE SPECTATOR SEATING IN THE ARENA TO KEEP OUT THE SUN, AND THE SHADOWS THAT THEY CAST OVER THE INSIDE OF THE CYLINDER ARE A LITTLE COMPLICATED, SO IT'S EXTREMELY DIFFICULT TO REPRODUCE THOSE ACCURATELY BY HAND. ONCE I'VE DRAWN UP THE LINES USING THE NORMAL 3-D SOFTWARE, I THEN ESTABLISH A LIGHT SOURCE WITHIN THE 3-D SPACE AND PAINT IN THE SHADOWS AT THE SAME TIME, SO THEY'RE REPRODUCED ACCURATELY.

LEXICON NEGIMARIUM

[*Negima!* 196th Period Lexicon Negimarium]

■ **"Sprouting young buds, become a chain and bind my enemy."**

(pullulantes pulli, vinculum facti inimicum captent)

•A spell that uses plant vines as a medium to restrain its target. It's very basic magic, and easier to use by beginners than magic arrows.

■ **"Come, earth, flower spirits, gather with dreaming flowers under the blue sky and create a storm. SPRING TEMPEST"**

(veniant, spiritus terreteres florentes, cum flores somniali sub caelo percurrat una tempestas. VERIS TEMPESTAS FLORENS)

•A tactical hypnosis spell that causes all targets in range to fall unconscious. It is effective as a military spell because it can knock out several targets.

[*Negima!* 197th Period Lexicon Negimarium]

■ **The Old World**

Mundus Vetus

•Mundus vetus is Latin for "old world." In the Magical World (Mundus Magicus), the world where wizards live with their culture unique to wizards, "Mundus Vetus" is what they call the space where we live with the culture unique to us. With Europe at the center, our world has stripped itself of magic, but since long ago, and even today, we maintain our cultures of sorcery and mythology, so it would not be appropriate to call it the "non-magical world."

As for why the Magical World calls our world the Old World, that is because the relationship between our world and the magical world is the same as the relationship that calls the Americas the "New World," and Asia, Africa, and Europe the "Old World." Also, in keeping with this, people from the Old World are called "veteres."

Furthermore, on page 29, they call Mundus Vetus "the real world," but this is a mistranslation. This is because the Magical World and the Old World are both real worlds, and the Latin for "real world" would be

"mundus actualis." That interpretation is an expression of the feeling of distance Asakura, Chisame, and the others still feel toward the Magical World.

[*Negima!* 198th Period Lexicon Negimarium]

■ **One Hundred Shadow Spears**
(CENTUM LANCEAE UMBRAE)

•An attack spell of sōei jutsu, the magic that controls manifestations of shadows. It generates an object from the shadows and mounts a physical attack that pierces magic barriers. For more on "shadows" and "sōei jutsu," please refer to the lexicon in the extras at the end of *Negima!* volume 12. [Note—in the volume 12 lexicon, sōei jutsu is listed not as soei jutsu, but as "the ultimate technique of a Shadow Master." In volume 12 itself, Takane calls herself a Shadow User, who uses sōei jutsu.]

■ **"Executioner's Sword, Imperfect"**
(IMPERFECTUS ENSIS EXSEQUENS)

•A spell with high destructive capabilities that mounts a two-stage, phase transition and low-temperature attack by forcing matter to change phase from solid or liquid to gas. For details, see the lexicon in the extras in the back of *Negima!* volume 12. It is a difficult magic to master, and while Evangeline can use it without any problems, Negi has yet to master it fully, and so his is "imperfect."

[*Negima!* 199th Period Lexicon Negimarium]

■ **Chirurgicum**

•Chirurgicum is the neuter gender, singular noun form of the Latin adjective "chirurgicus." The neuter gender noun meaning room, "spatium," is omitted. According to *Lewis & Short,* "chirurgicus" translates to "surgical," but it comes the Greek χειρουργία (cheirourgia), "work of the hand," which leads to the Japanese for surgery, "*shujutsu.*"

Before modern times, a lot of medicine was performed by high-ranking clergy, so they avoided surgical treatments that would get blood on them, and left these procedures to barbers and bathhouses (it is said that the red, blue, and white barber poles in use by barbershops today signify the arteries, veins, and lymph fluid or bandages in memory of that). But until L. Pasteur (1822–1895), H.H.R. Koch (1843–1910), and others pioneered bacteriology, no one prepared the sanitary

environment needed for surgery, and they couldn't utilize its true power as medical treatment.

Nevertheless, for medical magic, sanitation poses little to no problem, so in medical magic, they have developed unique "chirurgia" (work of the hand), which leads to the Japanese "*teate*," for "medical care," literally "put a hand to."

[*Negima!* 200th Period Lexicon Negimarium]

■ The Hero with a Thousand Faces

O Iros Meta Chilion Prosopon
(ὁ ἥρως μετὰ χίλιων πρόσωπων)

• Jack Rakan is awarded this tool for his use by the power of the pactio with Nagi.

A supreme artifact that can change shape freely to any weapon from stockings to a catapult.

[*Negima!* 201st Period Lexicon Negimarium]

■ "The Raven's Eye"

Oculus Corvinus

• Kazumi Asakura is awarded this tool for her use by the power of the pactio with Negi, Japanese name: *watarigarasu no hitomi*. It is a spy device that can be remote-controlled from exceedingly long distances. "Oculus" means "eye," or in other words "*hitomi*," which, with different kanji, means "people watcher." "Corvinus" is the adjective form of "corvus," or the common raven (scientific name, "corvus corax"). Because of their great intelligence, ravens are believed to watch the earth as messengers of the gods. For example, in Norse mythology, legend has it that "two ravens sit on his (Odin's) shoulders and whisper in his ears all that they see. The two ravens' names are Huginn and Muninn. When dawn breaks, Odin sends the two ravens out. He does so to let them fly around the entire world. At breakfast time, the two ravens return. Odin hears a multiplicity of tidings from the ravens." (*Snorri's Edda*, part 1, chapter 38), and in the Japanese myth of Emperor Jimmu's Eastern Expedition, it says "Takagi no Ōkami (Takamimusuhi no Kami) no Mikoto spoke, saying...I will send Yatagarasu (raven) from heaven. And the raven will guide you," (Kojiki, middle section) and according to legend, the raven preceded Kamuyamato Iwarebiko no Mikoto (Emperor Jimmu) in his eastward migration and surveyed the way ahead.

■ "Dispel"

DISPULSATIO

• A midlevel spell that students are required to learn at the magic academy. It terminates the paranormal phenomena brought about by magic. The caster's magical power collides with the magical power from the paranormal phenomena, and if the caster's power is greater, it can extinguish the phenomena in question. However, it can easily terminate paranormal phenomena brought into existence by the caster himself. Magic cancel can deploy this "magic erasing magic" voluntarily, constantly, and with maximum output. However, "magic erasing magic" is itself a contradictory magic, so no matter how powerful the wizard, it is impossible to deploy it constantly (with special exceptions).

■ Final pose

• The English social anthropologist J.G. Frazer (1854–1941) said the following: "In many parts of Europe dancing or leaping high in the air are approved homoeopathic modes of making the crops grow high. Thus in Franche-Comté they say that you should dance at the Carnival in order to make the hemp grow tall." (*The Golden Bough*, ch.III, §2) If you were to peruse anthropological texts, you wouldn't have time to count the examples of dance accompanying the use of spells (ibid. ch.V, IX, XI, XII, XX, XXV, XXXIII, XLV, XLVIII, etc.). Dancing fulfills a role in spells that is no less important than singing (incanting). Rakan being so particular about striking a final pose comes from this basic characteristic of spells. It's not unreasonable for Chisame, who is unfamiliar with the culture of spells, to call Rakan a freak for his obsession, but even Negi sees it as "stupidity," which is an indication that Negi himself still has much to learn about magic.

[*Negima!* 202nd Period Lexicon Negimarium]

■ "Maximum Output"

vis maxima

• A spell that maximizes the effects of such spells as "cantus bellax (song of battle)" and "melodia bellax (melody of battle)." It consumes a great amount of magic power, so it only lasts a very short time.

■ **Examination in Progress**

examinamus

●The present indicative first person plural form of the verb "examinare," which means "to examine." It's what the sprites say when the school nurse at the Academic City Ariadne summons them. They're saying, "We're examining you!"

■ **Ariadne**

[Αριάδνη] Ariadne

●The name of the biggest independent academic city-state in the Magical World. Ariadne is the daughter of Minos, king of Crete, and she is the one who gave the ball of thread to Theseus, the hero who fought the Minotaur, to help him find his way out of the Labyrinth (*Plutarch's Parallel Lives,* Theseus 19:1, etc.). From this story, clues that help people escape from enigmas and dilemmas have come to be called "Ariadne's thread." In keeping with this story, the symbol on the emblem of the Academic City Ariadne is a spindle with thread around it.

The Academic City Ariadne is neutral from all political force and is a free place of learning, governed by the Ariadne Magic Knights (Ariadniensis Magus Ordo).

"Ordo" is translated as "*kishidan*" or "knights," but should really be translated as "order." The Japanese "*kishidan*" and English "knights" could give the wrong impression that it's simply a military group. The famous Knights Templar and Knights of Malta, too, are orders like the Franciscan and Dominican orders of Catholicism. These organizations were orders of knights who participated in the Crusades and organized themselves after the model of other orders. For that reason, the "knights" are not merely armed groups, but are organizations with a set constitution that perform operations such as learning, medical care, and missionary work.

Like the Teutonic Knights and Knights of Malta of old, knightly orders also have their own territory (but it was difficult to distinguish between their territory and the donated land that made up the orders' property). The Ariadne Magic Knights have the Academic City and its surroundings as their territory, and they protect the place of learning from intervention by outside powers. Because of this, the Ariadne Magic Knights have a division responsible for using military force to defend their territory.

■ **"Aviation! Levitation! Fly, Broom!"**

(volatio, levitatio, scopae volent)

• As the words suggest, these are spells for flying on a broom. Flying on a broom without incantations is the basic of the basics, and Negi, Anya, and the other Ariadne Magic Knight trainees *1, etc. don't incant spells unless suddenly accelerating or decelerating.

[*Negima!* 204th Period Lexicon Negimarium]

■ **"Come, darkness from the abyss, blazing sword!! Great flame of darkness and shadow, of hatred and destruction, of vengeance!! Burn him, burn me, burn all to nothing, Flames of Hell!"**

(Agite, tenebrae abyssi, ensis incendens, et incendium caliginis umbrae inimicitiae destructionis ultionis, incendant et me et eum, sint solum incendentes, INCENDIUM GEHENNAE)

• In Latin, there are many words that mean fire or flame, such as "ignis" (fire), "flamma" (flame), "flagrantia" (blaze), "ardor" (burning heat), "incendium" (big fire), but of them, "incendium" signifies a very large flame. Up to this point, the basic "magic archer" is incanted with "IGNIS," the midlevel "Red Blaze" is incanted with "FLAGRANTIA," and the binding spell "Purple Flame Captor" is incanted with the adjective form of "FLAMMA" (see *Negima!* volume 13, 113th Period; volume 16, 141st Period).

Furthermore, "gehennae" is the singular, genitive case of the Latin used in the Vulgate translation of the New Testament, meaning "hell." This word comes from the Hebrew "gehinom"*2, or the "Valley of Hinnom." This valley was a place in the south of Jerusalem where they burned garbage and the bodies of criminals.

■ **"Stabilize. Seize. Load magic. 'Armament'"**

(stagnet, complexio, supplementum pro armationem.)

• Stops the magical power that was supposed to leave and be released from a spell caster in their hand and absorbs it. "pro" is a preposition meaning "for, in order to," "armationem" is the singular accusative case of the abstract noun that comes from the verb "armare (to arm)."

*1. Order members in training are called novices (novitius). Misora Kasuga isn't a member of the order, but a novice (novitia).

*2. Written in Roman letters instead of Hebrew.

魔法先生ネギま!
MAGISTER NEGI MAGI

赤松 健 SHONEN MAGAZINE COMICS
KEN AKAMATSU

22

・なぜなにネギま!
THE WHAT AND WHY OF NEGIMA!

Q. 変装してない夕映が
YUE ISN'T IN DISGUISE. WHY HASN'T SHE
指名手配で捕まらないのは
BEEN CAPTURED AS A WANTED
なぜ?
CRIMINAL?

A. 学術都市アリアドネー
IN THE ACADEMIC CITY ARIADNE
では、学ぼうという
IT IS FORBIDDEN TO
意志のある
ARREST ANYONE
者を捕え
WITH THE WILL
ることは
TO STUDY. (WHETHER
禁止されています。
THEY BE CRIMINALS OR
(例え犯罪者や
MONSTERS, IT'S ALL
魔物であっても
THE SAME.) YUE
同様です)
PROBABLY
夕映なら
WON'T BE
一生捕まること
CAPTURED
は無さそう
HER WHOLE
ですね。(笑)
LIFE. (LAUGH)

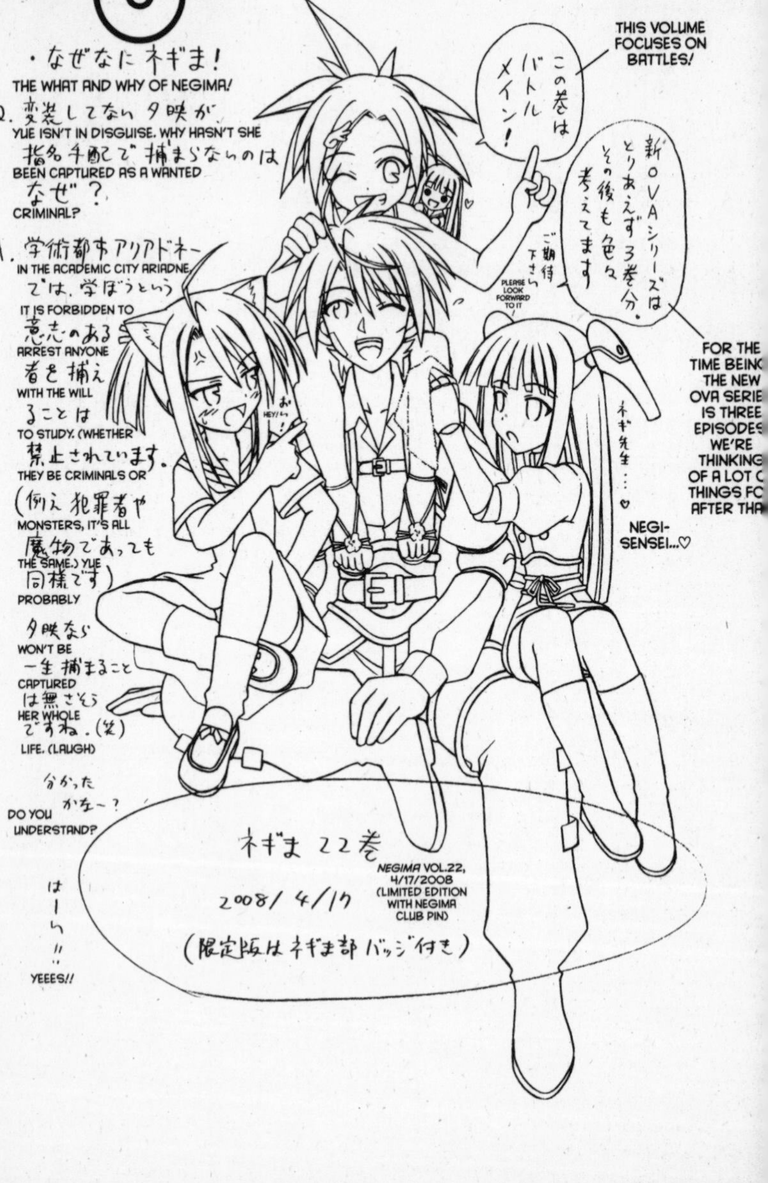
この巻はバトルメイン!
THIS VOLUME FOCUSES ON BATTLES!
新OVAシリーズはとりあえず3巻分。その後も色々考えてます
FOR THE TIME BEING THE NEW OVA SERIES IS THREE EPISODES. WE'RE THINKING OF A LOT OF THINGS FOR AFTER THAT.
ご期待下さい
PLEASE LOOK FORWARD TO IT!
おい!
HEY!
ネギ先生…♡
NEGI-SENSEI...♡
分かったかなー?
DO YOU UNDERSTAND?
はーい!!
YEEES!!
ネギま 22巻
2008/4/17
(限定版はネギま部バッジ付き)
NEGIMA VOL.22, 4/17/2008 (LIMITED EDITION WITH NEGIMA CLUB PIN)

キャラ解説
CHARACTER PROFILE

⑪ 釘宮円
⑪ MADOKA KUGIMIYA

ボーイッシュな釘宮ですが、亜子編での活躍に
BOYISH KUGIMIYA HAD A SUDDEN RISE IN POPULARITY WITH HER INVOLVEMENT
より人気は急上昇！大人版コタローとの
IN THE AKO EPISODES! HER RELATIONSHIP WITH ADULT-VERSION NEGI HAS
関係も浮上してきて、今後に期待の持てる
COME TO THE SURFACE, AS WELL, SO SHE'S BECOME A CHARACTER YOU CAN
キャラになりましたね。
HAVE HIGH HOPES FOR IN THE FUTURE.

髪型が難しくて、なかなか可愛く描けません。
HER HAIRSTYLE IS DIFFICULT, AND I JUST CAN'T DRAW IT CUTELY.
（…っていうか、ほとんどショート版モトコ？）
(…ER, I GUESS SHE'S LIKE A SHORT-HAIRED MOTOKO?)

チア3人組の中では、色気は少ない方ですが、
OF THE THREE CHEERLEADERS, SHE'S THE LEAST SEXY, BUT I THINK IF I WERE TO
女嫁にするなら 最適だと思います。（笑）
CHOOSE A BRIDE FROM THEM, SHE WOULD BE THE MOST SUITABLE. (LAUGH)
しっかりしてるから…。
BECAUSE SHE'S GOT IT TOGETHER…

アニメ版CVは 出口茉美さん。元気っ娘＝
THE ACTRESS WHO VOICES HER IN THE ANIME IS MAMI DEGUCHI-SAN.
デビュー当時はまだ10代で、かなり緊張した
SHE'S A CHEERFUL GIRL WHO WAS STILL IN HER TEENS WHEN SHE DEBUTED,
様子でしたが、最近は余裕が出てきたみたい。（^^）
AND SHE LOOKED LIKE SHE WAS PRETTY NERVOUS, BUT IT LOOKS LIKE
ドラマ版は 市川円香さん。
SHE'S MORE CONFIDENT RECENTLY. (^^) IN THE DRAMA, SHE IS PLAYED BY
元リネージュガールで、ネギまでも水着姿を
MADOKA ICHIKAWA-SAN. SHE USED TO BE A LINEAGE GIRL, AND SHE LETS
披露してくれました！ よし、!! ありがとー
US SEE HER IN A SWIMSUIT IN NEGIMA, TOO! ALL RIGHT!! THANK YOU!

赤松
AKAMATSU

About the Creator

Negima! is only Ken Akamatsu's third manga, although he started working in the field in 1994 with *AI Ga Tomaranai* (released in the United States with the title *A.I. Love You*). Like all of Akamatsu's work to date, it was published in Kodansha's *Shonen Magazine*. *AI Ga Tomaranai* ran for five years before concluding in 1999. In 1998, however, Akamatsu began the work that would make him one of the most popular manga artists in Japan: *Love Hina*. *Love Hina* ran for four years, and before its conclusion in 2002, it would cause Akamatsu to be granted the prestigious Manga of the Year award from Kodansha, as well as going on to become one of the bestselling manga in the United States.

Translation Notes

Japanese is a tricky language for most Westerners, and translation is often more art than science. For your edification and reading pleasure, here are notes on some of the places where we could have gone in a different direction with our translation of the work, or where a Japanese cultural reference is used.

That song, page v

Anyone who has seen the *Negima!* anime would be familiar with its opening theme, "Happy [STAR] Material." This popular theme song is making a comeback for the new original animation DVD (OAD), *Negima ~ Ala Alba ~*.

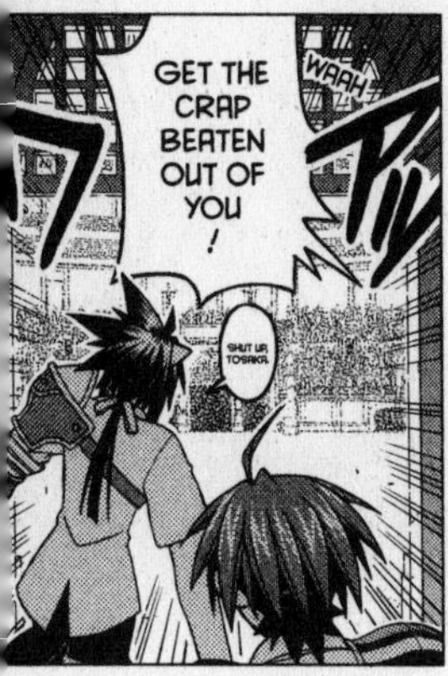
WAAAH
GET THE CRAP BEATEN OUT OF YOU !
SHUT UP, TOSAKA.

Tosaka, page 3

Literally, *tosaka* refers to the crest chicken's have on their heads. Kotarō isn't the only one to call this guy Tosaka, so it's unclear whether he's only calling him by name or insulting his hairstyle by calling him "chickenhead."

Kanji obsession, page 104

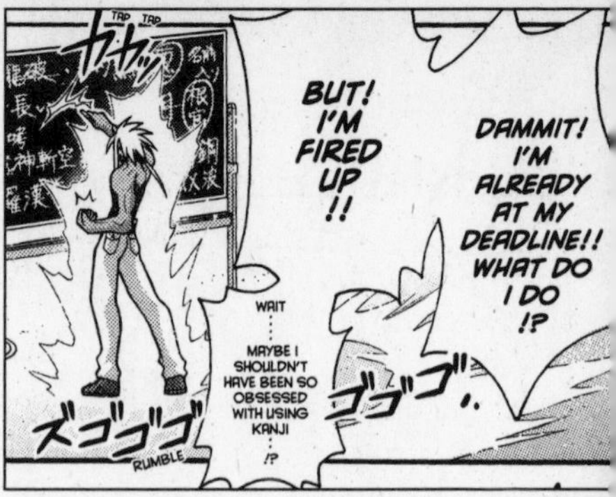

DAMMIT! I'M ALREADY AT MY DEADLINE!! WHAT DO I DO !?
BUT! I'M FIRED UP !!
TAP TAP
WAIT
MAYBE I SHOULDN'T HAVE BEEN SO OBSESSED WITH USING KANJI !?
RUMBLE

Up until now, Rakan's ideas for attack names have been made entirely of kanji, or Chinese characters, because, as we all know, attack names look that much more awesome when written out in Chinese. Unfortunately, he's having a hard time finding the right Chinese characters to look cool and sound cool at the same time. It probably doesn't help that the kanji that would be pronounced "Negi" means "spring onion."

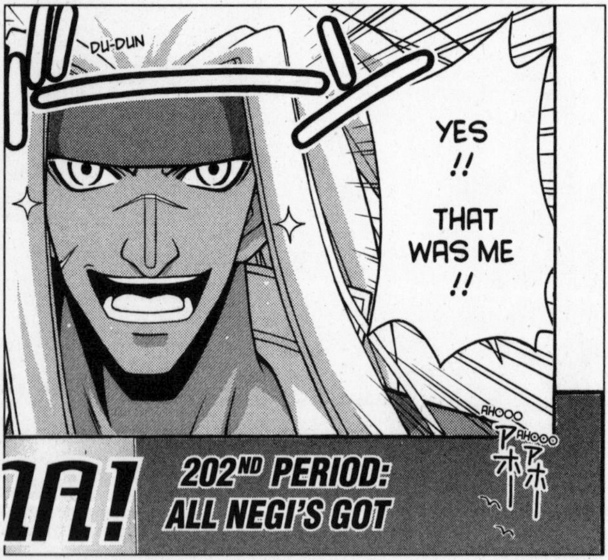

DU-DUN
YES !! THAT WAS ME !!
AHOOO
AHOOO
アホー
アホー
202ND PERIOD: ALL NEGI'S GOT

Aho, page 112

The *Negima!* world isn't the only one where the birds have the slightly unusual cry of "aho." They tend to fly by crying it when characters are being especially silly or moronic, as *aho* is Japanese for "moron."

YOU FIGHT ON YOUR OWN; A FITTING PATH FOR A SHUT-IN... A LONE WOLF LIKE YOURSELF.

Shut-in, page 157

In Japan, a shut-in, or *hikikomori*, is someone who has such a hard time dealing with the social pressures of life that they completely refuse to leave their home, and sometimes even refuse to leave their room, for an extended period of time. Negi obviously isn't quite that bad yet, but the way he keeps worrying so much about everything and taking everything onto himself, if he's not careful, Rakan can see where he might end up as one.

Lineage Girl, page 178

When the video game Lineage II came out in Japan, they promoted it by having young idols cosplay as Lineage characters and make appearances at stores and events. Madoka Ichikawa was one of these girls.

Princess Resurrection

BY YASUNORI MITSUNAGA

HAVE A NICE AFTERLIFE!

Werewolves, demons, vampires, and monsters all thrive on fear, but now there's one new warrior who has them quaking in their supernatural boots: the beautiful Princess Hime, who fights the forces of evil with a chainsaw and a smile.

Not only does she look great in a tiara, she has magical powers that allow her to raise the dead. She's a girl on a mission, and with the help of her undead servant and a supercute robot, there's no creature of darkness she can't take down!

Special extras in each volume! Read them all!

VISIT WWW.DELREYMANGA.COM TO:
- Read sample pages
- View release date calendars for upcoming volumes
- Sign up for Del Rey's free manga e-newsletter
- Find out the latest about new Del Rey Manga series

RATING | AGES OT 16+.

DEL REY MANGA デルレイ

The Otaku's Choice.™

TOMARE!

[STOP!]

You're going the wrong way!

Manga is a completely different type of reading experience.

To start at the *beginning*,
go to the *end*!

That's right! Authentic manga is read the traditional Japanese way—from right to left, exactly the *opposite* of how American books are read. It's easy to follow: Just go to the other end of the book, and read each page—and each panel—from right side to left side, starting at the top right. Now you're experiencing manga as it was meant to be.

Negima! volume 22 is a work of fiction. Names, characters, places, and incidents are the products of the author's imagination or are used fictitiously. Any resemblance to actual events, locales, or persons, living or dead, is entirely coincidental.

A Del Rey Manga/Kodansha Trade Paperback Original

Published in the United States by Del Rey, an imprint of The Random House Publishing Group, a division of Random House, Inc., New York.

Publication rights arranged through Kodansha Ltd.

First published in Japan in 2008 by Kodansha Ltd., Tokyo

ISBN 978-0-345-51030-3

Printed in the United States of America

www.delreymanga.com

9 8 7 6 5 4 3 2 1

Translator/adapter: Alethea Nibley and Athena Nibley
Lettering and retouch: Steve Palmer

NEGIMA!

22

Ken Akamatsu

TRANSLATED AND ADAPTED BY
Alethea Nibley and Athena Nibley

LETTERING AND RETOUCH BY
Steve Palmer

BALLANTINE BOOKS • NEW YORK